CW00821736

Complete Biblical Hebrew

Sarah Nicholson

First published in Great Britain in 2010 by Hodder Education

This revised and updated edition published in 2021 by Teach Yourself

An imprint of John Murray Press

A division of Hodder & Stoughton Ltd,

An Hachette UK company

Copyright © Sarah Nicholson 2010, 2021

The right of Sarah Nicholson to be identified as the Author of the Work has been asserted by her in accordance with the Copyright, Designs and Patents Act 1988.

All rights reserved. No part of this publication may be reproduced, stored in a retrieval system, or transmitted, in any form or by any means without the prior written permission of the publisher, nor be otherwise circulated in any form of binding or cover other than that in which it is published and without a similar condition being imposed on the subsequent purchaser.

A CIP catalogue record for this title is available from the British Library

ISBN 978 1 473 62783 3

Typeset by KnowledgeWorks Global Ltd.

Printed and bound by CPI Group (UK) Ltd, Croydon, CR0 4YY

John Murray Press policy is to use papers that are natural, renewable and recyclable products and made from wood grown in sustainable forests. The logging and manufacturing processes are expected to conform to the environmental regulations of the country of origin.

John Murray Press

Carmelite House

50 Victoria Embankment

London EC4Y 0DZ

www.teachyourself.com

Contents

About the author

My passion for biblical Hebrew began in my first week as a university student. I hadn't intended to take Hebrew; I'd done modern languages at school and enjoyed them, but I wanted to do something completely different, so my intention was to focus on history. However, my academic adviser strongly encouraged me to take Hebrew and I didn't like to refuse. (Guess what subject he taught?) In those days the usual approach was to teach all the grammar first and then come to the biblical texts themselves, which meant we spent several weeks mostly learning verbs, but the promise of reading Ruth in Hebrew got us all through the first term. Over the course of four years we read a wide range of biblical texts (Genesis, Amos, Ecclesiastes, Job and more) and moved out into the Dead Sea Scrolls and postbiblical Hebrew poetry which offered some alternative perspectives on both language and culture. I wasn't ready to stop, so I decided to do a PhD on the story of King Saul.

I was fortunate that a job came up in Theology and Religious Studies at the University of Glasgow not long after I finished my PhD, and I have been there ever since. I have been teaching biblical Hebrew for about 20 years and I have experimented quite a bit with the texts I use to introduce the language. I eventually settled on Genesis 21 and 22 as the texts with which to begin reading longer passages because they are straightforward enough for beginners but also raise a number of interpretive questions that have engaged readers of the Bible for centuries. I usually encourage students to propose their favourite texts for the whole class to work on, and this approach led to the range of additional texts at the end of this course. There were others that were perhaps of more marginal interest (prohibitions against witchcraft, Eglon's unfortunate end, and the revenge of the bald prophet) but if you would like to read those, or anything else, you should be able to do so by the time you have worked through the material here.

Acknowledgements

I would like to thank Ginny Catmur for her encouragement when I set out to write the first edition of this course, and Emma Green and Victoria Roddam for all their assistance and advice during the preparation of this edition. Thanks are also due to Calum Smith for correcting many typographical errors that were invisible to me, and to Anna Smith for suggesting clearer explanations. I am grateful to Zanne Domoney-Lyttle for her contributions both as test subject and as an experimenter at different stages in the evolution of the material, and to Jim Hamilton for astute questions and constructive comments about my approach. Finally, I wish to thank my many students over the last 20 years: their enthusiasm and perseverance have made teaching biblical Hebrew an immense pleasure.

Introduction

Biblical Hebrew

This course is about biblical Hebrew, which is an ancient language. There are other forms of Hebrew, such as Mishnaic Hebrew and modern Hebrew, which are somewhat different and, though interesting, beyond the scope of this course. Hebrew is a Semitic language and has features in common with other Semitic languages such as Arabic. By contrast, English is Indo-European, and more closely related to languages like French and German. There are some notable differences between the two language families, and hence between Hebrew and English.

In English, we write from left to right but in Hebrew it is the other way around: right to left. This means that books written in Hebrew usually open at what looks (to English speakers) like the back cover. In English, we write the vowels next to the consonants; in Hebrew, we usually write them underneath, above, or next to the consonants. In Hebrew, most words seem to be derived from a three-letter verbal root. For example, there is a verb **shamar** (*to guard*), and from the three-letter root שמר we get words like the following:

shomer	שֹׁמֵר	*a guard*
shamrah	שָׁמְרָה	*a watch*; i.e. a period where one guards
shemurah	שְׁמֻרָה	*an eyelid*, because it guards the eye
shimur	שִׁמֻּר	*a vigil*
mishmar	מִשְׁמָר	*a prison*
mishmeret	מִשְׁמֶרֶת	*an injunction* (like a law; something you have to keep)

Notice how the shape שמר occurs in the words. When you have learned the alphabet, you will be able to pronounce these words for yourself. Note: the words in the list are not the only words from the root שמר. Many other words come from the same root, such as words meaning *they have guarded*, and *we will be guarded* and *I am guarding*. The words above are simply examples.

Biblical Hebrew is not a difficult language to learn. Native English speakers might initially feel daunted at the prospect of learning a new alphabet, or learning to read from right to left, and yet these two aspects of biblical Hebrew can usually be mastered very quickly indeed.

Because Hebrew and English are in different language families, Hebrew words may sound very 'foreign' to us. Learning other Indo-European languages might feel easier because of their similarities to English. Those who have learned German, for example, may have taken comfort from the familiarity of the sounds of basic words: the word for *she* is pronounced 'zee', the word for *me* is pronounced 'meekh' and the word for *fish* is pronounced 'fish'. In contrast, the Hebrew for *she* is pronounced 'he'; the word for *he* is pronounced 'who' and the word for *who* is pronounced 'me'. The word for *fish* is pronounced 'dog'.

However, despite the unfamiliarity of Hebrew words, the vocabulary is actually quite small. Estimates vary as to the number of words in the Hebrew Bible (it depends how you count them), but a figure often mentioned is 4,000 words. Compare that with estimates of over 800,000 words in the English language! Readers of this course should not expect to learn all the words in the Hebrew Bible, but the small vocabulary does make the language easier to learn.

Moreover, the grammar of biblical Hebrew is (arguably) simpler than that of many Indo-European languages. For example, in biblical Hebrew there are no complex tense constructions like 'I would have had to leave'. The pronunciation is entirely regular, and there are none of the tricky combinations of letters that abound in the English language, such as the **ough** that sounds different in *cough*, *rough* and *though*.

Most importantly, though, learning biblical Hebrew can be very exciting. To engage with the biblical texts in their original languages can provide a sense of insight and a level of understanding that even the best translations cannot quite match. It can also be very interesting to discover how different translations have handled difficulties in the Hebrew text. But, ultimately, learning the language can give us a fresh perspective on texts that have prompted debate and provided inspiration for centuries.

How the course works

The aim of this course is to present the basics of biblical Hebrew clearly enough that in due course you will be able to read passages of the Bible in Hebrew. It can take time to achieve fluency in biblical Hebrew, and you should not expect to be fluent by the end of this course. However, the course should give you a fundamental knowledge of the language, and the skills to develop your Hebrew beyond the limits of an introductory course. By the time you reach the end of this course, you should have acquired a knowledge of some fundamental vocabulary and grammar and should have acquired the skills to read and translate simple passages from the biblical text.

This course contains 20 units and two sets of additional texts. Each unit explains some points of Hebrew grammar and then discusses a passage from the Bible, with plenty of activities to practice grammar and translation. It is best to work through it in order, since later units build on material presented in earlier units. The additional texts in the form of narrative texts and poetic texts at the end of the course build on everything outlined in the units, and offer further translation practice. These sections begin with shorter texts and increase in length to provide more challenges as the reader gains more experience.

In the early units, the Hebrew words are accompanied by approximate pronunciation. The suggestions in this course represent one way of pronouncing Hebrew, but this is by no means the only way. The suggestions in this course are also very approximate and may be open to debate. The approximate pronunciation is intended to be of use to people who are trying to learn Hebrew by themselves and who need support in pronouncing the words. If you are reading this course to supplement a Hebrew class, you should be guided by your teacher's pronunciation. And of course if you find the approximate pronunciation unhelpful you should simply ignore it.

Much of the textual focus of this course is on translation. Learning an ancient language is not a conversational enterprise in the same way as learning a modern language, and so understanding the texts often involves translating them. Naturally, there are differing ideas about what a translation should be and how we should go about it. The method used in this course involves translating into idiomatic English, since understanding a text in one's own language is a crucial step towards learning how the language works. There is a place for more literal translation, but it is generally most useful to people who are already very familiar with the vocabulary and syntax of the original language. Therefore this course emphasizes idiomatic translation.

▶ **What you will learn** gives an overview of the main topics of each unit.
▶ **What you will read** identifies the biblical passage used to demonstrate the language taught in the unit.
▶ **Vocabulary builder** organizes each unit's vocabulary into categories.

- ▶ **Grammar** sections will explain three or four points of language usage. The more straightforward aspects of Hebrew grammar are presented in the early units, and more challenging material is presented in the second half of the book.
- ▶ **Language discovery** encourages you to read a biblical text and answer questions based on language patterns. Producing an accurate translation will indicate that you have answered these questions correctly.
- ▶ **Practice** offers a variety of exercises, including comprehension, gap-fill and parsing, to give you a chance to see and understand words and phrases in context.
- ▶ **Reading sections** are intended to show the language in context and provide opportunities for translation, to improve your knowledge of the language.
- ▶ **Language insight** boxes aim to give you additional information about vocabulary, word usage and grammar points.
- ▶ **Test yourself** gives you some brief questions to test your understanding of the material in each unit.
- ▶ **Self-check** gives an overview of what you should now be able to do after completing the work in each unit.
- ▶ **Additional texts** provide further translation practice of narrative and poetic texts, building on the grammar presented in the units.
- ▶ The **Answer key** provides answers to all the exercises in each unit. Note that answers for Language discovery questions are given within each section with possible translations provided. Translations of the narrative and poetic texts can be found in printed Bibles or are widely available online.
- ▶ The **Glossary** offers a brief explanation of English and Hebrew grammatical terms.
- ▶ The **Verb tables** set out examples of the strong verbs in all stems and the weak verbs in the Qal stem, which is the basic stem.
- ▶ The **Lexicon** is a list of vocabulary in the course, in alphabetical order, although it is not exhaustive. This lexicon is shorter and less complex than the available published lexicons and therefore should be easier for a beginner to use.

To help you through the course, a system of icons indicates the actions to take:

 Figure something out

 Check your progress

Learning to learn

Some readers enjoy learning lists of vocabulary and grammatical forms; others find it easier to learn how words function within a text. Most people learn best if they employ a variety of approaches, and so this course encourages you to do that. If you find some of the suggestions unhelpful or irrelevant you can simply ignore them, but you are advised at least to try them for a few weeks to see if they work for you.

The method used in this course is as inductive as possible. In addition to setting exercises for the purpose of memorizing points of grammar, readers are encouraged to see how Hebrew is actually used in the Bible. Therefore, some of the work involves reading and translating real biblical passages. It is hoped that engaging with the Bible as soon as possible might be more motivating than working through a series of grammatically correct but sterile exercises.

To get the best results you should spend up to ten hours of learning time on each unit. This is not just the time taken to read the unit and do the exercises and translations, but also to re-read and to practise using the new material in the unit. Learning a language can take time, and most people find that doing a little each day is more effective than attempting to work through a whole unit at once.

Further reading

This course is an introduction to biblical Hebrew. It is not an Introduction to the Old Testament/Tanakh; neither is it a traditional grammar of biblical Hebrew. There are many very interesting things to learn about the Bible that are outside the scope of this course, and so it may be useful to read other books as well if you are curious about questions such as the history, authorship, contents or theology of the Bible.

You might be interested in reading an Introduction to the Hebrew Bible alongside or after this course. An Introduction will often be entitled just that: Introduction to the Hebrew Bible, or alternatively Introduction to the Old Testament. There are many of them available and they encompass a range of academic and theological perspectives. It is not the intention to recommend a particular Introduction; you are advised to visit a library and browse. Of course, the internet can also be a useful source.

There are, naturally, many websites that focus on biblical Hebrew and on issues of biblical interpretation. Many of them are very good; many others are mediocre. If you are interested in exploring the material available online, you are reminded that almost anyone can put up a web page, so information found online may not be accurate, or may represent a very minority position.

Although this course introduces the basics of the grammar of biblical Hebrew, it is not exhaustive. A traditional grammar will set out these points in more detail, often without the textual work that appears in this course. There are many grammars available and they might be useful to a reader who has worked through this course and wishes to continue learning Hebrew.

Commentaries are books that seek to explain in some detail each verse of a particular book of the Bible. Some commentaries discuss the whole Bible. Some commentaries have a devotional leaning; others focus on academic matters. Some, though not all, discuss the Hebrew. Readers of this course might be interested in reading a commentary on Genesis, particularly one that comments on the use of Hebrew.

If you wish to continue with Hebrew after this course you should invest in a dictionary or a lexicon. Dictionaries and lexicons for biblical Hebrew (as opposed to modern Hebrew) are usually Hebrew to English only and list the grammatical roots of words. It can be difficult to get the hang of using a dictionary until you have a good grasp of Hebrew grammar and it can take time to learn how to use a Hebrew dictionary or lexicon. There is a basic lexicon at the end of this course, but it does not cover the vocabulary of the entire biblical text, so a lexicon will be invaluable if you wish to pursue biblical Hebrew further.

1 Consonants

In this unit you will learn about:
▶ **all the biblical Hebrew consonants**
▶ **two of the biblical Hebrew vowels**

Grammar

THE ALPHABET

In English, the vowels are *a, e, i, o* and *u*. All the other letters are consonants. In English the vowels appear in the alphabet mixed in with the consonants, but in Hebrew the vowels are learned separately from the consonants.

'The Hebrew alphabet' really means the Hebrew consonants, and there are 22 of them. In Hebrew, the vowels are considered to be quite separate from the consonants and sometimes the vowels are simply left out. It is easy enough to understand a sentence written without vowels in a language you already know, but it is hard to learn to pronounce words with no vowels. So in this course, we are going to use the vowels. However, we will focus on the consonants first. Hebrew consonants have names that recall earlier pictogram forms of the letters. For example the first letter, **alef**, is derived from the word for *ox* and was originally a representation of ox horns. The second letter is the word for *house*.

There are different ways of pronouncing biblical Hebrew. The version presented in this course is common in universities, but in synagogues several other pronunciations are used. Modern Hebrew is slightly different again. Pronunciation isn't as crucial as it might be if you were learning to speak a modern language. However, it is much easier to read the text if you learn to pronounce the words properly. Mixing up letters, for example, could lead to misunderstanding the text. Do take as much time as you need to learn how the letters sound. You can find a summary pronunciation chart in Appendix 2. You can also find the Hebrew **alef bet** (*alphabet*) song online, and it will help you to learn the order of the consonants, which will be useful later when you use dictionaries.

HEBREW CONSONANTS

The very first letter is called **alef**: א. It is a silent letter so when you see it in a word, you pronounce the vowel underneath it. This is how you write it: start with a diagonal line, like the line on the right opposite, and add two more short lines.

Try writing it a few times. Remember to read and write from right to left.

The second letter is called **bet** (pronounced as English *bait*): בּ. Sometimes there is a dot, called a **dagesh**, inside it: בּ. Without the **dagesh** it's **v** (as in *van*); with the **dagesh** it's **b** (as in *book*). **Dagesh** will be explained in more detail in Unit 3.

Practise writing it a few times. Start with the bottom line and add the 'house' around the open 'door'. Notice that the bottom line extends beyond the vertical line.

The third letter is called **gimel** (say **gimel** with a hard **g**; not *jimel*): ג. It is always pronounced with a hard **g** (as in *gold*); never with a soft **g** (as in *gin*). It's a narrower letter than **alef** and **bet**.

Try writing it a few times. Start with the top and then add the other two diagonal lines.

The fourth letter is **dalet**: ד. It is pronounced **d** (as in *door*).

Practise writing it a few times. Start with the top line. Notice that the horizontal line extends beyond the vertical line.

The fifth letter is **he** (say it *hay*). It looks like this: ה and is pronounced **h** (as in *help*), although it is silent at the end of a word.

Try writing it a few times. Start with the top line. Make sure you leave a gap between the horizontal line and the left vertical line. Like **dalet**, the top (horizontal) line extends to the right.

The best way to practise pronouncing these is with a vowel, so we'll look at two vowels to begin with. The first is a short **a** vowel, pronounced **a** as in *pat* and called **patach**. It is a short line written underneath a consonant; e.g. אַ. The second is a short **e** vowel, pronounced **e** as in *set* and called **segol**. It is made up of three little dots written underneath a consonant; e.g. בֶ.

Try pronouncing these, reading from right to left (the first few have a pronunciation key to guide you):

הַ	דַ	גַ	בַּ	אַ
ha	da	ga	ba	a
הֶ	דֶ	גֶ	בֶּ	אֶ
heh	deh	geh	beh	e

Here are some more to try:

דְּ   דֱּ   בָ   בֶּ   גִ

אֱ   גֵ   דֶ   אָ   הֲ

The next consonant is **vav**: ו. It is pronounced **v** as in *van*, just the same as ב without **dagesh**. It's a very narrow letter. In some fonts it's just a straight line but in Hebrew Bibles and Tanakh scrolls it has a small stroke at the top.

Write it a few times.

Then we have **zayin**: ז. It is pronounced **z** as in *zone*. Like **vav**, it is a narrow letter, but the stroke at the top is larger, so be sure not to confuse the two.

Write it a few times. Start with the down stroke.

After that comes **chet**: ח. Be sure to distinguish it from ה. **Chet** is pronounced **ch** as in the Scottish word *loch*. It is never **ch** as in *cheese*. This can be a challenging sound for some, particularly for people from England or North America (to whom it's not unlike the sound of gargling), but with a bit of practice it can be achieved.

Write it a few times. Notice that the horizontal line at the top extends beyond the left vertical line.

The ninth consonant is **tet**: ט, which is pronounced **t** as in *time*.

Practise writing it.

And then the tenth letter is **yod** י, which is pronounced **y** as in *young*. It is a very small letter: both narrow and short compared with the other consonants. Here it is in the middle of a word חָיָה (this word is **chayah** meaning *to live*).

Write it a few times.

Now practise saying these consonants with vowels (read from right to left):

יַ	טַ	חַ	זַ	וַ
ya	ta	cha	za	va
יֶ	טֶ	חֶ	זֶ	וֶ
ye	te	che	ze	ve
חָ	יֵ	זַ	טֶ	וַ
יֶ	טַ	וַ	יֶ	חֶ

The Hebrew consonants also have a numerical value; if you look in a Hebrew Bible, you may see the verses are numbered with these consonants, so these letters have the values 1 to 10. The letters do not actually translate the numbers; while you can use ד as the equivalent of 4, if you want to say *four* in Hebrew you have to say **arbah**. It's not too confusing when we remember that when Italian speakers see 4 they say *quattro*, while Scottish Gaelic speakers say *ceithir*. However, when we see א at the beginning of a verse, we know it's verse 1.

The next consonant is **kaf**: כ. Like **bet**, it's pronounced differently when written with **dagesh** (כּ), in which case it is pronounced **k** as in *king*. Without **dagesh** (כ) it is pronounced **ch** as in *loch* (just the same as ח). Be sure not to confuse its shape with **bet** (ב).

Write it a few times, starting with the top line.

Then comes **lamed**: ל. It is pronounced **l** as in *land*.

Write it a few times, starting with the top stroke. This letter is slightly taller than the others.

It is followed by **mem** (say **mem** like the English word *maim*): מ, which is pronounced **m** as in *milk*.

Write it a few times.

The next letter is **nun** (say it *noon*): נ, which is pronounced **n** as in *not*. Be sure not to confuse it with **gimel** (ג).

Write it a few times. This is another narrow letter; be sure to distinguish it from **kaf**.

Then comes **samech** ס, which is pronounced **s** as in *sock*. Be sure not to confuse it with **tet** (ט).

Write it a few times. Note that the top line extends to the left.

And next there is **ayin** ע (say it **eye-in**), which is silent, like **alef**.

Write it a few times.

Here are some syllables to help you practise pronouncing these consonants. Remember: **a** as in *pat* and **e** as in *sĕt*.

עַ	סַ	נַ	מַ	לַ	כַ
a	sa	na	ma	la	cha
עֶ	סֶ	נֶ	מֶ	לֶ	כֶ
e	se	ne	me	le	ke
מֶ	סֶ	כַ	נֶ	עַ	לֶ
סַ	עֶ	לַ	כֶ	נַ	מֶ

There are only a few more consonants to learn. The next one is **pe** (say **pay**) פ, which is another letter that changes pronunciation with **dagesh**. Without **dagesh** it's pronounced **f**, as in *fin*, and with **dagesh** (פּ) it's pronounced **p** as in *pin*.

Write it a few times.

Then there is **tsade** צ (say it *tsad-ay*), which is pronounced **ts**, as in *tsar*. Be sure not to confuse it with **ayin** (ע).

Write it a few times.

Next comes **qof** ק (say it *kofe*), pronounced **k** as in *king*. This letter is slightly longer than the others and extends below the other letters. You can see this if you look at the whole alphabet written in a line (see page 8).

Write it a few times.

After **qof** is **resh** ר, pronounced **r** as in *run*. Be sure not to confuse it with **dalet** (ד).

Write it a few times.

The next letter is really two letters, distinguished by the placing of the dot.

This one שׂ is called **sin**, and is pronounced **s** as in *sock*.

Write **sin** (שׂ) a few times:

This one שׁ is called **shin** and is pronounced **sh** as in *shock*.

Write **shin** (שׁ) a few times:

And the last letter of the alphabet is **tav**: ת, which, just like ט, is pronounced **t** as in *time*.

Write it a few times. Notice the 'foot' in the lower left corner which helps distinguish ת from ה.

Reading

First, look at the whole alphabet and notice which letters look similar to help you distinguish them. Also take note of which letters are narrower than the others (**gimel**, **vav**, **zayin**, **yod**, **nun**) and which letters are taller (**lamed**) or longer (**qof**). Remember to read from right to left.

Practise writing the whole alphabet a few times.

א ב ג ד ה ה ו ז ח ט י כ ל מ נ ס ע פ צ ק ר ש ת

It is very important to be able to remember and pronounce the letters. The consonants are set out here, at random and with vowels, to give you the opportunity to practise. Most people find they learn best if they read out loud, rather than silently. Do this every day for a few days until you feel confident.

שָׁ קְ אָ זֻ סֻ צֵ שֵׁ דַ כָ רַ פְּ וְ
תַ גַ בְּ יְ הֶ נְ טֶ מַ עֲ חַ לְ קָ
שֵׁ תָ עַ סֹ פֶּ הַ חַ זְ כַ בָ מֶ שֵׁ
רְ יֵ אָ דְ גְ פֶ כְ לְ צַ וַ נֶ עַ

And some practice at distinguishing letters of similar appearance:

בָ כָ עַ צַ וַ זְ סֶ טֶ הַ חַ תַ

נַ גַ דַ רַ שֵׁ שֵׁ

Finally, here are some real Hebrew words to pronounce. Suggested pronunciation and meanings are below the words (*light* here is *light* as in *not heavy* rather than *light* as in *not dark*). Remember that ה is silent at the end of a word. Try to learn both the spelling and the meaning of these words.

אֶל	קַל	חַד	פַּח	עַז	שֶׂה	רַב	עַד	מָה
el	kal	chad	pach	az	se	rav	ad	ma
to	*light*	*sharp*	*snare*	*strong*	*lamb*	*many*	*until*	*what*

💡 Language discovery

Here are some verses from the Hebrew Bible. Without vowels you will struggle to read them. However, you should be able to identify each consonant. Look through them and ensure you can distinguish between consonants that are similar in appearance:

ב and כ, ג and נ, ד and ר, ה and ח, ז and ו, ח and ת, ט and ס, ע and צ, שׁ and שׁ.

Psalm 18:32 [English 18:31]	כי מי אלוה מבלעדי יהוה ומי צור זולתי אלהינו
Psalm 34:9 [English 34:8]	טעמו וראו כי טוב יהוה אשרי הגבר יחסה בו
Psalm 71:9	אל תשליכני לעת זקנה ככלות כחי אל תעזבני
Psalm 100:2	עבדו את יהוה בשמחה באו לפניו ברננה

Although you cannot yet read or translate these verses, you can look them up to see how others have translated them. Three of these verses contain the tetragrammaton (God's name, usually translated *the LORD*). Can you find it above? Hint: it has four letters: **yod**, **he**, **vav** and **he**. It will be discussed more fully in Unit 3.

❓ Test yourself

Write out all the consonants in order, from memory. Then check you have done it correctly: see the answer key at the back of this course. It is easy to get a bit lost after **mem**, so be sure you have the second half perfect. This will be very useful when you come to use a dictionary.

_____

_____

SELF-CHECK	
I CAN...	
○	identify and write all the Hebrew consonants in the correct order
○	pronounce the consonants in simple syllables with two vowels

2 Vowels

In this unit you will learn about:
▶ the vowels in biblical Hebrew
▶ how to pronounce simple syllables and words
▶ the final forms of consonants

Grammar

SHORT AND LONG VOWELS

The distinction between short and long vowels is convenient rather than strictly accurate, but useful for learning biblical Hebrew.

We have learned two of the vowels so far. This unit will introduce the others.

Short vowels

Name	Shape	Pronunciation
patach	ַ	**a** as in *pat*
segol	ֶ	**e** as in *set*
chireq	ִ	**i** as in *hit*
qamets chatuf	ָ	**o** as in *hot*
qibbuts	ֻ	**u** as in *put*

It is easier to see how the vowels work when they are put together with a consonant. Remember to pronounce the vowels as described above.

שֻׁ	שָׁ	שִׁ	שֶׁ	שַׁ
su	so	si	se	sa

Try reading these out loud, from right to left (don't forget: ח and כ are **ch** as in *loch*):

כְּ   יְ   פֻ   חַ   זֶ   נ   הָ   דָ   גִ   בֶּ   א

חַ   שֻׁ   רֻ   קִ   צַ   פֶּ   עַ   סֻ   נְ   מֻ   לֶ

Long vowels

Consonants appear in three of the long vowels. This might appear confusing at first but in practice it causes few difficulties. You might like to think of the ו as holding the dot in place in long *o* and long *u*, whereas the י simply lengthens the short-*i* vowel, and is also sometimes used with the long *e*-vowel.

Name	Shape	Pronunciation
qamets	ָ	**a** as in *pa*
tsere	ֵ	**e** as in *blasé*
hireq yod	ִי	**i** as in *routine*
cholem	וֹ	**o** as in *cone*
shureq	וּ	**u** as in *Peru*

Vowels are almost always written with a consonant, as here. The approximate pronunciation is based on the table in Appendix 2.

תּוּ	תּוֹ	תִּי	תֵּ	תָּ
too	tō	tee	tay	tā

Here are the long vowels with random consonants. The first line includes approximate pronunciation. Can you attempt to pronounce the second line?

כָּ	בִי	יֵ	טוֹ	זוּ	אָ	דֵ	הִי	גוֹ	וָ	חָ
kā	vee	yay	tō	zoo	ā	day	hee	gō	vā	chā

תָּ	צִי	קוֹ	סוּ	שָ	פֵּ	מִי	נוֹ	רוּ	עַ	לֵ

Note: the vowel ָ is sometimes pronounced **ah** (when used as a long vowel) and sometimes pronounced **o** as in *hot* (when used as a short vowel). In practice it is almost always **ah**, but later we will learn the contexts in which it is pronounced **o**. However, in some accents, e.g. North American accents, these two sounds are indistinguishable. The names of the vowels are sometimes transliterated differently (**qamats**, **hiriq**, **holem**, **shuruq**, etc.) but are usually easy enough to identify once you are familiar with them.

The syllables above are meaningless, but now we can try some more real Hebrew words.

טוֹב	tōv	*good*
רַע	ra	*evil, bad*
עִם	im	*with*
עַל	al	*on*
חָר	chur	*white*
כֵּן	kayn	*therefore*
הוּא	hoo	*he*
הִיא	hee	*she*
אִישׁ	eesh	*man*
הַר	har	*mountain*

Note: sometimes **cholem** is written without the וֹ. If טוֹב were written that way, it would look like this: טֹב. It would be pronounced just the same, though: **tōv**. Some words are always spelled without the **cholem vav**, e.g. the word for *priest*, כֹּהֵן (pronounced **kō-HAYN**).

PRACTICE 1

1 **Write the words in the list above in Hebrew.**

2 **Write the following words in Hebrew (from Unit 1) and give their meanings.**

a מֶה   d שֶׂה   g חַד

b עַד   e עַז   h קֵל

c רַב   f פַּח   i אֵל

SHEVA AND COMPOSITE VOWELS

Sheva

There is a vowel called **sheva** (pronounced **sha-VA**) that corresponds to the way we usually pronounce the first **o** in *tomato*. It is written ְ **and** is sometimes silent, but is sometimes vocalized. When vocalized, it is simplest to represent its pronunciation with a symbol: ə. For example, if we were to write the way *tomato* is pronounced, we could write **tə-MA-to.**

Here are a couple of examples:

| silent **sheva** | מִדְבָּר | mid-BAR (*a desert*) |
| vocalized **sheva** | מְשֹׁל | mə-SHŌL (*to rule*) |

Composite vowels

The last three vowels are composite vowels made up of the **sheva** and one of the short **a**, **e** or **o** vowels.

Name	Shape	Pronunciation
chatef patach	ֲ	a as in *pat*
chatef segol	ֱ	e as in *set*
chatef qamets chatuf	ֳ	o as in *hot*

These are pronounced just like their short-vowel equivalents and occur with the letters ע א ה and ח. These letters can take other vowels, but they cannot usually take a simple **sheva**.

PRACTICE 2

1 **Practise saying these out loud (approximate pronunciation is suggested).**

חֹ   חֱ   חֲ   הֹ   הֶ   הֲ   עֹ   עֶ   עֲ   אֹ   אֶ   אֲ

cho   che   cha   ho   he   ha   o   e   a   o   e   a

2 **Complete the table of vowels and write their names.**

	Short vowels	Long vowels	Composite vowels
a			ֲ
e	ֶ		
i		ִי	
o	ָ		
u		וּ	

FINAL FORMS OF CONSONANTS

Five of the consonants change shape if they are the last letter of a word. They are:

	tsade	pe	nun	mem	kaf
beginning or middle	צ	פ	נ	מ	כ
end of word	ץ	ף	ן	ם	ך

Notice how four of them (except **mem**) seem to grow a tail that comes straight down below the line. Be sure to distinguish final **kaf** ך from **dalet** ד; final **mem** ם from **samek** ס; and final **nun** ן from **vav** ו.

Try writing them a few times.

Final **kaf** ך

Final **mem** ם

Final **nun** ן

Final **pe** ף

Final **tsade** ץ

Here are some examples of how they are used in words:

אַך	ach	*but, except*
עַם	am	*people, nation, community*
מִן	min	*from*
כַּף	kaf	*palm* (of hand)
עֵץ	ayts	*tree*

The words אַת and אַך are pronounced the same way but are spelled differently, and they mean different things, so be careful not to confuse them.

LANGUAGE INSIGHT

In English we can string several consonants together, such as the combination 'tchphr' in *catchphrase*, but in Hebrew this kind of consonant string would be unpronounceable. In Hebrew, every consonant in a word takes a vowel, except the very last consonant. There are occasional exceptions, such as final **kaf**, which is usually written with **sheva** (ךְ) but can sometimes take **qamets**: ךָ.

Reading

Here are some more Hebrew words. Read them out loud, from right to left. Approximate pronunciation and meanings are given below the words. Learn this new vocabulary: some of these words are very common in biblical Hebrew.

שַׂר	אָח	בַּת	בֵּן	אֵם	אָב
sār	ach	bat	bayn	aym	āv
prince	*brother*	*daughter*	*son*	*mother*	*father*

פַּר	יוֹם	סוּס	יָד	חוֹל	יָם
pār	yōm	soos	yād	chōl	yām
ox	*day*	*horse*	*hand*	*sand*	*sea*

שְׁבָעָה	שִׂמְחָה	אֱלֹהִים	חֳלִי	אֲנִי	כָּל
shə-voo-AH	sim-CHAH	e-lo-HEEM	cho-LEE	a-NEE	kol
oath	*rejoicing*	*God*	*grief*	*I*	*all, every*

Here are some combinations of vowels and consonants to read out loud. Most are random or parts of real words. Practise reading the syllables and words in this unit every day until you are confident about pronouncing them.

מְ	בְּ	כְּ	זְ	נְ	וְ	צוֹ	לְ	טוּ	גִ	דֵ	סִי
חֶ	פֻ	תָ	הַ	רֶ	אִ	שִׁי	עֲ	קֵ	שְׁ	בָּ	כַ
זְק	כֵשׁ	בֵּן	מוּל	צֵת	נֵף	אַד	דוֹב	גִין	מֵם	לַד	אַף
פֵּק	חַס	קִיד	שֵׁן	הֵם	תוּג	עַף	רֵךְ	שׁוֹה	יַיִן	תוֹם	הֵל
עֹז	בֵּל	אָה	דַן	בֵּר	בֹּעַ	יָח	מַר	לֵב	חוּס	קֵל	בִּיל
טִישׁ	מֵה	נֵא	פָּד	מַן	עוּל	צוֹן	שֵׁץ	גֵּל	פִּית	נוֹךְ	חוֹשׁ

💡 Language discovery

The first four examples in this table were seen without vowels in Unit 1. The other examples include final forms of consonants. At this stage you may be able to pronounce some of these words, but it will be difficult. However, you should be able to identify all the vowels and the final forms. Find an example of each vowel and each of the final consonantal forms in the following verses.

Psalm 18:32	כִּי מִי אֱלוֹהַּ מִבַּלְעֲדֵי יְהוָה וּמִי צוּר זוּלָתִי אֱלֹהֵינוּ
Psalm 34:9	טַעֲמוּ וּרְאוּ כִּי־טוֹב יְהוָה אַשְׁרֵי הַגֶּבֶר יֶחֱסֶה־בּוֹ
Psalm 71:9	אַל־תַּשְׁלִיכֵנִי לְעֵת זִקְנָה כִּכְלוֹת כֹּחִי אַל־תַּעַזְבֵנִי
Psalm 100:2	עִבְדוּ אֶת־יְהוָה בְּשִׂמְחָה בֹּאוּ לְפָנָיו בִּרְנָנָה
Genesis 2:9b	וְעֵץ הַחַיִּים בְּתוֹךְ הַגָּן וְעֵץ הַדַּעַת טוֹב וָרָע
Genesis 8:3a	וַיָּשֻׁבוּ הַמַּיִם מֵעַל הָאָרֶץ הָלוֹךְ וָשׁוֹב
Genesis 37:5	וַיַּחֲלֹם יוֹסֵף חֲלוֹם וַיַּגֵּד לְאֶחָיו וַיּוֹסִפוּ עוֹד שְׂנֹא אֹתוֹ
Genesis 41:26b	וְשֶׁבַע הַשִּׁבֳּלִים הַטֹּבֹת שֶׁבַע שָׁנִים הֵנָּה

N.B. If you attempt to read these verses, bear in mind that יְהוָה (the tetragrammaton) is not pronounced as it is written. See Unit 3 for further details.

❓ Test yourself

Here is Genesis 1:1, the first verse of the Hebrew Bible, written in syllables. Read them out loud. There is a *dagesh* (dot) in a *shin* in the second line but this does not affect its pronunciation.

אֵת   הִים   לֹ   אֱ   רָא   בָּ   שִׁית   רֵא   בְּ

רֶץ   אָ   הָ   אֵת   וְ   יִם   מַ   שָׁ   הַ

SELF-CHECK	
I CAN...	
⚪	identify and write all the Hebrew vowels
⚪	pronounce Hebrew syllables and simple words
⚪	identify and write the final forms of consonants

3 Dagesh *and the conjunction* וֹ

In this unit you will learn about:
▶ some of the functions of **dagesh**
▶ how the conjunction וֹ is used

You will read:
▶ part of Psalm 25:8, including the name of God

Vocabulary builder

NOUNS

אָחֹת	ach-ŌT	sister
אֶרֶץ	ER-ets	land, earth
אִשָּׁה	ish-ĀH (spelled with **dagesh** in שׁ)	woman
גַּן	gan	garden
דֶּרֶךְ	DER-ech	way, path
חַטָּא	cha-TĀ (spelled with **dagesh** in ט)	sinner
יְהוָה	a-dō-NĪ *or* ha-SHEM	Yhwh, name of God
לֵבָב	lay-VĀV	heart
קוֹל	kōl	voice

ADJECTIVES

טוֹב	tōv (from Unit 2)	good
יָשָׁר	yā-SHĀR	just, upright

VERBS

יָרָה	yā-RĀ	to show, teach, instruct

ADVERBS

עַל־כֵּן	alkayn	therefore

Grammar

DAGESH

In Unit 1, we noted the occasional presence of a dot inside a letter: a dot called **dagesh**. **Dagesh** is sometimes described as a kind of doubling of the letter without writing it twice. However, there are various reasons for using **dagesh**, as we will discover.

The three letters we previously noted in connection with **dagesh** (בּ כּ and פּ) were pronounced differently when they took a **dagesh**. A reminder:

v as in *van*	ב	**b** as in *book*	בּ
ch as in *loch*	כ	**k** as in *king*	כּ
f as in *fin*	פ	**p** as in *pin*	פּ

Other letters can take **dagesh**, but none of the others changes the way it is pronounced when it takes **dagesh**. A consonant can take **dagesh** for various reasons.

One reason is that certain letters take **dagesh** when they come at the beginning of a word or syllable. The letters in question are ב ג ד כ פ and ת. These are sometimes called the **begadkefat** letters (the sounds of the Hebrew letters with vowels to aid pronunciation: בְּגַדְכְּפַת). So in the word בַּת (*daughter*), the ב has a **dagesh** because it comes at the beginning of a word. And because it has a **dagesh**, the word is pronounced **bat** rather than **vat**. Similarly, in the word גַּן (*garden*) the ג has a **dagesh** because it comes at the beginning of the word, but **gimel** doesn't change its pronunciation with **dagesh**. (In fact, the letters ג ד and ת used to change pronunciation, but the change is no longer widely observed in the pronunciation system we are following.)

Five letters never take **dagesh**: א ע ה ח and ר. Four of these consonants, א ע ה and ח, are commonly known as gutturals. There is some debate about the accuracy of the term, but the four letters do have particular properties. The letter ר is not really a guttural, but sometimes behaves like one.

PRACTICE 1

Write out the alphabet in order, from memory, with a *dagesh* in each letter that can take *dagesh*.

Then check your work against Unit 1. Did you get the order right? Did you remember which letters do not take *dagesh*?

THE CONJUNCTION ו

Consider these sentences:

The daughter is good and the son is good.

The daughter is good but the son is evil.

> The words *and* and *but* in these two sentences are conjunctions. Conjunctions join words or phrases together. Other examples in English are words like *if*, *because* and *that*.

In English *and* is a word in its own right, but in Hebrew it is the letter וֹ added to the beginning of a word. The vowel it takes is usually a **sheva**. Here are some examples:

רַע וְטוֹב   ra ve-tōv   *bad and good*

חוֹל וְיָם   chōl və-yām   *sand and sea*

When the conjunction וֹ comes before the letters מ ב and פ, it changes to a **shureq** to make the word easier to pronounce:

בַּת וּבֵן   bat oo-VAYN   *daughter and son*   (or *a daughter and a son*)

אִישׁ וּפָר   eesh oo-FĀR   *man and ox*   (or *a man and an ox*)

Note: we would normally expect the word בֵּן to be written with **dagesh** in the ב. However, when a **begadkefat** letter follows a long vowel it no longer requires **dagesh**; the same is true in פָר. Note also that when וֹ changes to a **shureq**, it is no longer written with **sheva**. Since it has become a vowel, it no longer takes a vowel.

The change from וְ to וּ also happens when the conjunction is placed in front of a word whose first vowel is a **sheva**. For example, the first vowel in the name דְּבוֹרָה (pronounced de-vō-RĀ; the name usually rendered *Deborah* in English) is a **sheva**. So *David and Deborah* would be דָּוִד וּדְבוֹרָה.

LANGUAGE INSIGHT

The conjunction וֹ can also mean *but* in sentences where a contrast is implied. This will be discussed in more detail later.

PRACTICE 2

Read aloud in Hebrew and translate into English:

a   אָב וְאֵם

b   גַּן וְעֵץ

c   סוּס וְשֶׂה

d   יָם וְהַר

e   אָחוֹת וְאָח

f   יָד וְכַף

g   חַד וְקַל

h   אִשָּׁה וְאִישׁ

i   אֶרֶץ וְעַם

j   לֵבָב וְקוֹל

THE NAME OF GOD

In biblical Hebrew there are two words for the deity. One is אֱלֹהִים, pronounced **el-ō-HEEM**, which simply means *God*. The other is God's name, יְהֹוָה or יְהוָֹה. The latter is sometimes called the tetragrammaton, because it has four letters and is often represented in English translations as *the LORD*. The convention is not to pronounce it as written, but instead to say אֲדֹנָי, pronounced **a-dō-NĪ**, which means *my Lord*, and it is the vowels of אֲדֹנָי that we see in יְהוָֹה. Another convention is to say **ha-SHEM**, which means *the name*. The word אֱלֹהִים is usually translated *God*, except on occasions where it refers to several gods. The word יְהוָה may be translated *the LORD* or *Yhwh*. The *w* in *Yhwh* dates from a time when **vav** was called **waw** and pronounced **w**.

Reading

PSALM 25:8

It is always challenging to find simple and appropriate texts in biblical Hebrew with which to demonstrate points of grammar. Sometimes it is easier to invent non-biblical sentences, or to adapt biblical texts to simplify their grammar. However, looking at the real biblical text can be tremendously exciting, even if it may be a little more ambitious. Learning grammatical points can be supported with exercises, but in order to get a sense of how the grammar is used in the Bible it is necessary to look at the real thing.

Reading real biblical texts will involve encountering some grammatical ideas before we have properly dealt with them. For example, we have not yet looked at verbs, and so if we would like to look at a real biblical passage at this point we will have to accept that we will not understand the verbs. This can be a little frustrating, but this frustration may be tempered with patience, and the thrill of reading the Bible itself may compensate for the delay in understanding every word perfectly. You may return to these texts later, with greater knowledge.

Points to look out for in this text:

▸ words you have already encountered
▸ the divine name
▸ **dagesh**
▸ use of the conjunction וְ.

Read the verse aloud two or three times to be sure you know how the words sound. These words are longer than the words we've seen already, but there are only a few of them.

Text	Approximate pronunciation
טוֹב־וְיָשָׁר יְהוָה	**TŌV və-yā-SHĀR a-dō-NĪ**
עַל־כֵּן יוֹרֶה חַטָּאִים בַּדָּרֶךְ׃	**al kayn yō-RE cha-tā-EEM ba-DĀ-rech**

Now match each word of the text with the vocabulary at the beginning of the unit, as far as you can. Some of the words are not precisely the same as the words in the list of vocabulary. The words in the vocabulary are the dictionary forms. In English, if we want to know the meaning of the word *brought* we need to look up *bring* in the dictionary. Similarly, if we want to know the meaning of יוֹרֶה, we have to look up יָרָה in the dictionary. Once you have matched the words in the text with the vocabulary, you should begin to have a sense of the meaning of the verse.

Language discovery

It should have been possible to match the first few words of the text to the vocabulary without too much difficulty. The last three words of the text are a little more complicated. There are also a few other points to deal with, so we will look at each word in the text.

טוֹב־

The line joining this word to the next word is called **maqqef**. It joins words in a manner rather like a hyphen in English, as in the phrase *happy-go-lucky*.

וְיָשָׁר

What is the וְ at the beginning of the word?

עַל־כֵּן

This word is made up of two words: עַל and כֵּן, joined by **maqqef**. Together they mean *therefore*.
Why is there a **dagesh** in the כ?

יוֹרֶה

Were you able to find a similar word in the vocabulary? Can you work out what this form might mean in context?

חַטָּאִים

Could you find a word that looks similar to this in the vocabulary? If the ending ים indicates a plural, how would you translate חַטָּאִים?

There is a **dagesh** in the ט simply because that is how the word is spelled. Something similar happens in the word אִשָּׁה (*woman*). There is a more complex orthographical explanation, but it requires an advanced understanding of Hebrew nouns.

בַּדָּרֶךְ

Did you find a word that looks like this in the vocabulary? The first letter, בַּ, is a preposition meaning *in the*. With this additional knowledge can you translate בַּדָּרֶךְ? Do you know why there is a **dagesh** in the ד?

We will learn about prepositions later. But it is worth noting that בַּ is a single letter attached to the front of the word, just like וְ. The symbol : after בַּדָּרֶךְ is called *sof pasuk* and it indicates that this is the end of the verse. It is not the same as a full stop (or period) in English; it occurs only at the end of a verse, even if the verse is made up of several sentences. Notice also that there is an *a* vowel instead of an *e* vowel in the middle syllable of the word. This has happened because it is the last word in the verse. It is said to be 'in pause', because a reader pauses at the last word in the verse and, in Hebrew, this can mean a vowel is lengthened (in this case from **segol** to **qamets**).

By this point your word-matching should have produced something like: *good and just Yhwh therefore he teaches sinners in the way.*

It is now necessary to turn this into a sentence in idiomatic English, which is (arguably) the most difficult task of translation. Hebrew word order is not the same as English word order. You will need to juggle the words until they make sense in English, while still retaining the meaning of the Hebrew.

> **LANGUAGE INSIGHT**
>
> You may have noticed **dagesh** in letters that are not **begadkefat** letters. There are other reasons for the presence of **dagesh** and they will be addressed later.

POSSIBLE TRANSLATION

Yhwh is good and just; therefore he teaches sinners in the way.

There are two points to note here. First, there is no word meaning *is* in the Hebrew text. It is common for this word to be absent in Hebrew, and we need to add the word *is* if the sentence is to make sense in English. This way of constructing sentences will be explained in more detail later. Second, the word order has been changed in the possible translation. This is because in today's English, we usually say *the house is white* rather than *white is the house*. But of course, this is a psalm; it is poetry and we can be a little more flexible with word order than we can in prose. It would be perfectly appropriate to translate the phrase: *Good and just is Yhwh*. And, of course, we can substitute *the LORD* for *Yhwh*.

❓ Test yourself

1 Place **dagesh** in the following words where appropriate.

אוֹר	ōr	*light*
בַּיִת	BĀ-yit	*house*
גָּמָל	gā-MĀHL	*camel*
דֶּלֶת	DE-let	*door*
חֵץ	chayts	*arrow*
כּוֹל	kōl	*all (totality)*
לֶחֶם	LE-chem	*bread*
נָבִיא	nā-VEE	*prophet*
עַז	az	*strength*
פֶּה	peh	*mouth*
שֵׁם	shaym	*name*
תּוֹרָה	tō-RĀH	*instruction, law*

2 Translate the following into Hebrew.

a Light and strength. _____

b Land and sea. _____

c A horse and a camel. _____

d A name and a house. _____

e A prince and a prophet. _____

SELF-CHECK

I CAN...
describe how **dagesh** is used in **begadkefat** letters
recognize the various forms of the conjunction ו
read and translate a verse from Psalm 25:8

4 The definite article, gender and number

In this unit you will learn about:
▶ the definite article
▶ singular, plural and dual forms of nouns
▶ masculine and feminine forms of nouns

You will read:
▶ Genesis 1:1

Vocabulary builder

NOUNS

חַג	chāg	*feast*
לַיְלָה	lī-LĀ	*night*
עִיר	eer	*city* (f)
פָּרָה	pā-RĀ	*cow* (f)
רֵאשִׁית	ray-SHEET	*beginning, a former time*
שָׁמַיִם	sha-MĪ-yim	*heaven, sky*
שָׂרָה	sā-RĀ	*princess* (f)

VERBS

בָּרָא	bā-RĀ	*to create, form, make*

OTHER

אֵת	ayt	object marker (no English word translates it)

Grammar

THE DEFINITE ARTICLE

In English, we have definite and indefinite articles. The word *the* is the definite article, as in *the house*, meaning a particular house. The word *a* is the indefinite article, as in *a house*, meaning an unspecified house.

24

The definite article in Hebrew is not a separate word (as it is in English), but instead is attached to the word that follows it, just like the conjunction וְ. The definite article comprises the letter הַ, usually with a **patach**, and a **dagesh** in the following letter. Here are some examples:

הַיּוֹם   *the day*

הַסּוּס   *the horse*

Note the **dagesh** in י and ס.

As we have noted, some letters take **dagesh** at the beginning of a word, and these continue to take a **dagesh** (only one **dagesh**: we do not add a second **dagesh** to indicate the definite article). Here are some examples:

הַבֵּן   *the son*

הַגָּמָל   *the camel*

And some letters do not take **dagesh** at all, so they cannot take **dagesh** with the definite article. However, in these cases the vowel under the ה usually lengthens to a **qamets**. Here are some examples:

הָאִישׁ   *the man*

הָאָב   *the father*

The use of **qamets** is not inevitable. For example, *the sand* is הַחוֹל with a **patach**.

Occasionally the vowel under the ה will change to a **segol**:

חַג   *a feast*   הֶחָג   *the feast*

There are a few common words that change vowels with the definite article, and it is worth learning the change:

אֶרֶץ	*land*	הָאָרֶץ	*the land*
גַּן	*garden*	הַגָּן	*the garden*
הַר	*mountain*	הָהָר	*the mountain*
עַם	*people*	הָעָם	*the people*

LANGUAGE INSIGHT

There is no indefinite article in Hebrew. The word סוּס can mean either *horse* or *a horse*. Context will usually determine whether we translate it with an indefinite article in English.

PRACTICE 1

1 **Put the definite article in front of the following words and write the meaning of the word next to it (the first is done for you). Don't forget to add the *dagesh* in letters that take *dagesh*.**

a הַיּוֹם   *the day*

b בַּת

c גָּמָל

d חוֹל

e יָד

f לֵבָב

g דֶּרֶךְ

h קוֹל

i אֶרֶץ

j אוֹר

k נָבִיא

2 **Translate into English.**

a הָאִישׁ וְהָאִשָּׁה

b הָאָב וְהָאֵם

c הַחוֹל וְהַיָּם

d הַסּוּס וְהַפָּר

e הָאָח וְהָאָחוֹת

NUMBER AND GENDER

In English, words can be singular (s) (e.g. *the apple*) or plural (p) (e.g. *the oranges*). We call this number. The word *banana* is singular whereas *bananas* is plural. This can apply to other kinds of words: *she* is singular; *they* is plural. Some plurals are irregular: the plural of *child* is *children*, not *childs*.

In Hebrew, as well as being singular or plural, words can be masculine (m) or feminine (f). The word for *land* is feminine and the word for *garden* is masculine. English does not have gender so gardens are neither masculine nor feminine in English. We might assume that *a prince* is masculine and *a princess* is feminine, but they are (arguably) not grammatically so.

In Unit 6 we will also encounter common (c) gender: things that can be grammatically either masculine or feminine.

A number of the words we have learned already are feminine. Here are some examples:

אַחַת   אֵם   אֶרֶץ   אִשָּׁה   בַּת   הִיא   יָד   כַּף

It is unsurprising that words for female people are grammatically feminine, though this is not inevitable. There is no particular logic to the gender of other words. One might guess at reasons why a *tree* should be masculine and a *spring* feminine, but often there is no way to predict a word's gender, and it must be learned. However, in Hebrew words that end with הָ are usually feminine, e.g.:

אִשָּׁה	i-SHĀ	woman
פָּרָה	pa-RĀ	cow
שָׂרָה	sa-RĀ	princess

> **LANGUAGE INSIGHT**
> A notable exception is the word for night, לַיְלָה, which ends in הָ but is masculine.

PLURAL NOUNS

It can be useful to distinguish different categories of words. This can be complicated, because some words are categorized according to context. In the sentence *I respect you* the word *respect* is a verb. But in the sentence *Please treat everybody with respect* the word *respect* is a noun.

A verb is often described as a 'doing word'. It describes activities like *walk*, *run*, *swim*; and also other things we do, like *think*, *owe*, *respect*. If you can put *to* in front of it, it's probably a verb. *To think* makes sense; *to window* doesn't. But many words, like *respect*, can be either nouns or verbs.

A noun is often described as an 'object' or a 'thing'. It can be a real object, like *window*, *fish*, *shoe*; or it can be abstract, like *integrity*, *love*, *respect*. If you can put *the* in front of it, it's probably a noun. *The window* makes sense; *the think* doesn't. Names are sometimes known as proper nouns. Most of the words we have learned so far are nouns.

Plurals are formed by adding suffixes (extra letters at the end of a word). In English, we usually add *s* (*cow*; *cows*), though some words in English have no distinct plural (*sheep*; *sheep*) and some have irregular plurals, which are left over from an earlier stage in the development of the English language (*ox*; *oxen*). Hebrew also adds suffixes to make plurals.

In Hebrew, masculine plurals add the suffix ים. We have already seen a masculine plural in Psalm 25: the word חַטָּא has the plural חַטָּאִים. Here are some more examples:

סוּס	soos	horse	סוּסִים	soos-EEM	horses
פַּר	par	ox	פָּרִים	par-EEM	oxen
שַׂר	sar	prince	שָׂרִים	sar-EEM	princes

Feminine plurals change the הָ to וֹת:

סוּסָה	soo-SĀ	mare	סוּסוֹת	soo-SŌT	mares
פָּרָה	pa-RĀ	cow	פָּרוֹת	pa-RŌT	cows
שָׂרָה	sa-RĀ	princess	שָׂרוֹת	sa-RŌT	princesses

DUAL FORM

In Hebrew there is a special ending for things that come in pairs, such as *hands* and *feet*. These words are typically feminine. This form is called the dual form and looks very much like the masculine ending, but with an extra **patach**:

יָד	yād	hand	יָדַיִם	yā-DĪ-im	hands
רֶגֶל	RE-gel	foot	רַגְלַיִם	rag-LĪ-im	feet
בֶּרֶךְ	BE-rek	knee	בִּרְכַּיִם	bir-KĪ-im	knees
שָׂפָה	sā-FĀ	lip	שְׂפָתַיִם	sə-fā-TĪ-im	lips
אֹזֶן	Ō-zen	ear	אָזְנַיִם	oz-NĪ-yim	ears
עַיִן	A-yin	eye	עֵינַיִם	ay-NĪ-yim	eyes

Notice that the vowels have changed in most of the plural forms: e.g. the ֶ vowels in רֶגֶל have changed to ַ and ְ in רַגְלַיִם. There are reasons for this, and we will discuss these later. For now it is important merely to notice that there are differences.

PRACTICE 2

1 Write the plurals of the following nouns and give the plural meaning. Some have a definite article. The first two have been done for you.

a	סוּסָה	סוּסוֹת	*mares*
b	הַפָּר	הַפָּרִים	*the oxen*
c	סוּס		
d	עַיִן		
e	הַשַּׂר		
f	הַשָּׂדֶה		
g	קוֹל		
h	פָּרָה		
i	הַיָּד		
j	רֶגֶל		

2 Write out the following in English.

a יָדַיִם וְרַגְלַיִם

b סוּסִים וְסוּסוֹת

c הֶהָרִים וְהַיַּמִּים

d הַגַּנִּים וְהַדְּרָכִים

Hint: If the last of these seems difficult, perhaps it is because both nouns end in letters that have final forms. They have appeared before in this course.

IRREGULAR PLURALS

Not all feminine nouns end in **הָ**; e.g., **בַּת** is feminine but doesn't end in **הָ**. Sometimes these feminine nouns form plurals differently, and indeed some of the common masculine nouns have irregular plurals. Moreover, we have already encountered a word that appears to have the form of a feminine plural, since it ends with **וֹת**, but in fact it is singular. The word is **אָחוֹת** (*sister*). Common irregular plurals must be learned:

אִישׁ	*man*	אֲנָשִׁים	a-nā-SHEEM	*men*
אִשָּׁה	*woman*	נָשִׁים	nā-SHEEM	*women*
בֵּן	*son*	בָּנִים	bā-NEEM	*sons*
בַּת	*daughter*	בָּנוֹת	bā-NŌT	*daughters*
אָח	*brother*	אַחִים	a-CHEEM	*brothers*
אָחוֹת	*sister*	אֲחָיוֹת	ach-AĪ-ōt	*sisters*
אָב	*father*	אָבוֹת	ā-VŌT	*fathers*
אֵם	*mother*	אִמּוֹת	im-MŌT	*mothers*

A feminine word with an apparently masculine ending:

עִיר	*city*	עָרִים	ā-REEM	*cities*

A masculine word with an apparently feminine ending:

לַיְלָה	*night*	לֵילוֹת	LAY-lōt	*nights*

Plurals that are easily confused:

יוֹם	*day*	יָמִים	yā-MEEM	*days*
יָם	*sea*	יַמִּים	ya-MEEM	*seas*

The plurals of two of these words take a definite article pointed with **segol** for reasons to do with where the stress falls in the word:

הֶהָרִים	*the mountains*
הֶעָרִים	*the cities*

PRACTICE 3

Translate into Hebrew.

a a man   the men
b a daughter   the daughters
c the mother   mothers
d night   nights
e the days and the nights
f cities and princes

Reading

GENESIS 1:1

There is no ideal verse in the Bible with which to demonstrate the definite article and the use of plurals at this stage. Verses with straightforward plurals often have complicated verbs or other difficult grammatical features. The advantage of Genesis 1:1 is that it is familiar to many people and it shows definite articles and plurals in action.

Points to look out for in this text:

▶ words we have already encountered
▶ use of the definite article
▶ plural forms.

Read the verse aloud a few times to be sure of the pronunciation.

Text	Approximate pronunciation
בְּרֵאשִׁית בָּרָא אֱלֹהִים אֵת הַשָּׁמַיִם וְאֵת הָאָרֶץ׃	bə-ray-SHEET bā-RĀ elō-HEEM ayt ha-shā-MĪ-yim ve-ayt hā-ĀR-ets

As you did in Unit 3, try to match each word of the text with the vocabulary list at the beginning of the unit, as far as you can. Remember, some of the words are not precisely the same as the words in the list of vocabulary. The words in the vocabulary are the dictionary forms. Once you have matched the words in the text with the vocabulary, you should begin to have a sense of the meaning of the verse. Of course, many readers will find this verse very familiar: the meaning is obvious. Or is it?

💡 Language discovery

בְּרֵאשִׁית

The letter בְּ at the beginning of this word means *in*. What do you think the whole word means?

It is usually translated *in the beginning*, though translations vary – look up a few and see. Notice that the **alef** has no vowel. This is fairly common in Hebrew; **alef** is often left unvocalized.

בָּרָא

Did you find this word in the vocabulary? Notice that the meaning given in the vocabulary for בָּרָא is *to create* but we are translating exactly the same word here as *he created*. Also, the word for *he* (הוּא) is not used here. We will explore the reasons for this later.

אֱלֹהִים

You might already know this word; it has been used before in this course.

This word is plural in form but is not usually translated as a plural, unless it refers to the gods of other nations.

אֵת

This word is known as the 'object marker', and will be discussed later. There is no English word for אֵת, so we leave it untranslated.

הַשָּׁמַיִם

What is the best way of translating this word? It has a dual ending, but usually in idiomatic English we use the singular, except sometimes in religious contexts.

וְאֵת

The conjunction וְ (clearly meaning *and* rather than *but* in this context) and the object marker again. How would you translate it?

הָאָרֶץ

This word was encountered earlier in the unit. How would you translate it?

POSSIBLE TRANSLATIONS

In the beginning God created the heavens and the earth.

In the beginning God created heaven and earth.

 Test yourself

Translate the following into Hebrew.

a The sea and the sky. _____

b Sisters and brothers. _____

c The city and the mountain. _____

d The people and the land. _____

e Oxen and cows. _____

f Hands and feet. _____

g Mothers and fathers. _____

h The men and the women. _____

i The cities and the seas. _____

j The sons and the daughters. _____

SELF-CHECK

I CAN...
○ recognize the definite article in Hebrew
○ recognize singular, plural and dual forms of nouns
○ recognize masculine and feminine forms of nouns
○ read and translate Genesis 1:1

5 Subject pronouns and verbless sentences

In this unit you will learn about:
▶ Hebrew subject pronouns
▶ how sentences without verbs work in Hebrew

You will read:
▶ 2 Samuel 12:7a

Vocabulary builder

NOUNS

דָּוִד	dā-VID	David
מֶלֶךְ	MEL-ech	king
נָתָן	nā-TĀN	Nathan

VERBS

אָמַר	ā-MAR	to say

Grammar

SUBJECT PRONOUNS

A pronoun is a word that takes the place of a noun. Examples are words like *she* and *they*.

The subject of a verb is the person or people doing whatever the verb indicates. In the sentence *She gave the book to him, she* is the subject of *gave*; the object is *him*.

There are many pronouns in Hebrew (just like in English). In this unit we are going to look at the subject pronouns meaning *he, she, you, I, they* and *we*. Personal pronouns in Hebrew have to be learned by heart so you should repeat them daily for a few days until they are familiar.

Singular			Plural		
he	הוּא	hoo	*they* (m)	הֵם or הֵמָּה	haym or HAY-mā
she	הִיא	hee	*they* (f)	הֵנָּה	HAY-nā
you (m)	אַתָּה	at-TĀ	*you* (m)	אַתֶּם	a-TEM
you (f)	אַתְּ	at	*you* (f)	אַתֶּן	a-TEN
I	אֲנִי or אָנֹכִי	a-NEE or ā-no-CHEE	*we*	אֲנַחְנוּ	a-NACH-noo

These pronouns are used only when they are the subject of a verb. So הוּא is the pronoun used as the subject: it means *he* but not *him*. The object pronouns will be discussed in Unit 10 (words for *me*, *him*, *her*, etc.).

In biblical Hebrew, there are four ways of saying *you*; it depends on how many people are being addressed, and whether those people are male or female. If addressing a group of men or a mixed group the masculine plural is used. The feminine plural is used only for addressing two or more women. Since there aren't many groups of women in the Hebrew Bible, we don't see feminine plurals much, though there are quite a few in the book of Ruth.

PRACTICE 1

Fill in the blanks.

Singular		Plural	
he		*they* (m)	
	הִיא		הֵנָּה
you (m)			אַתֶּם
you	אַתְּ	*you* (f)	
I			אֲנַחְנוּ

SENTENCES WITHOUT VERBS

If we want to use English grammar correctly, we need to put verbs in our sentences (e.g. *I am the king*). However, in Hebrew we can make simple sentences using just pronouns and nouns.

In Hebrew, the present tense of the verb *to be* is understood without needing to be written. If you know the Hebrew for *I* (אֲנִי) and for *king* (מֶלֶךְ **MEL-ech**), you can say *I am the king*: אֲנִי הַמֶּלֶךְ.

Here are some more examples of verbless sentences:

אַתָּה הָאָב *You are the father.*

הִיא הַשָּׂרָה *She is the princess.*

The words הוּא and הִיא can also mean *it*:

הוּא הַגָּן *It is the garden.*

הִיא הָאָרֶץ *It is the land.*

LANGUAGE INSIGHT

We use הוּא with הַגָּן because גַּן is masculine, and הִיא with הָאָרֶץ because אֶרֶץ is feminine.

PRACTICE 2

Complete the following sentences.

a   He is the prince.   _____ הוּא

b   She is the woman.   _____ הִיא

c   You are the brother.   הָאָח _____

d   You are the princess.   _____ אַתְּ

e   I am the king.   הַמֶּלֶךְ _____

f   It is the mountain.   הָהָר _____

g   It is the city.   _____ הִיא

h   They are the sons.   הַבָּנִים _____

i   They are the women.   הַנָּשִׁים _____

j   You are the fathers.   _____ אַתֶּם

k   You are the daughters.   _____ אַתֶּן

l   We are the princes.   הַשָּׂרִים _____

m   They are the horses.   הַסּוּסִים _____

n   They are the cows.   _____ הֵנָּה

Reading

2 SAMUEL 12:7A

Read the verse aloud a few times to be sure of the pronunciation.

Text   Approximate pronunciation

וַיֹּאמֶר נָתָן אֶל־דָּוִד אַתָּה הָאִישׁ:   va-YO-mer nā-TĀN el dā-VID at-TĀ hā-EESH

💡 Language discovery

וַיֹּאמֶר

We have not learned about verbs yet; we will learn this form later. Verbs in biblical Hebrew are quite unlike verbs in Indo-European languages such as English, so it is easier to learn them once we have a good understanding of the other words around them. Notice, though, the ו at the beginning of the word: you have learned this conjunction, although with different vowels. This is the 'he' form of the verb, and we will translate it with a past tense. With this information, can you figure out how to translate it?

נָתַן

This appears in the vocabulary section. What does it mean?

אֶל־דָּוִד

We have seen the word אֶל before, in Unit 1. Here it is joined with **maqqef** to a name. Can you translate it?

אַתָּה

This is one of the pronouns. Which one?

הָאִישׁ

You have encountered this word several times already and can probably work out what it means.

By now you should have something like: *And he said Nathan to David you (are) the man.* Notice that the word order in Hebrew differs from English. The verb comes first in the sentence (*and he said*), followed by the subject (*Nathan*) and then the object (*David*). Also, Hebrew has no quotation marks for indicating direct speech. But when we translate into English, it is appropriate to use quotation marks if a person in the text speaks directly to another. If you are unfamiliar with the context of this phrase, read 2 Samuel 11–12 in English.

POSSIBLE TRANSLATION

And Nathan said to David, 'You are the man.'

 Test yourself

These questions are intended to test your knowledge and understanding of the points of grammar covered in Units 1 to 5. Answer all questions as fully as possible. Try to answer the questions without looking up the answers.

1 Write out the alphabet in order (it's easy to forget the order after the first couple of weeks). Include final forms where they exist.

_____

2 Write out the following:

   a   short vowels _____
   b   long vowels _____
   c   **sheva** _____
   d   composite **sheva** vowels _____

3 Answer the following questions.

   a   Which letters always take **dagesh** at the beginning of a word? _____
   b   Which letters never take **dagesh**? _____

4 Write out the following in Hebrew.

    a   the king _____

    b   the land _____

    c   the hands _____

    d   the men _____

5 Write out the following in Hebrew.

    a   man and woman _____

    b   princess and prince _____

    c   night and day _____

    d   the mountain and the city _____

    e   the horse and the mare _____

    f   the garden and the sea _____

6 Write out the following in English.

    a   הוּא הָאִישׁ _____

    b   הֵמָּה הַשָּׂרִים _____

    c   אֲנַחְנוּ הַבָּנוֹת _____

    d   הִיא הָעִיר _____

    e   אַתֵּן הַנָּשִׁים _____

    f   אֲנִי הָאָחוֹת _____

SELF-CHECK

	I CAN...
○	recognize the personal pronouns for the subject of the verb
○	understand Hebrew verbless sentences
○	read and translate 2 Samuel 12:7a

6 Possessives, adjectives and negatives

In this unit you will learn about:
▶ how to indicate possession with pronominal suffixes
▶ how negatives are formed in Hebrew
▶ how adjectives work in verbless sentences

You will read:
▶ Psalm 76:2

Vocabulary builder

NOUNS

אַהֲבָה	a-ha-VĀ	*love* (f)
אָכְלָה	och-LĀ	*food* (f)
בַּיִת	BA-yit (p בָּתִּים bāt-TEEM)	*house* (m)
בְּרָכָה	bərā-CHĀ (p בְּרָכוֹת bə-rā-CHŌT)	*blessing* (f)
דָּבָר	dā-VĀR (p דְּבָרִים də-vā-REEM)	*word, thing* (m)
דַּעַת	DA-at	*knowledge* (f)
חֶרֶב	CHE-rev (p חֲרָבוֹת cha-rā-VŌT)	*sword* (f)
יְהוּדָה	yə-hoo-DĀ	*Judah*
יִשְׂרָאֵל	yis-rā-AYL	*Israel*
כֹּהֵן	cō-HAYN (p כֹּהֲנִים cō-ha-NEEM)	*priest* (m)
מָקוֹם	mā-KŌM (p מְקוֹמוֹת me-kō-MŌT)	*place* (m)
שֵׁם	shaym	*name* (m)

> **LANGUAGE INSIGHT**
> Note that מָקוֹם is a masculine noun with an irregular plural ending that looks feminine. It takes masculine adjectives.

ADJECTIVES

גָּדוֹל	**gā-DŌL**	*great, large, big*
חָדָשׁ	**chā-DĀSH**	*new*
חָכָם	**chā-CHĀM**	*wise*
יָפֶה	**yā-FE (f** יָפָה **yā-FĀ)**	*beautiful*
קָדוֹשׁ	**kā-DŌSH**	*holy*
קָטֹן	**kā-TŌN (f** קְטַנָּה **kə-ta-NĀ)**	*small*
רֵיק	**rayk**	*empty*

VERBS

יָדַע	**yā-DĀ**	*to know*
שָׁבַת	**shā-VAT**	*to rest*

Grammar

NOUNS WITH PRONOMINAL SUFFIXES

The idea of *person* is used to indicate the relationship between the speaker or writer and the listener or reader. It is probably easiest to grasp by means of an example:

I told you that he was happy.

If we describe the pronouns in this sentence, we would say that *I* is first person, *you* is second person and *he* is third person.

Here are the English pronouns categorized by person:

I, me, my, mine, we, our, ours	first person
you, your, yours	second person
he, him, his, she, her, hers, it, its, they, their, theirs	third person

These pronouns can be singular: *I, you, he, she, it;* or plural: *we, you* (as in *all of you*), *they*.

In Hebrew, the pronouns can be masculine (m) הוּא אַתָּה הֵמָּה אַתֶּם; feminine (f) אַתֶּן הֵנָּה אַתְּ הִיא; or common (c) אֲנַחְנוּ אָנֹכִי. Common gender is not exactly like the concept of neuter gender in other languages, but it is similar. In Hebrew, first-person pronouns are always common gender. However, Hebrew nouns are rarely common gender.

The idea of person does not apply only to pronouns; it can also apply to verbs, as we will discover in due course.

We can use shorthand to indicate person, gender and number. For example, הוּא is 3ms (third person masculine singular).

In English, if we want to indicate that a horse belongs to me, we can use the possessive pronoun *my*: *my horse*. In Hebrew the idea is conveyed by adding an ending to the word for *horse*. These suffixes are called pronominal suffixes because they are endings that indicate a pronoun.

Here is the word סוּס with pronominal suffixes:

סוּסוֹ	**soo-SŌ**	*his horse* (3ms)
סוּסָהּ	**soo-SĀCH**	*her horse* (3fs)
סוּסְךָ	**soo-sə-CHĀ**	*your horse* (2ms)
סוּסֵךְ	**soo-SAYCH**	*your horse* (2ms)
סוּסִי	**soo-SEE**	*my horse* (1cs)
סוּסָם	**soo-SĀM**	*their horse* (3mp)
סוּסָן	**soo-SĀN**	*their horse* (3fp)
סוּסְכֶם	**soo-sə-CHEM**	*your horse* (2mp)
סוּסְכֶן	**soo-sə-CHEN**	*your horse* (2fp)
סוּסֵנוּ	**soo-SAY-noo**	*our horse* (1cp)

Four words can be translated *your horse*. The word used depends on whether the *you* referred to is one man (2ms), one woman (2fs), a group of men or a mixed group (2mp), or a group of women (2fp).

Note the dot in the final ה of סוּסָהּ, *her horse*. This looks exactly the same as a **dagesh** but is called **mappiq**. Of course, ה cannot take **dagesh**, so if you see a dot in a ה it must be **mappiq**. When you see ה you pronounce it **ch** as in *loch*. Thus סוּסָהּ is **soos-ACH**.

The same suffixes are used if a noun is feminine, although if the noun ends in הָ, the ה changes to ת. Here is the word סוּסָה with pronominal suffixes:

סוּסָתוֹ	**soo-sā-TŌ**	*his mare* (3ms)
סוּסָתָהּ	**soo-sā-TĀCH**	*her mare* (3fs)
סוּסָתְךָ	**soo-sā-tə-CHĀ**	*your mare* (2ms)
סוּסָתֵךְ	**soo-sā-TAYCH**	*your mare* (2fs)
סוּסָתִי	**soo-sā-TEE**	*my mare* (1cs)
סוּסָתָם	**soo-sā-TĀM**	*their mare* (3mp)
סוּסָתָן	**soo-sā-TĀN**	*their mare* (3fp)
סוּסַתְכֶם	**soo-sa-tə-CHEM**	*your mare* (2mp)
סוּסַתְכֶן	**soo-sa-tə-CHEN**	*your mare* (2fp)
סוּסָתֵנוּ	**soo-sā-TAY-noo**	*our mare* (1cp)

If more than one horse is being described, slightly different suffixes are added to a modified form of the plural noun. Here is the word סוּסִים with pronominal suffixes:

סוּסָיו	soo-SAV	*his horses*
סוּסֶיהָ	soo-SAY-hā	*her horses*
סוּסֶיךָ	soo-SAY-chā	*your horses*
סוּסַיִךְ	soo-SĪ-yich	*your horses*
סוּסַי	soo-SĪ	*my horses*
סוּסֵיהֶם	soo-say-HEM	*their horses*
סוּסֵיהֶן	soo-say-HEN	*their horses*
סוּסֵיכֶם	soo-say-CHEM	*your horses*
סוּסֵיכֶן	soo-say-CHEN	*your horses*
סוּסֵינוּ	soo-SAY-noo	*our horses*

The pronominal suffixes for feminine plural nouns are the same, even to the extent of preserving the י of the masculine plural. Here is the word סוּסוֹת with pronominal suffixes:

סוּסוֹתָיו	soo-sō-TĀV	*his mares*
סוּסוֹתֶיהָ	soo-sō-TAY-hā	*her mares*
סוּסוֹתֶיךָ	soo-sō-TAY-chā	*your mares*
סוּסוֹתַיִךְ	soo-sō-TĪ-yich	*your mares*
סוּסוֹתַי	soo-sō-TĪ	*my mares*
סוּסוֹתֵיהֶם	soo-sō-tay-HEM	*their mares*
סוּסוֹתֵיהֶן	soo-sō-tay-HEN	*their mares*
סוּסוֹתֵיכֶם	soo-sō-tay-CHEM	*your mares*
סוּסוֹתֵיכֶן	soo-sō-tay-CHEN	*your mares*
סוּסוֹתֵינוּ	soo-sō-TAY-noo	*our mares*

PRACTICE 1

1 Write the following in the correct places in the table and give the English translation.

קוֹלִי קוֹלִי קוֹלְכֶם קוֹלֵךְ קוֹלְךָ קוֹלָן קוֹלְכֶן קוֹלֵנוּ קוֹלָהּ קוֹלָם קוֹלֵךְ

3ms			3mp		
3fs			3fp		
2ms			2mp		
2fs			2fp		
1cs			1cp		

2 Write out פָּרָה with pronominal suffixes.

3ms			3mp		
3fs			3fp		
2ms			2mp		
2fs			2fp		
1cs			1cp		

3 Translate the following into English.

a אָבִי

b יָדְךָ

c אֱלֹהֵינוּ

d מַלְכֵיהֶם

e אִמּוֹ

Hint: the absolute forms of the words (i.e. the forms you would find in a dictionary) are:

אָב יָד אֱלֹהִים מֶלֶךְ אֵם

ADJECTIVES IN VERBLESS SENTENCES

An adjective is a word that describes a noun. In the phrase *the door is red* the word *door* is a noun and the word *red* is an adjective. Other examples of adjectives are *good, bad,* etc.

We have already encountered several Hebrew adjectives:

קַל		רַב	חָר	עַז	יָשָׁר	חַד	רַע	טוֹב
light (in weight)		*many*	*white*	*strong*	*just (upright)*	*sharp*	*bad*	*good*

In Unit 5, we looked at sentences without verbs; e.g. אֲנִי הַמֶּלֶךְ *I am the king*. The present tense of the verb *to be* is understood without being written.

Similarly, if we want to say *the man is good* or *the horse is strong* in Hebrew, we leave out the verb *to be*. We also have to put the adjective before the noun. Read these examples out loud:

טוֹב הָאִישׁ   *the man is good*

עַז סוּסִי   *my horse is strong*

We have already seen an example of this construction in Psalm 25:8 (see Unit 3).

In English, adjectives generally do not change. We can say *the door is red* or *the doors are red*; *red* remains the same. In Hebrew, all adjectives have to agree in gender and number with the noun they are describing. If the adjective describes a feminine noun, it takes a feminine form:

טוֹבָה הָאִשָּׁה   **tō-VĀ hā-i-SHĀ**   *the woman is good*

עַזָּה סוּסָתוֹ   **a-ZĀ soo-sā-TŌ**   *his mare is strong*

If the adjective describes a plural noun, it takes a plural form:

טוֹבִים הָאֲנָשִׁים	tō-VEEM hā-a-nā-SHEEM	*the men are good*
רָעִים בָּנֵינוּ	rā-EEM bā-NAY-noo	*our sons are bad*

A noun that is both feminine and plural requires an adjective that is both feminine and plural:

טוֹבוֹת הָאִמּוֹת	tō-VŌT ha-i-MŌT	*the mothers are good*
רָעוֹת הַשָּׂרוֹת	rā-ŌT ha-sā-RŌT	*the princesses are bad*

You may remember that some nouns have irregular forms. For example, לַיְלָה looks like a feminine noun but is in fact masculine. And the word for *women* looks like a masculine plural but is in fact feminine. In cases like this, the form of the adjective should be the usual form. The same applies to nouns with dual endings. For example:

טוֹבִים הַלֵּילוֹת	tō-VEEM ha-lay-LŌT	*the nights are good*
טוֹבִים הָאָבוֹת	tō-VEEM hā-a-VŌT	*the fathers are good*
טוֹבוֹת הַנָּשִׁים	tō-VŌT ha-nā-SHEEM	*the women are good*
טוֹבוֹת הַיָּדַיִם	tō-VŌT ha-yā-DĪ-yim	*the hands are good*

Many nouns and adjectives are vocalized differently (i.e. they have different vowels) when they appear in feminine or plural forms. Others acquire a **dagesh**. For example, compare the adjectives in the following:

עַז הַסּוּס	*the horse is strong*
עַזָּה הַסּוּסָה	*the mare is strong*

Note the **dagesh** in עַזָּה. There are complex reasons for such changes which can be learned later. The changes do not usually interfere with recognition; if you know a word in its absolute (i.e. basic) form, you should be able to recognize it in plural or feminine forms. And even if you don't know the word, the changes are not usually significant enough to cause difficulty in finding the word in a dictionary.

NEGATIVES

In Hebrew, negatives are introduced with the negative particle לֹא. This is how it works:

טוֹב הַמֶּלֶךְ	*the king is good*
לֹא טוֹב הַמֶּלֶךְ	*the king is not good*
עַז הַסּוּס וְלֹא עַזָּה הַסּוּסָה	*the horse is strong but the mare is not strong*

You might remember that the conjunction וְ can mean *but* when a contrast is implied.

PRACTICE 2

Choose the correct adjective from the options given, and give the meanings of the sentences. The adjective must agree in gender and number with the noun.

a	קְטַנָּה	קָטֹן	קְטַנִּם	הַכֹּהֵן
b	חַד	חַדָּה	חַדּוֹת	חֲרָבוֹת
c	קְדוֹשׁוֹת	קְדוֹשִׁים	קָדוֹשׁ	הַמְּקוֹמוֹת
d	רָעוֹת	רָעָה	רַע	הַשַּׂר
e	טוֹב	טוֹבָה	טוֹבוֹת	הָאָכְלָה
f	רֵיק	רֵיקָה	רֵיקוֹת	הַבַּיִת
g	יָפֶה	יָפָה	יָפוֹת	אַהֲבָתוֹ
h	חָכָם	חַכְמוֹת	חֲכָמִים	דְּבָרֵינוּ
i	גְּדוֹלוֹת	גָּדוֹל	גְּדוֹלָה	דַּעְתִּי
j	חֲדָשִׁים	חֲדָשָׁה	חֲדָשׁוֹת	בִּרְכוֹתֵיכֶם

ADJECTIVES (ATTRIBUTIVE)

There are other ways to use adjectives in English. Compare the following:

The man is good.

the good man

Both of these describe the man in the same way and have much the same meaning. However, the first example is a complete sentence, whereas the second example is just part of a sentence. The second example needs more information (generally a verb) to make it a sentence; e.g. *The good man rested*, or *Abraham is a good man*. This kind of use of adjectives is called attributive.

In English, an attributive adjective comes before the noun, but in Hebrew (like French and many other languages) it comes after the noun. Notice also that both words have the definite article:

הָאִישׁ הַטּוֹב	*the good man*
הַדָּבָר הַקָּדוֹשׁ	*the holy word*

If we wanted to say *a good man* or *a holy word*, we would omit the definite articles on both noun and adjective:

אִישׁ טוֹב	*a good man*
דָּבָר קָדוֹשׁ	*a holy word*

The adjective must always agree with the noun:

ms	הַכֹּהֵן הַגָּדוֹל	*the great priest (high priest)*
mp	הַכֹּהֲנִים הַגְּדוֹלִים	*the great priests (high priests)*
fs	הַפָּרָה הַקְּטַנָּה	*the small cow*
fp	הַפָּרוֹת הַקְּטַנּוֹת	*the small cows*

To use this kind of adjectival construction in a sentence, a verb is needed. Verbs generally come at the beginning of a sentence in Hebrew. The verb in this example is *to rest*:

שָׁבַת הָאִישׁ הַטּוֹב	**shā-VAT hā-EESH ha-TŌV**	*The good man rested.*

Literally this means *He rested the man the good* but in English we would say *The good man rested*.

If the verb is the present tense of the verb *to be*, it is not necessary to write it in Hebrew because the sense is understood implicitly, as we have seen previously. For example:

אִישׁ טוֹב אַבְרָהָם	*Abraham is a good man.*

Literally, this means *A man a good (is) Abraham* but in English we would say *Abraham is a good man*.

PRACTICE 3

Write the following in English.

a	הַחֶרֶב הַחֲדָשָׁה
b	הָעִיר הַגְּדוֹלָה
c	הַשָּׂרוֹת הֶחֲכָמוֹת
d	הַדְּבָרִים הַקְּדוֹשִׁים
e	הַנָּשִׁים הַיָּפוֹת

Reading

PSALM 76:2 (76:1 IN ENGLISH)

Points to look out for in this text:
- words we have already encountered
- use of pronominal suffixes
- use of adjectives.

Read the verse aloud a few times.

> **LEARNING INSIGHT**
>
> The psalm titles have no verse numbers in English translations, which leads to differences in verse numbering.

נוֹדָע בִּיהוּדָה אֱלֹהִים	**nō-DĀ bee-hoo-DĀ e-lo-HEEM**
בְּיִשְׂרָאֵל גָּדוֹל שְׁמוֹ׃	**bə-yis-rā-AYL gā-DŌL shə-MŌ**

Language discovery

נוֹדָע

If you connected this word to the verb יָדַע or the noun דַּעַת in the vocabulary, you have good instincts, but it isn't necessarily obvious! This form is passive and 3ms. Can you work out what it means?

בִּיהוּדָה

We have previously encountered the prefix בְּ. Do you remember what it means? And can you work out what the whole word means? In this context, it is a place name.

אֱלֹהִים

This word should be familiar now. Did you remember it?

בְּיִשְׂרָאֵל

This is also a place name with the prefix בְּ. What does the whole word mean?

גָּדוֹל

Did you find this word in the vocabulary? What does it mean?

שְׁמוֹ

Did you find this word in the vocabulary? What is the i at the end? How would you translate it?

POSSIBLE TRANSLATION

God is known in Judah;

In Israel his name is great.

We could, of course, translate the second phrase as *His name is great in Israel*, which would also be correct English. The choice involves deciding which translation best captures the meaning and style of the Hebrew. This verse is a psalm and therefore poetry; if it were prose we might expect to see:

גָּדוֹל שְׁמוֹ בְּיִשְׂרָאֵל

? Test yourself

1 Write out the following in English.

‫קוֹלוֹ סוּסְךָ קוֹלָם סוּסֵנוּ‬.

_____

2 Write out the following in English.

‫קוֹלֵיהֶם סוּסָתָהּ פָּרוֹתֵינוּ סוּסוֹתֵיכֶן‬.

_____

3 Write out the following in Hebrew.

a my father _____

b his princess _____

c our voices _____

4 Translate this sentence into Hebrew.

The cities are bad but the king is good.

_____

5 Translate the following into English.

‫טוֹבִים פָּרֵינוּ וְרָעוֹת פָּרוֹתֵינוּ‬.

_____

SELF-CHECK

	I CAN...
○	recognize pronominal suffixes
○	recognize the negative
○	understand how adjectives are used in verbless sentences
○	read and translate Psalm 76:2 [Engl. 76:1]

7 Demonstratives and the construct

In this unit you will learn about:
▶ how demonstratives work in biblical Hebrew
▶ the construct: another way of indicating possession

You will read:
▶ Exodus 15:1a

Vocabulary builder

NOUNS

יְרוּשָׁלַיְם	yə-roo-shā-LĀ-yim	*Jerusalem*
מֹשֶׁה	mō-SHE	*Moses*
שִׁירָה	shee-RĀ	*song* (f)

VERBS

שִׁיר	sheer	*to sing*

ADVERBS

אָז	āz	*then, therefore*

Grammar

DEMONSTRATIVES

Demonstratives indicate which particular thing (or things) is (or are) being referred to. Demonstratives can be used as adjectives or as pronouns. In English, demonstratives are words like *this*, *these*, *that* and *those*.

When they are used as adjectives, they describe a noun; e.g.:

This house is new.

When they are used as pronouns they stand in place of a noun; e.g.:

This is new (i.e. *this house is new*).

This is the new house (i.e. *this house is the new house*).

These sentences are similar in meaning:

This house is new.

This is the new house.

In fact, the distinction between them can usually be understood without determining whether the demonstrative is being used as an adjective or as a pronoun.

The demonstratives in Hebrew are:

זֶה	ze	*this* (m)
זֹאת	zōt	*this* (f)
אֵלֶּה	AY-le	*these* (m and f)
הוּא	hoo	*that* (m)
הִיא	hee	*that* (f)
הֵם	haym	*those* (m)
הֵנָּה	HAY-nā	*those* (f)

Note: the words for that and those are the same as the subject pronouns meaning *he, she, they* (m) and *they* (f).

When they are used to qualify a noun, they come after the noun (like other adjectives) and they take the definite article:

הָאִישׁ הַזֶּה	*this man*
הָאִשָּׁה הַזֹּאת	*this woman*
הָאֲנָשִׁים הָאֵלֶּה	*these men*
הַנָּשִׁים הָאֵלֶּה	*these women*
הַבֵּן הַהוּא	*that son*
הַבַּת הַהִיא	*that daughter*
הַבָּנִים הָהֵם	*those sons*
הַבָּנוֹת הָהֵנָּה	*those daughters*

When demonstratives are used as pronouns they follow the usual word order for pronouns. Remember:

אַתָּה הָאָב	*You are the father.*

Similarly:

זֶה הָאָב	*This is the father.*
זֹאת הָאֵם	*This is the mother.*
אֵלֶּה הָאַחִים	*These are the brothers.*
אֵלֶּה הָאֲחָיוֹת	*These are the sisters.*

הוּא הָאָב	*That is the father.*
הִיא הָאֵם	*That is the mother.*
הֵם הָאַחִים	*Those are the brothers.*
הֵנָּה הָאֲחָיוֹת	*Those are the sisters.*

Of course, since the word הוּא also means *he*, we could translate the sentences *He is the father, She is the mother,* etc. The context will determine whether to translate with a personal pronoun or a demonstrative pronoun. If it is not clear from the context of the Hebrew text, then the sense will always be ambiguous.

A noun with a pronominal suffix does not need a definite article, since the suffix makes it definite:

זֹאת אִמִּי	*This is my mother.*
הוּא אָבִי	*That is my father.*

Again, the second example could also be translated as *He is my father.*

A noun can be qualified by several words at the same time, by adjectives and demonstrative pronouns:

חָדָשׁ הַבַּיִת הַזֶּה	*This house is new.*

This means literally *New (is) this house.* Compare the word order with טוֹב הָאִישׁ.

זֶה הַבַּיִת הֶחָדָשׁ	*This is the new house.*

This means literally *This (is) the house the new one.* Compare the word order with הָאִישׁ הַטּוֹב.

זֶה הָאִישׁ הַטּוֹב וְהַיָּשָׁר	*This is the good and just man.*

This means literally *This (is) the man the good and the just.*

טוֹב וְיָשָׁר הָאִישׁ הַזֶּה	*This man is good and just.*

This means literally *Good and just (is) the man the this.*

זֹאת פָּרָתִי הַקְּטַנָּה	*This is my small cow.*

This means literally *This is my cow the small.*

PRACTICE 1

1 Translate the following into English.

Example: הַסּוּס הַזֶּה   *this horse*

a   הַשֵּׁם הַזֶּה
b   הָאֲכִלָה הַזֹּאת

c   הַדְּבָרִים הָאֵלֶּה

d   הַבְּרָכוֹת הָאֵלֶּה

e   הַבַּיִת הַהוּא

f   הָאַהֲבָה הַהִיא

g   הַמְּקוֹמוֹת הָהֵם

h   הֶחֳרָבוֹת הָהֵנָּה

2 **Choose the appropriate demonstrative and translate into English.**

a	אֵלֶּה	הֵנָּה	זֶה	הַכֹּהֵן
b	הוּא	הִיא	זֹאת	הַלֵּבָב
c	הוּא	זֹאת	אֵלֶּה	הָאָרֶץ
d	אֵלֶּה	זֶה	הֵנָּה	הַלֵּילוֹת
e	זֹאת	הֵם	הֵנָּה	הַשָּׁמַיִם
f	אֵלֶּה	הוּא	זֹאת	סוּסוֹתֵיכֶם
g	אֵלֶּה	הוּא	הִיא	פָּרָתוֹ
h	הֵנָּה	הֵם	זֹאת	הַנָּשִׁים

THE CONSTRUCT

There is no word for *of* in Hebrew. To indicate possession, Hebrew places one noun before another:

קוֹל הַמֶּלֶךְ

           the voice of the king

In idiomatic English, we would be more likely to say *the king's voice*.

In this sentence, the word קוֹל is said to be in a construct relationship to the word הַמֶּלֶךְ.

The word קוֹל does not change when it is in a construct relationship to another noun. Many words do not change in the construct state (for more about different kinds of nouns see Unit 15).

However, many words do change a little. If we were talking about *the king's word* or *his law* (תּוֹרָה toh-RAH) rather than *his voice*, for example, we would say:

דְּבַר הַמֶּלֶךְ	də-VAR ha-ME-lech	*the king's word* (ms)
דִּבְרֵי הַמֶּלֶךְ	div-RAY ha-ME-lech	*the king's words* (mp)
תּוֹרַת הַמֶּלֶךְ	tō-RAT ha-ME-lech	*the king's law* (fs)
תּוֹרוֹת הַמֶּלֶךְ	tō-RŌT ha-ME-lech	*the king's laws* (fp)

These forms are the most straightforward and are very common. The main points to note are as follows:

▶ Masculine singular: shortened vowels. The two long *a* vowels in דָּבָר have reduced to ְ and ַ.
▶ Masculine plural: shortened vowels and the י of the plural form without the ם.
▶ Feminine singular: the וֹת ending changes to ַת (as it does before pronominal suffixes).
▶ Feminine plural: frequently unchanged, though there are sometimes vowel changes.

It is usually possible to recognize a construct form even if you do not recognize the word.

PRACTICE 2

Translate these phrases into English.

a   כֹּהֲנֵי יהוה

b   מַלְכֵי הָאָרֶץ

c   אַהֲבַת הָאִשָּׁה

d   חַרְבוֹת דָּוִד

e   אֱלֹהֵי אָבִי

A number of construct forms are irregular or unusual. These are the construct forms of some common words:

Singular	Construct singular	Plural	Construct plural	Meaning
אָב	אֲבִי	אָבוֹת	אֲבוֹת	father
אָח	אֲחִי	אַחִם	אֲחֵי	brother
אִישׁ	אִישׁ	אֲנָשִׁים	אַנְשֵׁי	man
אִשָּׁה	אֵשֶׁת	נָשִׁים	נְשֵׁי	woman
אֶרֶץ	אֶרֶץ	אֲרָצוֹת	אַרְצוֹת	land
בַּיִת	בֵּית	בָּתִּים	בָּתֵּי	house
בֵּן	בֶּן	בָּנִים	בְּנֵי	son
בַּת	בַּת	בָּנוֹת	בְּנוֹת	daughter
יוֹם	יוֹם	יָמִים	יְמֵי	day
עַיִן	עֵין	עֵינַיִם	עֵינֵי	eye
עִיר	עִיר	עָרִים	עָרֵי	city

In Hebrew, we sometimes encounter several construct forms in a chain, e.g.:

דִּבְרֵי בְּנוֹת אַנְשֵׁי יִשְׂרָאֵל   *the words of the daughters of the men of Israel*

We could translate this as *Israel's men's daughters' words*. With a construct chain it can be clumsy to translate in this way. However, there can be exceptions. In Hebrew, the words אִישׁ and אִשָּׁה (and their construct forms) can be used to indicate *husband* and *wife*. The phrase בְּנוֹת אֵשֶׁת הָאִישׁ is probably better translated as *the man's wife's daughters* rather than *the daughters of the wife of the man*.

The examples used so far are definite: the *voice of* the *king*. The word קוֹל does not need a definite article: it is assumed to be definite, because it is in construct relationship to *the king* which is definite. Similarly, a name is always definite; hence:

קוֹל דָּוִד	*the voice of David* (or *David's voice*)
מֶלֶךְ יִשְׂרָאֵל	*the king of Israel* (or *Israel's king*)
אַנְשֵׁי יְרוּשָׁלַיִם	*the men of Jerusalem*

An indefinite example, *a voice of a king*, would be קוֹל מֶלֶךְ without the definite article on מֶלֶךְ. It is understood that קוֹל is indefinite, because מֶלֶךְ is indefinite.

Clearly, it would be impossible to use the construct to say a *son of* the *man* or the *son of* a *man*. There are other ways of expressing these ideas in Hebrew, as we will see later.

LANGUAGE INSIGHT

Sometimes the **dagesh** is missing at the beginning of the word in the construct state, as in the כ in כֹּהֲנֵי יהוה. Sometimes the words in a construct relationship are joined by **maqqef**; e.g. בֶּן־דָּוִד *the son of David*.

PRACTICE 3

1 **Translate the English phrases into Hebrew using the words below. You will need to think about word order and you will need to work out the construct forms.**

אָבִי אִשָּׁה בֵּן בַּיִת דָּבָר דָּוִד הָאִישׁ יְהוּדָה יִשְׂרָאֵל הַכֹּהֵן הָעָם מֶלֶךְ סוּסוֹ עַיִן עִיר שֵׁם

   a The man's wife.
   b The priest's word.
   c The kings of Israel.
   d David's son.
   e The people's eyes.
   f The cities of Judah.
   g His horse's name.
   h My father's house.

2 **Translate the following into English.**

   a זֹאת אֵשֶׁת אָבִי
   b אֵלֶּה דִּבְרֵי מַלְכְּךָ
   c הוּא קוֹל בְּנוֹ
   d הֵנָּה שִׂפְתֵי שָׂרוֹתֵינוּ

Reading

EXODUS 15:1A

This text introduces a passage known as the Song of Moses, which takes up most of Exodus 15. The song focuses on motifs important throughout the Hebrew Bible: on Yhwh's deliverance of his people and his incomparable power, and on the fulfilment of the promise of descendants and land.

Points to look out for in this text:

▶ words we have already encountered
▶ demonstratives
▶ use of the construct.

Read the verse aloud a few times to be sure of the pronunciation.

אָז יָשִׁיר־מֹשֶׁה וּבְנֵי יִשְׂרָאֵל אֶת־הַשִּׁרָה הַזֹּאת לַיהוה

Approximate pronunciation:

āz yā-SHEER mō-SHE oo-vǝ-NAY yis-rā-AYL et ha-shee-RĀ ha-ZŌT lā-dō-NĪ

(**lā-dō-NĪ** could also be **la-SHEM**)

Write the words you know beneath the words in the text, and match the others to the words in the vocabulary.

💡 Language discovery

יָשִׁיר

This is related to a verb in the vocabulary . It is 3ms and we will translate it with a past tense. Can you work out what it means?

וּבְנֵי

This is a common noun in construct state, with the conjunction **וּ**. Why has **וְ** become **וּ**? Can you work out whether the word is singular or plural? Is it definite or indefinite? How would you translate the whole word?

אֶת

Do you remember this word from Genesis 1:1? It has a segol instead of tsere here.

הַשִּׁרָה הַזֹּאת

Can you translate this phrase?

לַיהוה

You may remember that the letter **בּ** at the beginning of a word means *in*. Similarly, the letter **לּ** at the beginning of a word indicates *to* (we will learn about these in Unit 8). This word means *to Yhwh* or *to the LORD*. Although the word **יָשִׁיר** means *he sang* (singular), it seems that the subject of the verb is *Moses and the sons of Israel* (plural). This kind of construction is common in biblical Hebrew. Sometimes the phrase בְּנֵי יִשְׂרָאֵל is translated *the children of Israel* rather than *the sons of Israel*. Another word for *song* is שִׁיר (which is masculine and looks exactly like the verb *to sing*). It occurs in the title of the book Song of Songs: שִׁיר הַשִּׁירִים.

POSSIBLE TRANSLATION

Then Moses and the children of Israel sang this song to Yhwh.

Test yourself

1 List the words for *this*, giving their gender and number.

2 List the words for *those*, giving their gender and number.

3 Write the following in Hebrew.

   a *these horses* _____

   b *those mares* _____

4 Translate the following into English.

   זֹאת אֵשֶׁת אָבִי וְהוּא סוּסוֹ

   _____

5 Translate the following into English.

   אֵלֶּה דִבְרֵי כֹּהֲנֵי אֱלֹהֵי יִשְׂרָאֵל

   _____

6 Translate the following sentences into Hebrew.

   a This is my horse and that is your horse. _____

   _____

   b These horses are big but that mare is small. _____

   _____

   c This is the king's wife. _____

   d That is the voice of the princess of the city of Jerusalem. _____

   _____

SELF-CHECK

I CAN...

○ use demonstratives (*this, these, that, those*)

○ understand and translate the construct

○ read and translate Exodus 15:1a

8 Prepositions

In this unit you will learn about:
- ▶ the simple prepositions in biblical Hebrew
- ▶ inseparable prepositions
- ▶ prepositions with pronominal suffixes
- ▶ idiomatic uses of prepositions

You will read:
- ▶ Ruth 1:1

Vocabulary builder

NOUNS

אֹיֵב	Ō-yayv	enemy
בֵּית לֶחֶם	bayt LE-chem	Bethlehem (literally *house of bread*. The word for *bread* is לֶחֶם.)
דּוֹד	dōd	beloved
דָּנִאֵל	dā-nee-AYL	Daniel
חָכְמָה	choch-MĀ	wisdom (f)
חֲלוֹם	cha-LŌM	dream
חֶסֶד	CHE-sed	love, kindness
יְהוֹשֻׁעַ	yə-hō-SHOO-a	Joshua
יוֹסֵף	yō-SAYF	Joseph
יֵשׁ or יֵשׁ־	yaysh or yesh	there is, there are
כֹּל or כָּל־	kōl or kol	all, entirety, the whole
כָּנָף	kā-NĀF	wing, skirt (of a robe) (f)
מוֹאָב	mō-ĀV	Moab
מָוֶת	MĀ-vet (construct: מוֹת mōt)	death
נַעַר	NA-ar	young man, servant

עֶבֶד	E-ved	*servant*
פֶּה	pe	*mouth*
רָעָב	rā-ĀV	*famine*
שָׂדֶה	sā-DE	*field*
שֶׁמֶשׁ	SHE-mesh	*sun* (m and f)
שֹׁפֵט	shō-FAYT	*judge*

VERBS

גּוּר	goor	*to live* (temporarily)
הָיָה	hā-YĀ	*to be*
הָלַךְ	hā-LACH	*to go, walk*
עָמַד	ā-MAD	*to stand*
פָּתַח	pā-TACH	*to open*
שָׁפַט	shā-FAT	*to judge*

OTHER

אֵין	ayn	*there is not, there are not*
שְׁנַיִם	shə-NĪ-im	*two, both*

Grammar

PREPOSITIONS

In English, prepositions indicate relationships between a noun or pronoun and other words in the sentence. For example:

The angel	*stood*	*under*	*the tree.*
noun	verb	preposition	noun

In this sentence, *under* describes the angel's location in relation to the tree.

In Hebrew, many prepositions work in a similar way to English prepositions. We have seen one example of a preposition in Unit 5:

וַיֹּאמֶר נָתָן אֶל־דָּוִד   *and Nathan said to David*

So the word אֶל means *to*. Here it is joined to דָּוִד by **maqqef**, which is common. However, prepositions are found without **maqqef** more often than with it.

Other prepositions are:

עַד	ad	until, as far as
עַל	al	on, upon, against
תַּחַת	TA-chat	beneath
בֵּין	bayn (to be distinguished from בֵּן, meaning son)	between

Here are some examples of how these prepositions are used in Hebrew:

עַד הָעֵץ	as far as the tree
עַל הָעֵץ	upon the tree
תַּחַת הָעֵץ	beneath the tree
בֵּין הָעֵצִים	between the trees

The word בֵּין is used twice if something is between two different things:

| בֵּין הַבַּיִת וּבֵין הָעֵץ | between the house and the tree |

Literally: between the house and between the tree.

There are two words in Hebrew for *with*: עִם and אֵת:

| עִם הָאִישׁ | with the man |
| אֵת הָאִישׁ | with the man |

LANGUAGE INSIGHT

The word אֵת is spelled the same way as the object marker (which we saw in Unit 4 and will learn more about later) but the context should indicate when it is the object marker and when it means *with*.

There is another preposition that is very common and worth learning. The word לִפְנֵי (lif-NAY) literally means *before the face of*. It means *before*, usually in the sense of *in front of*. For example:

| וַיַּעַמְדוּ לִפְנֵי יוֹסֵף | and they stood before (in front of) Joseph | (Genesis 43:15) |

Finally, the preposition אַחֲרֵי (a-cha-RAY) means *after*. For example:

| אַחֲרֵי מוֹת יְהוֹשֻׁעַ | after the death of Joshua | (Judges 1:1) |

PRACTICE 1

1 Match the English with the Hebrew.

a	as far as the city	1	בֵּין הָאֲנָשִׁים
b	on the skirt	2	תַּחַת הַשֶּׁמֶשׁ
c	with my servant	3	אֶל אִשְׁתּוֹ
d	between the men	4	עַד הָעִיר
e	with the young men	5	עִם עַבְדִּי
f	beneath the sun	6	עִם אֹיֵב
g	with an enemy	7	אֵת הַנְּעָרִים
h	to his wife	8	עַל הַכָּנָף

2 Translate the following into Hebrew.
   a Then David sang before the people.
   b And Moses said to his wife, 'You are the princess'.
   c The man rested between the city and the mountain.

INSEPARABLE PREPOSITIONS

Three prepositions in Hebrew work as prefixes: they are joined to a word rather like the definite article is joined to a word. These three prepositions are:

בְּ	in, with
כְּ	as, like
לְ	to, at, for

When the noun is indefinite, these prepositions are usually vocalized with **sheva**:

בְּבָיִת	in a house
כְּבָיִת	like a house
לְבָיִת	to a house

Notice that there is no need for **dagesh** in the בְּ of בָּיִת.

If the noun is definite, the definite article הַ is omitted but the preposition is vocalized with ַ or another vowel:

בַּבָּיִת	in the house
כַּבָּיִת	like the house
לַבָּיִת	to the house

Notice that the **dagesh** is now required in the ב of בַּיִת because the **dagesh** is part of the definite article, even though the ה has dropped out.

Prefixing an inseparable preposition to אֱלֹהִים and יהוה is slightly different:

בֵּאלֹהִים	in/with God	בַּיהוה	in/with the LORD
כֵּאלֹהִים	like God	כַּיהוה	like the LORD
לֵאלֹהִים	to God	לַיהוה	to the LORD

The distinction between definite and indefinite nouns can be confusing if the first vowel in the noun is a composite **sheva**, because even indefinite nouns will take a vocalized preposition. So:

חֲלוֹם	cha-LŌM	a dream (m)
בַּחֲלוֹם	ba-cha-LŌM	in a dream

We have already seen inseparable prepositions in previous units:

בַּדֶּרֶךְ	in the path	(Psalm 25:8)
בְּרֵשִׁית	in the beginning	(Genesis 1:1)
בִּיהוּדָה	in Judah	(Psalm 76:2)
בְּיִשְׂרָאֵל	in Israel	(Psalm 76:2)
לַיהוה	to Yhwh	(Exodus 15:1a)

> **LANGUAGE INSIGHT**
>
> If you are wondering why we usually translate בְּרֵשִׁית as *in the beginning* rather than *in a beginning* you have noticed something that has occupied scholars for centuries. Good commentaries on the Hebrew Bible will outline the technical issues and some of the possible answers.

The preposition ב can be used to mean *with* in the instrumental sense; e.g.:

פִּיהָ פָּתְחָה בְחָכְמָה	She opens her mouth with wisdom.
(Proverbs 31:26)	(literally *her mouth she opens with wisdom*)

It never means *with* in the sense of *together with*, as עִם and אֵת do.

The preposition ל can indicate possession. For example:

יֵשׁ־לַמֶּלֶךְ סוּס	The king has a horse.

(literally *there is to the king a horse*)

אֵין־לַשָּׂרִים נָשִׁים	The princes have no wives.

(literally *there are not to the princes women*)

Another preposition can either stand alone or be joined to the noun rather like an inseparable preposition. The word is מִן and means *from*. It usually remains separate from the noun when the noun has a definite article. For example:

מִן הָאָרֶץ	*from the earth*
מִן הַבַּיִת הַזֶּה	*from this house*

The word is often joined to the noun with **maqqef**; e.g.:

מִן־הַשָּׁמַיִם	*from heaven (from the heavens)*

When a word has no definite article, מִן is often attached to the word as a prefix, like an inseparable preposition. When it is prefixed in this way, it loses its final נ, but a **dagesh** in the first letter of the noun replaces the נ. For example:

מִבַּיִת	*from a house*
מִמֶּלֶךְ	*from a king*
מֵעִירְךָ	*from your city*
מִיהוּדָה	*from Judah*

Notice that in מֵעִירְךָ, the vowel under מ is an *e* vowel rather than an *i* vowel. This is because עִיר begins with a guttural and so cannot take a **dagesh**; the vowel under מ is lengthened. The same would be true of words beginning with other gutturals and ר.

Notice also that in מִיהוּדָה, the **sheva** under the י of יְהוּדָה has dropped out.

The preposition מִן is used idiomatically in Hebrew for comparing things. For example:

חָכָם אַתָּה מִדָּנִאֵל	*You are wiser than Daniel.*

(Ezekiel 28:3)

This is literally *wise are you from Daniel*; i.e. you are wise in comparison to Daniel. Similarly:

גָּדוֹל יהוה מִכָּל־הָאֱלֹהִים	*Yhwh is greater than all the gods.*

(Exodus 18:11 adapted)

This is literally *great is Yhwh from all the gods*; i.e. Yhwh is great in comparison to all the gods.

PRACTICE 2

Translate the following into Hebrew.

    a In the night
    b Like a voice
    c To the heavens
    d From this city
    e She opens her mouth with knowledge.

f The woman has a daughter.

g The people have no king.

h My horse is bigger than all your horses.

PREPOSITIONS WITH PRONOMINAL SUFFIXES

Ideas like *to him* or *in them* are expressed in Hebrew by adding a suffix to the preposition. The suffixes are the pronominal suffixes we learned in Unit 6. The most straightforward forms are the inseparable prepositions בְּ and לְ. We will look at more complicated forms later.

These are the forms with pronominal suffixes:

בּוֹ	bō	*in/with him (or it)*
בָּהּ	bāch	*in/with her (or it)*
בְּךָ	ba-chā	*in/with you (ms)*
בָּךְ	bāch	*in/with you (fs)*
בִּי	bee	*in/with me*
בָּהֶם	bā-HEM	*in/with them (mp)*
בָּהֶן	bā-HEN	*in/with them (fp)*
בָּכֶם	bā-CHEM	*in/with you (mp)*
בָּכֶן	bā-CHEN	*in/with you (fp)*
בָּנוּ	bā-NOO	*in/with us*
לוֹ		*to/at/for him (or it)*
לָהּ		*to/at/for her (or it)*
לְךָ		*to/at/for you (ms)*
לָךְ		*to/at/for you (fs)*
לִי		*to/at/for me*
לָהֶם		*to/at/for them (mp)*
לָהֶן		*to/at/for them (fp)*
לָכֶם		*to/at/for you (mp)*
לָכֶן		*to/at/for you (fp)*
לָנוּ		*to/at/for us*

> **LANGUAGE INSIGHT**
>
> The approximate pronunciation for בְּ should serve as a guide for לְ.

The preposition לְ with pronominal suffixes can indicate possession, just like לְ as an inseparable preposition. For example:

| יֶשׁ־לוֹ עֶבֶד | *he has a servant* |

(literally *there is to him a servant*)

| יֶשׁ־לָנוּ אָחוֹת | *we have a sister* |
| אֵין־לָהּ אִישׁ | *she has no husband* |

(literally *there is not to her a husband*)

| אֵין־לִי אֹיֵב | *I have no enemy* |

Here's an example from the Hebrew Bible:

| דּוֹדִי לִי וַאֲנִי לוֹ | *My beloved is mine and I am his.* |

(Song of Songs 2:16)

PRACTICE 3

1 Fill in the prepositions.

a   כְּאֹיֵב   _____ an enemy

b   בְּקוֹל־גָּדוֹל   _____ a loud voice

c   מֵעֶרֶב עַד־בֹּקֶר   _____ evening _____ morning

d   לִפְנֵי הַמֶּלֶךְ   _____ the king

e   מִן־הָאִשָּׁה הַזֹּאת   _____ this woman

2 Translate the following into English.

a   טוֹב חֶסֶד מִדַּעַת

b   רַע הָעָם וְלֹא בָּהֶם דַּעַת

c   אַתֶּם בְּיָדִי

d   יֶשׁ לָהּ בֵּן

e   הַסּוּסִים הַגְּדוֹלִים הָאֵלֶּה לָנוּ

Reading

RUTH 1:1

Points to look out for in this text:

▸ words we have already encountered

▸ simple prepositions

▸ inseparable prepositions.

וַיְהִי בִּימֵי שְׁפֹט הַשֹּׁפְטִים וַיְהִי רָעָב בָּאָרֶץ וַיֵּלֶךְ אִישׁ מִבֵּית לֶחֶם יְהוּדָה לָגוּר בִּשְׂדֵי מוֹאָב הוּא וְאִשְׁתּוֹ וּשְׁנֵי בָנָיו :

Approximate pronunciation:

va-yə-HEE bee-MAY shə-FŌT ha-shō-fə-TEEM va-yə-HEE rā-ĀV bā-ĀR-ets va-YAY-lech eesh mi-BAYT LE-chem yə-HOO-dā lā-GOOR bis-DAY mō-ĀV hoo və-ish-TŌ oo-shə-NAY vā-NĀV.

Write the words you know beneath the words in the text, and match the others to the words in the vocabulary.

💡 Language discovery

וַיְהִי

Did you find this verb in the vocabulary? It is 3ms and we will translate it with a past tense. It is a very common word in the Hebrew Bible and is often found at the beginning of a story, rather like *once upon a time* in English. It used to be translated *and it came to pass*, though that phrase is now associated almost exclusively with biblical language. How would you translate it?

בִּימֵי

Did you spot the inseparable preposition? Which one is it? If the noun is a masculine plural construct, what might it mean? Clue: it is one of the nouns with irregular construct forms.

שְׁפֹט

This is a verbal form we haven't seen before, and means *the judging of*.

הַשֹּׁפְטִים

Can you find this noun in the vocabulary and identify its gender and number?

בָּאָרֶץ

What does the **qamets** under the **bet** tell you about this preposition?

וַיֵּלֶךְ

Another verb: did you find something that looked like it in the vocabulary? It is 3ms and we will translate it with a past tense.

מִבֵּית לֶחֶם

This phrase involves a preposition and a construct relationship. Can you identify them?

לָגוּר

This verbal form is easier to find in the vocabulary. What is the לְ here? Can you translate the word?

בִּשְׂדֵי

What is the בְ doing here? Will you translate it with a definite article or an indefinite article? Can you identify the gender and number of שְׂדֵי?

וְאִשְׁתּוֹ

The conjunction וְ prefixed to a feminine irregular noun, with a pronominal suffix. Can you identify which pronominal suffix? Can you translate it?

וּשְׁנֵי

The conjunction וּ prefixed to the word for *two* or *both* in construct form. Why is the conjunction וּ rather than וְ? Can you identify the gender and number of this word?

בָנָיו

This is the plural of בֵּן with a pronominal suffix: can you identify which suffix? If you are wondering why there is no **dagesh** in the בְ, it is because of the construct relationship with וּשְׁנֵי. The construct relationship treats the two words as if they were one, and often there is no **dagesh** in the second word where we might expect one.

You should now have something like *And it happened in the days of the judging of the judges and there was a famine in the land and a man from Bethlehem of Judah went to live in the fields of Moab, he and his wife and both of his sons.*

POSSIBLE TRANSLATIONS

Fairly literal:

And it happened in the days when the judges judged, there was a famine in the land, and a man from Bethlehem in Judah went to live as a resident alien in the fields of Moab, he and his wife and his two sons.

Somewhat freer:

In the days when the judges ruled, there was a famine in the land. So a man from Bethlehem in Judah went to live in Moab with his wife and both his sons.

Test yourself

1 Write out the following in Hebrew.

    a to   _____

    b on   _____

    c under   _____

    d between _____

2 Translate the following into Hebrew.

    He has a son.

    _____

3 Translate the following into English.

גָּדוֹל הַמֶּלֶךְ מִן־הָאֲנָשִׁים

_____

4 Write out the following in Hebrew, using בְּ and לְ.

a to me _____

b in her _____

c to them (m) _____

d in us _____

5 Write out the following in English.

כַּעֲבָדִי בָּעִיר לְנַעַר

_____

SELF-CHECK	
I CAN...	
⬤	use simple prepositions
⬤	understand in separable prepositions
⬤	identify prepositions with pronominal suffixes
⬤	understand the idiomatic uses of prepositions
⬤	read and translate Ruth 1:1

9 The object marker, more prepositions, and comparatives

In this unit you will learn about:
▶ the object marker
▶ further prepositions with pronominal suffixes
▶ how comparatives and superlatives work

You will read:
▶ Deuteronomy 10:17

Vocabulary builder

NOUNS

אֵל	ayl	God/god
עֶבֶד	E-ved	servant
פָּנִים	pā-NEEM	face

VERBS

אָהַב	ā-HAV	to love
לָקַח	lā-KACH	to take
נוֹרָא	nō-RĀ	participle: terrible, wonderful
נָשָׂא	nā-SĀ	to lift up, take
סוּר	soor	to turn, depart

ADJECTIVES

גִּבֹּר	gib-BŌR	strong
חָזָק	chā-ZĀK	strong, powerful
כָּבֵד	kā-VAYD	heavy, difficult
קָטֹן	kā-TŌN	small, young

OTHER

אֲשֶׁר	a-SHER	*that, which, who*
הִנֵּה	hi-NAY	*behold, look*
כִּי	kee	*because, that*

Grammar

THE OBJECT MARKER

Look at this sentence:

The woman wore a hat.

In this sentence, *the woman* is the subject of the verb *wore*, and *a hat* is the object.

Another example:

The cat climbed the tree.

In this sentence *the cat* is the subject of *climbed*, and *the tree* is the object.

A verb can have several subjects and several objects; e.g.:

The boy and the girl ate a pizza, a hamburger and an apple pie.

In this sentence, *the boy* and *the girl* are the subjects; *the pizza*, *the hamburger* and *the apple pie* are the objects.

And a slightly more complicated example:

This morning my mother filled a cup with water.

Here *my mother* is the subject of the verb *filled* and the objects are *a cup* and *water*. The phrase *This morning* is neither the subject nor the object.

At a glance:

Subject	Verb	Object
The woman	*wore*	*a hat.*
The cat	*climbed*	*the tree.*
The boy and the girl	*ate*	*a pizza, a hamburger and an apple pie.*
My mother	*filled*	*a cup, water.*

In Hebrew, there is a word we sometimes see before the object of a verb, so it is known as the 'object marker'. The word is אֵת and we have already encountered it in Genesis 1:1. It can also be attached to the object with **maqqef**, in which case the vowel changes and it is written אֶת־. There is no word we can use to translate it into English. That does not mean it is untranslatable, however. It is translated when we translate using an object in English.

The object marker is especially helpful in Hebrew because it is not always immediately obvious from the word order what the subject or object is. In English, the word order determines which part of the sentence is the subject and which is the object. For example, in the English sentence *The father loved the son* we know that it is *the father* doing the loving, because of the word order.

However, in Hebrew the verb usually comes first in a sentence: אָהַב הָאָב הַבֵּן. Without אֵת this could mean either *the father loved the son* or *the son loved the father*. To make the Hebrew clear we might see:

אָהַב הָאָב אֶת הַבֵּן   *The father loved the son.*

or

אָהַב אֶת הָאָב הַבֵּן   *The son loved the father.*

Although the word אֵת occurs frequently, it is not inevitably found before the object, so we should not expect to see it every time we encounter an object. Moreover, it has exactly the same spelling as אֵת meaning *with*, but the context should indicate whether it is an object marker or a preposition.

PRACTICE 1

Match the Hebrew to the English, and identify the subject and object.

a	אָהַב הָאָח אֶת הָאֲחָיוֹת	1	The king lifted up the sword.
b	לָקַח הָאִישׁ אֶת־הַסּוּסִים	2	David knew that song.
c	נָשָׂא הַמֶּלֶךְ אֶת הָחֶרֶב	3	The priest judged this city.
d	שָׁפַט הַכֹּהֵן אֶת־הָעִיר הַזֹּאת	4	The brother loved the sisters.
e	יָדַע דָּוִד אֶת־הַשִּׁירָה הַהִיא	5	The man took the horses.

FURTHER PREPOSITIONS WITH PRONOMINAL SUFFIXES

In Unit 8, we learned בְּ and לְ with pronominal suffixes. Other prepositions are slightly more complicated, because they introduce extra letters into the suffix. However, if you have learned the pronominal suffixes, it should be possible to identify the forms and translate them.

Often the extra letter is י, which can make the forms look like plurals. However, if you learn them carefully now, you will not be confused when you encounter them in the text; and in fact, some of the forms are so common that you will soon become familiar with them.

Reading all of these out loud several times (or even copying them out) can help you learn them. It can seem tedious, but it is much easier to read Hebrew if you don't need to look up endings on prepositions.

One of the most common words is אֶל (*to*) with pronominal suffixes:

אֵלָיו	**ay-LĀV**	*to him* (or *it*)
אֵלֶיהָ	**ay-LAY-hā**	*to her* (or *it*)
אֵלֶיךָ	**ay-LAY-chā**	to you (ms)
אֵלַיִךְ	**ay-LĪ-yik**	*to you* (fs)

אֵלַי	ay-LĪ	to me
אֲלֵיהֶם	a-lay-HEM	to them (m)
אֲלֵיהֶן	a-lay-HEN	to them (f)
אֲלֵיכֶם	a-lay-CHEM	to you (mp)
אֲלֵיכֶן	a-lay-CHEN	to you (fp)
אֵלֵינוּ	ay-LAY-noo	to us

The stress pattern in the approximate pronunciation should be familiar from סוּסוֹ. The same pattern works for all the prepositions with suffixes.

The preposition עַל (*on*) is formed in the same way:

עָלָיו	on him (or *it*)	עֲלֵיהֶם	on them (mp)
עָלֶיהָ	on her (or *it*)	עֲלֵיהֶן	on them (fp)
עָלֶיךָ	on you (ms)	עֲלֵיכֶם	on you (mp)
עָלַיִךְ	on you (fs)	עֲלֵיכֶן	on you (fp)
עָלַי	on me	עָלֵינוּ	on us

And similarly עַד (*as far as, until*):

עָדָיו	as far as him (or *it*)	עֲדֵיהֶם	as far as them (mp)
עָדֶיהָ	as far as her (or *it*)	עֲדֵיהֶן	as far as them (fp)
עָדֶיךָ	as far as you (ms)	עֲדֵיכֶם	as far as you (mp)
עָדַיִךְ	as far as you (fs)	עֲדֵיכֶן	as far as you (fp)
עָדַי	as far as me	עָדֵינוּ	as far as us

Another preposition you will see frequently with pronominal suffixes is מִן (*from*).

מִמֶּנּוּ	from him (or *it*)	מֵהֶם	from them (mp)
מִמֶּנָּה	from her (or *it*)	מֵהֶן	from them (fp)
מִמְּךָ	from you (ms)	מִכֶּם	from you (mp)
מִמֵּךְ	from you (fs)	מִכֶּן	from you (fp)
מִמֶּנִּי	from me	מִמֶּנּוּ	from us

LANGUAGE INSIGHT

Notice that the word for *from him* is the same as the word for *from us*. Context should help determine which is meant.

The pronominal suffixes on both words for *with*, אֵת and עִם, should be instantly recognizable. The main point to note about these prepositions is the **dagesh** in the ת and the מ when suffixes are added:

אִתּוֹ	*with him* (or *it*)	אִתָּם	*with them* (mp)
אִתָּהּ	*with her* (or *it*)	אִתָּן	*with them* (fp)
אִתְּךָ	*with you* (ms)	אִתְּכֶם	*with you* (mp)
אִתָּךְ	*with you* (fs)	אִתְּכֶן	*with you* (fp)
אִתִּי	*with me*	אִתָּנוּ	*with us*
עִמּוֹ	*with him* (or *it*)	עִמָּם	*with them* (mp)
עִמָּהּ	*with her* (or *it*)	עִמָּן	*with them* (fp)
עִמְּךָ	*with you* (ms)	עִמָּכֶם	*with you* (mp)
עִמָּךְ	*with you* (fs)	עִמָּכֶן	*with you* (fp)
עִמִּי	*with me*	עִמָּנוּ	*with us*

The suffixes on the word for *between* (בֵּין) are similar to בְּ and לְ until you get to the second column, where they resemble those in the second half of אֶל, עַל and עַד:

בֵּינוֹ	*between him* (or *it*)	בֵּינֵיהֶם	*between them* (mp)
בֵּינָהּ	*between her* (or *it*)	בֵּינֵיהֶן	*between them* (fp)
בֵּינְךָ	*between you* (ms)	בֵּינֵיכֶם	*between you* (mp)
בֵּינֵךְ	*between you* (fs)	בֵּינֵיכֶן	*between you* (fp)
בֵּינִי	*between me*	בֵּינֵינוּ	*between us*

When the prepositions אַחֲרֵי (*after*) and תַּחַת (*under*) take suffixes, they are formed rather like the second half of בֵּין; see also אֶל, עַל and עַד:

אַחֲרָיו	*after him* (or *it*)	אַחֲרֵיהֶם	*after them* (mp)
אַחֲרֶיהָ	*after her* (or *it*)	אַחֲרֵיהֶן	*after them* (fp)
אַחֲרֶיךָ	*after you* (ms)	אַחֲרֵיכֶם	*after you* (mp)
אַחֲרַיִךְ	*after you* (fs)	אַחֲרֵיכֶן	*after you* (fp)
אַחֲרַי	*after me*	אַחֲרֵינוּ	*after us*
תַּחְתָּיו	*under him* (or *it*)	תַּחְתֵּיהֶם	*under them* (mp)
תַּחְתֶּיהָ	*under her* (or *it*)	תַּחְתֵּיהֶן	*under them* (fp)

תַּחְתֶּיךָ	under you (ms)	תַּחְתֵּיכֶם	under you (mp)
תַּחְתַּיִךְ	under you (fs)	תַּחְתֵּיכֶן	under you (fp)
תַּחְתַּי	under me	תַּחְתֵּינוּ	under us

The preposition לִפְנֵי (*before*) follows the same form as אַחֲרֵי and תַּחַת.

The inseparable preposition כְּ is a little different:

כָּמוֹהוּ	*like him* (or *it*)	כָּהֶם	*like them* (mp)
כָּמוֹהָ	*like her* (or *it*)	כָּהֵן	*like them* (fp)
כָּמוֹךָ	*like you* (ms)	כָּכֶם	*like you* (mp)
כָּמוֹךְ	*like you* (fs)	כָּכֶן	*like you* (fp)
כָּמוֹנִי	*like me*	כָּמוֹנוּ	*like us*

Note the additional מ before the endings are added. These are not precisely the same as the endings on מִן, but are similar.

One further point about prepositions: they can be combined. For example:

מֵעִם	*away from*
וּמֵעִם שָׁאוּל סָר	*and it left Saul* (literally: *and from with Saul it departed*)

(1 Samuel 18:12)

PRACTICE 2

1 Complete the columns in the tables.

a Prepositions אֶל עַל and עַד:

3ms	on him/it	עָלָיו	3mp	as far as them	
3fs	to her/it		3fp	on them	
2ms	as far as you		2mp	to you	
2fs	to you		2fp	on you	
1s	on me		1p	as far as us	

b Prepositions אַחֲרֵי לִפְנֵי and תַּחַת:

3ms	after him/it	אַחֲרָיו	3mp	under them	
3fs	before her/it		3fp	after them	
2ms	after you		2mp	after you	
2fs	under you		2fp	before you	
1s	before me		1p	under us	

d Prepositions כְּ and מִן (remember, the suffixes on כְּ are not identical to those on מִן):

3ms	from him/it	מִמֶּנּוּ	3mp	from them	
3fs	from her/it		3fp	like them	
2ms	like you		2mp	from you	
2fs	like you		2fp	like you	
1s	from me		1p	from us	

2 Translate the following into English.

a נָשָׂא הַמֶּלֶךְ אֶת הַחֶרֶב עִמָּנוּ

b לָקַח הָאִישׁ אֶת־הַסּוּסִים מֵהֶם

c שָׁפַט הַכֹּהֵן אֶת־הָעִיר לְפָנָיו

COMPARATIVES AND SUPERLATIVES

In English, we make comparatives and superlatives either by adding endings to an adjective:

holy

holier (comparative)

holiest (superlative)

or we do it by using the words *more* and *most*:

beautiful

more beautiful (comparative)

most beautiful (superlative)

Some of these forms are irregular in English; e.g.:

good

better (comparative)

best (superlative)

It is helpful to bear this in mind, and avoid translations like *to obey is more good than sacrifice*.

As we have seen, the preposition מִן is used idiomatically in Hebrew for comparing things. For example:

חָכָם אַתָּה מִדָּנִיֵּאל   *you are wiser than Daniel*

(Ezekiel 28:3)

Literally *wise are you from Daniel*, i.e. *you are wise in comparison to Daniel*.

Similarly:

גָּדוֹל יהוה מִכָּל־
הָאֱלֹהִים   *Yhwh is greater than all the gods*

(Exodus 18:11 adapted)

74

The מִן construction can also be used in the sense of *to … for…*. For example:

חֲזָקִים הֵמָּה מִמֶּנּוּ   *they were too strong for him*

(Judges 18:26)

כִּי כָבֵד מִמֶּנִּי   *because it is too difficult for me*

(Numbers 11:14)

A number of Hebrew idioms may be translated with a superlative in English. An adjective can be used with the definite article; e.g.:

הַקָּטֹן אֶת־אָבִינוּ   *the youngest is with our father*

                                    (Genesis 42:32 adapted)

                                    Literally *the young (one) is with our father.*

הִנֵּה בִתִּי הַגְּדוֹלָה   *here is my eldest daughter*

                                    (1 Samuel 18:17)

                                    Literally *behold my daughter, the large one.*

Alternatively, a construct relationship can be used; e.g.:

קְטֹן בָּנָיו   *the youngest of his sons*

                                    (2 Chronicles 21:17)

                                    Literally *the small of his sons.*

The word קְטֹן is the construct form of the adjective קָטֹן. Adjectives can have construct forms, just like nouns, and this one works like דְּבָר. See e.g. דְּבַר הַמֶּלֶךְ in Unit 7.

Another way of expressing a superlative is to use a noun in a construct relationship to its plural; e.g.:

שִׁיר הַשִּׁירִים   *the greatest song*

(Song 1:1) Literally *the song of songs*

קֹדֶשׁ הַקֳּדָשִׁים   *the holiest place*

(Exodus 26:33) Literally *the holy of holies*

הֲבֵל הֲבָלִים   *the worst vanity*

(Ecclesiastes 1:2) Literally *vanity of vanities*

Superlatives can also be expressed by use of words that indicate divinity or death. For example:

נְשִׂיא אֱלֹהִים   *a mighty prince*

(Genesis 23:6)

Literally *a prince of gods*

כִּי־עַזָּה כַמָּוֶת אַהֲבָה   *for love is exceedingly strong*

(Song 8:6)

Literally *for love is as strong as death*

It is this construction that gives rise to differing translations of Genesis 1:2, in which, moving over the surface of the water, there is either *a mighty wind* or *the spirit of God*. The phrase רוּחַ אֱלֹהִים can be translated either way, so translators must decide which seems most appropriate.

PRACTICE 3

Translate the following into English.

a   וְדָוִד הוּא הַקָּטָן בָּנָיו
b   וַיְהִי הָאִישׁ הַהוּא גָּדוֹל מִכָּל־אַנְשֵׁי הָעִיר
c   אַתָּה מֶלֶךְ מְלָכִים וְאֲנִי עֶבֶד עֲבָדִים
d   זֶה מֶלֶךְ יִשְׂרָאֵל הַטּוֹב וְהַגָּדוֹל וְאֲנִי בִּתּוֹ הַגְּדוֹלָה

Reading

DEUTERONOMY 10:17

Points to look out for in this text:

▶ words we have already encountered
▶ superlatives.

כִּי יְהוָה אֱלֹהֵיכֶם הוּא אֱלֹהֵי הָאֱלֹהִים וַאֲדֹנֵי הָאֲדֹנִים הָאֵל הַגָּדֹל הַגִּבֹּר וְהַנּוֹרָא אֲשֶׁר לֹא־יִשָּׂא פָנִים וְלֹא יִקַּח שֹׁחַד :

Approximate pronunciation:

kee a-don-Ī e-lō-HAY-chem hoo e-lō-HAY hā-e-lō-HEEM va-a-dō-NAY hā-a-dō-NEEM, hā-AYL ha-gā-DŌL ha-gib-BŌR və-ha-nō-RĀ a-SHER lō yis-SĀ fā-NEEM və-lō yi-KACH SHŌ-chad.

Write the words you know beneath the words in the text, and match the others to the words in the vocabulary.

💡 Language discovery

כִּי

This is in the vocabulary and has two possible meanings. Which one would you choose?

יְהוָה

This should be familiar by now.

אֱלֹהֵיכֶם

Did you correctly identify the pronominal suffix?

הוּא אֱלֹהֵי הָאֱלֹהִים

Which verb is implied but not written in this clause? Is אֱלֹהֵי definite or indefinite? (Hint: it's in construct relationship to a noun with a definite article.)

וַאֲדֹנֵי הָאֲדֹנִים

A similar phrase to that above. Would you translate it literally, or would you prefer a freer translation?

הָאֵל הַגָּדֹל הַגִּבֹּר וְהַנּוֹרָא

Is this a verbless clause or not? Think about the word order. If the distinction between טוֹב הָאִישׁ (the man is good) and הָאִישׁ הַטּוֹב (the good man) is still a little confusing, look at Unit 6 again.

אֲשֶׁר

This is in the vocabulary and is known as the relative pronoun. Many people translate it intuitively. In this verse it refers to God, so which English word would you use to translate it?

לֹא־יִשָּׂא פָנִים

The word יִשָּׂא means *he lifts up*; the נ in the verb has disappeared. It is common for the letter נ to disappear, especially if it comes at the beginning of a word. It is said to be assimilated into the next letter, which gives the שׂ a **dagesh**. We will learn more about verbs later. This whole phrase means literally *he does not lift up faces*. A more idiomatic translation into English requires a little interpretation of the text. Have a look at several translations and see which one you prefer – and think about why.

יִקַּח

This verbal form means *he takes*; the ל in the verb has disappeared. This is not as common as the disappearance of the letter נ; in fact, it really only happens in לָקַח. How would you translate וְלֹא יִקַּח שֹׁחַד?

POSSIBLE TRANSLATIONS

You should now have something like *Because Yhwh your God is the God of gods and the Lord of lords; the great, strong and terrible God who does not lift up the face and does not take a bribe.* This is fairly literal.

Somewhat freer:

Because the LORD your God is the highest God and the holiest Lord; the great, strong and wonderful God who is impartial and takes no bribes.

❓ Test yourself

1 Write the object marker both with and without **maqqef**. _____

_____

2 Write out the following in English.

עָלֶיךָ מִמֶּנִּי בֵּינֵיהֶם כָּמוֹהוּ

_____

3 Translate the following into English.

הֲבֵל הֲבָלִים

_____

4 Translate the following into English.

וְשָׁאוּל הוּא חָזָק מִן־הָאֲנָשִׁים

_____

5 Translate the following into English.

וְיִשְׂרָאֵל אָהַב אֶת־יוֹסֵף מִכָּל־בָּנָיו (Genesis 37:3)

_____

SELF-CHECK

	I CAN...
○	understand the object marker
○	identify prepositions with pronominal suffixes
○	identify and translate comparatives and superlatives
○	read and translate Deuteronomy 10:17

10 The Perfect and how to parse verbs

In this unit you will learn about:
▶ forms of the Perfect
▶ uses of the Perfect
▶ how to parse verbs

You will read:
▶ Job 1:21

Vocabulary builder

NOUNS

בְּרִית	bə-REET	covenant (f)
בֶּטֶן	BE-ten	belly, womb (f)
גְּאוּלִים	gə-oo-LEEM	the redeemed
גּוֹאֵל	gō-AYL	redeemer
מִיכַל	mi-CHAL	Michal
מִצְרַיִם	mits-RĀ-yeem	Egypt
מִקֶּדֶם	mi-KE-dem	olden time, of old
שְׁלֹמֹה	shə-LŌ-mō	Solomon

VERBS

בָּרַךְ	bā-RACH	to bless
חָיָה	chā-YĀ	to live
יָצָא	yā-TSĀ	to go out, to be born
נָתַן	nā-TAN	to give
קָטַל	kā-TAL	to kill
קָרָא	kā-RĀ	to call
שׁוּב	shoov	to return

OTHER

עָרֹם	ā-RŌM	*naked* (adjective)
שָׁם	shām	*there* (adverb)

Grammar

VERBS: PERFECT OR **QATAL**

Hebrew verbs work in a way quite different from English verbs. Some of the differences are straightforward; others take a little time to get used to. The first verb pattern we will learn is called the Perfect. In some grammars it is known as **Qatal**, because the term 'Perfect' can convey ideas about Indo-European languages irrelevant to Hebrew. However, since 'Perfect' is the term found in many grammars, it seems sensible to use it here.

The Perfect usually describes a completed action in the past, though sometimes it can describe things happening in the present or future. The verb קָטַל (*to kill*) is often used as a demonstration verb when discussing Hebrew grammar; hence the name **Qatal**. This is what it looks like:

קָטַל	kā-TAL	*he killed*
קָטְלָה	kā-tə-LĀ	*she killed*
קָטַלְתָּ	kā-TAL-tā	*you killed* (ms)
קָטַלְתְּ	kā-TALT	*you killed* (fs)
קָטַלְתִּי	kā-TAL-tee	*I killed*
קָטְלוּ	kā-tə-LOO	*they killed*
קְטַלְתֶּם	kə-tal-TEM	*you killed* (mp)
קְטַלְתֶּן	kə-tal-TEN	*you killed* (fp)
קָטַלְנוּ	kā-TAL-noo	*we killed*

In English we use the word *killed* for each person, but in Hebrew each word is slightly different. Another point to notice is that we talk about the verb קָטַל, which means literally *he killed*, whereas in English we would talk about the verb *to kill*. The reason is that קָטַל is the simplest form of the verb. In a Hebrew–English dictionary we look up the Perfect third person masculine singular. The dictionary will tell you that קָטַל means *to kill*, even though literally it means *he killed*.

The three letters that make up the third person masculine singular (in this case קטל) are known as the root, and endings are added to the root to form the different parts of the verb. So the first-person singular ending in the Perfect is תִּי, etc.

The verb קָטַל is the basis of the verb tables in many grammars because it is very regular, but its meaning is slightly unfortunate for a demonstration verb, so we will practise with other verbs.

מָשַׁל   *to rule*

מָשַׁל	mā-SHAL	*he has ruled*
מָשְׁלָה	mā-shə-LĀ	*she has ruled*
מָשַׁלְתָּ	mā-SHAL-tā	*you have ruled* (ms)
מָשַׁלְתְּ	mā-SHALT	*you have ruled* (fs)
מָשַׁלְתִּי	mā-SHAL-tee	*I have ruled*
מָשְׁלוּ	mā-shə-LOO	*they have ruled*
מְשַׁלְתֶּם	mə-shal-TEM	*you have ruled* (mp)
מְשַׁלְתֶּן	mə-shal-TEN	*you have ruled* (fp)
מָשַׁלְנוּ	mā-SHAL-noo	*we have ruled*

שָׁמַר   *to guard/keep*

שָׁמַר	shā-MAR	*he has guarded/kept*
שָׁמְרָה	shā-mə-RAH	*she has guarded/kept*
שָׁמַרְתָּ	shā-MAR-tā	*you have guarded/kept* (ms)
שָׁמַרְתְּ	shā-MART	*you have guarded/kept* (fs)
שָׁמַרְתִּי	shā-MAR-tee	*I have guarded/kept*
שָׁמְרוּ	shā-mə-ROO	*they have guarded/kept*
שְׁמַרְתֶּם	shə-mar-TEM	*you have guarded/kept* (mp)
שְׁמַרְתֶּן	shə-mar-TEN	*you have guarded/kept* (fp)
שָׁמַרְנוּ	shā-MAR-noo	*we have guarded/kept*

The approximate pronunciation for קָטַל should serve as a guide for other verbs in the Perfect.

אָכַל   *to eat*

אָכַל	*he has eaten*
אָכְלָה	*she has eaten*
אָכַלְתָּ	*you have eaten* (ms)
אָכַלְתְּ	*you have eaten* (fs)

אָכַלְתִּי	I have eaten
אָכְלוּ	they have eaten
אֲכַלְתֶּם	you have eaten (mp)
אֲכַלְתֶּן	you have eaten (fp)
אָכַלְנוּ	we have eaten

הָלַךְ **to walk**

הָלַךְ	he has walked
הָלְכָה	she has walked
הָלַכְתָּ	you have walked (ms)
הָלַכְתְּ	you have walked (fs)
הָלַכְתִּי	I have walked
הָלְכוּ	they have walked
הֲלַכְתֶּם	you have walked (mp)
הֲלַכְתֶּן	you have walked (fp)
הָלַכְנוּ	we have walked

> **LANGUAGE INSIGHT**
>
> Note: in the word קְטַלְתֶּם, the first vowel is a simple **sheva**, whereas in אֲכַלְתֶּם and הֲלַכְתֶּם the first vowel is a compound **sheva**. The reason is that gutturals do not usually take a simple **sheva**. However, this should not cause any difficulty in understanding the word.

לָקַח **to take**

לָקַח	he has taken
לָקְחָה	she has taken
לָקַחְתָּ	you have taken (ms)
לָקַחַתְּ	you have taken (fs)
לָקַחְתִּי	I have taken
לָקְחוּ	they have taken
לְקַחְתֶּם	you have taken (mp)
לְקַחְתֶּן	you have taken (fp)
לָקַחְנוּ	we have taken

LANGUAGE INSIGHT

Note: in קָטְלָה there are two **sheva** vowels next to each other. This is rare in Hebrew in general, although it is usual in the Perfect. However, gutturals do not usually take a simple **sheva**. That is why in לְקַחַת the first **sheva** has been replaced by a **patach**.

Vowel changes under gutturals are common, but should not usually cause problems in understanding the Perfect.

PRACTICE 1

Using קָטַל as a model, write out the Perfect of the following verbs.

	to visit פָּקַד	to write כָּתַב	to remember זָכַר
3ms			
3fs			
2ms			
2fs			
1s			
3p			
2mp			
2fp			
1p			

HOW THE PERFECT IS USED

Hebrew word order is generally different from English. In Hebrew, the verb usually comes first in a sentence or phrase, followed by the subject, and then the object. However, a few words or phrases may come before the verb. For example:

לֹא שָׁמְרוּ בְּרִית אֱלֹהִים   *They have not kept the covenant of God.*

(Psalm 78:10)

עַל־כֵּן קָרְאָה שְׁמוֹ דָּן   *Therefore she called his name Dan.*

(Genesis 30:6)

(We have seen something similar in Genesis 1:1, Unit 4.)

In English, if we want to say *he walked* or *they walked* we always have to use the pronoun so that it is clear who walked. In Hebrew, the pronoun is unnecessary because it is clear from the form of the verb. The word הָלַכְנוּ means *we walked*, with no need for אֲנַחְנוּ. If a pronoun is used, it usually indicates emphasis:

וַאֲנִי יָדַעְתִּי גֹּאֲלִי חָי   *And I know that my redeemer lives.*

(Job 19:25)

or *As for me, I know that my redeemer lives.*

Another technique used in Hebrew to indicate emphasis is to change the word order, placing the object before the verb:

וְלַחֹשֶׁךְ קָרָא לָיְלָה   *And the darkness he called night.*

(Genesis 1:5)

Notice the difference in nuance between this and the phrase we might have expected: *and he called the darkness night*. The word לָיְלָה is in pause and so the first vowel has lengthened. This should not present any difficulties in understanding.

In Hebrew, a verb always has to agree with its subject. If the subject is masculine and singular, the verb has to be masculine and singular. In the phrase אָהֲבָה מִיכַל דָּוִד, it is clear from the verb that Michal loved David and it would mean the same even if the word order were changed to אָהֲבָה דָּוִד מִיכַל.

Verbs in biblical Hebrew do not express time in quite the same way as English verbs. The Perfect can sometimes be translated with an English past tense, sometimes with a present tense, and sometimes with a future tense. Sometimes it is clear from the context, although not always. Here are some examples of the Perfect translated with different English tenses.

Past tense:

בְּרֵאשִׁית בָּרָא אֱלֹהִים אֵת הַשָּׁמַיִם
וְאֵת הָאָרֶץ   *In the beginning God created the heavens and the earth.*

(Genesis 1:1)

Present tense:

זָכַרְתִּי יָמִים מִקֶּדֶם   *I remember the days of old.*

(Psalm 143:5)

Future tense:

וְהָלְכוּ גְאוּלִים   *And (or but) the redeemed shall walk.*

(Isaiah 35:9)

However, for now it is probably easiest to think of the Perfect as a past tense and to translate it as demonstrated.

PRACTICE 2

Match the Hebrew sentences to the English translations:

a	עָמַדְתִּי בַּגָּן בֵּין הָעֵצִים	1	The priest called to the people from his house.
b	בָּרָאתָ אֶת־עֲצֵי הַשָּׂדֶה	2	She remembered the name of my father's servant.
c	מָשְׁלוּ דָּוִד וּשְׁלֹמֹה בִּיהוּדָה	3	This cow ate all my bread.
d	זָכְרָה שֵׁם עֶבֶד אָבִי	4	You created the trees of the field.

e	אֲמַרְתֶּן אֵלֵינוּ אֵין מֶלֶךְ בְּיִשְׂרָאֵל 5	You guarded the beautiful princess.
f	אָכְלָה הַפָּרָה הַזֹּאת אֶת־כָּל־לַחְמִי 6	I stood in the garden between the trees.
g	קָרָא הַכֹּהֵן אֶל־הָעָם מִבֵּיתוֹ 7	David and Solomon ruled in Judah.
h	שְׁמַרְתְּ אֶת־הַשָּׂרָה הַיָּפָה 8	You kept the law of the LORD your God.
i	לֹא שָׁבַתְנוּ בְּאֶרֶץ מִצְרַיִם 9	You said to us, 'There is no king in Israel.'
j	שְׁמַרְתֶּם אֶת־תּוֹרַת יְהוָה אֱלֹהֵכֶם 10	We did not rest in the land of Egypt.

PARSING VERBS

To parse a verb is to analyse it by describing it in terms of its constituent elements. This can be useful when translating. So far we have looked almost exclusively at Perfect forms, so we will see how parsing works in these. We identify the tense, person, gender and number, and then the verbal root, and we offer a translation. Some forms do not distinguish between masculine and feminine, e.g. the first-person forms. So we can use c (common to both grammatical genders) or simply leave it out.

קָטַל	Perfect 3ms	קָטַל	*he has killed*
שְׁמַרְתֶּם	Perfect 2mp	שָׁמַר	*you have guarded*
אָכַלְתִּי	Perfect 1cs	אָכַל	*I have eaten*

PRACTICE 3

Parse the following.

קָרָא			
קָטַלְתָּ			
שָׁמַרְנוּ			
הֲלַכְתֶּן			
זָכְרוּ			

Reading

JOB 1:21

Points to look out for in this text:

▶ words we have already encountered
▶ forms of the Perfect
▶ superlatives.

וַיֹּאמֶר עָרֹם יָצָתִי מִבֶּטֶן אִמִּי וְעָרֹם אָשׁוּב שָׁמָּה יְהוָה נָתַן וַיהוָה לָקָח יְהִי שֵׁם יְהוָה מְבֹרָךְ׃

Approximate pronunciation:

va-YŌ-mer ā-RŌM yā-TSĀ-tee mi-BE-ten im-MEE vǝ-ā-RŌM ā-SHOOV SHĀ-mā ā-dō-NĪ nā-TAN vā-dō-NĪ lā-KACH ya-HEE shaym ā-dō-NĪ mǝ-vō-RĀCH.

Write the words you know beneath the words in the text, and match the others to the words in the vocabulary.

💡 Language discovery

וַיֹּאמֶר

We have seen this word before, in 2 Samuel 12. Do you remember what it means?

יָצָתִי

The usual spelling of this word is יָצָאתִי. It's a Perfect form. Can you work out which one (e.g. 3ms, etc.)? Can you translate it?

מִבֶּטֶן

This is a preposition attached to a noun; we saw examples of this in Unit 8. The noun is in construct relationship to the following noun. Can you translate the phrase?

אָשׁוּב

This is a verbal form we have not encountered yet. The word means *I shall return*.

שָׁמָּה

This is the word שָׁם with a ה attached to it. It is known as a ה of direction or locative ה because it indicates movement towards a place or thing. So this word means *towards there*, although often it is better English to translate it simply *there*.

נָתַן

A verb in the Perfect: this should be simple enough to parse (analyse) and translate.

לָקָח

This is another verb in the Perfect; also fairly straightforward to parse and thus translate.

There are usually two pause points in a verse in biblical Hebrew: one about halfway through, and another at the end. This sometimes results in a lengthening of a vowel of the word in pause, and לָקָח is the pausal form of the 3ms of לָקַח.

יְהִי

This is a verb form we have not looked at yet. The word means *may it be* or *it will be*.

מְבֹרָךְ

Another verb form we have not yet encountered. This word means *blessed*.

POSSIBLE TRANSLATIONS

You should now have something like *And he said, 'Naked I was born from my mother's womb, and naked I shall return there. Yhwh has given and Yhwh has taken. May Yhwh's name be blessed.'*

Somewhat more conventional: *And he said, 'Naked I came out of my mother's womb and naked I shall return. The LORD has given and the LORD has taken away; blessed be the name of the LORD.'*

Test yourself

1 Write out the whole of the Perfect of קָטַל in Hebrew.

_____

2 Write in Hebrew: he has ruled, she has eaten, I have walked, they have guarded.

_____

3 Translate the following into English.

הָלְכָה עַד הָעִיר

_____

4 Translate the following into English.

אָכְלוּ דָוִד וְדָנִאֵל אֶת הַלֶּחֶם

_____

5 Translate the following into English.

מָשַׁל הַמֶּלֶךְ בְּכָל־אֶרֶץ יְהוּדָה הוּא וּבָנָיו

_____

SELF-CHECK	
I CAN...	
⬤	identify and parse verbs in the Perfect
⬤	explain some basic features of the Perfect
⬤	parse verbs
⬤	read and translate Job 1:21

11 *The Imperfect and numerals*

In this unit you will learn about:
▸ forms and uses of the Imperfect
▸ counting in Hebrew

You will read:
▸ Judges 8:22–3

Vocabulary builder

NOUNS

גִּדְעוֹן	gid-ŌN	*Gideon*
חַטָּאת	cha-TĀT	*sin* (f)
מִדְיָן	mid-YĀN	*Midian*
סָךְ	sāk	*crowd*
סֵפֶר	SAY-fer	*book*

VERBS

יָשַׁע	yā-SHA	*to deliver, save*
עָבַר	ā-var	*to pass over, go*
עָרַג	ā-RAG	*to bless*

OTHER

גַּם	gam	*also, even* (adverb)

Grammar

VERBS: IMPERFECT OR YIQTOL

The Imperfect in Hebrew used to be called the Future because it can be translated by the English future tense. And in fact it is commonly used to describe an incomplete action in the future. But, like the Perfect, it is impossible to map the Imperfect to a single English tense. Hebrew verbs really do not correspond directly to English verbs. Nevertheless, for now we will translate the Hebrew Imperfect with an English future.

When we learned the Perfect, we saw that the root קטל acquired endings in order to indicate who was doing the acting, e.g.:

קָטַלְתִּי	*I have killed*
קָטַלְתֶּם	*you have killed*

But in the Imperfect we find that the root acquires additional letters at the beginning and in some cases at the end as well. This is how it works, using קָטַל again as a demonstration verb:

יִקְטֹל	**yik-TŌL**	*he will kill*
תִּקְטֹל	**tik-TŌL**	*she will kill*
תִּקְטֹל	**tik-TŌL**	*you will kill* (ms)
תִּקְטְלִי	**tik-tə-LEE**	*you will kill* (fs)
אֶקְטֹל	**ek-TŌL**	*I will kill*
יִקְטְלוּ	**yik-tə-LOO**	*they will kill* (mp)
תִּקְטֹלְנָה	**tik-TŌL-nā**	*they will kill* (fp)
תִּקְטְלוּ	**tik-tə-LOO**	*you will kill* (mp)
תִּקְטֹלְנָה	**tik-TŌL-nā**	*you will kill* (fp)
נִקְטֹל	**nik-TŌL**	*we will kill*

Note the identical forms: 3fs is identical to 2ms, and 2fp is identical to 3fp. Context should help with translation. Unlike the Perfect, the third-person plural is divided into masculine and feminine.

By this point you are probably more confident about reading the Hebrew aloud and less dependent on approximate pronunciations (if indeed you used them). It should now be possible to attempt to pronounce most new Hebrew vocabulary; remember that the stress usually goes at the end (e.g. **da-VAR, yik-tə-LOO**), although exceptions will be noted. There will still be some help with pronunciation, but it will diminish over the next few units.

Here are some more examples of the Imperfect. Use the previous model to work out how they are pronounced.

מָשַׁל   *to rule*

יִמְשֹׁל	*he will rule*
תִּמְשֹׁל	*she will rule*
תִּמְשֹׁל	*you will rule* (ms)
תִּמְשְׁלִי	*you will rule* (fs)
אֶמְשֹׁל	*I will rule*
יִמְשְׁלוּ	*they will rule* (mp)
תִּמְשֹׁלְנָה	*they will rule* (fp)

תִּמְשְׁלוּ	you will rule (mp)
תִּמְשֹׁלְנָה	you will rule (fp)
נִמְשֹׁל	we will rule

שָׁמַר   *to keep, guard*

יִשְׁמֹר	he will guard
תִּשְׁמֹר	she will guard
תִּשְׁמֹר	you will guard (ms)
תִּשְׁמְרִי	you will guard (fs)
אֶשְׁמֹר	I will guard
יִשְׁמְרוּ	they will guard (mp)
תִּשְׁמֹרְנָה	they will guard (fp)
תִּשְׁמְרוּ	you will guard (mp)
תִּשְׁמֹרְנָה	you will guard (fp)
נִשְׁמֹר	we will guard

In Unit 10, we noted that the Perfect is sometimes known as the **Qatal**. In a similar way, the Imperfect is sometimes known as the **Yiqtol**. For example, the **Qatal** of שָׁמַר is שָׁמַר and the **Yiqtol** of שָׁמַר is יִשְׁמֹר.

Here is another example verb:

עָמַד   *to stand*

יַעֲמֹד	he will stand
תַּעֲמֹד	she will stand
תַּעֲמֹד	you will stand (ms)
תַּעַמְדִי	you will stand (fs)
אֶעֱמֹד	I will stand
יַעַמְדוּ	they will stand (mp)
תַּעֲמֹדְנָה	they will stand (fp)
תַּעַמְדוּ	you will stand (mp)
תַּעֲמֹדְנָה	you will stand (fp)
נַעֲמֹד	we will stand

Note: the vowels differ somewhat from קָטַל. This is because of the guttural at the beginning of עָמַד. If you look above at the Imperfect of קָטַל you will see that beneath the first root letter (ק) there is always a **sheva**. Gutturals generally do not take a simple **sheva** and so the vowel changes to a composite **sheva** or a full vowel. This attracts a **patach** in the prefix.

However, at this stage it is usually possible to make a good translation from Hebrew into English without knowing all the rules about vowels in verbal forms.

We have encountered one Imperfect form already, in Unit 7. The word is יָשִׁיר and is usually translated with a past tense: he sang. The word יְהִי in Job 1:21 (Unit 10) is also an Imperfect form meaning it will be or may it be. As you can see, neither of these follows the pattern we have just learned. This is because of the changes to the pattern that occur when the verbal root contains ו or י or gutturals. This will be explained in more detail in Unit 13.

PRACTICE 1

Write out the Imperfect of the following verbs, using the model of קָטַל.

These are some of the same verbs you learned in the Perfect. Remember that the **dagesh** in the פ will not be necessary when פָּקַד has the Imperfect prefixes, since פ will no longer be the first letter of the syllable. The same applies to כָּתַב, which will now require **dagesh** in the **tav**. The verb also contains a **begadkefat** letter which will need a **dagesh** in the Imperfect.

	to visit פָּקַד	to write כָּתַב	to remember זָכַר
3ms	יִפְקֹד	יִכְתֹּב	יִזְכֹּר
3fs			
2ms			
2fs			
1s			
3p			
3mp			
3fp			
2mp			
2fp			
1p			

HOW THE IMPERFECT IS USED

Like the Perfect, the Imperfect cannot be translated by a single English tense. Although we usually translate it with a future tense, there are times when it can be translated by a present or a past.

Future tense:

וְחַטֹּאתֶיךָ לֹא אֶזְכֹּר   *and your sins I will not remember*

(Isaiah 43:25)

Note the change from the usual word order in this phrase. We might have expected לֹא אֶזְכֹּר to come before חַטֹּאתֶיךָ. This can have the effect of emphasizing חַטֹּאתֶיךָ and it is also a poetic device, but thorough discussion would require us to look more closely at the context.

Present tense:

נַפְשִׁי תַעֲרֹג אֵלֶיךָ   *My soul longs for you.*

(Psalm 42:2; Engl. 42:1)

Notice that the Imperfect form here resembles the vowel pattern in עָמַד.

Past tense:

אֶעֱבֹר בַּסָּךְ   *I used to go with the crowd.*

(Psalm 42:5; Engl. 42:4)

Again, the vowel pattern is like עָמַד.

The circumstances in which we would translate the Hebrew Imperfect with a present or a past tense in English can be complicated and a Hebrew grammar should provide a more detailed explanation. For now, we will translate the Imperfect with an English future tense.

PRACTICE 2

Match the English to the Hebrew.

a	נִשְׁפֹּט אֶת־הֶעָרִים הָאֵלֶּה	1	You will rule over all the land of Israel.
b	תִּשְׁבְּתְנָה תַּחַת הָעֵץ אֲשֶׁר בְּשָׂדֶה	2	I will remember this day.
c	יְהִי מְבֹרָךְ	3	We will judge these cities.
d	תִּמְשֹׁל בְּכָל־אֶרֶץ יִשְׂרָאֵל	4	He will be blessed.
e	תַּעַמְדוּ לִפְנֵי הַמֶּלֶךְ וְלִפְנֵי עֲבָדָיו	5	They will keep the law.
f	יִשְׁמְרוּ אֶת־הַתּוֹרָה	6	They will remember the name of Yhwh the God of gods.
g	אֶזְכֹּר הַיּוֹם הַזֶּה	7	She will visit the women of Judah.
h	תִּכְתְּבִי בְּסִפְרַיִךְ	8	You will stand before the king and his servants.
i	תִּזְכֹּרְנָה שֵׁם יְהוָה אֱלֹהֵי הָאֱלֹהִים	9	You will rest under the tree which is in the field.
j	תִּפְקֹד אֶת־נְשֵׁי יְהוּדָה	10	You will write in your books.

NUMERALS

Numbers in biblical Hebrew can be complicated: they can change spelling and meaning according to their number and gender, and in fact their gender can be counter-intuitive. They can be found in the construct state and can have pronominal suffixes. However, it is useful to learn to count to ten at this point, and to learn additional features along the way.

אֶחָד	1
שְׁתַּיִם	2
שָׁלוֹשׁ	3

אַרְבַּע	4
חָמֵשׁ	5
שֵׁשׁ	6
שֶׁבַע	7
שְׁמוֹנֶה	8
תֵּשַׁע	9
עֶשֶׂר	10

PRACTICE 3

Translate the following into English. The first two have been done for you.

a	אָב אֶחָד	*one father*
b	נָשִׁים שְׁתַּיִם	*two women*
c	שָׁלוֹשׁ אֲרָצוֹת	
d	אַרְבַּע בָּנוֹת	
e	חָמֵשׁ עָרִים	
f	שֵׁשׁ סוּסוֹת	
g	שֶׁבַע פָּרוֹת	
h	שְׁמוֹנֶה שָׂרוֹת	
i	תֵּשַׁע חֲרָבוֹת	
j	עֶשֶׂר בְּרָכוֹת	

Reading

JUDGES 8:22–3

Points to look out for in this text:

▶ words we have already encountered
▶ verbs in the Imperfect
▶ word order and use of prepositions.

וַיֹּאמְרוּ אִישׁ־יִשְׂרָאֵל אֶל־גִּדְעוֹן מְשָׁל־בָּנוּ גַּם־אַתָּה גַּם־בִּנְךָ גַּם בֶּן־בְּנֶךָ כִּי הוֹשַׁעְתָּנוּ מִיַּד מִדְיָן: וַיֹּאמֶר אֲלֵהֶם גִּדְעוֹן לֹא־אֶמְשֹׁל אֲנִי בָּכֶם וְלֹא־יִמְשֹׁל בְּנִי בָּכֶם יְהוָה יִמְשֹׁל בָּכֶם:

Approximate pronunciation:

va-yō-mə-ROO eesh yis-rā-AYL el gid-ŌN, mə-SHĀL bā-NOO gam at-TĀ gam bin-CHĀ gam bayn bə-NAY-chā, kee hō-sha-TĀ-noo mi-YAD mid-YĀN. va-YŌ-mer a-lay-HEM gid-ŌN lō em-SHŌL a-NEE bā-CHEM, və-lō yim-SHŌL bə-NEE bā-CHEM; a-dō-NĪ yim-SHŌL bā-CHEM.

Language discovery

וַיֹּאמְרוּ

We have seen וַיֹּאמְרוּ before, but this is slightly different. Can you work out what it means?

אִישׁ־יִשְׂרָאֵל

Two nouns in construct relationship. The first is usually translated with a plural here: although it is grammatically singular it has the sense of a collective noun. How would you translate the phrase?

מְשָׁל־בָּנוּ

This is a verb form we haven't seen before. It is an imperative used with a preposition, and you should be able to identify the latter. The phrase means *rule over us*.

גַּם־אַתָּה

You may be able to work out the literal meaning, but it requires idiomatic translation into English.

גַּם־בִּנְךָ גַּם בֶּן־בְּנֶךָ

The word גַּם here is usually translated *and* for the sake of correct grammar in English. How would you translate בֶּן־בְּנֶךָ?

הוֹשַׁעְתָּנוּ

This is a verbal form we have not yet learned. The word means *you have saved us*.

מִיַּד

The first letter here is the preposition מִן attached to the word יַד which is the construct form of יָד. How would you translate it?

אֲלֵהֶם

The usual spelling is אֲלֵיהֶם. Do you recognize it? It's a preposition with a pronominal suffix.

לֹא־אֶמְשֹׁל

The particle means *not*. Can you parse and translate the verb?

אֲנִי בָּכֶם

The pronoun אֲנִי is not strictly necessary for the verb to be understood, but here it is being used for emphasis. The preposition is used with the verb: see מְשָׁל־בָּנוּ.

וְלֹא־יִמְשֹׁל בְּנִי

The Hebrew word order is rather different from English word order: the negative comes before the verb in Hebrew. Can you make a grammatically correct translation of this phrase?

יְהוָה יִמְשֹׁל

In English we could insert the word *but* or *rather* since the contrast is so strongly implied in the Hebrew. Is it clear who will rule over the people?

POSSIBLE TRANSLATIONS

Here are two possible translations: one more literal and the other freer. Which appeals most, and why? What would you change?

And the men of Israel said to Gideon, 'Rule over us: you and also your son and also your son's son, because you have delivered us from the hand of Midian.' And Gideon said to them, 'I will not rule over you and my son will not rule over you; the LORD will rule over you.'

The people of Israel said to Gideon, 'Rule over us: you and your son and your grandson, because you have saved us from the Midianites.' But Gideon said to them, 'It is not I who shall rule over you, nor my son; instead Yhwh shall rule over you.'

Test yourself

1 Write out the whole of the Imperfect of שָׁמַר in Hebrew.

_____

2 Write in Hebrew: he will judge, she will rule, I will kill, they will stand.

_____

3 Translate the following into English.

יִקְטֹל אֶת הָאֲנָשִׁים

_____

4 Write the following in Hebrew.

You (ms) will remember the wife of the king.

_____

5 Translate the following into Hebrew.

I will rule over all the cities of Judah.

_____

SELF-CHECK	
I CAN...	
○	identify and translate verbs in the Imperfect
○	count to ten in Hebrew
○	read and translate Judges 8:22–3.

11 *The Imperfect and numerals*   **97**

12 *Vav Consecutive*

In this unit you will learn about:
▶ the use of the Vav Consecutive

You will read:
▶ Isaiah 12:1–2

Vocabulary builder

NOUNS

אֵל	ayl	God
אַף	af	nose, anger
זִמְרָה	zim-RĀ	song, praise, music
יָהּ	yāch	abbreviation of יְהֹוָה: the LORD
יְשׁוּעָה	yə-shoo-Ā	help, salvation
עֹז	ōz	strength, power

VERBS

אָנַף	ā-NAF	to be angry
בָּטַח	bā-TACH	to cling to, trust, rely on
יָדָה	yā-DĀ	to thank, praise
נָחַם	nā-cham	to comfort, console
פָּחַד	pā-CHAD	to tremble, be afraid

OTHER

הִנֵּה	hin-NAY	behold, look, notice (demonstrative particle)

Grammar

VERBS: THE VAV CONSECUTIVE

The verbal forms we have learned so far are the most straightforward forms, but not necessarily the most common forms. The Vav Consecutive is more common in biblical narrative than the less complex forms we have learned so far. The principle seems surprising: adding the conjunction *and* to the beginning of a verb can change the way we translate it.

We have learned that the Perfect is usually translated with a past tense:

קָטַל   *he has killed*

and the Imperfect is usually translated with a future tense:

יִקְטֹל   *he will kill*

However, the Vav Consecutive is translated differently:

וְקָטַל   *and he will kill*
וַיִּקְטֹל   *and he killed*

The first is a Perfect with the conjunction וְ. The second is an Imperfect with the conjunction וַ and **dagesh** in the verbal prefix (in this case **yod**).

Here are some more examples:

Perfect	VC Perfect	Imperfect	VC Imperfect
שָׁמַר	וְשָׁמַר	יִשְׁמֹר	וַיִּשְׁמֹר
he has guarded	*and he will guard*	*he will guard*	*and he guarded*
שָׁמַרְתִּי	וְשָׁמַרְתִּי	אֶשְׁמֹר	וָאֶשְׁמֹר
I have guarded	*and I will guard*	*I will guard*	*and I guarded*
זָכַר	וְזָכַר	יִזְכֹּר	וַיִּזְכֹּר
he has remembered	*and he will remember*	*he will remember*	*and he remembered*
זָכְרוּ	וְזָכְרוּ	יִזְכְּרוּ	וַיִּזְכְּרוּ
they have remembered	*and they will remember*	*they will remember*	*and they remembered*

These forms are called Vav Consecutive Perfect and Vav Consecutive Imperfect, though there is some scholarly debate about the use of the term 'consecutive', and indeed whether the Vav Consecutive Perfect really is just that. For extra confusion, the form of the Vav Consecutive Imperfect is frequently a jussive (which will be introduced later). These distinctions may be of limited use to learners but excite grammarians.

Nevertheless, the term reflects the phenomenon in biblical narrative in which a number of successive verbs are found in the Imperfect prefixed by וַ, conveying a sense of *then*; of what happened next. For example:

וַתֵּלַכְנָה שְׁתֵּיהֶם עַד־בּוֹאָנָה בֵּית לָחֶם וַיְהִי כְּבוֹאָנָה בֵּית לֶחֶם וַתֵּהֹם כָּל־הָעִיר עֲלֵיהֶן
וַתֹּאמַרְנָה הֲזֹאת נָעֳמִי ׃

(Ruth 1:19)

This verse contains numerous verbal forms and words that have not yet been introduced in this course. Notice, however, the sequence of Imperfect forms prefixed by וַ:

וַתֹּאמַרְנָה ... וַתֵּהֹם ... וַיְהִי ... וַתֵּלַכְנָה

A rough translation might be:

And they walked, both of them, until they came to Bethlehem. And it happened when they came to Bethlehem and (that) the whole city was in a commotion about them, and they said, 'Is this Naomi?'

An alternative term for VC Imperfect is **Vayyiqtol** and an alternative term for VC Perfect is **Veqatal**, just as the Perfect and Imperfect are sometimes known as **Qatal** and **Yiqtol**. However, the term 'consecutive' is widely used and may be the most accessible term for the time being. We will look at the Vav Consecutive (VC or, in some grammars, WC) Imperfect first because it is extremely common in biblical narrative. In fact we have already seen examples of it in 2 Samuel 12:7a and in Judges 8:23: וַיֹּאמֶר means *and he said*, which comes from אָמַר *to say*. This form is actually a little unusual, but the word וַיֹּאמֶר is so common in the Hebrew Bible that it becomes familiar very quickly. The form וַיֹּאמְרוּ occurs in Judges 8:22, and is also VC Imperfect.

The וֹ in the VC Imperfect is pointed with a **patach**, and the next letter takes **dagesh**: וַיִּכְתֹּב. If the next letter is a guttural it cannot take **dagesh** and so the vowel under the וֹ is lengthened: וָאֶזְכֹּר (see also וָאֶשְׁמֹר).

Here are some examples from the Hebrew text:

וַיִּכְתֹּב בַּסֵּפֶר   *and he wrote in the book*

(1 Samuel 10:25)

וָאֶזְכֹּר אֶת־בְּרִיתִי   *and I have remembered my covenant*

(Exodus 6:5)

PRACTICE 1

Complete the table with the correct English translations.

3ms	יִשְׁמֹר	*he will guard*	וַיִּשְׁמֹר	*and he guarded*
3fs	תִּשְׁמֹר		וַתִּשְׁמֹר	
2ms	תִּשְׁמֹר		וַתִּשְׁמֹר	
2fs	תִּשְׁמְרִי		וַתִּשְׁמְרִי	
1s	אֶשְׁמֹר		וָאֶשְׁמֹר	
3mp	יִשְׁמְרוּ		וַיִּשְׁמְרוּ	
3fp	תִּשְׁמֹרְנָה		וַתִּשְׁמֹרְנָה	
2mp	תִּשְׁמְרוּ		וַתִּשְׁמְרוּ	
2fp	תִּשְׁמֹרְנָה		וַתִּשְׁמֹרְנָה	
1p	נִשְׁמֹר		וַנִּשְׁמֹר	

Some very common verbs have unusual forms in the Imperfect, and they occur frequently in the VC Imperfect. Two such words are:

הָלַךְ	to walk, go	יֵלֵךְ	he will walk/go	וַיֵּלֶךְ	and he walked/went
לָקַח	to take	יִקַּח	he will take	וַיִּקַּח	and he took

VAV CONSECUTIVE PERFECT

The Perfect can also change meaning when prefixed by וֹ. However, it is vocalized differently. The וֹ in the VC Perfect is pointed with a **sheva**, for example, just like the usual pointing of the conjunction:

וְלָקַחְתָּ אִשָּׁה לִבְנִי   *and you will take a wife for my son*

(Genesis 24:7)

This usage is less common than the VC Imperfect, but worth knowing about.

Compare the previous sentence (VC Perfect) with the same sentence in the VC Imperfect:

וְלָקַחְתָּ אִשָּׁה לִבְנִי   *and you will take a wife for my son*

וַתִּקַח אִשָּׁה לִבְנִי   *and you took a wife for my son*

Note that in the second-person plural forms with an initial **sheva** the **vav** will be pointed as **shureq**:

וּשְׁמַרְתֶּם   *and you will guard*

You may read elsewhere that the Vav Consecutive changes the Imperfect into a Perfect or the Perfect into an Imperfect; or that the Vav Consecutive changes a future tense into a past tense and vice versa. In my view this is an oversimplification; the sense of reversal relates to the English tense with which we translate these different forms. However, for now it may be helpful to think of the VC as a transformative **vav**. And if these ideas sound difficult, that is because they are difficult. The VC should become clearer when you are more familiar with the Hebrew text.

However difficult it may be to learn about Hebrew verbs by reading grammatical descriptions, the fact remains that with some practice and experience it is not too difficult to understand them. The best way to come to understand Hebrew verbs is probably to read as much Hebrew as possible, all the while keeping in mind that the idea of tense in biblical Hebrew can be rather provisional.

PRACTICE 2

1 Translate the following into English.

a   וַיִּזְכֹּר אֶת־בְּרִיתְכֶם:

b   וְתִכְתֹּב דִּבְרֵיכֶם בְּסֵפֶר:

c   וְאָמְשֹׁל בָּהֶם:

d	וַתֵּלַכְנָה בְּדַרְכֵי צְדָקָה:
e	וַתֹּאכְלוּ הַלֶּחֶם:
f	וַיִּשְׁמְרוּ אֶת־תּוֹרַת יְהֹוָה:
g	וַתִּקְטֹל אִישׁ:
h	וַיִּקְרָא שֵׁם בְּנוֹ שְׁלֹמֹה:
i	וַיֹּאמֶר אֶשְׁפֹּט אֶת־כָּל־אֶרֶץ יְהוּדָה:
j	וַיֹּאמְרוּ נִשְׁמֹר אֶת בֵּית הַמֶּלֶךְ:

2 Write out the VC Perfect of זָכַר and translate into English. The first one has been done for you.

3ms		וְזָכַר	and he will remember
3fs			
2ms			
2fs			
1s			
3p			
2mp			
2fp			
1p			

Reading

ISAIAH 12:1–2

Points to look out for in this text:

▶ words we have already encountered
▶ occurrences of the VC with Imperfect and Perfect forms.

וְאָמַרְתָּ בַּיּוֹם הַהוּא אוֹדְךָ יְהֹוָה כִּי אָנַפְתָּ בִּי יָשֹׁב אַפְּךָ וּתְנַחֲמֵנִי: הִנֵּה אֵל יְשׁוּעָתִי אֶבְטַח
וְלֹא אֶפְחָד כִּי־עָזִּי וְזִמְרָת יָהּ וַיְהִי־לִי לִישׁוּעָה:

Approximate pronunciation:

və-ā-mar-TĀ bā-YŌM ha-HOO ōd-CHĀ ā-dō-NĪ kee ā-NAF-tā bee yā-SHŌV ap-CHĀ
oot-na-cha-MAY-nee. hin-NAY ayl yə-shoo-ā-TEE ev-TACH və-LŌ ef-CHĀD; kee ā-ZEE və-
zim-RĀT yāch ā-dō-NĪ va-yə-hee-LEE lee-shoo-Ā.

Language discovery

וְאָמַרְתָּ

This comes from the verb אמר meaning *to say*. Can you translate it? Notice that when we discuss verbal roots we can write them without the vowels, though out loud we would still say ā-MAR.

בַּיּוֹם הַהוּא

This phrase should be straightforward. How would you translate the preposition?

אוֹדְךָ

This is an Imperfect, though not one of the forms we have learned. (It is a form called **Hifil**, which we will learn about in Unit 18.) It comes from ידה meaning *to praise* or *to give thanks*. It also has a pronominal suffix: an ending associated with a pronoun. In this case the ending is ךָ, which means *you*. It is the same as the ending on סוּסְךָ *your horse* so it should be easy to recognize. What does the initial א tell you? Despite a lack of knowledge of Hifil forms, you may have enough information to translate it.

כִּי אָנַפְתָּ בִּי

This comes from the verb אנף. Since it begins with א, it might be easily mistaken for an Imperfect, presumably from a hypothetical verb נפת. However, the תָּ ending should indicate that it is a Perfect. Is it Vav Consecutive? How will you translate it? The preposition בְּ is used to indicate *with* as in *angry with someone or something*; here with the 1s suffix it means *with me*. The word כִּי can sometimes be translated *although*, which might make sense here.

יָשֹׁב

This is an Imperfect, from the verb שׁוּב *to turn*, *return*, or *turn back*. It is not formed in the same way as the Imperfect of קטל because it is spelled with a וֹ in the middle. This verb is commonly confused with יָשַׁב *to sit, live*. The subject is אַפְּךָ so consider which pronoun you will use. Most English translations use a past tense to translate this word, which demonstrates the difficulties of mapping Hebrew verbs to English tenses.

אַפְּךָ

If this is the noun אַף with a 2ms suffix, how will you translate it?

וּתְנַחֲמֵנִי

This is another Imperfect form but again a version we have not yet learned about (this one is called **Piel**). Like אוֹדְךָ it has a pronominal suffix which is 1cs. Is this verb VC? How would you translate it? Incidentally, this root is the origin of the name of the prophet Nahum, in Hebrew נַחוּם.

הִנֵּה

This word is often translated *behold*. Perhaps in today's English we might translate it *look* or *notice*.

אֵל

This is another word, or name, for God. We have seen it already in Unit 9. Be sure to distinguish it from אֶל meaning *to*.

יְשׁוּעָתִי

The noun יְשׁוּעָה with a first-person singular suffix. How would you translate it?

אֶבְטַח

Another Imperfect 1cs from בטח. Is it VC? What tense would you use to translate it?

אֶפְחָד

Imperfect 1s from פחד. Is it VC? How will you incorporate the negative particle into your translation?

עָזִּי

This is עֹז with a pronominal suffix, but which one? Be sure to distinguish it from אָז, which means *then*.

וְזִמְרָת

The construct singular form of זִמְרָה.

יָהּ

An abbreviation of יְהֹוָה and usually translated the same way. Many English translations take this with the following word and translate it *the LORD GOD*.

לִישׁוּעָה

We have seen יְשׁוּעָה but this time it is found with the preposition לְ. This construction is common in Hebrew and is often translated as an idiomatic expression of becoming. How might you work this into your translation?

After working on your translation, you should have something like:

And you will say in that day I will praise/thank you LORD because/although you were/have been angry with me your anger will turn away and you comforted me. Look, God is my salvation; I will trust and I will not fear because my strength and the song of the LORD, the LORD is to me for salvation.

This is a good start, but needs to be polished. However, there are some decisions to be made. How will we decide where the sentences begin and end? What will we do with that Imperfect יָשֹׁב which seems to be anomalous? Do we simply translate it with a past tense or should we leave it as a future? How do we deal with the construct form וְזִמְרָת in verse 2? Can we translate it *my song*? These kinds of questions are discussed in good commentaries, and it can be very helpful to read some commentaries while translating a passage so that you can come to your own conclusions about the most appropriate way to translate difficult passages. However, each decision may involve matters of theology as well as matters of language, and theology is beyond the scope of this course. It is probably impossible to be theologically neutral, but the following possible translation is an attempt to deal with some of the difficulties in the language and is not intended to provide any theological solutions!

POSSIBLE TRANSLATION

And you will say on that day, 'I will thank you, Yhwh, although you were angry with me. Your anger will turn away, and you have comforted me. Look, God is my salvation; I will trust and I will not be afraid, because Yhwh is my strength and my song. Yhwh has become my salvation.'

One solution to the difficulty posed by יָשֹׁב is to translate both יָשֹׁב and וּתְנַחֲמֵנִי with English verbs in the present tense: *your anger turns away and you comfort me*. The other common solution is to translate יָשֹׁב as a past tense, and then it fits in more easily with the other English past tenses: *your anger has turned away and you have comforted me*. Meanwhile, most translations render וְזִמְרָת *my song*.

Translation is partly a science and partly an art. There can be no perfection, but some solutions may seem more suitable than others. Sometimes it may seem as if very little is at stake; other times it may seem as if a fundamental principle depends on correctly understanding the meaning of the Hebrew. This can be difficult, but it can also be very rewarding.

Test yourself

1 Which English tense do we usually use to translate a VC Imperfect?

_____

2 What vowel would we usually find underneath the וֹ in a VC Imperfect?

_____

3 Translate the following into English.

וַיֵּלֶךְ עַד יְהוּדָה

_____

4 Translate the following into English.

אָנַף וַיִּקַּח חַרְבוֹ וָאֶפְחַד

_____

5 Parse this verbal form.

וַתִּפְקְדִי.

_____

SELF-CHECK

I CAN...

○	recognize and translate Vav Consecutive Imperfect and Perfect forms
○	read and translate Isaiah 12:1–2, with particular reference to the difficulties in deciding which English tense to use

13 Weak verbs: Perfect and Imperfect

In this unit you will learn:
▶ what weak verbs are in biblical Hebrew
▶ how weak verbs are conjugated in the Perfect
▶ how weak verbs are conjugated in the Imperfect

You will read:
▶ Jonah 2:1–3 and 11

Vocabulary builder

NOUNS

בֶּטֶן	belly, womb, inside
דָּג	fish
יַבָּשָׁה	dry land
יוֹנָה	Jonah
מֵעֶה	intestines, belly, womb, heart
צָרָה	distress
שְׁאוֹל	Sheol

VERBS

בּוֹא	to come
בָּלַע	to swallow
בָּנָה	to build
גָּלָה	to reveal
יָלַד	to give birth
יָצָא	to go out
יָרַד	to go down (e.g. to Egypt)
יָשַׁב	to sit, live (dwell)
מָנָה	to assign, appoint
מָצָא	to find

נָגַשׁ	to approach
סָבַב	to turn, go around
עָלָה	to go up
עָנָה	to answer
עָשָׂה	to make, do
פָּלַל	to intercede, pray
קוֹא	to vomit
קוּם	to get up
רָאָה	to see
שָׁוַע	to implore, ask for help
שָׁחַט	to kill, slaughter
שִׂים	to place, put
שָׁלַח	to send, stretch out
שָׁמַע	to hear
שָׁתָה	to drink

Grammar

WEAK VERBS

Weak verbs are verbs with patterns that differ from those of קָטַל. Many of them are similar but have slightly different vowels and are usually easy enough to recognize. Others change their spelling so that it is difficult to guess the verbal root in order to look it up in a dictionary, so it is useful to know what kinds of changes are possible. The word 'weak' suggests that the vowels will be forced to change (e.g. if they occur under a guttural), or that some consonants in the word may disappear when prefixes and suffixes are added to make pronunciation easier.

Verbs in English sometimes differ from the standard form: for example, we might expect the past tense of *feed* and *put* to be *feeded* and *putted*, but instead they are *fed* and *put*. In English these verbs are usually irregular. There are a few irregular verbs in Hebrew but weak verbs are actually different patterns rather than irregular verbs.

We have already seen examples of weak verbs in Hebrew. One example is the verb עָמַד: in Unit 11, we saw that its vowels are different from קָטַל.

Verb	Imperfect 3ms	Meaning
קָטַל *to kill*	יִקְטֹל	he will kill
עָמַד *to stand*	יַעֲמֹד	he will stand

We might have expected the Imperfect 3ms of עָמַד to be יַעְמֹד. However, gutturals tend not to take a simple **sheva**. They usually take a composite **sheva** instead: עֲ. The guttural also affects the vowel under the letter that comes before it, so instead of יְ we have יַ.

There are ten categories of weak verbs. Verbs can be weak if:

the first letter of the root is a guttural	עָמַד	I-guttural
the second letter is a guttural	שָׁחַט	II-guttural
the third letter is a guttural	שָׁלַח	III-guttural
the first letter is א (rather than one of the other gutturals)	אָכַל	I- א
the first letter is ו or י	יָשַׁב	I- ו or י
the second letter is ו or י	קוּם	II- ו or י / hollow
the first letter is נ	נָגַשׁ	I- נ
the second letter is the same as the third letter	סָבַב	geminate
the third letter is א	מָצָא	III- א
the third letter is ה	גָּלָה	III- ה

In Hebrew grammars there is sometimes a kind of shorthand for 'first letter', 'second letter' and so on.

The first letter is the פ letter.

The second letter is the ע letter.

The third letter is the ל letter.

If we want to say the first letter of the verbal root is **alef**, we say the verb is פ״א (**pe alef**). The mark that looks like an apostrophe, ׳, is called a **geresh** (pl **gershayim** or **gerashayim**). It can be used singly or doubled, depending on context, e.g. פ״י or ק׳. The mark means 'not a word' and is used for abbreviations.

If we want to say the second letter of the verbal root is **vav** we say the verb is ע״ו (**ayin vav**). Verbs in this category are also called hollow verbs.

If we want to say the third letter of the verbal root is **he** we say the verb is ל״ה (**lamed he**).

The letters פ, ע and ל are not random; in fact פָּעַל means *to make* or *to form*, which is quite an appropriate verb in the circumstances. As a noun, it can mean *verb* (פֹּעַל). In fact, if it weren't for the weakness in פָּעַל (it is, of course, **ayin** guttural), it might be more appropriate as a demonstration verb than קָטַל. Many recent grammars of biblical Hebrew use I, II and III instead to classify weak verbs. However, it is useful to know the פעל system as well, since this system is used in older dictionaries and grammars available online and as reprints.

The weaknesses have various effects, and the effects can be found in the Perfect or Imperfect or other forms. Here are the most likely departures from the regular verb, somewhat oversimplified for convenience:

Weakness type	Alternative name	Example	Effect
I-guttural	פ guttural	עָמַד	changes to the vowel patterns
II-guttural	ע guttural	שָׁחַט	changes to the vowel patterns
III-guttural	ל guttural	שָׁלַח	changes to the vowel patterns
I-ו or י	פ״י and פ״ו	יָשַׁב	disappearing י and vowel changes
hollow	ע״ו and ע״י	קוּם	disappearing י or ו and vowel changes
I-נ	פ״נ	נָגַשׁ	disappearing נ and vowel changes
geminate	ע״ע	סָבַב	disappearing third letter and vowel changes
I-א	פ״א	אָכַל	changes to the vowel patterns
III-א	ל״א	מָצָא	changes to the vowel patterns
III-ה	ל״ה	גָּלָה	disappearing ה and vowel changes

We have already seen some weak verbs in Units 10 and 11 and they were very similar to the קָטַל pattern. The weak verbs we have already encountered are: עָמַד אָכַל הָלַךְ לָקַח נָתַן שׁוּב הָיָה, and others have appeared in the examples. Some verbs can be doubly weak; for example עָשָׂה is both I-guttural and III-ה and has features of both types.

PRACTICE 1

Identify the weaknesses in the following verbs and complete the table.

Note: some are doubly weak.

Verb	Meaning	Weakness(es)
עָמַד	to stand	
שָׁלַח	to send, stretch out	
שִׂים	to put, place	
רָאָה	to see	
שָׁמַע	to hear	
שָׁתָה	to drink	
עָלָה	to go up	
בּוֹא	to come	
יָלַד	to give birth	

יָצָא	to go out	
יָרַד	to go down	
מוּת	to die	
בָּנָה	to build	

WEAK VERBS IN THE PERFECT

Many weak verbs in the Perfect are easily recognizable despite their vowel changes. In most cases it is useful to learn the principles of the effect of the weakness in the verb, but it is not generally necessary to commit the paradigm to memory.

Verbs with an initial guttural take composite **sheva** instead of simple **sheva** in the second-person plural forms, i.e. where the first letter of the root is usually pointed with **sheva**. All the other parts of the verb are formed like קָטַל.

	I-guttural	Strong	
3ms	עָמַד	קָטַל	he stood
3fs	עָמְדָה	קָטְלָה	she stood
2ms	עָמַדְתָּ	קָטַלְתָּ	you stood
2fs	עָמַדְתְּ	קָטַלְתְּ	you stood
1cs	עָמַדְתִּי	קָטַלְתִּי	I stood
3cp	עָמְדוּ	קָטְלוּ	they stood
2mp	עֲמַדְתֶּם	קְטַלְתֶּם	you stood
2fp	עֲמַדְתֶּן	קְטַלְתֶּן	you stood
1cp	עָמַדְנוּ	קָטַלְנוּ	we stood

Verbs with a middle guttural take composite **sheva** instead of simple **sheva** in the third feminine singular and third common plural forms. All the other parts of the verb are formed like קָטַל.

	II-guttural	Strong	
3ms	שָׁחַט	קָטַל	he killed
3fs	שָׁחֲטָה	קָטְלָה	she killed
2ms	שָׁחַטְתָּ	קָטַלְתָּ	you killed
2fs	שָׁחַטְתְּ	קָטַלְתְּ	you killed
1cs	שָׁחַטְתִּי	קָטַלְתִּי	I killed
3cp	שָׁחֲטוּ	קָטְלוּ	they killed

2mp	שְׁחַטְתֶּם	קְטַלְתֶּם	*you killed*
2fp	שְׁחַטְתֶּן	קְטַלְתֶּן	*you killed*
1cp	שְׁחַטְנוּ	קָטַלְנוּ	*we killed*

Verbs with a final guttural are formed just like קָטַל in the Perfect even though they have a **sheva** under the guttural. This is because, in these verbs, the **sheva** is silent rather than vocalized.

	III-guttural	Strong	
3ms	שָׁלַח	קָטַל	*he sent*
3fs	שָׁלְחָה	קָטְלָה	*she sent*
2ms	שָׁלַחְתָּ	קָטַלְתָּ	*you sent*
2fs	שָׁלַחְתְּ	קָטַלְתְּ	*you sent*
1cs	שָׁלַחְתִּי	קָטַלְתִּי	*I sent*
3cp	שָׁלְחוּ	קָטְלוּ	*they sent*
2mp	שְׁלַחְתֶּם	קְטַלְתֶּם	*you sent*
2fp	שְׁלַחְתֶּן	קְטַלְתֶּן	*you sent*
1cp	שָׁלַחְנוּ	קָטַלְנוּ	*we sent*

Verbs with an initial **yod** are formed just like קָטַל in the Perfect.

	I-ו or י	Strong	
3ms	יָשַׁב	קָטַל	*he sat*
3fs	יָשְׁבָה	קָטְלָה	*she sat*
2ms	יָשַׁבְתָּ	קָטַלְתָּ	*you sat*
2fs	יָשַׁבְתְּ	קָטַלְתְּ	*you sat*
1cs	יָשַׁבְתִּי	קָטַלְתִּי	*I sat*
3cp	יָשְׁבוּ	קָטְלוּ	*they sat*
2mp	יְשַׁבְתֶּם	קְטַלְתֶּם	*you sat*
2fp	יְשַׁבְתֶּן	קְטַלְתֶּן	*you sat*
1cp	יָשַׁבְנוּ	קָטַלְנוּ	*we sat*

Verbs with a middle **yod** or **vav** lose this vowel in the Perfect. These forms can be recognized by their suffixes, which are the same suffixes usually found in the Perfect, even though they look as if they do not have enough letters.

	Hollow	Strong	
3ms	קָם	קָטַל	*he got up*
3fs	קָמָה	קָטְלָה	*she got up*
2ms	קַמְתָּ	קָטַלְתָּ	*you got up*
2fs	קַמְתְּ	קָטַלְתְּ	*you got up*
1cs	קַמְתִּי	קָטַלְתִּי	*I got up*
3cp	קָמוּ	קָטְלוּ	*they got up*
2mp	קַמְתֶּם	קְטַלְתֶּם	*you got up*
2fp	קַמְתֶּן	קְטַלְתֶּן	*you got up*
1cp	קַמְנוּ	קָטַלְנוּ	*we got up*

Verbs with an initial nun are are formed just like קָטַל in the Perfect.

	I-נ	Strong	
3ms	נָגַשׁ	קָטַל	*he approached*
3fs	נָגְשָׁה	קָטְלָה	*she approached*
2ms	נָגַשְׁתָּ	קָטַלְתָּ	*you approached*
2fs	נָגַשְׁתְּ	קָטַלְתְּ	*you approached*
1cs	נָגַשְׁתִּי	קָטַלְתִּי	*I approached*
3cp	נָגְשׁוּ	קָטְלוּ	*they approached*
2mp	נְגַשְׁתֶּם	קְטַלְתֶּם	*you approached*
2fp	נְגַשְׁתֶּן	קְטַלְתֶּן	*you approached*
1cp	נָגַשְׁנוּ	קָטַלְנוּ	*we approached*

Verbs where the second and third letters are the same take **dagesh** in the second letter as a way of doubling it, although not in every form. These verbs are also called double **ayin** or reduplicated verbs.

	Geminate	Strong	
3ms	סָבַב	קָטַל	*he turned*
3fs	סָבְבָה	קָטְלָה	*she turned*
2ms	סַבּוֹתָ	קָטַלְתָּ	*you turned*

2fs	סַבּוֹת	קָטַלְתְּ	*you turned*
1cs	סַבּוֹתִי	קָטַלְתִּי	*I turned*
3cp	סָבְבוּ	קָטְלוּ	*they turned*
2mp	סַבּוֹתֶם	קְטַלְתֶּם	*you turned*
2fp	סַבּוֹתֶן	קְטַלְתֶּן	*you turned*
1cp	סַבּוֹנוּ	קָטַלְנוּ	*we turned*

Verbs with an initial **alef** take a composite **sheva** in the 2mp and 2fp forms (just like I-guttural verbs).

	א-I	Strong	
3ms	אָכַל	קָטַל	*he ate*
3fs	אָכְלָה	קָטְלָה	*she ate*
2ms	אָכַלְתָּ	קָטַלְתָּ	*you ate*
2fs	אָכַלְתְּ	קָטַלְתְּ	*you ate*
1cs	אָכַלְתִּי	קָטַלְתִּי	*I ate*
3cp	אָכְלוּ	קָטְלוּ	*they ate*
2mp	אֲכַלְתֶּם	קְטַלְתֶּם	*you ate*
2fp	אֲכַלְתֶּן	קְטַלְתֶּן	*you ate*
1cp	אָכַלְנוּ	קָטַלְנוּ	*we ate*

Verbs with a final **alef** lose the **sheva** under the **alef** in some of the forms, which affects the **dagesh** in the suffix retain. In practice these are nevertheless easy to recognize and translate.

	א-III	Strong	
3ms	מָצָא	קָטַל	*he found*
3fs	מָצְאָה	קָטְלָה	*she found*
2ms	מָצָאתָ	קָטַלְתָּ	*you found*
2fs	מָצָאת	קָטַלְתְּ	*you found*
1cs	מָצָאתִי	קָטַלְתִּי	*I found*
3cp	מָצְאוּ	קָטְלוּ	*they found*
2mp	מְצָאתֶם	קְטַלְתֶּם	*you found*
2fp	מְצָאתֶן	קְטַלְתֶּן	*you found*
1cp	מָצָאנוּ	קָטַלְנוּ	*we found*

Verbs with a final **he** involve multiple changes, replacing the **he** with other letters (**tav** or **yod**). According to language scholars this reflects the historical development of this class of verbs in biblical Hebrew. This type of weak verb should be learned in full.

	III-הַ		Strong	
3ms	גָּלָה		קָטַל	he revealed
3fs	גָּלְתָה		קָטְלָה	she revealed
2ms	גָּלִיתָ		קָטַלְתָּ	you revealed
2fs	גָּלִית		קָטַלְתְּ	you revealed
1cs	גָּלִיתִי		קָטַלְתִּי	I revealed
3cp	גָּלוּ		קָטְלוּ	they revealed
2mp	גְּלִיתֶם		קְטַלְתֶּם	you revealed
2fp	גְּלִיתֶן		קְטַלְתֶּן	you revealed
1cp	גָּלִינוּ		קָטַלְנוּ	we revealed

The verb נָתַן is irregular and should also be learned in full. Note the disappearing **nun**.

	נָתַן		Strong	
3ms	נָתַן		קָטַל	he gave
3fs	נָתְנָה		קָטְלָה	she gave
2ms	נָתַתָּ		קָטַלְתָּ	you gave
2fs	נָתַתְּ		קָטַלְתְּ	you gave
1cs	נָתַתִּי		קָטַלְתִּי	I gave
3cp	נָתְנוּ		קָטְלוּ	they gave
2mp	נְתַתֶּם		קְטַלְתֶּם	you gave
2fp	נְתַתֶּן		קְטַלְתֶּן	you gave
1cp	נָתַנּוּ		קָטַלְנוּ	we gave

PRACTICE 2

Parse the following forms. The first one has been done for you.

These are the same verbs whose weaknesses have been identified.

a עָמַדְנוּ   Perfect 3cp עָמַד we have stood
b שָׁלְחָה
c שָׁמָה
d רָאִינוּ

114

e	שָׁמַעְתִּי
f	שְׁתִיתֶם
g	עָלְתָה
h	בָּא
i	יָלַדְתְּ
j	יָצָאת
k	יָרְדוּ
l	מַתֶּן
m	בָּנוּ

WEAK VERBS IN THE IMPERFECT

Weak verbs have more departures from the strong verb pattern in the Imperfect than in the Perfect. Some of the weak verbs that were identical to the קָטַל form in the Perfect are quite different from the קָטַל pattern in the Imperfect. Again, learning lists of verbs is not usually necessary at this stage, although some forms are less recognizable than others and should be committed to memory if possible.

Verbs with an initial guttural take composite **sheva** instead of simple **sheva** under the first letter of the verbal root, which generates a vowel change in the Imperfect prefix.

	I-guttural	Strong	
3ms	יַעֲמֹד	יִקְטֹל	*he will stand*
3fs	תַּעֲמֹד	תִּקְטֹל	*she will stand*
2ms	תַּעֲמֹד	תִּקְטֹל	*you will stand*
2fs	תַּעֲמְדִי	תִּקְטְלִי	*you will stand*
1cs	אֶעֱמֹד	אֶקְטֹל	*I will stand*
3mp	יַעֲמְדוּ	יִקְטְלוּ	*they will stand*
3fp	תַּעֲמֹדְנָה	תִּקְטֹלְנָה	*they will stand*
2mp	תַּעַמְדוּ	תִּקְטְלוּ	*you will stand*
2fp	תַּעֲמֹדְנָה	תִּקְטֹלְנָה	*you will stand*
1cp	נַעֲמֹד	נִקְטֹל	*we will stand*

Verbs with a middle guttural take patach instead of cholem under the second root letter. Gutturals are often found with a-type vowels (patach or qamets)

	II-guttural	Strong	
3ms	יִשְׁחַט	יִקְטֹל	*he will kill*
3fs	תִּשְׁחַט	תִּקְטֹל	*she will kill*
2ms	תִּשְׁחַט	תִּקְטֹל	*you will kill*

2fs	תִּשְׁחֲטִי		תִּקְטְלִי	you will kill
1cs	אֶשְׁחַט		אֶקְטֹל	I will kill
3mp	יִשְׁחֲטוּ		יִקְטְלוּ	they will kill
3fp	תִּשְׁחַטְנָה		תִּקְטֹלְנָה	they will kill
2mp	תִּשְׁחֲטוּ		תִּקְטְלוּ	you will kill
2fp	תִּשְׁחַטְנָה		תִּקְטֹלְנָה	you will kill
1cp	נִשְׁחַט		נִקְטֹל	we will kill

Verbs with a final guttural take **patach** instead of **cholem** under the second root letter.

	III-guttural		Strong	
3ms	יִשְׁלַח		יִקְטֹל	he will send
3fs	תִּשְׁלַח		תִּקְטֹל	she will send
2ms	תִּשְׁלַח		תִּקְטֹל	you will send
2fs	תִּשְׁלְחִי		תִּקְטְלִי	you will send
1cs	אֶשְׁלַח		אֶקְטֹל	I will send
3mp	יִשְׁלְחוּ		יִקְטְלוּ	they will send
3fp	תִּשְׁלַחְנָה		תִּקְטֹלְנָה	they will send
2mp	תִּשְׁלְחוּ		תִּקְטְלוּ	you will send
2fp	תִּשְׁלַחְנָה		תִּקְטֹלְנָה	you will send
1cp	נִשְׁלַח		נִקְטֹל	we will send

Verbs with initial **yod** usually drop the initial **yod** and take **tsere** vowels. Some verbs of this type do not lose their **yod** and follow a pattern more similar to יִקְטֹל although they tend to be less common. Therefore, this is the paradigm you will encounter more often. There are a great many common verbs of this type, so this paradigm should be learned.

	I-ו or י		Strong	
3ms	יֵשֵׁב		יִקְטֹל	he will sit
3fs	תֵּשֵׁב		תִּקְטֹל	she will sit
2ms	תֵּשֵׁב		תִּקְטֹל	you will sit
2fs	תֵּשְׁבִי		תִּקְטְלִי	you will sit
1cs	אֵשֵׁב		אֶקְטֹל	I will sit

3mp	יֵשְׁבוּ	יִקְטְלוּ	they will sit
3fp	תֵּשַׁבְנָה	תִּקְטֹלְנָה	they will sit
2mp	תֵּשְׁבוּ	תִּקְטְלוּ	you will sit
2fp	תֵּשַׁבְנָה	תִּקְטֹלְנָה	you will sit
1cp	נֵשֵׁב	נִקְטֹל	we will sit

Verbs with a middle vowel retain it in the Imperfect, although the vowel in the prefix changes to **qamets** in most forms. A few verbs have **vav** as a consonant and conjugate like קטל: for example the root צוה *to command*, from which we get the noun מִצְוָה, *commandment*. Nevertheless, the following paradigm is very common and should be memorized.

	Hollow	Strong	
3ms	יָקוּם	יִקְטֹל	he will get up
3fs	תָּקוּם	תִּקְטֹל	she will get up
2ms	תָּקוּם	תִּקְטֹל	you will get up
2fs	תָּקוּמִי	תִּקְטְלִי	you will get up
1cs	אָקוּם	אֶקְטֹל	I will get up
3mp	יָקוּמוּ	יִקְטְלוּ	they will get up
3fp	תְּקוּמֶינָה	תִּקְטֹלְנָה	they will get up
2mp	תָּקוּמוּ	תִּקְטְלוּ	you will get up
2fp	תְּקוּמֶינָה	תִּקְטֹלְנָה	you will get up
1cp	נָקוּם	נִקְטֹל	we will get up

Verbs with an initial **nun** lose the **nun** in the Imperfect. It is assimilated into the second root letter, as long as that letter can take **dagesh**. This generates vowel changes: **cholem** becomes **patach**.

	נ-I	Strong	
3ms	יִגַּשׁ	יִקְטֹל	he will approach
3fs	תִּגַּשׁ	תִּקְטֹל	she will approach
2ms	תִּגַּשׁ	תִּקְטֹל	you will approach
2fs	תִּגְּשִׁי	תִּקְטְלִי	you will approach
1cs	אֶגַּשׁ	אֶקְטֹל	I will approach

3mp	יִגְּשׁוּ	יִקְטְלוּ	they will approach
3fp	תִּגַּשְׁנָה	תִּקְטֹלְנָה	they will approach
2mp	תִּגְּשׁוּ	תִּקְטְלוּ	you will approach
2fp	תִּגַּשְׁנָה	תִּקְטֹלְנָה	you will approach
1cp	נִגַּשׁ	נִקְטֹל	we will approach

Double **ayin**, or geminate, verbs have the **ayin** letter only once, sometimes with **dagesh** (in the forms of the Imperfect where there is a suffix as well as a prefix). Like other weak verbs, this generates a **qamets** in the prefix in most forms.

	Geminate	Strong	
3ms	יָסֹב	יִקְטֹל	he will turn
3fs	תָּסֹב	תִּקְטֹל	she will turn
2ms	תָּסֹב	תִּקְטֹל	you will turn
2fs	תָּסֹבִּי	תִּקְטְלִי	you will turn
1cs	אָסֹב	אֶקְטֹל	I will turn
3mp	יָסֹבּוּ	יִקְטְלוּ	they will turn
3fp	תְּסֻבֶּינָה	תִּקְטֹלְנָה	they will turn
2mp	תָּסֹבּוּ	תִּקְטְלוּ	you will turn
2fp	תְּסֻבֶּינָה	תִּקְטֹלְנָה	you will turn
1cp	נָסֹב	נִקְטֹל	we will turn

As in the Perfect, the **alef** in I-א verbs loses its vowel. This time the vowel in the prefix changes to **cholem**.

	I-א	Strong	
3ms	יֹאכַל	יִקְטֹל	he will eat
3fs	תֹּאכַל	תִּקְטֹל	she will eat
2ms	תֹּאכַל	תִּקְטֹל	you will eat
2fs	תֹּאכְלִי	תִּקְטְלִי	you will eat
1cs	אֹכַל	אֶקְטֹל	I will eat
3mp	יֹאכְלוּ	יִקְטְלוּ	they will eat
3fp	תֹּאכַלְנָה	תִּקְטֹלְנָה	they will eat
2mp	תֹּאכְלוּ	תִּקְטְלוּ	you will eat

2fp	תֹּאכַלְנָה	תִּקְטֹלְנָה	you will eat
1cp	נֹאכַל	נִקְטֹל	we will eat

In verbs with final **alef**, similarly, the **alef** loses its vowel in the plural forms and causes vowel changes in most of the other forms.

	III-א	Strong	
3ms	יִמְצָא	יִקְטֹל	he will find
3fs	תִּמְצָא	תִּקְטֹל	she will find
2ms	תִּמְצָא	תִּקְטֹל	you will find
2fs	תִּמְצְאִי	תִּקְטְלִי	you will find
1cs	אֶמְצָא	אֶקְטֹל	I will find
3mp	יִמְצְאוּ	יִקְטְלוּ	they will find
3fp	תִּמְצֶאנָה	תִּקְטֹלְנָה	they will find
2mp	תִּמְצְאוּ	תִּקְטְלוּ	you will find
2fp	תִּמְצֶאנָה	תִּקְטֹלְנָה	you will find
1cp	נִמְצָא	נִקְטֹל	we will find

Verbs that end with **he** are more recognizable in the Imperfect than in the Perfect. The **he** drops out in some of the forms, and tends to favour **segol**.

	III-ה	Strong	
3ms	יִגְלֶה	יִקְטֹל	he will reveal
3fs	תִּגְלֶה	תִּקְטֹל	she will reveal
2ms	תִּגְלֶה	תִּקְטֹל	you will reveal
2fs	תִּגְלִי	תִּקְטְלִי	you will reveal
1cs	אֶגְלֶה	אֶקְטֹל	I will reveal
3mp	יִגְלוּ	יִקְטְלוּ	they will reveal
3fp	תִּגְלֶינָה	תִּקְטֹלְנָה	they will reveal
2mp	תִּגְלוּ	תִּקְטְלוּ	you will reveal
2fp	תִּגְלֶינָה	תִּקְטֹלְנָה	you will reveal
1cp	נִגְלֶה	נִקְטֹל	we will reveal

And, finally, the irregular verb נָתַן. This time the initial **nun** disappears and is assimilated into the **tav**: note the **dagesh** in the **tav**.

		III-ה	Strong
3ms	he will give	יִתֵּן	יִקְטֹל
3fs	she will give	תִּתֵּן	תִּקְטֹל
2ms	you will give	תִּתֵּן	תִּקְטֹל
2fs	you will give	תִּתְּנִי	תִּקְטְלִי
1cs	I will give	אֶתֵּן	אֶקְטֹל
3mp	they will give	יִתְּנוּ	יִקְטְלוּ
3fp	they will give	תִּתֵּנָּה	תִּקְטֹלְנָה
2mp	you will give	תִּתְּנוּ	תִּקְטְלוּ
2fp	you will give	תִּתֵּנָּה	תִּקְטֹלְנָה
1cp	we will give	נִתֵּן	נִקְטֹל

PRACTICE 3

Translate the following into Hebrew.

a The king will sit under the tree.

b Deborah will get up and she will hear my voice.

c You (ms) will not approach the city.

d You (mp) will go around the mountain.

e I will eat bread in the house.

f They (f) will give horses to our sons.

Reading

JONAH 2:1–3, 11 [ENGL. 1:17–2:2, 10]

Points to look out for in this text:

▶ words we have already encountered

▶ weak verbs in a variety of forms.

1 וַיְמַן יְהוָה דָּג גָּדוֹל לִבְלֹעַ אֶת־יוֹנָה וַיְהִי יוֹנָה בִּמְעֵי הַדָּג שְׁלֹשָׁה יָמִים וּשְׁלֹשָׁה לֵילוֹת:

2 וַיִּתְפַּלֵּל יוֹנָה אֶל־יְהוָה אֱלֹהָיו מִמְּעֵי הַדָּגָה:

3 וַיֹּאמֶר קָרָאתִי מִצָּרָה לִי אֶל־יְהוָה וַיַּעֲנֵנִי מִבֶּטֶן שְׁאוֹל שִׁוַּעְתִּי שָׁמַעְתָּ קוֹלִי:

11 וַיֹּאמֶר יְהוָה לַדָּג וַיָּקֵא אֶת־יוֹנָה אֶל־הַיַּבָּשָׁה:

💡 Language discovery

Sometimes the Hebrew Bible and the English translation have slightly different chapter and verse numbers. This course will follow the numbering of the Hebrew text.

There are several verbal forms in this text that have not yet been explored. However, it is usually better to learn by reading real biblical texts, even with some explanations, than by reading texts that perfectly clarify points of grammar but lack familiarity or interpretive challenges.

VERSE 1

וַיְמַן יְהוָה דָּג גָּדוֹל

Can you identify which verbal root (in the vocabulary) the first word comes from? Sometimes in the VC Imperfect 3ms of III-ה verbs the **he** disappears. Therefore this does not match the table of III-ה verbs; and also because it is in a form we have not yet encountered, called Piel.

לִבְלֹעַ אֶת־יוֹנָה

If the first word is an inseparable preposition and an infinitive, what might it mean? Infinitives will be examined in more detail in the next unit, but the word is in the vocabulary. What kind of weakness does the verb have?

וַיְהִי יוֹנָה בִּמְעֵי הַדָּג

We saw וַיְהִי in Unit 8, before we had learned about verbs. This is a doubly weak verb in a VC Imperfect form, and does not quite match the forms in the III-ה table. There are complex reasons for this, but the word is so common that it presents no difficulties in translation.

שְׁלֹשָׁה יָמִים וּשְׁלֹשָׁה לֵילוֹת

The numeral is in a different form from that presented in Unit 11, but should still be identifiable, and the nouns are some of the first nouns encountered in this course. This period of time is important in a number of biblical narratives (e.g. Genesis 42:17–18; Esther 4:15–16), and its resonance continues into the New Testament (e.g. Matthew 12:38–42) and the Talmud (e.g. Baba Mezi'a 86a). What do you think is the significance of this?

VERSE 2

וַיִּתְפַּלֵּל יוֹנָה אֶל־יְהוָה אֱלֹהָיו מִמְּעֵי הַדָּגָה

The verb is in a form we have not yet encountered, but despite the extra **tav** you might be able to identify the verbal root from the vocabulary. What is this verb's weakness?

What has happened to the fish? Is it the same thing that happens to סוּס and פַּר when הַ is added? The rabbis explained this apparent sex change by introducing a pregnant fish in Midrash Jonah. How might this idea influence your translation of מְעֵי? Your answer may depend on your theoretical orientation: feminists might prefer a female fish; scientists might argue that most fish don't have wombs; and linguists might insist that the grammatical gender of a noun does not necessarily reflect the biological sex of an animal.

VERSE 3

וַיֹּאמֶר קָרָאתִי מִצָּרָה לִי אֶל־יְהוָה וַיַּעֲנֵנִי

There are three verbs in this clause and all of them are weak. Can you identify how they are weak? Can you parse the first two? The third has a pronominal suffix which is 1cs. How would you translate it?

The phrase מִצָּרָה לִי uses a preposition to express an idea that requires a possessive pronoun in English. The other preposition behaves like an inseparable preposition. How would you translate this phrase?

מִבֶּטֶן שְׁאוֹל שִׁוַּעְתִּי שָׁמַעְתָּ קוֹלִי

Sheol is the underworld in the Hebrew Bible: the place where the dead go. Some translations have *Sheol*, some have *hell*, and some explain the term with *world of the dead* or similar. Which approach do you find preferable, and why?

The verb שׁוע behaves like צוה rather than like the II-ו paradigm in the table. However, it is another Piel form. Can you translate it nevertheless?

The last two words of this clause should be recognizable. Can you parse the verb?

This verse, and the next seven verses, are in the style of a Psalm and therefore in poetic form rather than prose. Poetry is generally more difficult to translate than prose in the early stages of learning a language. However, if you read it in translation you will get a sense of Jonah's change of perspective.

VERSE 11

וַיֹּאמֶר יְהוָה לַדָּג וַיָּקֵא אֶת־יוֹנָה אֶל־הַיַּבָּשָׁה

The first word should be familiar, but usually introduces speech. Since there is no reported speech here, how would you translate it?

The word וַיָּקֵא is in yet another form that we have not encountered at this point, called Hifil. Are you able to identify it from the vocabulary? It is VC Imperfect 3ms; can you translate it?

POSSIBLE TRANSLATION

After working on your translation, you should have something like:

Then God assigned a big fish to swallow Jonah, and he was in the intestines of the fish for three days and three nights. So Jonah prayed to Yhwh his God from the intestines of the fish. And he said, 'I called to Yhwh out of my distress and he answered me. From the belly of Sheol I implored; you heard my voice.' ... And Yhwh spoke to the fish and it vomited Jonah onto the dry land.

Test yourself

1 What effect does a guttural have on a verb's vowels?

_____

2 Which letters are likely to disappear in forms of the Imperfect in weak verbs?

_____

3 Translate the following into English.

מָצָאתָ אֶת־סוּסֵי הַמֶּלֶךְ

_____

4 Translate the following into English.

וַתֵּלֶד הָאִשָּׁה בֵּן וַתִּקְרָא שְׁמוֹ אַבְרָהָם

_____

5 Parse this verbal form: give the tense, person, gender, number, root and meaning of וַיִּשְׁמְעוּ.

_____

SELF-CHECK

I CAN...
recognize weak verbs
understand how weak verbs are conjugated in the Perfect
understand how weak verbs are conjugated in the Imperfect
read and translate Jonah 2:1–3, 11 considering some of the decisions that must be made in translating an ancient text

14 Imperatives, participles and infinitives

In this unit you will learn about:
- ▶ imperatives (instructions) in biblical Hebrew
- ▶ participles as verbs and as nouns
- ▶ the two Hebrew infinitives

You will read:
- ▶ Genesis 3:1–5

Vocabulary builder

NOUNS

אֶבֶן	stone
זְמָן	time
חַיָּה	living thing
חֵפֶץ	pleasure, matter
מִלְחָמָה	war, battle
נָחָשׁ	snake, serpent
עֵת	time
פְּרִי	fruit
צִיּוֹן	Zion
רֵעַ	friend
שַׁבָּת	Sabbath
שָׁלוֹם	safety, peace
שִׁמְשׁוֹן	Samson
תָּוֶךְ	middle

VERBS

בָּכָה	to weep, lament
מוּת	to die

נָגַע	*to touch*
נָשָׂא	*to lift up*
סָפַד	*to mourn*
פָּרָה	*to be fertile, fruitful*
פָּקַח	*to open*
קָדַשׁ	*to honour as sacred* (in Piel form)
רָאָה	*to see*
רָבַב	*to become many*
רָקַד	*to leap, dance*
שָׂחַק	*to joke, play* (in Piel form)
שָׁכַר	*to get drunk*

OTHER

אַף	*indeed* (conjunction)
אֹתָם	*them* (pronoun mp)
חָדָשׁ	*new* (adjective)
פֹּה	*here* (adverb)
פֶּן	*lest, or else* (conjunction)
עָרוּם	*clever, cunning, prudent* (adjective)

Grammar

IMPERATIVES

Imperatives are for telling people what to do. Since we usually command people directly, imperatives are in the second person. An example in English is *Look at the moon!* In this sentence, *look* is in the imperative. In Hebrew the form used depends on who is being addressed.

In biblical Hebrew, if you tell a man to guard you say: שְׁמֹר (ms).

If you were addressing one woman: שִׁמְרִי (fs).

Addressing a group of men or a mixed group you would say: שִׁמְרוּ (mp).

Addressing two or more women: שְׁמֹרְנָה (fp).

In each case we would translate the Hebrew with the English *guard!*

Here is an example with the verb כָּתַב:

כְּתֹב	write! (ms)
כִּתְבִי	write! (fs)
כִּתְבוּ	write! (mp)
כְּתֹבְנָה	write! (fp)

The word in Hebrew for *please* is known as the particle of entreaty, נָא. It comes after the Imperative, to which it is joined with **maqqef**:

| שְׁמָר־נָא | please guard |
| כְּתָב־נָא | please write |

At a glance (masculine singular only):

Verb type	Example verb	Imperative	Meaning
Regular (strong) verb	קָטַל	קְטֹל	kill!
I-guttural	עָמַד	עֲמֹד	stand!
II-guttural	שָׁחַט	שְׁחַט	kill!
III-guttural	שָׁלַח	שְׁלַח	send!
I-ו or י	יָשַׁב	שֵׁב	sit!
hollow	קוּם	קוּם	arise!
I-נ	נָגַשׁ	גַּשׁ/גְּשָׁה	approach!
geminate	סָבַב	סֹב	turn!
I-א	אָכַל	אֱכֹל	eat!
III-א	מָצָא	מְצָא	find!
III-ה	גָּלָה	גְּלֵה	reveal!

PRACTICE 1

Translate these examples from the Hebrew Bible.

a Deuteronomy 6:4   שְׁמַע יִשְׂרָאֵל יְהוָה אֱלֹהֵינוּ יְהוָה אֶחָד

b from Exodus 20:7 (adapted)   זָכוֹר אֶת־יוֹם הַשַּׁבָּת לְקַדְּשׁוֹ

c from Judges 16:25   וַיֹּאמְרוּ קִרְאוּ לְשִׁמְשׁוֹן וִישַׂחֶק־לָנוּ

d from Qohelet 1:10   רְאֵה־זֶה חָדָשׁ הוּא

e from 1 Samuel 1:17   וַיַּעַן עֵלִי וַיֹּאמֶר לְכִי לְשָׁלוֹם

f from Song of Songs 5:1

אִכְלוּ רֵעִים שְׁתוּ וְשִׁכְרוּ דּוֹדִים

g from Isaiah 51:6

שְׂאוּ לַשָּׁמַיִם עֵינֵיכֶם

h from Ruth 4:2

וַיֹּאמֶר שְׁבוּ־פֹה וַיֵּשֵׁבוּ

LANGUAGE INSIGHT

Note: in the example from Samuel, Eli is speaking to Hannah. Remember that הָלַךְ behaves like a verb beginning with **yod**.

PARTICIPLES

A participle is a verbal form that functions as an adjective. In English we have two kinds of participle:

present participle

he is starting, she was stopping; a running river, a compelling reason

past participle

he has started, she had stopped; a painted fence, an edited book

The form of the participle in Hebrew is קֹטֵל. It is usually translated with an English present participle or with a noun. Here are some examples of how it can work.

| הוּא שֹׁפֵט אֶת־עַם הָאָרֶץ | *He was judging the people of the land.* |

(2 Kings 15:5 adapted)

Note that in the absence of a verb and further context, this phrase could also be translated *He is judging the people of the land.*

| כִּי־אֱלֹהִים שֹׁפֵט הוּא | *For God is a judge.* |

(Psalm 50:6)

Literally *for God a judge is he.* This is often translated *for God himself is judge* with the pronoun הוּא understood as emphatic.

The participle in the weak verbs is very regular, with just a few exceptions to the קֹטֵל model. Notice that the participle in the hollow verbs is identical to the Perfect 3ms: קָם. Context will usually help to determine which it is.

At a glance:

Verb type	Example verb	Participle	Meaning
Regular (strong) verb	קָטַל	קֹטֵל	*killing*
I-guttural	עָמַד	עֹמֵד	*standing*
II-guttural	שָׁחַט	שֹׁחֵט	*killing*

III-guttural	שָׁלַח	שֹׁלֵחַ	sending
I-ו or י	יָשֵׁב	יֹשֵׁב	sitting
hollow	קוּם	קָם	arising
I-נ	נָגַשׁ	נֹגֵשׁ	approaching
geminate	סָבַב	סוֹבֵב	turning
I-א	אָכַל	אֹכֵל	eating
III-א	מָצָא	מֹצֵא	finding
III-ה	גָּלָה	גֹּלֶה	revealing

If you are wondering about how to pronounce יֹשֵׁב, it is **yō-SHAYV**. The dot on the שׁ doubles as a **cholem**. Instead of writing יׁשֵׁב, it is written with a single dot.

The **patach** under the ח in שֹׁלֵחַ is called a **patach** furtive because it is pronounced before the consonant; the word is pronounced **sho-LAY-ach**. Verbs ending in ע also have a **patach** furtive in the participle form, e.g. שֹׁמֵעַ, *hearing*.

You may occasionally encounter passive participles in the form קָטוּל which are translated with a passive in English: *being killed*.

PRACTICE 2

Fill in the blanks.

Root	Participle	Meaning	Imperative	Meaning
אָכַל	אֹכֵל	eating		eat!
גָּלָה		revealing	גְּלֵה	reveal!
יָרַד		going down	רֵד	go down!
	יֹשֵׁב	sitting	שֵׁב	sit!
מוּת	מֵת	dying		die!
	מֹצֵא	finding	מְצָא	find!
נָגַשׁ		approaching	גַּשׁ/גְּשָׁה	approach!
נָפַל	נֹפֵל	falling		fall!
סָבַב		turning	סֹב	turn!
עָמַד		standing	עֲמֹד	stand!
	קָם	arising	קוּם	arise!
קָטַל	קֹטֵל	killing		kill!
שָׁחַט	שֹׁחֵט	killing		kill!
שִׂים		putting	שִׂים	put!

INFINITIVE CONSTRUCT

In English, an infinitive is a verbal form often preceded by *to*, e.g. *to say*. It is infinitive because it could apply to anyone at any time. This is in contrast to finite verbal forms like *he said*, which applies specifically to a man or boy who has spoken in the past, or *they will say*, which applies specifically to a group of people who will speak in the future. However, the form *to say* has no person, no number, no gender and no tense, and so it has an infinite quality about it.

In Hebrew, there are two infinitives. We will learn the Infinitive Construct first. The Infinitive Construct works rather like the English infinitive and is formed like this:

קְטֹל

It can be translated *to kill* or *killing*. For example:

עֵת סְפוֹד וְעֵת רְקוֹד   *a time to mourn and a time to dance*

(Ecclesiastes 3:4b)

This is sometimes translated as *a time for mourning and a time for dancing*.

Notice that the Infinitive Construct forms in this example are written with a וֹ (**cholem vav**) rather than just a dot for the **cholem**. This is simply an alternative spelling.

The Infinitive Construct is often found with לְ prefixed to it, and the לְ usually takes a **chireq** instead of a **sheva** because the first vowel of the Infinitive Construct takes a **sheva** and Hebrew tends to avoid placing two **shevas** together:

לִקְטֹל   *to kill*

לִמְשֹׁל   *to rule*

לִשְׁמֹר   *to guard*

Here's another example:

עֵת לִבְכּוֹת וְעֵת לִשְׂחוֹק   *a time to weep and a time to laugh*

(Ecclesiastes 3:4a)

Again, these Infinitive Constructs are written with וֹ, as in the example given.

Gutturals cannot usually take a simple **sheva**, but a **sheva** is the first vowel of the Infinitive Construct. This means that verbs that begin with a guttural must take a composite **sheva** in the Infinitive Construct, so if they are prefixed with לְ it will take the corresponding short vowel, usually **chatef patach** and **patach**:

לַעֲמֹד   *to stand*

Sometimes the Infinitive Construct is found with the prefix כְּ or בְּ, in which case we can translate כְּ or בְּ as *when*. For example:

| כִּזְכֹּר הַכֹּהֵן אֶת־דְּבָרַי שָׁר | *When the priest remembered my words he sang.* |
| בִּזְכֹּר הַכֹּהֵן אֶת־דְּבָרַי יָשִׁיר | *When the priest remembers my words he will sing.* |

Notice the form of the verb שִׁיר, which is a hollow verb. In the first sentence it appears in the Perfect 3ms (שָׁר) and so we translate both it and the Infinitive Construct (כִּזְכֹּר) with an English past tense (*he remembered, he sang*).

In the second sentence it appears in the Imperfect 3ms (יָשִׁיר) and so we translate both it and the Infinitive Construct (בִּזְכֹּר) with an English future tense (*he will remember, he will sing*).

The Infinitive Construct can be found with both a preposition as a prefix and a pronominal suffix, for example בְּזָכְרֵנוּ in the following verse:

| בְּזָכְרֵנוּ אֶת־צִיּוֹן | *when we remembered Zion* |

(Psalm 137:1)

The vowels in the Infinitive Construct have changed because the suffix has been added. It is important to distinguish it from זְכַרְנוּ (*we have remembered*), which would not make sense with the prefix בְּ.

A very common (and slightly irregular) word in the Infinitive Construct is לֵאמֹר from אָמַר (*to say*). It comes after words introducing speech and it means *saying*. For example:

| וַיְבָרֶךְ אֹתָם אֱלֹהִים לֵאמֹר פְּרוּ וּרְבוּ | *And God blessed them, saying 'Be fruitful and multiply'.* |

(Genesis 1:22)

This phrase also uses masculine plural imperatives of two weak verbs. Can you identify them?

Infinitive Constructs of weak verbs can vary quite a bit from the קָטֹל model. It is worth looking at the following table to see how they work. Notice that the Infinitive Construct of the hollow verbs is the citation or dictionary form: קוּם is an Infinitive Construct (the Perfect 3ms is קָם). Notice also that in many cases the masculine singular form of the Imperative is identical to the Infinitive Construct.

Verb type	Example verb	Infinitive Construct	Meaning
Regular (strong) verb	קָטַל	קָטֹל	*to kill*
I-guttural	עָמַד	עֲמֹד	*to stand*
II-guttural	שָׁחַט	שְׁחֹט	*to kill*
III-guttural	שָׁלַח	שְׁלֹחַ	*to send*
I-נ or י	יָשַׁב	שֶׁבֶת	*to sit*

hollow	קוּם	קוּם	to arise
נ-I	נָגַשׁ	גֶּשֶׁת	to approach
geminate	סָבַב	סֹב	to turn
א-I	אָכַל	אֱכֹל	to eat
א-III	מָצָא	מְצֹא	to find
ה-III	גָּלָה	גְּלוֹת	to reveal

> **LANGUAGE INSIGHT**
>
> Some נ-I verbs, such as נָפַל, form their Infinitive Construct according to the strong verb pattern: נְפֹל.

PRACTICE 3

This passage from Chapter 3 of Ecclesiastes (also known as Qohelet) contains a series of infinitive constructs. Read it through and identify as many verbal roots as you can. A few of the infinitives are in forms such as Piel that we haven't looked at yet, but most match the table. Then find a translation (in print or online) for comparison. Would you translate all the Hebrew infinitives with English infinitives?

1 לַכֹּל זְמָן וְעֵת לְכָל־חֵפֶץ תַּחַת הַשָּׁמָיִם׃ 2 עֵת לָלֶדֶת וְעֵת לָמוּת עֵת לָטַעַת וְעֵת לַעֲקוֹר
נָטוּעַ׃ 3 עֵת לַהֲרוֹג וְעֵת לִרְפּוֹא עֵת לִפְרוֹץ וְעֵת לִבְנוֹת׃ 4 עֵת לִבְכּוֹת וְעֵת לִשְׂחוֹק עֵת סְפוֹד
וְעֵת רְקוֹד׃ 5 עֵת לְהַשְׁלִיךְ אֲבָנִים וְעֵת כְּנוֹס אֲבָנִים עֵת לַחֲבוֹק וְעֵת לִרְחֹק מֵחַבֵּק׃ 6 עֵת
לְבַקֵּשׁ וְעֵת לְאַבֵּד עֵת לִשְׁמוֹר וְעֵת לְהַשְׁלִיךְ׃ 7 עֵת לִקְרוֹעַ וְעֵת לִתְפּוֹר עֵת לַחֲשׁוֹת וְעֵת
לְדַבֵּר׃ 8 עֵת לֶאֱהֹב וְעֵת לִשְׂנֹא עֵת מִלְחָמָה וְעֵת שָׁלוֹם׃

INFINITIVE ABSOLUTE

The Infinitive Absolute is a second infinitive in Hebrew. It is formed like this: קָטוֹל (sometimes קָטֹל with **cholem** instead of **cholem vav**). Note the difference from the Infinitive Construct: the first vowel is a **qamets**.

The Infinitive Absolute can be used like the Infinitive Construct, and translated with an English infinitive, or it can be translated with an English participle. It is quite frequently found in a particular idiomatic construction in Hebrew. It is often used in combination with a finite verb in order to intensify the idea contained in the verb. Here are some examples:

מָשׁוֹל מָשַׁלְתִּי בָּהֶם   *I did indeed rule over them.*

(Literally: *ruling I ruled over them.*)

דַּע כִּי־מוֹת תָּמוּת   *Know that you will certainly die.*

(Genesis 20:7) (Literally: *know that dying you will die.*)

Notice that the tense we use in English depends on whether the Hebrew finite verb is Perfect or Imperfect. In the examples given, the Perfect מָשַׁלְתִּי is translated with a past tense (*I did indeed rule*) and the Imperfect תָּמוּת with a future tense (*you will die*). This is fairly intuitive.

The Infinitive Absolute can be used in other ways (less frequently) and a Hebrew grammar should explain all the possibilities.

There are very few variations in form among the weak verbs. III-guttural verbs take a **patach** furtive, just like in the other infinitive. Thus the Infinitive Absolute of שָׁלַח is שָׁלוֹחַ (pronounced **sha-LŌ-ach**). The other exception is the hollow verbs: their Infinitive Absolute is formed קוֹם.

At a glance:

Verb type	Example verb	Infinitive Absolute	Meaning
Regular (strong) verb	קָטַל	קָטוֹל	*killing*
I-guttural	עָמַד	עָמוֹד	*standing*
II-guttural	שָׁחַט	שָׁחוֹט	*killing*
III-guttural	שָׁלַח	שָׁלוֹהַ	*sending*
I-ו or י	יָשַׁב	יָשׁוֹב	*sitting*
hollow	קוּם	קוֹם	*arising*
I-נ	נָגַשׁ	נָגוֹשׁ	*approaching*
geminate	סָבַב	סָבוֹב	*turning*
I-א	אָכַל	אָכוֹל	*eating*
III-א	מָצָא	מָצוֹא	*finding*
III-ה	גָּלָה	גָּלֹה	*revealing*

Some I-נ verbs, such as נָפַל, form their Infinitive Construct according to the strong verb pattern: נְפֹל.

PRACTICE 4

Read through the following verses and find:
   a   an Imperative
   b   a Participle
   c   an Infinitive Construct
   d   an Infinitive Absolute
   e   a verb in the Perfect
   f   a verb in the Imperfect

You may find more than one form in a single verse but you will not find all five forms in a single verse.

Translations are not provided here; you will need to find the words purely by their forms without the clues that translations can give. However, references are given so that you can look them up after you have completed the exercise.

Exodus 3:5b	הַמָּקוֹם אֲשֶׁר אַתָּה עוֹמֵד עָלָיו אַדְמַת־קֹדֶשׁ הוּא
Jeremiah 24:7a	וְנָתַתִּי לָהֶם לֵב לָדַעַת אֹתִי כִּי אֲנִי יְהוָה
Deuteronomy 6:4	שְׁמַע יִשְׂרָאֵל יְהוָה אֱלֹהֵינוּ יְהוָה אֶחָד
1 Samuel 26:25	גַּם עָשֹׂה תַעֲשֶׂה וְגַם יָכֹל תּוּכָל

Reading

GENESIS 3:1 – 5

Points to look out for in this text:
- ▶ verbal forms we have already encountered
- ▶ use of the Infinitive Absolute.

1 וְהַנָּחָשׁ הָיָה עָרוּם מִכֹּל חַיַּת הַשָּׂדֶה אֲשֶׁר עָשָׂה יְהוָה אֱלֹהִים וַיֹּאמֶר אֶל־הָאִשָּׁה אַף כִּי־אָמַר אֱלֹהִים לֹא תֹאכְלוּ מִכֹּל עֵץ הַגָּן:

2 וַתֹּאמֶר הָאִשָּׁה אֶל־הַנָּחָשׁ מִפְּרִי עֵץ־הַגָּן נֹאכֵל:

3 וּמִפְּרִי הָעֵץ אֲשֶׁר בְּתוֹךְ־הַגָּן אָמַר אֱלֹהִים לֹא תֹאכְלוּ מִמֶּנּוּ וְלֹא תִגְּעוּ בּוֹ פֶּן־תְּמֻתוּן:

4 וַיֹּאמֶר הַנָּחָשׁ אֶל־הָאִשָּׁה לֹא־מוֹת תְּמֻתוּן:

5 כִּי יֹדֵעַ אֱלֹהִים כִּי בְּיוֹם אֲכָלְכֶם מִמֶּנּוּ וְנִפְקְחוּ עֵינֵיכֶם וִהְיִיתֶם כֵּאלֹהִים יֹדְעֵי טוֹב וָרָע:

 Language discovery

VERSE 1

וְהַנָּחָשׁ הָיָה עָרוּם מִכֹּל חַיַּת הַשָּׂדֶה

Many narratives start with the VC Impf 3ms of the verb הָיָה but this story starts with the verb's subject. The phrase כֹּל חַיַּת הַשָּׂדֶה is a construct chain, and the מְ is a preposition used here to make a comparison. How would you translate the phrase?

אֲשֶׁר עָשָׂה יְהוָה אֱלֹהִים

There is no pluperfect in Hebrew, but English seems to require it here: *had made* instead of just *made*. Here the verb comes before the subject. How would you translate it?

אַף־כִּי־אָמַר אֱלֹהִים

This phrase is difficult to translate into English. Many translations include some form of words to indicate that the serpent is asking a question, e.g. *is it true that God said … ?*.

לֹא תֹאכְלוּ

This could be understood as *you will not eat*, but the word לֹא followed by an Imperfect is usually a way of prohibiting things … in this case *do not eat*. How will you translate the reported speech within reported speech?

VERSE 2

מִפְּרִי עֵץ־הַגָּן נֹאכֵל

Notice the construct chain: how will you translate it? The word for *tree* can be a collective noun. The word is Imperfect 1cp (first person plural) and can mean *we will eat*, but is usually translated here as *we may eat*.

VERSE 3

הָעֵץ אֲשֶׁר בְּתוֹךְ־הַגָּן

Notice the use of אֲשֶׁר in this verbless clause. Where will you put the verb in your translation?

לֹא תֹאכְלוּ מִמֶּנּוּ וְלֹא תִגְּעוּ בּוֹ

These two verbs are used in the same way as לֹא תֹאכְלוּ in verse 1. How will you translate them? Both verbs are used with prepositions to indicate the object: מִמֶּנּוּ and בּוֹ. Can you identify their suffixes?

פֶּן־תְּמֻתוּן

The verb is an Imperfect 2mp with an extra letter ן at the end (the technical term is a paragogic **nun**). This kind of feature is unusual in English, but perhaps the extra *y* in *scaredy cat* might be considered paragogic. How would you translate the phrase?

VERSE 4

לֹא־מוֹת תְּמֻתוּן

This is an example of an infinitive absolute (מוֹת) used with a finite form (תְּמֻתוּן) of the same verb (מוּת). How will you translate it? Which tense will you use in English to translate תְּמֻתוּן?

VERSE 5

יֹדֵעַ אֱלֹהִים

Notice the participle here. Why is there a **patach** under the **ayin**?

בְּיוֹם אֲכָלְכֶם מִמֶּנּוּ

The verb here is an Infinitive Construct from אכל with a pronominal suffix 2mp. Literally this means *in the day of your eating from it*. How would you render this in idiomatic English?

וְנִפְקְחוּ עֵינֵיכֶם

The verb means *they will be opened*. In English we would not use a conjunction (*and*) here, but in Hebrew it is quite common. Is the verb VC or is this a simple conjunction? The word עֵינֵיכֶם is the dual form of עַיִן with a 2mp suffix. What does it mean?

וִהְיִיתֶם כֵּאלֹהִים יֹדְעֵי טוֹב וָרָע

The verb is a VC Perfect 2mp. Notice that the וֹ is pointed וִ instead of the usual VC Perfect pointing וֹ. This is because the first vowel in הְיִיתֶם is a **sheva** and so the vowel under the וֹ changes. The question of how to translate כֵּאלֹהִים is difficult: it can mean *like God* or *like gods* and both approaches can be found in reputable translations. Which do you prefer, and why?

POSSIBLE TRANSLATION

And the serpent was more cunning than all the living things of the field which the LORD God had made. And he said to the woman, 'Did God really say, "Do not eat from all the trees of the garden"?' And the woman said to the serpent, 'We may eat the fruit of the trees of the garden. But [concerning] the fruit of the tree which is in the middle of the garden God said, 'Do not eat of it and do not touch it or you will die.' And the serpent said to the woman, 'You certainly will not die. For God knows that in the day that you eat of it your eyes will be opened and you will be like God, knowing good and evil.'

Test yourself

1 Translate the following into English.

כְּתֹב סְפָרִים

_____

2 Why does the form שֹׁלֵחַ differ from other Participle forms such as אֹכֵל and נֹפֵל?

_____

3 Translate the following into English.

וַיַּעַן דָּנִאֵל אוֹתִי לֵאמֹר שֵׁב־נָא וְאֶכָל־נָא

_____

4 How can an Infinitive Absolute be used to intensify the verbal idea?

_____

5 Translate the following into Hebrew.

And he said, 'You [ms] are a guard and this is a time to guard. Guard my horses or you will certainly die.'

_____

SELF-CHECK	
I CAN...	
○	recognize imperatives and participles
○	recognize both forms of the Infinitive
○	read and translate Genesis 3:1–5

15 Object, relative and interrogative pronouns, and noun declensions

In this unit you will learn about:
- ▶ how object pronouns work in biblical Hebrew
- ▶ how relative and interrogative pronouns work
- ▶ the role of **patach** furtive
- ▶ about noun declensions

You will read:
- ▶ Genesis 21:1–6

Vocabulary builder

NOUNS

בֹּקֶר	*morning*
זְקֻנִים	*old age*
מוֹעֵד	*time*
צְחֹק	*laughter, ridicule*
שָׁנָה	*year* (f)
שָׂרָה	*Sarah*

VERBS

בָּחַן	*to try, test*
בָּלַע	*to swallow*
דִּבֵּר	*to speak* (Piel)
הָרָה	*to conceive, be pregnant*
כָּרַת	*to cut*
יָסַף	*to add*
יָרֵא	*to fear*
מוּל	*to circumcise*

| עָנָה | to answer |
| צָחַק | to laugh |

OTHER

| כַּאֲשֶׁר | as, when (preposition + pronoun) |
| מֵאָה | one hundred (numeral) |

Grammar

OBJECT PRONOUNS

Consider these sentences:

He gave a hammer to Mark.

Mark gave a saw to him.

In the first sentence, the pronoun is the subject of the verb: the person who is doing the action. We do not know the subject's name; only that he is male. The pronoun *he* is the subject of the verb *gave*, and *Mark* is the object.

In the second sentence, *Mark* is the subject, the one who is doing the giving. The object of the verb *gave* is the pronoun *him*.

Similarly:

Subject	Verb	Object
My friend	likes	me.
The cat	climbed	it.
The computer	will calculate	them.
Newspapers	popularized	her.
Nobody	saw	us.

Hebrew object pronouns are formed by adding a pronominal suffix to the object marker. The object pronouns are:

אֹתוֹ	him	אֹתָם	them (mp)
אֹתָהּ	her	אֹתָן	them (fp)
אֹתְךָ	you (ms)	אֹתְכֶם	you (mp)
אֹתָךְ	you (fs)	אֹתְכֶן	you (fp)
אֹתִי	me	אֹתָנוּ	us

Here are some examples of Hebrew object pronouns used in sentences:

בָּרָא יְהוָה אֹתוֹ	Yhwh has created it.
יָרֵא הַמֶּלֶךְ אֹתָהּ	The king has feared her.
לֹא בָחַן דָּוִד אֹתְךָ	David has not tested you.
רָאֲתָה אִמִּי אֹתָן	My mother has seen you.
כָּרְתָה הַחֶרֶב אֹתִי	The sword has cut me.
בָּלַעְנוּ אֹתָם	We have swallowed them.
לָקְחוּ הַנָּשִׁים אֹתָן	The women have taken them.
שָׁלַחְתִּי אֶתְכֶם	I have sent you.
מָצָא גִּדְעוֹן אֹתְכֶן	Gideon has found you.
עָנָה אֹתָנוּ	He has answered us.

PRACTICE 1

Translate the following variations on the above sentences, using verbs in the Imperfect. The verbs you will need are given.

יִבְרָא יִירָא יִבְחַן תִּרְאֶה תִּכְרֹת נִבְלַע תִּקַּחְנָה אֶשְׁלַח יִמְצָא יַעֲנֶה

   a Yhwh will create them.
   b The king will fear you.
   c David will not test me.
   d My mother will see them.
   e The sword will cut you.
   f We will swallow it.
   g The women will take you.
   h I will send her.
   i Gideon will find us.
   j He will answer you.

RELATIVE AND INTERROGATIVE PRONOUNS

We have already encountered the relative pronoun אֲשֶׁר: it means *that, which* or *who*. There is nothing particularly difficult about the meaning of אֲשֶׁר but when we translate it into English we need to choose the most appropriate word.

In English we need different relative pronouns (or adverbs) in the following sentences:

זֹאת בְּרִיתִי אֲשֶׁר תִּשְׁמְרוּ	This is my covenant which *you will keep*. (Genesis 17:10)
זֶה הָאִישׁ אֲשֶׁר יִשְׁמֹר אֶת־הַבְּרִית	This is the man who *will keep the covenant*.

(Literally *this is the man which he will keep the covenant*.)

זֶה הָאִישׁ אֲשֶׁר תִּשְׁמְרוּ — *This is the man* whom *you will guard.*

(Literally *this is the man which you will guard*.)

זֶה הָאִישׁ אֲשֶׁר תִּשְׁמְרוּ
אֶת־עֲבָדָיו — *This is the man* whose *servants you will guard.*

(Literally *this is the man which you will guard his servants*.)

Notice that אֲשֶׁר does not have masculine, feminine or plural forms: it is used with בְּרִיתִי (feminine) and with הָאִישׁ (masculine) without changing its spelling. Similarly, עֲבָדָיו is plural but אֲשֶׁר remains the same.

We sometimes find אֲשֶׁר with the inseparable preposition כְּ: כַּאֲשֶׁר. It is often translated *when* or *as.*

Other pronouns that do not have masculine or feminine forms are the interrogative pronouns. Just like English, Hebrew has special words for questions: pronouns, known as interrogative pronouns. Here are the most common:

מִי	*Who …?*
מֶה or מַה	*What …?*
לְמֶה or לָמָה	*Why …?*
אֵי or אַי	*Where …?*
מָתַי	*When …?*
אֵיךְ	*How …?*

Here are examples of how they are used:

מִי אָנֹכִי	*Who am I?* (Exodus 3:11)
מֶה עָשִׂיתִי	*What have I done?* (Jeremiah 8:6)
לָמָה עֲזַבְתָּנִי	*Why have you deserted me?* (Psalm 22:2 [Engl. 22:1])
אֵי הֶבֶל אָחִיךָ	*Where is Abel your brother?* (Genesis 4:9)
וּכְסִילִים מָתַי תַּשְׂכִּילוּ	*You fools, when will you be wise?* (Psalm 94:8)
אֵיךְ תֹּאמַר אֲהַבְתִּיךְ	*How can you say, 'I love you'?* (Judges 16:15)

Note: the **dagesh** in the מ of לָמָה can be absent before gutturals.

It is important to remember that each of the above phrases is asking a question. The interrogative pronouns are always used in contexts where a question is implied. For example, the word מִי only means *who?* as in *who am I?* It does not mean *who* as in *You are the man who wrote that book.* In that case אֲשֶׁר would be used: אַתָּה הָאִישׁ אֲשֶׁר כָּתַב הַסֵּפֶר הַהוּא.

PRACTICE 2

Fill in the blanks using the appropriate interrogative or relative pronoun. You may use them more than once.

Note: there are two words which you have not previously seen. They are וַיַּרְא and וַיַּעַן. The word וַיַּרְא is VC Imperfect 3ms from רָאָה and the word וַיַּעַן is VC Imperfect 3ms from עָנָה. In both cases the final ה of the root is missing. This is very common in VC Imperfect forms of verbs that end in ה. The technical term for a shortened form like this is apocopated.

בָּא דָוִד אֶל־הַבַּיִת _____ בֵּין הֶהָרִים וַיַּרְא הַנַּעַר

שֹׁמֵר הַבָּיִת: וַיֹּאמֶר אֵלָיו _____ הָאִשָׁה _____ אָבָה יָשֵׁב

בְּבַיִת הַזֶּה: וַיַּעַן דָוִד אֲנִי הַמֶּלֶךְ וַיֹּאמֶר הַנַּעַר _____ אַתָּה:

_____ בָּאתָ וַיֹּאמֶר דָוִד בָּאתִי לִפְקֹד שָׂרָה _____ שְׁמֵךְ:

Hint: it might be easier to translate it first.

PATCH FURTIVE

We have seen already how in some verbal forms that end in a guttural an extra *a* vowel (**patach**) creeps in underneath the guttural. For example, in Unit 14 we saw that the Participle of שָׁלַח is not שֹׁלֵח but rather שֹׁלֵחַ, pronounced **shō-LAY-ach**. Similarly, the Infinitive Construct of שָׁלַח is not שְׁלֹח as we might expect, but rather שְׁלֹחַ, pronounced **shə-LŌ-ach**, and the Infinitive Absolute is not שָׁלֹח but rather שָׁלֹחַ, pronounced **shā-LŌ-ach**. The likely function of **patach** furtive is to make the guttural easier to pronounce. The rule generally applies to verbs ending in ח or ע rather than in א or ה.

Here are some more examples:

Verb	Participle		Infinitive Construct		Infinitive Absolute	
שָׁמַע	שֹׁמֵעַ	hearing	שְׁמֹעַ	to hear	שָׁמֹעַ	hearing
יָדַע	יוֹדֵעַ	knowing	דַּעַת	to know	יָדֹעַ	knowing
לָקַח	לֹקֵחַ	taking	קַחַת	to take	לָקֹחַ	taking
נָגַע	נֹגֵעַ	touching	נְגֹעַ	to touch	נָגֹעַ	touching
שָׂמַח	שָׂמֵחַ	rejoicing	שְׂמֹחַ	to rejoice	שָׂמוֹחַ	rejoicing
שָׁכַח	שֹׁכֵחַ	forgetting	שְׁכֹחַ	to forget	שָׁכוֹחַ	forgetting

Notice that the Infinitive Construct of יָדַע is דַּעַת. This is because it is I-י (or, some might argue, I-ו) as well as III-guttural. Remember that the Infinitive Construct of יָשֵׁב is שֶׁבֶת; so similarly the Infinitive Construct of יָדַע is דַּעַת, which is also the word for *knowledge*. And likewise the verb לָקַח, although it begins with **lamed** in the Perfect, behaves like a I-י verb in the Imperfect and other forms, and so its Infinitive Construct follows the I-י pattern.

Some nouns have **patach** furtive, for example רוּחַ meaning *wind* or *spirit* and pronounced **roo-ACH**, which we saw in Unit 9.

PRACTICE 3

Work out the Participle and Infinitive Construct of the following verbs and fill in the blanks.

Verb	Participle		Infinitive Construct	
בָּלַע		swallowing		
נָטַע		planting		
קָרַע				to tear
פָּקַח				to open

NOUN DECLENSIONS

LANGUAGE INSIGHT

Declensions are different patterns that nouns can have. In English, it is difficult to categorize nouns according to declension, but in other languages declension categories are common. For example, Greek and Latin nouns can be grouped according to how they behave. At the risk of over-simplifying, here are some examples of nouns that have retained some of their original characteristics after being adopted into English:

Singular	Plural
antenna	antennae
focus	foci
medium	media
crisis	crises
octopus	octopodes*

LANGUAGE INSIGHT

* Well, not really. But some grammarians prefer this to the equally incorrect *octopi*. There are probably good reasons to prefer *octopuses*.

The number of Hebrew declensions is somewhat disputed. Some grammars list as many as 13; others list as few as four. It is worth being aware of some of the patterns because it will be easier to identify plural nouns or nouns with pronominal suffixes if you are aware of some of the basic patterns.

Nouns with a **qamets** (most nouns containing a **qamets** follow this pattern). The word absolute here means the dictionary form (i.e. the word is not in plural or construct form).

Singular absolute	דָּבָר	word	נָבִיא	prophet
Plural absolute	דְּבָרִים	words	נְבִיאִים	prophets

Singular construct	דְּבַר	word of	נְבִיא	prophet of
Plural construct	דִּבְרֵי	words of	נְבִיאֵי	prophets of
Singular with 1cs suffix	דְּבָרִי	my word	נְבִיאִי	my prophet

Notice that the first vowel becomes shorter (reducing to **sheva** or **chireq**) in all the forms except the singular absolute.

Nouns with **segol** are sometimes called segolates (some nouns without **patach** follow the same pattern, such as נַעַר).

The singular absolute and the singular construct forms are always accented on the first syllable: **ME-lech, SAY-fer, BŌ-ker, NA-ar**. Notice also that their vowels do not shorten in the singular construct: the construct is the same as the absolute. Notice also that several of them lose their **segol** in favour of a **patach**, **chireq** or short **qamets** when they become construct plural or gain a suffix. Thus בָּקְרֵי is pronounced **bok-RAY** and בָּקְרִי is pronounced **bok-REE**.

Singular absolute	מֶלֶךְ	king	סֵפֶר	book
Plural absolute	מְלָכִים	kings	סְפָרִים	books
Singular construct	מֶלֶךְ	king of	סֵפֶר	book of
Plural construct	מַלְכֵי	kings of	סִפְרֵי	books of
Singular with 1cs suffix	מַלְכִּי	my king	סִפְרִי	my book

Singular absolute	בֹּקֶר	morning	נַעַר	young man
Plural absolute	בְּקָרִים	mornings	נְעָרִים	young men
Singular construct	בֹּקֶר	morning of	נַעַר	young man of
Plural construct	בָּקְרֵי	mornings of	נַעֲרֵי	young men of
Singular with 1cs suffix	בָּקְרִי	my morning	נַעֲרִי	my young man

Nouns with participle-type vowels (the קֹטֵל pattern of the Qal Participle: see Unit 14) are another category. In these nouns the singular construct is the same as the singular absolute (like מֶלֶךְ type nouns) but the second vowel reduces in the plural absolute and construct, and with the addition of a suffix.

Singular absolute	אֹיֵב	enemy	כֹּהֵן	priest
Plural absolute	אֹיְבִים	enemies	כֹּהֲנִים	priests
Singular construct	אֹיֵב	enemy of	כֹּהֵן	priest of
Plural construct	אֹיְבֵי	enemies of	כֹּהֲנֵי	priests of
Singular with 1cs suffix	אֹיְבִי	my enemy	כֹּהֲנִי	my priest

Some single syllable nouns double their second consonant when they form plurals or acquire suffixes:

Singular absolute	יָם	sea	עַם	people
Plural absolute	יַמִּים	seas	עַמִּים	peoples
Singular construct	יַם	sea of	עַם	people of
Plural construct	יַמֵּי	seas of	עַמֵּי	peoples of
Singular with 1cs suffix	יַמִּי	my sea	עַמִּי	my people

All the nouns given here, in all types, are masculine. Feminine nouns tend to match the patterns of the masculine nouns, but with the addition of feminine endings.

It should be noted that adjectives decline just like nouns, and so they follow one of these patterns. For example רָשָׁע (wicked) follows the דָּבָר model:

רָשָׁע *wicked*   רְשָׁעִים *wicked* (pl)   רְשַׁע *wicked of*   רִשְׁעֵי *wicked of* (pl)

PRACTICE 4

Fill in the table by giving the singular construct of the following words and meanings.

Singular absolute	Meaning	Singular construct	Meaning
חֶרֶב			
גּוֹאֵל			
רָעָב			
נָחָשׁ			
יָשָׁר			

Reading

GENESIS 21:1–6

From now on the texts at the ends of the units will follow part of the story of Abraham and Sarah in Genesis. For background and context, read Genesis 12–20 in translation. We pick up the story where Sarah becomes pregnant at an advanced age in Genesis 21.

Points to look out for in this text:

▶ verbal forms we have already encountered
▶ object pronouns
▶ relative and interrogative pronouns
▶ examples of **patach** furtive.

1 וַיהוָה פָּקַד אֶת־שָׂרָה כַּאֲשֶׁר אָמָר וַיַּעַשׂ יְהוָה לְשָׂרָה כַּאֲשֶׁר דִּבֵּר :

2 וַתַּהַר וַתֵּלֶד שָׂרָה לְאַבְרָהָם בֵּן לִזְקֻנָיו לַמּוֹעֵד אֲשֶׁר־דִּבֶּר אֹתוֹ אֱלֹהִים :

3 וַיִּקְרָא אַבְרָהָם אֶת־שֶׁם־בְּנוֹ הַנּוֹלַד־לוֹ אֲשֶׁר־יָלְדָה־לּוֹ שָׂרָה יִצְחָק :

4 וַיָּמָל אַבְרָהָם אֶת־יִצְחָק בְּנוֹ בֶּן־שְׁמֹנַת יָמִים כַּאֲשֶׁר צִוָּה אֹתוֹ אֱלֹהִים :

5 וְאַבְרָהָם בֶּן־מְאַת שָׁנָה בְּהִוָּלֶד לוֹ אֵת יִצְחָק בְּנוֹ :

6 וַתֹּאמֶר שָׂרָה צְחֹק עָשָׂה לִי אֱלֹהִים כָּל־הַשֹּׁמֵעַ יִצְחַק־לִי :

💡 Language discovery

VERSE 1

The verb וַיַּעַשׂ is an apocopated (shortened) form. We saw the same phenomenon in וַיַּרְא and וַיַּעַן. What does it mean?

How would you translate the preposition in לְשָׂרָה?

Although we have not yet looked at the Piel the form דִּבֵּר is Perf 3ms. Can you translate it?

VERSE 2

The form וַתַּהַר is also apocopated. What does it mean?

If we assume that Sarah does not give birth to Abraham, how would you translate לְאַבְרָהָם?

The word לִזְקֻנָיו means, literally, *for his old age*. The idea is that the child is born when the father is old.

לַמּוֹעֵד אֲשֶׁר־דִּבֶּר אֹתוֹ אֱלֹהִים

Notice the relative pronoun and the object pronoun in this phrase. Also, the subject of the verb דִּבֶּר is אֱלֹהִים, which comes after the object. The usual word order in biblical Hebrew is verb, subject, object. Here the relative pronoun can be translated *when*. How would you render the phrase in English?

VERSE 3

וַיִּקְרָא אַבְרָהָם אֶת־שֶׁם־בְּנוֹ

This is a common formula following the birth of a child in Hebrew narrative: one of the parents will name the baby. It is simple enough to make a literal translation, but how would you translate it into idiomatic English?

הַנּוֹלַד־לוֹ

The word לוֹ is simply the preposition ל with the 3ms pronominal suffix. The word הַנּוֹלַד is from יָלַד but it is a form we have not encountered before. This form is called Nifal and we will learn about it in Unit 16. It is passive. Can you attempt to translate it?

אֲשֶׁר־יָלְדָה־לּוֹ שָׂרָה

Notice the relative pronoun again. The word יָלְדָה is a simple Perfect 3fs. The word לוֹ is spelled with **dagesh** here, but it means the same as the earlier לוֹ. Again, the subject is at the end of the clause. How would you render this?

יִצְחָק

The name of the child is withheld until the end of the verse, which perhaps creates some suspense. It is an Imperfect 3ms form. What does the name mean? How would you make the whole verse grammatically correct in English? It may help to compare translations and see what others have done.

VERSE 4

בֶּן־שְׁמֹנַת יָמִים

Literally *the son of eight days*. This is an idiomatic expression meaning *when he was eight days old*.

כַּאֲשֶׁר צִוָּה אֹתוֹ אֱלֹהִים

Notice the object pronoun. The verb צִוָּה is in Piel form, and we will find out more about Piel in Unit 16. Can you translate the phrase nevertheless?

VERSE 5

וְאַבְרָהָם בֶּן־מְאַת שָׁנָה

Just as in the previous verse, this is a way of indicating a person's age. The word שָׁנָה usually remains singular when it comes after a number. How old is Abraham at this point in the story?

בְּהִוָּלֶד

The preposition בְּ is sometimes used to mean *when*, as it does here. The verb is another Nifal form and means *was born*.

צְחֹק עָשָׂה לִי אֱלֹהִים

Literally *laughter he has made for me God*. What would be better idiomatic English?

כָּל־הַשֹּׁמֵעַ

The word הַשֹּׁמֵעַ is a participle; what kind of weak verb is it from? If participles can be translated with English nouns, how might you render this phrase? Can you make a grammatically correct sentence with an English noun here?

יִצְחַק־לִי

The verb is an Imperfect 3mp: *they will laugh*. When צָחַק is used with לְ it can mean *to mock* or *to laugh at*. Which do you think is more appropriate in this context?

POSSIBLE TRANSLATION

And Yhwh visited Sarah as he said, and Yhwh did for Sarah what he promised. So Sarah conceived and she bore a son for Abraham in his old age at the time when God promised him, and Abraham named his son, whom Sarah bore for him, Isaac. Abraham circumcised Isaac his son when he was eight days old as God commanded him, and Abraham was one hundred years old when Isaac his son was born. And Sarah said, 'God has made laughter for me; all who hear will laugh for me.'

The last verse could also be translated: *And Sarah said, 'God has made me an object of ridicule; all who hear will mock me.'* Which do you prefer, and why?

❓ Test yourself

1 Write out the Hebrew words for *why?, what?* and *who?*

_____

2 We have learned five ways that אֲשֶׁר can be translated into English. Which one would you use in the following sentence?

אֵלֶּה הָאֲנָשִׁים אֲשֶׁר קוֹלֵיהֶם יָשִׁירוּ שִׁירוֹת

_____

3 Give the Participle, the Infinitive Construct and the Infinitive Absolute of שָׁמַע .

_____

4 Translate the following into English.

בֶּן־שְׁמֹנַת שָׁנָה

_____

5 Translate the following into Hebrew.

David will fear me but all who touch my horse will laugh.

_____

SELF-CHECK	
I CAN...	
⚪	recognize object pronouns as the object marker with pronominal suffixes
⚪	translate the relative pronoun and interrogative pronouns depending on context
⚪	understand the **patach** furtive, which occurs in some forms of the III-guttural verbs
⚪	recognize noun declensions
⚪	read and translate Genesis 21:1–6

16 Verbal stems, Nifal and gentilic adjectives

In this unit you will learn about:
▶ how the verbal stems (**binyanim**) work in Hebrew
▶ forms and uses of the Nifal stem
▶ gentilic adjectives
▶ the Jussive

You will read:
▶ Genesis 21:7–13

Vocabulary builder

NOUNS

אָמָה	handmaid, female servant
בֹּקֶר	morning
גּוֹי	nation
הָגָר	Hagar
זֶרַע	seed, progeny, family
חָמַד	to desire
חֲמוֹר	donkey
יֶלֶד	child
מִשְׁתֶּה	banquet, feast
עֵד	testimony, witness
צְדָקָה	righteousness
קֹדֶשׁ	holiness, sanctuary
שׁוֹר	ox, bull
שֶׁקֶר	lie, falsehood

VERBS

מָלֵא	to be full, to fill
גָּדַל	to grow
גָּמַל	to wean
גָּנַב	to steal
גָּרַשׁ	to drive away, expel
יָנַק	to suck
יָרַשׁ	to inherit, take possession
מָלַל	to say, speak
נָאַף	to commit adultery, commit idolatry
נָתַשׁ	to pluck up, root out, destroy
עָנָה	to answer, give testimony
רָעַע	to be bad
רָצַח	to kill, murder

OTHER

כַּאֲשֶׁר	as, when (preposition + pronoun)
מְאֹד	very (adverb)
עַל אֹדֹת	because, on account of (adverb)

Grammar

VERBAL STEMS

Hebrew verbs are unlike English verbs in many respects, and one difference is that Hebrew verbs come in seven forms called stems or **binyanim** (*buildings*). The different stems indicate different meanings of the verb; for example, verbs can be passive in certain stems. It is usually easiest to see how this works in practice.

In English we use the term voice to describe whether the subject of the verb is doing the action or whether the subject is having something done to them. Here's an example:

Subject	Verb		Object
Ruth	*sent*		*the present.*
The present	*was sent*	*by*	*Ruth.*

Notice that the object of the first sentence is the subject of the second sentence. Other examples of sentences in the passive voice are:

Subject	Verb		Object
The movie	was praised	by	the critics.
The donations	will be given	to	charity.
Results of surveys	are published	in	magazines.

Some Hebrew stems are passive. Other stem modifications involve causative, intensive or reflexive functions which may overlap with active or passive voice.

These are the stems of the verb, with the functions and meanings rather oversimplified for now (more nuance will follow). The verb קָטַל does not occur in all seven stems but it is still best placed to demonstrate the forms because it is a strong verb and contains no **begadkefat** letters. The meanings of all but the Qal have been invented in order to demonstrate the basic principle of the function.

Stem	Hebrew name	Function	Example Perfect 3ms	Probable meaning
Qal	קַל	'Light'	קָטַל	to kill
Nifal	נִפְעַל	Passive	נִקְטַל	to be killed
Piel	פִּעֵל	Intensive active	קִטֵּל	to slaughter
Pual	פֻּעַל	Intensive passive	קֻטַּל	to be slaughtered
Hitpael	הִתְפַּעֵל	Intensive reflexive	הִתְקַטֵּל	to slaughter oneself
Hifil	הִפְעִיל	Causative active	הִקְטִיל	to make someone kill (someone else)
Hofal	הָפְעַל	Causative passive	הָקְטַל	to be made to kill (someone else)

The word **Qal** (קַל), as we learned in Unit 1, means *light*. Qal forms are light because they are not encumbered by the verb stem changes caused by Nifal, Piel and so on.

The names of the other stems are based on the root פעל in the Perfect 3ms. The names describe what happens to the root to change its meaning. As you can see, Nifal changes the root by adding a נ prefix in the Perfect tense and changing the first vowel to a **sheva**. Adding נ to פעל gives נִפְעַל.

Here is the complete Perfect of the Nifal of קָטַל:

3ms	נִקְטַל	he has been killed	3cp	נִקְטְלוּ	they have been killed
3fs	נִקְטְלָה	she has been killed			
2ms	נִקְטַלְתָּ	you have been killed	2mp	נִקְטַלְתֶּם	you have been killed
2fs	נִקְטַלְתְּ	you have been killed	2fp	נִקְטַלְתֶּן	you have been killed
1cs	נִקְטַלְתִּי	I have been killed	1p	נִקְטַלְנוּ	we have been killed

Here is the complete Imperfect of the Nifal of קָטַל. The נ prefix of the Nifal disappears; it is assimilated into the first root letter, which is therefore written with **dagesh**. The assimilation probably occurs because it is easier to say **yi-ka-tayl** than **yin-ka-tayl**. If you try to say **yin-ka-tayl** quickly, you may find yourself 'swallowing' the **n** sound.

3ms	יִקָּטֵל	he will be killed	3mp	יִקָּטְלוּ	they will be killed
3fs	תִּקָּטֵל	she will be killed	3fp	תִּקָּטַלְנָה	they will be killed
2ms	תִּקָּטֵל	you will be killed	2mp	תִּקָּטְלוּ	they will be killed
2fs	תִּקָּטְלִי	you will be killed	2fp	תִּקָּטַלְנָה	they will be killed
1cs	אֶקָּטֵל	I will be killed	1p	נִקָּטֵל	we will be killed

PRACTICE 1

Complete the tables by writing out the Nifal of the following verbs. Remember to consider the placement of *dagesh*.

Nifal Perfect	שָׁמַר	מָשַׁל	פָּקַד
3ms	נִשְׁמַר	נִמְשַׁל	נִפְקַד
3fs	נִשְׁמְרָה		
2ms	נִשְׁמַרְתָּ		
2fs	נִשְׁמַרְתְּ		
1cs	נִשְׁמַרְתִּי		
3cp	נִשְׁמְרוּ		
2mp	נִשְׁמַרְתֶּם		
2fp	נִשְׁמַרְתֶּן		
1p	נִשְׁמַרְנוּ		

Nifal Imperfect	שָׁמַר	פָּקַד	זָכַר
3ms	יִשָּׁמֵר	תִּפָּקֵד	יִזָּכֵר
3fs	תִּשָּׁמֵר		
2ms	תִּשָּׁמֵר		
2fs	תִּשָּׁמְרִי		
1cs	אֶשָּׁמֵר		
3mp	יִשָּׁמְרוּ		
3fp	תִּשָּׁמַרְנָה		

2mp	תִּשָּׁמְרוּ		
2fp	תִּשָּׁמַרְנָה		
1p	נִשָּׁמֵר		

USES OF THE NIFAL

Each stem can be found in the Perfect, Imperfect, Imperative, Infinitive and Participle. So we will encounter Nifal Perfects, Nifal Imperfects, Nifal Infinitives and so on.

However, not every root occurs in every form of every stem. Some roots occur almost exclusively in Qal, others occur almost exclusively in Piel (e.g. צוה *to command*) or Hifil (e.g. נגד *to tell*). So although the system is complicated, the Hebrew vocabulary itself is not necessarily so complicated. Very few verbal roots occur in all the stems, and most of those are weak verbs. The only strong verb that occurs in all the stems is פקד and so we will use this as a model for further examples.

In this unit we will concentrate on Nifal; the other stems will be addressed in later units. From the previous table we see that Nifal is described as passive. Essentially this means that with the addition of prefixes that indicate Nifal, the verb is usually translated with an English passive tense.

This is how we usually translate Qal and Nifal:

	Perfect 3ms	Imperfect 3ms	Infinitive Construct	Infinitive Absolute	Participle
Qal	פָּקַד *he has visited*	יִפְקֹד *he will visit*	פְּקֹד *to visit*	פָּקוֹד *visiting*	פֹּקֵד *visiting*
Nifal	נִפְקַד *he has been visited*	יִפָּקֵד *he will be visited*	הִפָּקֵד *to be visited*	הִפָּקֹד *being visited*	נִפְקָד *being visited*

Although we have learned that the verb פָּקַד means *to visit*, it can be translated in a variety of other ways (*to attend, take care of, count, appoint*). Furthermore, the infinitives can be translated in other ways (see Unit 14). So the table is an example rather than a comprehensive analysis of the root פָּקַד in Qal and Nifal.

Here are some examples of how the Nifal is used, compared with examples in Qal to demonstrate the difference.

Qal Perfect

פָּקַד יְהוָה אֶת־בְּנֵי יִשְׂרָאֵל   *Yhwh visited the sons of Israel.* (Exodus 4:31)

Nifal Perfect

וְנִפְקַדְתָּ כִּי יִפָּקֵד מוֹשָׁבֶךָ   *And you will be missed because your seat will be empty.* (1 Samuel 20:18)

(Note: the first word is a Nifal VC Perfect and the third word is a Nifal Imperfect.)

Qal Imperfect

וְכִי־יִפְקֹד מָה אֲשִׁיבֶנּוּ

And when he visits, what shall I answer him? (Job 31:14)

Nifal Imperfect

בַּל־יִפָּקֶד רָע

He shall not be visited with evil. (Proverbs 19:23)

RECOGNIZING THE NIFAL (MOST VERBS)

Perfect: נ prefixed to the root, usual Perfect suffixes, **sheva** under the first root letter.

Imperfect: **dagesh** in first letter of root, usual Imperfect prefixes and suffixes.

Imperative/Infinitive construct: הִ prefix, **dagesh** in first letter of root.

Infinitive absolute: נ prefixed to the root.

Participle: נ prefixed to the root.

WEAK VERBS AND THE NIFAL

As we have already seen when learning the Perfect and Imperfect, the weak verbs often undergo some departures from the pattern of the strong verbs. This is also true for verbs in the Nifal and other stems. Most of the differences are vowel changes, such as composite **shevas** instead of simple **shevas** under gutturals, and **patach** furtives in **lamed** guttural verbs. These should not present many problems in translation.

The basic patterns in Nifal forms of weak verbs are outlined here, although it is probably not necessary at this stage to learn them all. It is more important to learn the Qal forms. However, it can be useful to have an overview of the changes in other stems in the weak verbs so that they can be recognized.

In the Nifal, verbs that follow the יָשַׁב model regain their putative initial ו. This is why they are sometimes described as I-ו verbs.

Perfect	Qal	Nifal
3ms	יָשַׁב	נוֹשַׁב
3fs	יָשְׁבָה	נוֹשְׁבָה
2ms	יָשַׁבְתָּ	נוֹשַׁבְתָּ
2fs	יָשַׁבְתְּ	נוֹשַׁבְתְּ
1s	יָשַׁבְתִּי	נוֹשַׁבְתִּי
3p	יָשְׁבוּ	נוֹשְׁבוּ
2mp	יְשַׁבְתֶּם	נוֹשַׁבְתֶּם
2fp	יְשַׁבְתֶּן	נוֹשַׁבְתֶּן

Imperfect	Qal	Nifal
3ms	יֵשֵׁב	יִוָּשֵׁב
3fs	תֵּשֵׁב	תִּוָּשֵׁב
2ms	תֵּשֵׁב	תִּוָּשֵׁב
2fs	תֵּשְׁבִי	תִּוָּשְׁבִי
1s	אֵשֵׁב	אִוָּשֵׁב
3mp	יֵשְׁבוּ	יִוָּשְׁבוּ
3fp	תֵּשַׁבְנָה	תִּוָּשַׁבְנָה
2mp	תֵּשְׁבוּ	תִּוָּשְׁבוּ

				2fp	תִּוָּשַׁבְנָה	תֵּשָׁבַבְנָה
1p	יִשָּׁבְנוּ	נוֹשַׁבְנוּ		1p	נֵשֵׁב	נוֹשַׁב

There are a few other significant departures from the strong verb pattern in the Nifal:

Nifal Perfect	Strong verb	Hollow verbs	Geminate verbs	I-נ verbs
3ms	נִקְטַל	נָקוֹם	נָסַב	נִגַּשׁ
3fs	נִקְטְלָה	נָקוֹמָה	נָסַבָּה	נִגְּשָׁה
2ms	נִקְטַלְתָּ	נְקוּמֹתָ	נְסַבּוֹתָ	נִגַּשְׁתָּ
2fs	נִקְטַלְתְּ	נְקוּמֹתְ	נְסַבּוֹת	נִגַּשְׁתְּ
1s	נִקְטַלְתִּי	נְקוּמֹתִי	נְסַבּוֹתִי	נִגַּשְׁתִּי
3p	נִקְטְלוּ	נָקוֹמוּ	נָסַבּוּ	נִגְּשׁוּ
2mp	נִקְטַלְתֶּם	נְקוּמֹתֶם	נְסַבּוֹתֶם	נִגַּשְׁתֶּם
2fp	נִקְטַלְתֶּן	נְקוּמֹתֶן	נְסַבּוֹתֶן	נִגַּשְׁתֶּן
1p	נִקְטַלְנוּ	נְקוּמֹנוּ	נְסַבּוֹנוּ	נִגַּשְׁנוּ

Most other forms of the Nifal in weak verbs can be readily identified.

GENTILIC ADJECTIVES

When we discuss nationality in English we might refer to ourselves or others as Australian, or Scottish, or Chinese or Israeli. In Hebrew those words that describe nationality are called gentilic adjectives; 'gentilic' means *of the nations*. They are formed by adding particular endings, as these examples should demonstrate:

מוֹאָבִי	Moabite (ms)	מִצְרִי	Egyptian (ms)
מוֹאָבִית	Moabite (fs)	מִצְרִית	Egyptian (fs)
מוֹאָבִים	Moabite (mp)	מִצְרִים	Egyptian (mp)
מוֹאֲבִיּוֹת	Moabite (fp)	מִצְרִיּוֹת	Egyptian (fp)

In English we sometimes use the gentilic adjectives as nouns: *an Israeli, the Australians* (although it is not possible with adjectives like *Scottish*: we need to say *the Scots*). A similar thing happens in Hebrew: for example, the word מִצְרִי (*Egyptian*) can be used as an adjective or a noun. Hence:

Adjective:

He was the son of an Egyptian man. (Leviticus 24:10)   הוּא בֶּן־אִישׁ מִצְרִי

Noun:

And he was in the house of his master the Egyptian.
(Genesis 29:2)

וַיְהִי בְּבֵית אֲדֹנָיו הַמִּצְרִי

JUSSIVE

We have already looked at a number of forms related to the Imperfect, but there are still a couple that we have not yet learned about. One of these is the Jussive. However, we have seen an example of it: וְלֹא תִגְּעוּ and לֹא תֹאכְלוּ in Genesis 3:3.

Like the Imperative, the Jussive can be used for expressing commands. In Hebrew the Imperative is usually used when the commands are in the second person; the Jussive is used when the commands are in the third person. Here are some examples:

2nd person command (singular)   *Go away.*
3rd person command (singular)   *Let him leave.*

2nd person command (plural)   *Take your places.*
3rd person command (plural)   *Let them eat cake.*

In Hebrew the Jussive is almost always identical in form to the Imperfect:

Imperfect   יִקְטֹל   *he will kill*

Jussive   יִקְטֹל   *let him kill*

The only way to determine how to translate a Jussive is by examining the context.

JUSSIVE IN WEAK VERBS

The exceptions are in the hollow verbs and the **lamed he** verbs, in which the Jussive differs from the Imperfect:

Hollow verb   יָקוּם *he will arise*   יָקֹם *let him arise*

III-ה verb   יִגְלֶה *he will reveal*   יִגֶל *let him reveal*

JUSSIVE IN NIFAL

Jussives occur not just in Qal but in the other verb stems as well. Here are the examples in Nifal:

	Qal		Nifal	
Regular verb	יִקָּטֵל	*he will be killed*	יִקָּטֵל	*let him be killed*
III-ה verb	יִגָּלֶה	*it will be revealed*	יִגָּל	*let it be revealed*

JUSSIVE IN VC IMPERFECT: QAL

Strictly speaking, the VC Imperfect is really formed by adding **וַ** to the Jussive form. This causes no difficulties in the majority of verbs, where the Imperfect is identical to the Jussive. However, in hollow verbs and III-ה verbs the VC Imperfect is formed differently from the Imperfect.

	Imperfect	Jussive	VC Imperfect
Strong verb	יִקְטֹל *he will kill*	יִקְטֹל *let him kill*	וַיִּקְטֹל *and he killed*
Hollow verb	יָקוּם *he will arise*	יָקֹם *let him arise*	וַיָּקָם *and he arose* (the last vowel is a short o: va-YĀ-kom)
III-ה verb	יִגְלֶה *he will reveal*	יִגֶל *let him reveal*	וַיִּגֶל *and he revealed*

JUSSIVE IN VC IMPERFECT: NIFAL

	Imperfect	Jussive	VC Imperfect
Strong verb	יִקָּטֵל *he will be killed*	יִקָּטֵל *let him be killed*	וַיִּקָּטֵל *and he was killed*
III-ה verb	יִגָּלֶה *it will be revealed*	יִגָּל *let it be revealed*	וַיִּגָּל *and it was revealed*

NEGATIVE COMMANDS

There is one feature of the Jussive that is particularly important, and that is its usage in negative commands (prohibitions). Prohibitions use the negative particle **לֹא** or another negative particle **אַל**:

אַל תִּקְטֹל אוֹתָם	*Do not kill them.*	Jussive 2ms + negative particle אַל
לֹא תִקְטֹל אוֹתָם	*You absolutely must not kill them.*	Jussive 2ms + negative particle לֹא
אַל יִקְטֹל אוֹתָם	*Let him not kill them.*	Jussive 3ms + negative particle אַל

> **LANGUAGE INSIGHT**
> Prohibitions with לֹא are strong prohibitions. The prohibitions in the ten commandments are formulated with לֹא.

PRACTICE 2

1 Translate the following into English: Exodus 20:12–13 [Engl. 20: 12–17].

לֹא תִרְצָח לֹא תִנְאָף לֹא תִגְנֹב לֹא־תַעֲנֶה בְרֵעֲךָ עֵד שָׁקֶר ׃ לֹא תַחְמֹד בֵּית רֵעֶךָ לֹא־
תַחְמֹד אֵשֶׁת רֵעֶךָ וְעַבְדּוֹ וַאֲמָתוֹ וְשׁוֹרוֹ וַחֲמֹרוֹ וְכֹל אֲשֶׁר לְרֵעֶךָ ׃

2 Translate these sentences with either commands or prohibitions as appropriate and categorize the nouns according to whether they are formed like אֹיֵב or מֶלֶךְ or דָּבָר or יָם.

Three hints:

▶ the word תִּתֹּשׁ comes from the verb נָתַשׁ
▶ the א in גֹּאֲלִי needs a composite **sheva** because it cannot take a simple **sheva**
▶ The preposition מִן can be translated *of* when it is used with the verb יָרֵא

a	גּוּר־נָא בְּאַרְצִי
b	לֹא תִּקְטְלוּ אֶת־הַשֹּׁמְרִים
c	יִמְלָא לְבַב מֹשֶׁה
d	אַל תִּגַּע אֶת־אַפִּי
e	זְכֹר צִדְקַת שְׁלֹמֹה
f	יִשְׂמְחוּ שֹׁפְטֵי יִשְׂרָאֵל
g	אַל תִּתֹּשׁ אֶת־קָדְשֵׁי יְהוּדָה
h	יִפְקֹד אוֹתִי גֹּאֲלִי
i	לֹא תִּשְׁכַּח אֶת־אִמּוֹת בְּנֵי־יִשְׂרָאֵל
j	לֹא תִּרָא מִן דַּעְתִּי

Reading

GENESIS 21:7–13

Points to look out for in this text:

▶ words we have already encountered
▶ Nifal forms
▶ gentilic adjectives
▶ Jussive forms
▶ Segolate nouns.

7	וַתֹּאמֶר מִי מִלֵּל לְאַבְרָהָם הֵינִיקָה בָנִים שָׂרָה כִּי־יָלַדְתִּי בֵן לִזְקֻנָיו:
8	וַיִּגְדַּל הַיֶּלֶד וַיִּגָּמַל וַיַּעַשׂ אַבְרָהָם מִשְׁתֶּה גָדוֹל בְּיוֹם הִגָּמֵל אֶת־יִצְחָק:
9	וַתֵּרֶא שָׂרָה אֶת־בֶּן־הָגָר הַמִּצְרִית אֲשֶׁר־יָלְדָה לְאַבְרָהָם מְצַחֵק:
10	וַתֹּאמֶר לְאַבְרָהָם גָּרֵשׁ הָאָמָה הַזֹּאת וְאֶת־בְּנָהּ כִּי לֹא יִירַשׁ בֶּן־הָאָמָה הַזֹּאת עִם־בְּנִי עִם־יִצְחָק:
11	וַיֵּרַע הַדָּבָר מְאֹד בְּעֵינֵי אַבְרָהָם עַל אוֹדֹת בְּנוֹ:
12	וַיֹּאמֶר אֱלֹהִים אֶל־אַבְרָהָם אַל־יֵרַע בְּעֵינֶיךָ עַל־הַנַּעַר וְעַל־אֲמָתֶךָ כֹּל אֲשֶׁר תֹּאמַר אֵלֶיךָ שָׂרָה שְׁמַע בְּקֹלָהּ כִּי בְיִצְחָק יִקָּרֵא לְךָ זָרַע:
13	וְגַם אֶת־בֶּן־הָאָמָה לְגוֹי אֲשִׂימֶנּוּ כִּי זַרְעֲךָ הוּא:

⚙ Language discovery

VERSE 7

מִלֵּל

This is a Piel form, and we will learn about the Piel in the next unit. It means *he has said*.

הֵינִיקָה

This is a Hifil form. The Hifil is described as a causative: the sense is that someone is caused to do something. If יָנַק means *to suck*, what might the Hifil mean in this context?

The phrase מִי מִלֵּל לְאַבְרָהָם הֵינִיקָה ... שָׂרָה is usually translated: *Who would have said to Abraham that Sarah would breastfeed sons*. Hebrew does not have a way of framing conditional questions but English seems to demand it here. How would you translate the second half of the verse?

VERSE 8

וַיִּגְדַּל

If גָּמַל means *to wean*, what does the Nifal mean? How would you translate this form of the verb?

וַיַּעַשׂ

This is a very common word and you may recognize it from previous texts. It is VC Imperfect 3ms apocopated (shortened) from the verb עָשָׂה. What does it mean?

בְּיוֹם הִגָּמֵל אֶת־יִצְחָק

The word הִגָּמֵל is a Nifal infinitive construct, and could perhaps be translated as a noun (*on the day of the weaning*) or as a verb (*on the day he was weaned*). How would you translate the whole phrase?

VERSE 9

וַתֵּרֶא

This is VC Imperfect 3fs of רָאָה (*to see*). How would you render it?

אֶת־בֶּן־הָגָר הַמִּצְרִית

How would you translate the gentilic adjective?

אֲשֶׁר־יָלְדָה לְאַבְרָהָם

Read Genesis 20 to find out about Abraham and Hagar's son.

מְצַחֵק

Another Piel form; this time a participle. It can mean *playing* or *laughing*, or possibly *teasing* or *mocking*. It is difficult to know exactly what is meant, though an early Greek translation of the biblical text (called the Septuagint) adds the words *with Isaac*. So perhaps Ishmael is playing with Isaac or teasing Isaac. Would you include the Septuagint addition in your translation even though it is not in the Hebrew text?

VERSE 10

גָּרֵשׁ

This is a Piel Imperative. It means *expel* or *drive away*.

לֹא יִירַשׁ בֶּן־הָאָמָה הַזֹּאת עִם־בְּנִי

The verb יָרַשׁ, does not follow the I-י pattern we have seen before, but it is not difficult to identify. The subject of the verb is *the son of the handmaid* but how would you translate עִם־בְּנִי?

VERSE 11

וַיֵּרַע

The verb is VC Imperfect of רָעַע, and דָּבָר can mean *word*, but it can also mean *thing* or *matter*. *So the matter was very bad in Abraham's eyes*. This is a common Hebrew expression indicating a person's distress or displeasure. It is better to translate it into idiomatic English: e.g. *Abraham was very displeased*.

VERSE 12

אַל־יֵרַע בְּעֵינֶיךָ עַל־הַנַּעַר

If this is a prohibition, what form of רָעַע is this? How would you parse it? How would you translate the phrase?

כֹּל אֲשֶׁר תֹּאמַר אֵלֶיךָ שָׂרָה שְׁמַע בְּקֹלָהּ

To listen to someone's voice is often associated with obeying them or doing as they suggest. So this phrase is an exhortation to Abraham to do as Sarah has requested despite his misgivings. Would you use the word *obey* in your translation? If not, which word would feel more apt?

כִּי בְיִצְחָק יִקָּרֵא לְךָ זָרַע

You should be able to parse יִקָּרֵא even though it is not in the Qal stem. Since you have previously encountered the verb in the Qal you should be able to work out its literal meaning. However, rendering it in grammatical English is more of a challenge. The idea is that Abraham's descendants through Isaac will be particularly significant as Abraham's progeny. If you get stuck, compare translations and try to work out how they made their decisions.

VERSE 13

וְגַם אֶת־בֶּן־הָאָמָה

This refers to Hagar's son.

לְגוֹי אֲשִׂימֶנּוּ

The word is an Imperfect 1s of שִׂים (*to put, place*) and the suffix נּוּ indicates the object of the verb, which is 3ms. We will learn more about suffixes on verbs in the next unit. The whole word means *I will place him* or *I will establish him*. And לְגוֹי means *as a nation*.

כִּי זַרְעֲךָ הוּא

Literally *because your seed is he*. Ishmael is also Abraham's progeny. Notice that his name is not given in this chapter. What might be the reason for that? How will you translate זֶרַע?

POSSIBLE TRANSLATION

And she said, 'Who would have said to Abraham that Sarah would breastfeed sons? For I have given birth to a son in his old age.' And the child grew and was weaned and Abraham held a great feast on the day that Isaac was weaned. And Sarah saw the son of Hagar the Egyptian, whom she bore to Abraham, playing [with Isaac]. And she said to Abraham, 'Drive away this handmaid and her son, because the son of this handmaid will not inherit with my son, with Isaac.' And Abraham was very distressed because of his son. And God said to Abraham, 'Do not be distressed about the young man or about your handmaid. Listen to Sarah's voice in all that she has said to you, because your descendants will be recognized through Isaac.' And I will also make the handmaid's son into a nation because he is your offspring.

Test yourself

1 Translate the following into English.

a נִכְתַּב _____

b נֶאֶכְלוּ _____

c תִּזָּכֵר _____

2 Where do these people come from?

a מוֹאָבִית _____

b מִצְרִי _____

c יִשְׂרְאֵלִים _____

3 Translate the following into Hebrew.

let him remember; let them be remembered

_____

4 Translate the following into Hebrew.

a He was visited in the morning.

b The law of the king was remembered in Israel.

c The words of the prophets of Israel were written in the books of the priests.

SELF-CHECK

I CAN...
⚪ understand the system of verbal stems (**binyanim**)
⚪ recognise forms and uses of the Nifal stem
⚪ recognize gentilic adjectives
⚪ translate the Jussive in appropriate contexts
⚪ read and translate Genesis 21:7–13

17 Verbs with pronominal suffixes, cohortatives, Piel, Pual and Hitpael

In this unit you will learn about:
▶ how verbs take pronominal suffixes
▶ how the cohortative is used for first-person commands
▶ the verbal stems Piel, Pual and Hitpael

You will read:
▶ Genesis 21:14–21

Vocabulary builder

NOUNS

בְּאֵר	well (f)
בְּאֵר שֶׁבַע	Beersheba
דָּגָן	corn, grain
דֶּלֶת	door
הֵיכָל	temple, palace
חַיִּים	life (also living, alive)
חֵמֶת	container (f)
מָוֶת	death
מַיִם	water
מַלְאָךְ	angel, messenger
נֶפֶשׁ	soul, life
פָּארָן	Paran
קֶשֶׁת	bow
שִׂיחַ	shrub
שְׁכֶם	shoulder

VERBS

בָּכָה	to weep
הָלַל	Piel to praise
חָזַק	Hifil to hold (with בְּ)
טָחַה	to shoot
כָּלָה	to be finished
לָמַד	Piel to teach
מָלֵא	Qal to be full; Piel to fill
נָתַק	to tear away
סָגַר	to shut, close up
עָזַב	to abandon, forsake
פָּשַׁע	to turn away, sin
צָוָה	Piel to command
קָדַשׁ	to be holy
רָבָה	to shoot
רָחַק	to be distant
שָׁכַם	to get up early
שָׁבַר	to break
שָׁלַךְ	to throw
שָׁקָה	Hifil to give someone a drink
תָּעָה	to wander

OTHER

נֶגֶד	in front of, opposite
עוֹד	again, yet, still

Grammar

VERBS WITH SUFFIXES

So far we have learned about pronominal suffixes on nouns (e.g. סוּסוֹ) and on prepositions (e.g. לָהֶם) but we have not yet looked at how these suffixes are attached to verbs, although we have encountered a few examples.

With nouns and prepositions it was a fairly straightforward process of adding the appropriate endings. If the ending was 3fs, it was usually הָ. Some of the prepositions acquired a few extra letters (e.g. כְּ with 1s suffix became כְּמוֹנִי) but essentially it was somewhat predictable. Verbs are not so predictable: there are a variety of endings that can be applied to verbs and it is necessary to be aware of the possibilities in order to make sense of them. At this stage it is not necessary to learn the rules about the usage of particular suffixes; recognizing them is enough for now.

	Suffix on ל (for comparison)	Suffixes on verb					Meaning
3ms	וֹ	וֹ	תוֹ	תוֹ	הוּ	נּוּ	him
3fs	הָ	הָ	הָ	הָ	נָה		her
2ms	ךָ	ךָ	וּךָ				you
2fs	ךְ	ךְ	וּךְ				you
1s	ִי	נִי	תְנִי	תוּנִי	נִּי		me
3mp	הֶם	ָם	ַם	ָם	וּם	ָּ..	them
3fp	הֶן	ָן	ַן	ָן	וּן	ָּ..	them
2mp	כֶם	כֶם					you
2fp	כֶן	כֶן					you
1p	נוּ	נוּ	תְנוּ				us

When a suffix is added to a verb the vowels in the verb will often change. Sometimes extra vowels are added to make the word easier to pronounce. Here are some examples:

Without suffix		With suffix		Pronunciation
פָּקַד	he has visited	פְּקָדַנִי	he has visited me	pə-kā-DA-nee
פָּקְדוּ	they have visited	פְּקָדוּהוּ	they have visited him	pə-kā-DOO-hoo
יִפְקֹד	he will visit	יִפְקְדֵנִי	he will visit me	yif-kə-DAY-nee
יִפְקְדוּ	they will visit	יִפְקְדוּהוּ	they will visit him	yif-kə-DOO-hoo

Verbs with pronominal suffixes are very common in biblical Hebrew; much more common than using object pronouns such as אוֹתוֹ. Fortunately, despite the number of alternative suffixes for verbs there is not a great variety among them. The five possibilities for the 3mp, for example, are simply the letter ם with one of five vowels. The 3mp forms are the most important to learn, partly because they are very common, but also because they are less immediately recognizable than most of the others.

> **LANGUAGE INSIGHT**
>
> Verbs with pronominal suffixes can cause a little confusion at first. For example , פְּקַדְנוּ looks very like פְּקָדָנוּ but the two mean *we have visited* and *he has visited us* respectively. The 3ms pronominal suffix וֹ can also be tricky: it is easy to mistake it for the third-person Perfect suffix. However, context usually provides some assistance.

PRACTICE 1

Match the Hebrew to the English.

a	this great fire will consume us (Deuteronomy 5:25)	1	וַיֶּאֱהָבֵהוּ מְאֹד
b	and he took them from the middle of the tent (Joshua 7:3)	2	וַיִּזְכְּרֶהָ יְהוָה
c	and Yhwh remembered her (1 Samuel 1:19)	3	וְלֹא יְדַעְתָּם
d	and he loved him very much (1 Samuel 16:21)	4	בֵּרַכְנוּכֶם מִבֵּית יְהוָה
e	and you did not know them (Isaiah 48:6)	5	יְהוָה יִשְׁמָרְךָ מִכָּל־רָע
f	We bless you from the house of Yhwh (Psalm 118:26)	6	אֵלִי אֵלִי לָמָה עֲזַבְתָּנִי
g	Yhwh will guard you from all evil (Psalm 121:7)	7	תֹּאכְלֵנוּ הָאֵשׁ הַגְּדֹלָה הַזֹּאת
h	My God, my God, why have you abandoned me? (Psalm 22:2; Engl. 22:1)	8	וַיִּקָּחוּם מִתּוֹךְ הָאֹהֶל

COHORTATIVE

We have already learned the Imperative and the Jussive. The Cohortative is another way of issuing commands, and this time they are commands to oneself. This means they are first person. (Remember, Imperatives are second-person commands and Jussives can be second person or third person.) The Cohortative is formed by adding the ending הָ to the Imperfect form. This lengthens the word by one syllable, and so the **cholem** of the Imperfect changes to a **sheva** in the Cohortative.

I will visit	אֶפְקֹד	*I will remember*	אֶזְכֹּר	*I will write*	אֶכְתֹּב
let me visit	אֶפְקְדָה	*let me remember*	אֶזְכְּרָה	*let me write*	אֶכְתְּבָה
we will visit	נִפְקֹד	*we will remember*	נִזְכֹּר	*we will write*	נִכְתֹּב
let us visit	נִפְקְדָה	*let us remember*	נִזְכְּרָה	*let us write*	נִכְתְּבָה

Here are some examples of how the Cohortative is used:

אֶזְכְּרָה דְּבָרֶיךָ *Let me remember your words.*

נִכְרְתָה בְּרִית *Let us make a covenant.* (the verb used for making a covenant is כָּרַת *to cut*)

17 Verbs with pronominal suffixes, cohortatives, Piel, Pual and Hitpael **165**

Here are some examples from the Hebrew Bible:

וַיֹּאמֶר לוֹ אֵלְכָה נָּא וְאָשׁוּבָה
אֶל־אַחַי אֲשֶׁר־בְּמִצְרַיִם וְאֶרְאֶה
הַעוֹדָם חַיִּים

And he said to him, 'Let me go please, and let me return to my brothers who are in Egypt so that I may see if they are still alive.' (Exodus 4:18)

אַל־נָא נֹאבְדָה בְּנֶפֶשׁ הָאִישׁ הַזֶּה

Please do not let us die for the life of this man. (Jonah 1:14)

אֲלַמְּדָה פֹשְׁעִים דְּרָכֶיךָ
וְחַטָּאִים אֵלֶיךָ יָשׁוּבוּ

Let me teach sinners your ways so that sinners will return to you. (Psalm 51:15 [Engl. 51:13])

PRACTICE 2

Translate the following into English.

a Judges 15:1   וַיֹּאמֶר אָבֹאָה אֶל־אִשְׁתִּי

b Ruth 2:13   וַתֹּאמֶר אֶמְצָא־חֵן בְּעֵינֶיךָ

c Isaiah 2:5   לְכוּ וְנֵלְכָה בְּאוֹר יְהֹוָה

d Nehemiah 5:2   וְנִקְחָה דָגָן וְנֹאכְלָה

e Nehemiah 6:10   וְנִסְגְּרָה דַּלְתוֹת הַהֵיכָל

VERBS: PIEL, PUAL AND HITPAEL

We have seen a number of examples of verbs in the Piel in the biblical texts. The Piel is another of the verbal stems, like the Nifal we learned in Unit 16. As you probably remember, Nifal forms are usually translated with an English passive, so Nifal can be thought of as a passive stem. Piel is slightly different: Piel is traditionally described as intensive: it intensifies the verbal idea, although this is an oversimplification. It is known as Piel because in the Perfect 3ms its vowels are **chireq** and **tsere**. Applied to the verb פָּעַל (formerly the model verb) the intensive form is פִּעֵל, pronounced **pee-ayl**.

	Qal	Piel
שָׁבַר	*to break*	*to shatter*
נָתַק	*to pull off, tear away*	*to tear apart, tear to pieces*
קָדַשׁ	*to be holy*	*to sanctify, consecrate*

Other verbs have meanings in the Piel that are very similar to their Qal meanings:

	Qal	Piel
הָלַךְ	*to go, walk*	*to go, walk*
גָּלָה	*to uncover, reveal*	*to uncover, reveal*

And some meanings appear to be less similar to the Qal meanings:

	Qal	Piel
פָּקַד	to visit, take care of	to muster (Isaiah 13:4)

However, to muster is a possible meaning of the Qal of פָּקַד so it is not so dissimilar as it first appears.

Some verbs are never found in Qal in biblical Hebrew: they occur only in Piel form and their meanings are not necessarily inherently intensive.

	Qal	Piel
צָוָה	—	to command
הָלַל	—	to praise

The ו in the verb צָוָה is not a vowel as it is in קוּם; it is a consonant, even with **dagesh** (וּ) which makes it look like a vowel. Therefore it is pronounced **v** and not **oo**.

Like Nifal, Piel occurs in Perfect, Imperfect and the other forms.

Piel Perfect

3ms	פִּקֵּד	he has mustered	3p	פִּקְּדוּ	they have mustered
3fs	פִּקְּדָה	she has mustered			
2ms	פִּקַּדְתָּ	you have mustered	2mp	פִּקַּדְתֶּם	you have mustered
2fs	פִּקַּדְתְּ	you have mustered	2fp	פִּקַּדְתֶּן	you have mustered
1s	פִּקַּדְתִּי	I have mustered	1p	פִּקַּדְנוּ	we have mustered

There is, of course, a **dagesh** in the initial פ because it is a **begadkefat** letter and always takes **dagesh** at the beginning of a word. However, the **dagesh** to notice is the **dagesh** in the middle root letter (ק). All Piel forms have this **dagesh**. And for that reason פָּעַל is not an ideal model verb, because its middle letter is a guttural and so cannot take **dagesh**.

Piel Imperfect

3ms	יְפַקֵּד	he will muster	3p	יְפַקְּדוּ	they have mustered
3fs	תְּפַקֵּד	she will muster	3fp	תְּפַקֵּדְנָה	they have mustered
2ms	תְּפַקֵּד	you have mustered	2mp	תְּפַקְּדוּ	you have mustered
2fs	תְּפַקְּדִי	you have mustered	2fp	תְּפַקֵּדְנָה	you have mustered
1s	אֲפַקֵּד	I have mustered	1p	נְפַקֵּד	we have mustered

Piel Imperative ms

פַּקֵּד	muster!

Piel Infinitive Construct

(identical to the Imperative, as in Qal)

פַּקֵּד   *to muster*

Piel Infinitive Absolute

פַּקֹּד   *mustering*

Piel Participle

(Participles in all stems except Qal and Nifal begin with מ.)

מְפַקֵּד   *mustering*

PIEL AND WEAK VERBS

II-guttural verbs and verbs with a ר as the second root letter are the most obviously likely to deviate from the strong verb pattern, since the Piel employs a **dagesh** in the second letter. With the absence of **dagesh** the vowel under the first letter can change from **chireq** to **tsere**: for example בֵּרֵךְ (*he has blessed*) instead of the clearly wrong בֵּרֵךְ. Another possibility is that the **tsere** changes to **patach**, e.g. נָחַם (*he has comforted*). The word פָּעַל itself, from which we get the names of the roots, is a weak verb. In fact, instead of pronouncing it **piel**, it should probably be written פָּעַל and pronounced **pee-al**. However, the **Piel** of פָּעַל does not appear in biblical Hebrew so the correct spelling is only interesting as a point of grammar.

III-guttural verbs attract *a* vowels instead of **tsere**, thus שִׁלַּח is the Piel Perfect 3ms, and not שִׁלֵּחַ; and the same is true for any gender and number of this type of weak verbs. For the same reason the Piel Imperfect 3ms of שָׁלַח is יְשַׁלַּח. Similarly, III-ה verbs replace the **tsere** with **patach** in the Piel Perfect (e.g. גִּלָּה instead of גִּלֵּה) and replace **tsere** with **segol** in the Piel Imperfect (e.g. יְגַלֶּה). Other vowel changes occur in other forms, but they are usually recognizable if you are familiar with the general pattern of the Piel.

PUAL

In Unit 16 we learned that Nifal is usually translated with an English passive. The Pual is a passive stem that corresponds to the Piel. It is therefore both intensive and passive. It is formed in a similar way to Piel, with the **dagesh** in the middle root letter (with the exception of gutturals), but it is formed with *u* and *a* vowels, hence the name Pual. It is much less common than Piel, and there is no need at this stage to learn lists of verbal forms. Here are some examples of how it is used:

Qal		Piel		Pual	
שָׁבַר	*he has broken*	שִׁבֵּר	*he has shattered*	שֻׁבַּר	*he has been shattered*
נָתַק	*he has torn (something) away*	נִתֵּק	*he has torn (something) to pieces*	נֻתַּק	*he has been torn to pieces*
קָדֵשׁ	*he is holy*	קִדֵּשׁ	*he has consecrated*	קֻדַּשׁ	*he has been consecrated*

Notice the unusual Piel form קִדַּשׁ. We might have expected קִדֵּשׁ.

Although it is not necessary to learn verb lists, it may be useful to be aware of the five basic forms of the verb in Pual, with Qal and Piel for comparison:

	Qal	Piel	Pual
Perfect 3ms	קָטַל	קִטֵּל	קֻטַּל
Imperfect 3ms	יִקְטֹל	יְקַטֵּל	יְקֻטַּל
Imperative 2ms	קְטֹל	קַטֵּל	—
Infinitive Construct	קְטֹל	קַטֵּל	קֻטַּל
Participle	קֹטֵל	מְקַטֵּל	מְקֻטָּל

HITPAEL

The Hitpael, like the Pual, is related to the Piel. It is frequently used as a reflexive form of the Piel although it can carry other meanings and is sometimes translated with the same meaning as the Qal or Piel. It is formed with the prefix הִת and with **dagesh** in the second root letter and **patach** and **tsere** vowels. Here are some examples:

Qal	קָדַשׁ	*he is holy*
Piel	קִדַּשׁ	*he has consecrated*
Pual	קֻדַּשׁ	*he/it has been consecrated*
Hitpael	הִתְקַדֵּשׁ	*he has consecrated himself*

Qal	פָּקַד	*he has visited*
Piel	פִּקַּד	*he has mustered*
Pual	פֻּקַּד	*he has been mustered*
Hitpael	הִתְפַּקֵּד	*he has mustered*

In the Hitpael Imperfect the prefix changes according to the person and number, in a manner very similar to the Qal Imperfect prefix:

3ms	יִתְקַדֵּשׁ	*he will consecrate himself*
3fs	תִּתְקַדֵּשׁ	*she will consecrate herself*
2ms	תִּתְקַדֵּשׁ	*you will consecrate yourself*
2fs	תִּתְקַדְּשִׁי	*you will consecrate yourself*
1s	אֶתְקַדֵּשׁ	*I will consecrate myself*
3mp	יִתְקַדְּשׁוּ	*they will consecrate themselves*

3fp	תִּתְקַדֵּשְׁנָה	they will consecrate themselves
2mp	תִּתְקַדְּשׁוּ	you will consecrate yourselves
2fp	תִּתְקַדֵּשְׁנָה	you will consecrate yourselves
1p	נִתְקַדֵּשׁ	we will consecrate ourselves

Again, it is not necessary at this stage to learn lists of verbs in the Hitpael, but it may be useful to see how the five basic forms of the verb look in Hitpael with Qal and the other intensive stems for comparison:

	Qal	Piel	Pual	Hitpael
Perfect 3ms	קָטַל	קִטֵּל	קֻטַּל	הִתְקַטֵּל
Imperfect 3ms	יִקְטֹל	יְקַטֵּל	יְקֻטַּל	יִתְקַטֵּל
Imperative 2ms	קְטֹל	קַטֵּל	—	הִתְקַטֵּל
Infinitive Construct	קְטֹל	קַטֵּל	קֻטַּל	הִתְקַטֵּל
Participle	קֹטֵל	מְקַטֵּל	מְקֻטָּל	מִתְקַטֵּל

In verbal roots that begin with sibilants (**s**-sounds), that is ס צ שׁ and שׂ, the **tav** of the Hitpael switches places with the sibilant, probably for ease of pronunciation. This is called metathesis. Thus:

Verb	Stem	Meaning
שָׁבַר	Qal	to break
שִׁבֵּר	Piel	to shatter
הִשְׁתַּבֵּר	Hitpael	to shatter oneself

There is no Hitpael of שָׁבַר in biblical Hebrew, but it demonstrates the principle.

The simplified stem schema taught to beginners cannot capture the full range of meanings of each stem, but the Piel, Pual and Hitpael are particularly difficult to pin down. For some time the Piel and associated forms were understood to be intensive, but more recently a greater range of meaning is attributed to these stems. Some grammarians identify factitive or resultative meanings in which the subject of the verb acts on the object to change its state. For example, גָּדַל in Qal means *to be large* or *to grow*, whereas the Piel גִּדַּל means *to nourish* (to take care of something so that it grows, hence to bring up children) and the Hifil הִגְדִּיל means *to make great*. It can be quite difficult to use this principle to discern the meaning of the Piel from the meaning of the Qal, and in practice most beginners simply learn the Piel meanings as well as the Qal. Translation is a matter not just of science but also of poetry, so that establishing and rendering the meaning of a word depends not only on linguistic analysis but also on tradition, changes in semantic range, and occasionally inspiration.

Here are the verbs that are found in all seven common stems in biblical Hebrew: this should provide a sense of the variety of ways of understanding and translating the Piel, Pual and Hitpael. We will look at Hifil and Hofal in more depth in the next unit.

Verb / Stem	בקע	גלה	חלה	ידע	ילד	פקד
Qal	to split, break open	to uncover, depart, go into exile	to be weak, ill	to know	to bring forth, give birth, father a child	to attend to, visit, provide
Nifal	to be broken open	to be uncovered, uncover oneself	to be made ill, make oneself ill	to be made known, make oneself known	to be born	to visit, punish, appoint, be missing
Piel	to cut in pieces	to disclose, reveal	to make ill, diseased	to cause to know	to bring forth, act as a midwife	to muster (an army)
Pual	to be ripped open	to be uncovered	to be made weak	to be known, become known	to be born (to a parent)	to be missed, punished
Hitpael	to burst oneself open (wineskins)	to make oneself naked	to make oneself ill	to make oneself known	to declare one's ancestry	to be counted
Hifil	to break into	to take into exile	to make ill, become ill	to make known	to father a child	to appoint, entrust
Hofal	to be broken into	to be taken into exile	to be wounded	to be made known	to be born (usu. ref. a birthday)	to be appointed, punished

IDENTIFYING THE STEMS

There are certain factors to look for if you want to determine whether a verb is Piel or Pual or another stem. Here are the factors that can help you recognize one of the intensives:

Recognizing the Piel

Perfect: **Dagesh** in second root letter. E.g. קִטַּלְתִּי

Imperfect: **Dagesh** in second root letter, **sheva** under prefix (1s has a complex **sheva** because the prefix is א which cannot take a simple **sheva**). E.g. אֲקַטֵּל

Imperative and Infinitives: Short-*a* vowel under the first root letter. E.g. קַטֵּל

Participle: Begins with מ and has short-*a* vowel under the first root letter. E.g. מְקַטֵּל

Recognizing the Pual

Perfect: **Dagesh** in second root letter, ◌ֻ **vowel** in first syllable. E.g קֻטַּלְתִּי

Imperfect: **Dagesh** in second root letter, **sheva** under prefix, ◌ֻ **vowel** under first root letter. E.g. אֲקֻטַּל

Imperative: does not exist

Infinitives: ֵ vowel in first syllable. E.g. קַטֵּל

Participle: Begins with מ and has ֵ vowel under the first root letter. E.g. מְקַטֵּל

Recognizing the Hitpael

Perfect: **Dagesh** in second root letter, prefix הִת. E.g. הִתְקַטַּלְתִּי

Imperfect: **Dagesh** in second root letter, prefix incorporates a ת. E.g. אֶתְקַטֵּל

Imperative and infinitives: Prefix הִת. E.g. הִתְקַטֵּל

Participle: Prefix מִת. E.g. מִתְקַטֵּל

PRACTICE 3

Complete the second and third tables, using the meanings set out in the first table.

	קָדַשׁ	פָּקַד	אָסַף	בָּקַע	צָוָה
Qal	to be holy	to visit	to gather	to divide	—
Piel	to consecrate	to muster	to gather	to tear in pieces	to command
Pual	to be consecrated	to be mustered	to be gathered	to be torn in pieces	to be commanded
Hitpael	to consecrate oneself	to muster	to be gathered together	to be torn	—

	Perf. 3ms	Perf. 1s	Perf. 3mp	Impf. 3ms	Impv.
Qal	קָדַשׁ	פָּקַדְתִּי	בָּקְעוּ		פְּקֹד
Meaning	he is holy	I have visited		—	
Piel	קִדַּשׁ	פָּקַדְתִּי	בִּקְּעוּ	צִוָּה	פַּקֵּד
Meaning		I have mustered	they have torn in pieces		muster
Pual	קֻדַּשׁ	פֻּקַּדְתִּי	בֻּקְּעוּ	צֻוָּה	—
Meaning	he has been consecrated			he has been commanded	—
Hitpael	הִתְקַדֵּשׁ	הִתְפַּקַּדְתִּי	הִתְבַּקְּעוּ		הִתְפַּקֵּד
Meaning	he has consecrated himself		they have been torn	—	

	Impf. 1p	Impf. 3mp	Impv.	Part.	Inf. Cstr.
Qal	נִבְקַע	יַאַסְפוּ	קְדַשׁ	אֹסֵף	בְּקֹעַ
Meaning	we will divide		be holy	gathering	to divide
Piel	נְבַקַּע	יְאַסְפוּ	קַדֵּשׁ	מְאַסֵּף	בַּקַּע
Meaning		they will gather			to tear in pieces

Pual	נִבְקַע	יְאָסְפוּ	—	מְאֻסָּף	בְּקַע
Meaning	we will be torn in pieces	they will be gathered	—	being gathered	
Hitpael	נִתְבַּקַע	יִתְאַסְפוּ	הִתְקַדֵּשׁ	מִתְאַסֵּף	הִתְבַּקַע
Meaning					

Reading

GENESIS 21:14–21

Points to look out for in this text:

▸ words we have already encountered

▸ verbs with pronominal suffixes

▸ verbs in intensive stems.

14 וַיַּשְׁכֵּם אַבְרָהָם בַּבֹּקֶר וַיִּקַּח־לֶחֶם וְחֵמַת מַיִם וַיִּתֵּן אֶל־הָגָר שָׂם עַל־שִׁכְמָהּ וְאֶת־הַיֶּלֶד וַיְשַׁלְּחֶהָ וַתֵּלֶךְ וַתֵּתַע בְּמִדְבַּר בְּאֵר שָׁבַע :

15 וַיִּכְלוּ הַמַּיִם מִן־הַחֵמֶת וַתַּשְׁלֵךְ אֶת־הַיֶּלֶד תַּחַת אַחַד הַשִּׂיחִם :

16 וַתֵּלֶךְ וַתֵּשֶׁב לָהּ מִנֶּגֶד הַרְחֵק כִּמְטַחֲוֵי קֶשֶׁת כִּי אָמְרָה אַל־אֶרְאֶה בְּמוֹת הַיָּלֶד וַתֵּשֶׁב מִנֶּגֶד וַתִּשָּׂא אֶת־קֹלָהּ וַתֵּבְךְּ :

17 וַיִּשְׁמַע אֱלֹהִים אֶת־קוֹל הַנַּעַר וַיִּקְרָא מַלְאַךְ אֱלֹהִים אֶל־הָגָר מִן־הַשָּׁמַיִם וַיֹּאמֶר לָהּ מַה־לָּךְ הָגָר אַל־תִּירְאִי כִּי־שָׁמַע אֱלֹהִים אֶל־קוֹל הַנַּעַר בַּאֲשֶׁר הוּא־שָׁם :

18 קוּמִי שְׂאִי אֶת־הַנַּעַר וְהַחֲזִיקִי אֶת־יָדֵךְ בּוֹ כִּי־לְגוֹי גָּדוֹל אֲשִׂימֶנּוּ :

19 וַיִּפְקַח אֱלֹהִים אֶת־עֵינֶיהָ וַתֵּרֶא בְּאֵר מָיִם וַתֵּלֶךְ וַתְּמַלֵּא אֶת־הַחֵמֶת מַיִם וַתַּשְׁקְ אֶת־הַנָּעַר :

20 וַיְהִי אֱלֹהִים אֶת־הַנַּעַר וַיִּגְדָּל וַיֵּשֶׁב בַּמִּדְבָּר וַיְהִי רֹבֶה קַשָּׁת :

21 וַיֵּשֶׁב בְּמִדְבַּר פָּארָן וַתִּקַּח־לוֹ אִמּוֹ אִשָּׁה מֵאֶרֶץ מִצְרָיִם :

💡 Language discovery

VERSE 14

וַיַּשְׁכֵּם אַבְרָהָם בַּבֹּקֶר

The verb וַיַּשְׁכֵּם is in the Hifil stem, which we will learn in the next unit. It is related to שְׁכֶם (shoulder). It is VC Imperfect 3ms. Can you analyse and translate the word בַּבֹּקֶר ?

וַיִּקַּח־לֶחֶם וְחֵמַת מַיִם

Can you parse וַיִּקַּח ? The word חֵמַת is in the construct form, thus *a container of water*.

וַיִּתֵּן אֶל־הָגָר

The verb וַיִּתֵּן is from נָתַן, which is irregular. Can you parse and translate it? The object pronoun (or pronominal suffix) that we might expect, i.e. a word for *them* referring to the bread and water, is absent. This is commonplace in Hebrew.

שָׂם עַל־שִׁכְמָהּ וְאֶת־הַיֶּלֶד וַיְשַׁלְּחֶהָ

The word שָׂם is either Perfect 3ms or Qal Participle from שִׂים; they are spelled the same. As שִׂים is a hollow verb, the Perfect 3ms is not the same as the citation form; can you remember which form of the hollow verb is found in dictionaries? Again, the pronoun or pronominal suffix is absent. The noun שִׁכְמָהּ has a pronominal suffix 3fs. וְאֶת־הַיֶּלֶד means *and the child.* Can you parse וַיְשַׁלְּחֶהָ?

וַתֵּתַע בְּמִדְבַּר בְּאֵר שָׁבַע

The verb וַתֵּתַע is VC Imperfect 3fs from תָּעָה and is a shortened (or apocopated) form: the final ה is missing. בְּמִדְבַּר is מִדְבָּר with the preposition בְּ and is in construct relationship to בְּאֵר שָׁבַע; how would you translate it?

VERSE 15

וַיִּכְלוּ הַמַּיִם מִן־הַחֵמֶת

The verb is VC Imperfect 3mp from כָּלָה. Why is it missing the ה from the root? This verb is plural because the word מַיִם (*water*) is dual in form and therefore takes a plural verb.

וַתַּשְׁלֵךְ אֶת־הַיֶּלֶד

It is easy to confuse שָׁלַךְ with שָׁלַח but this is the former, meaning *to throw*, and only occurs in the Hifil. The form וַתַּשְׁלֵךְ is Hifil VC Imperfect 3fs.

תַּחַת אַחַד הַשִּׂיחִם

The word אַחַד is in construct relationship to הַשִּׂיחִם; how would you translate it?

VERSE 16

וַתֵּלֶךְ וַתֵּשֶׁב לָהּ

What is the verbal root of וַתֵּלֶךְ? The phrse וַתֵּשֶׁב לָהּ means *and she sat down.*

הַרְחֵק כִּמְטַחֲוֵי קֶשֶׁת

The word הַרְחֵק is a Hifil Infinitive Absolute from רָחַק and means *far away.* The word כִּמְטַחֲוֵי is an unusual form called Pilel, which you do not need to learn at this stage, although it is worth mentioning that it functions like the Piel stem. It is a Participle from טָחָה with the prefix כְּ so it means *like shooters* and is in construct relationship to קֶשֶׁת. Therefore the whole phrase means literally *far away like shooters of a bow.* Can you improve on this translation?

כִּי אָמְרָה אַל־אֶרְאֶה בְּמוֹת הַיָּלֶד

The verb usually means *to say.* However, it is also used in the sense of *to think.* אָמְרָה is Perfect 3fs. בְּמוֹת is the construct form of מָוֶת with the preposition בְּ.

וַתִּשָּׂא אֶת־קֹלָהּ וַתֵּבְךְ

The verb is VC Imperfect of נָשָׂא; the initial נ is incorporated into the שׂ, which acquires a **dagesh**. קֹלָהּ is קוֹל with a pronominal suffix 3fs, and וַתֵּבְךְ is VC Imperfect 3fs from בָּכָה. As we have seen frequently, the verb is shortened because the final ה is missing.

VERSE 17

וַיִּשְׁמַע אֱלֹהִים אֶת־קוֹל הַנַּעַר

The verb וַיִּשְׁמַע is VC Imperfect 3ms from שָׁמַע. What is the relationship between קוֹל and הַנַּעַר? We have seen that נַעַר is often translated *young man* but in this passage it is used alongside יֶלֶד (*child*) to describe Hagar's son, and so we might better translate נַעַר as *boy* in this context.

וַיִּקְרָא מַלְאַךְ אֱלֹהִים

What is the verbal root of וַיִּקְרָא? The word מַלְאַךְ is in construct relationship to אֱלֹהִים and is therefore definite: *the angel*, rather than *an angel*, because אֱלֹהִים is definite. All names are definite.

מַה־לָּךְ הָגָר

Literally *What is to you, Hagar?*

אַל־תִּירְאִי

This is a Jussive 2fs because it is a prohibition. It is the weaker kind of Jussive; which particle would be used with a stronger prohibition?

כִּי־שָׁמַע אֱלֹהִים אֶל־קוֹל הַנַּעַר

The verb שָׁמַע used with the preposition אֶל means *to listen to*.

בַּאֲשֶׁר הוּא־שָׁם

Literally *in which he was there*. How would you improve on this?

VERSE 18

קוּמִי שְׂאִי אֶת־הַנַּעַר

There are two Imperatives here: קוּמִי and שְׂאִי; what are the verbal roots from which they derive? They are both feminine forms of the Imperative (see Unit 14) because Hagar is a woman.

וְהַחֲזִיקִי אֶת־יָדֵךְ בּוֹ

This verb is a Hifil Imperative (see Unit 18) and when used with the preposition בְּ it means *to hold*. אֶת־ is not the object marker here; what is it?

כִּי־לְגוֹי גָּדוֹל אֲשִׂימֶנּוּ

Literally *because for a nation a great I will make him*. The word אֲשִׂימֶנּוּ was seen in verse 13.

VERSE 19

וַיִּפְקַח אֱלֹהִים אֶת־עֵינֶיהָ

Can you parse וַיִּפְקַח? The word עֵינֶיהָ is the f dual of עַיִן; what is the pronominal suffix?

וַתֵּרֶא בְּאֵר מָיִם וַתֵּלֶךְ

The verb is VC Imperfect 3fs from רָאָה but why is the final **he** missing? Can you parse וַתֵּלֶךְ ?

וַתְּמַלֵּא אֶת־הַחֵמֶת מַיִם

The verb is Piel VC Imperfect 3fs from מָלֵא. This verb can have two objects: in this case the subject is *she* and the objects are *the container* and *water*. So we would not translate this phrase: *she filled the container of water* because חֵמֶת is not in construct relationship to מַיִם in this phrase. The only way to know this is to know that the construct form of חֵמֶת is הֵמַת. We can find this in a good dictionary. How should we translate this phrase?

וַתַּשְׁקְ אֶת־הַנָּעַר

Another Hifil form, and we will learn more about it in the next unit. Literally *and she caused the boy to drink*. How could you express this in grammatical English?

VERSE 20

וַיְהִי אֱלֹהִים אֶת־הַנַּעַר

The verb וַיְהִי is VC Imperfect 3ms from הָיָה. It often introduces a new story, and a traditional translation is *and it came to pass*, although that particular phrase is not used in everyday English. However, it is not introducing a story here. How would you translate it? אֶת־ here is, again, not the object marker; what is it?

וַיִּגְדָּל וַיֵּשֶׁב בַּמִּדְבָּר

Can you parse וַיִּגְדָּל ? The second verb וַיֵּשֶׁב is VC Imperfect 3ms from יָשַׁב (*to sit, dwell*). It is easy to confuse יָשַׁב and שׁוּב (*to return*), especially in Imperfect forms. For the record they are as follows:

Verb	VC Imperfect 3ms	Meaning
יָשַׁב	וַיֵּשֶׁב	*and he sat/lived*
שׁוּב	וַיָּשָׁב	*and he returned*

וַיְהִי רֹבֶה קַשָּׁת

Literally *and he became a shooter of bow*. What form is רֹבֶה ?

VERSE 21

וַיֵּשֶׁב בְּמִדְבַּר פָּארָן

The word בְּמִדְבַּר is in construct relationship to the word פָּארָן.

וַתִּקַּח־לוֹ אִמּוֹ אִשָּׁה

Literally *and she took for him his mother a wife*. How should this be translated into grammatical English?

מֵאֶרֶץ מִצְרָיִם

Simply *from the land of Egypt*. Remember that Hagar herself is described as an Egyptian.

176

POSSIBLE TRANSLATION

And Abraham got up early in the morning and took bread and a water container and gave them to Hagar, putting them on her shoulder, and the child, and he sent her away. And she went and wandered in the desert of Beersheba. And the water in the container was finished and she threw the child under one of the shrubs. And she went and she sat down opposite, a bow-shot's distance, because she thought, 'Let me not see the death of the child.' And she sat opposite and she lifted her voice and wept. And God heard the voice of the boy and the angel of God called to Hagar from heaven and he said to her, 'What is wrong with you, Hagar? Do not be afraid, for God has listened to the voice of the boy where he was. Get up, lift up the boy and hold him with your hand, for I will make him a great nation.' And God opened her eyes and she saw a well of water and she went and she filled the container with water and she gave the boy a drink. And God was with the boy, and he grew and he lived in the desert, and he became an archer. And he lived in the desert of Paran and his mother chose a wife for him from the land of Egypt.

Test yourself

1 Parse (analyse) the following words.

Example: פְּקָדוּהוּ Qal Perfect 3rd person masculine plural with suffix 3rd person masculine singular from פָּקַד; *they have visited him* (or simply Qal Perf 3ms + suff 3ms פָּקַד; *they have visited him*)

a וַיְקַלְלֵם _____

b אֲהַבְתָּנִי _____

c יִשְׁמָרְךָ _____

2 The word אֶדְרֹשׁ means *I will ask*. How would you write *let me ask*?

_____

3 Identify the stems of the following words.

a בִּקֵּשׁ _____

b הִתְבָּרְכוּ _____

c לֻקְחָתָּ _____

d אֲדַבֵּר _____

SELF-CHECK

I CAN...
○ recognize pronominal suffixes on verbs
○ identify cohortative forms
○ recognize verbs in the Piel, Pual and Hitpael stems
○ read and translate Genesis 21:14–21

18 Hifil, Hofal, and more about stems

In this unit you will learn about:
- ▶ the causative verbal stems Hifil and Hofal
- ▶ how to recognize verbs in all the stems

You will read:
- ▶ Genesis 22:1–6

Vocabulary builder

NOUNS

אֵשׁ	*fire* (m and f)
חֲמוֹר	*donkey*
עוֹלָה	*burnt offering* (f)
מַאֲכֶלֶת	*knife* (f)

VERBS

בָּקַע	Piel *to divide, split*
חָבַשׁ	*to bind, saddle* (an animal)
נגד	Hifil *to tell*
נסה	Piel *to test, try*
עָלָה	Qal *to go up*; Hifil *to offer*
שׁחה	Hitpael *to bow down, worship*

Note: verbs that do not exist in Qal are sometimes written without vowels in dictionaries or vocabulary lists.

OTHER

אַחַר	*after* (preposition)
יַחְדָּו	*together* (adverb)

יָחִיד	*only* (adjective)
מֵרָחֹק	*in the distance* (adverb)
עַד־כֹּה	*over there* (adverb)
פֹּה	*here* (adverb)

Grammar

VERBS: HIFIL AND HOFAL

The last two stems of the verb are known as the causatives. Just as Nifal is often understood as a passive version of Qal, and Piel is understood to intensify the verbal idea, so Hifil and Hofal introduce the idea of cause to the verbal idea. And just as Pual was the passive form of Piel, Hofal is the passive form of Hifil. The names come, like most of the other verb stem names, from what the Perfect 3ms of פָּעַל does in that stem. So the Hifil of פָּעַל is הִפְעִיל. Some verbs are found only in the Hifil stem, e.g. נגד *to tell*.

Here are some examples:

Verb		Qal	Hifil	Hofal
בּוֹא		*to come*	*to bring (to cause to come)*	*to be brought (to be caused to come)*
יָלַד		*to give birth*	*to beget (to cause to give birth)*	*to be born*
פָּקַד		*to visit*	*to appoint*	*to be appointed*
רוּם		*to be high*	*to raise, exalt (to cause to be high)*	*to be exalted (to be caused to be high)*
שׁוּב		*to return*	*to restore (to cause to return)*	*to be restored (to be caused to return)*

Like the other stems, the Hifil and Hofal can be found in any form: Perfect, Participle etc. The Hofal is much less common than Hifil, and there is no need to learn it thoroughly at this stage, but it may be helpful to have a short look at it. Hifil Perfects begin with הַ, while Hifil Imperfects have the usual prefixes, but pointed with **patach**. In some (though not all) parts of the verb an extra י is inserted between the second and third root letters.

Hifil Perfect

3ms	הִפְקִיד	*he has appointed*	3p	הִפְקִידוּ	*they have appointed*
3fs	הִפְקִידָה	*she has appointed*			
2ms	הִפְקַדְתָּ	*you have appointed*	2mp	הִפְקַדְתֶּם	*you have appointed*
2fs	הִפְקַדְתְּ	*you have appointed*	2fp	הִפְקַדְתֶּן	*you have appointed*
1s	הִפְקַדְתִּי	*I have appointed*	1p	הִפְקַדְנוּ	*we have appointed*

Hifil Imperfect

3ms	יַפְקִיד	*he will appoint*	3mp	יַפְקִידוּ	*they will appoint*
3fs	תַּפְקִיד	*she will appoint*	3fp	תַּפְקֵדְנָה	*they will appoint*
2ms	תַּפְקִיד	*you will appoint*	2mp	תַּפְקִידוּ	*you will appoint*
2fs	תַּפְקִידִי	*you will appoint*	2fp	תַּפְקֵדְנָה	*you will appoint*
1s	אַפְקִיד	*I will appoint*	1p	נַפְקִיל	*we will appoint*

Hifil Imperative ms

הַפְקֵד   *appoint!*

Hifil Infinitive Construct

Differs from the Imperative, unlike Qal and Piel:

הַפְקִיד   *to appoint*

Hifil Infinitive Absolute

הַפְקֵד   *appointing*

Hifil Participle

Participles in all stems except Qal and Nifal begin with מ.

מַפְקִיד   *appointing*

PRACTICE 1

Identify Hifil forms in the following phrases. The first two should be familiar from previous units and you can check the others by comparing with an English translation.

a	וַיַּשְׁכֵּם אַבְרָהָם בַּבֹּקֶר	(Genesis 21:14)
b	וַתַּשְׁלֵךְ אֶת־הַיֶּלֶד תַּחַת אַחַד הַשִּׂיחִם	(Genesis 21:15)
c	מִי הִגִּיד לְךָ כִּי עֵירֹם אָתָּה	(Genesis 3:11)
d	וּמִכַּף מֶלֶךְ־אַשּׁוּר אַצִּילְךָ	(Isaiah 38:6)
e	כֹּה הִרְאַנִי אֲדֹנָי יְהוִה	(Amos 8:1)
f	בִּנְאוֹת דֶּשֶׁא יַרְבִּיצֵנִי	(Psalm 23:2)
g	וַיַּזְעֵק וַיֹּאמֶר בְּנִינְוֵה מִטַּעַם הַמֶּלֶךְ	(Jonah 3:7)
h	אֲבִיאֲךָ אֶל־בֵּית אִמִּי	(Song of Songs 8:2)

HIFIL AND WEAK VERBS

Like the other stems, some changes can be found when weak verbs occur in Hifil stems. Roots with gutturals experience some vowel changes: for example, the Hifil Perfect 3ms of the guttural verb עָמַד cannot be הֶעְמִיד because the ע will not take a simple **sheva**. Instead it must take the composite **sheva**: עֲ. This e-type vowel attracts a **segol** underneath the ה of the Hifil. Therefore the Hifil Perfect 3ms is הֶעֱמִיד. Similarly, in III-guttural verbs we find a **patach** furtive in some forms: the Hifil Perfect 3ms of שָׁלַח is הִשְׁלִיחַ. The I-**yod** and **vav** verbs take a longer vowel than the usual ה of the Hifil, so the Hifil Perfect 3ms of יָשַׁב is הוֹשִׁיב and the Hifil Perfect 3ms of יָנַק is הֵינִיק. The נ of I-**nun** verbs is assimilated into the second root letter, which acquires a **dagesh**: the Hifil Perfect 3ms of נָגַשׁ is הִגִּישׁ. And the Hifil Perfects of the hollow verbs and the reduplicated verbs are formed with הֵ instead of ה, while the Imperfects are formed with **qamets**. So, for example the Hifil Perfect 3ms of קוּם is הֵקִים and the Hifil Perfect 2ms of סָבַב is הֵסֵב. The Hifil Imperfect 3ms of קוּם is יָקִים and of סָבַב is יָסֵב.

At a glance:

I-gutturals; III-gutturals	vowel changes (הֶ instead of ה; **patach** furtive)
I-**yod** and **vav** verbs	vowel lengthening: הוֹ or הֵי instead of ה
I-**nun** verbs	**nun** assimilated
Hollow and reduplicated verbs	vowel lengthening: הֵ instead of ה

HOFAL

We have seen that the Hofal is the passive form of Hifil. So Hofal is both causative and passive. Where Hifil indicates that something causes something to happen, Hofal indicates that something is caused to happen. It is much less common than Hifil, and there is no need at this stage to learn lists of verbal forms. However, it may be useful to know the five basic forms, also known as principal parts, of the Hofal. Here they are with Qal and Hifil for comparison:

Verb	Qal	Hifil	Hofal
Perfect 3ms	קָטַל	הִקְטִיל	הָקְטַל
Imperfect 3ms	יִקְטֹל	יַקְטִיל	יָקְטַל
Imperative 2ms	קְטֹל	הַקְטֵל	—
Infinitive Construct	קְטֹל	הַקְטִיל	הָקְטַל
Participle	קֹטֵל	מַקְטִיל	מָקְטָל

Notice that the first vowel in the Hofal forms is ָ. This is a short **qamets** rather than a long **qamets**, if your accent distinguishes between the two.

As with other stems, there are factors that help to determine whether a verb is Hifil or Hofal.

RECOGNIZING THE HIFIL

Perfect: Begins with הִ. Some forms have an extra י between the second and third root letters. E.g. הִקְטִילוּ

Imperfect: Vowel in prefix is ַ, e.g. אַקְטִיל

Imperative and Infinitives: Begin with הַ, e.g. הַקְטֵל (Imperative)

Participle: Begins with מַ, e.g. מַקְטִיל

RECOGNIZING THE HOFAL

Perfect: Begins with הָ, e.g. הָקְטַלְתִּי

Imperfect: Vowel in prefix is ָ ,e.g. אָקְטַל

Imperative: Does not exist

Infinitives: Begin with הָ, e.g. הָקְטַל (Infinitive Construct)

Participle: Begins with מָ, e.g. מָקְטַל

PRACTICE 2

We have encountered a number of Hifil forms in previous units. Here is a list of those we have seen before, and parsed (analysed). Can you give meanings for them? If you have a good memory, you may be able to remember their meanings from previous units, but it may still be useful to look at them carefully in order to understand their meanings.

a הוֹשַׁעְתָּנוּ (Unit 11)   Hifil Perf 2ms + suffix 1p יָשַׁע

b אוֹדְךָ (Unit 12)   Hifil Impf 1s + suff 2mp from ידה

c הֵינִיקָה (Unit 16)   Hifil Perf 3fs from יָנַק

d וְהַחֲזִיקִי (Unit 17)   Hifil Impv 2fs from חָזַק with simple **vav**

e וַתַּשְׁקְ (Unit 17)   Hifil VC Imperfect apocopated 3fs from שָׁקָה

RECOGNIZING THE STEMS

Identifying the Perfect in the various stems is not too difficult; usually there is some change to the consonants in the root that makes the stem obvious. The following table explains this in more detail.

Stem	Description	Example
Qal	—	קָטַל
Nifal	begins with נִ	נִקְטַל
Piel	**dagesh** in second root letter, first vowel ִ	קִטֵּל
Pual	**dagesh** in second root letter, first vowel ֻ	קֻטַּל
Hitpael	begins with הִתְ, **dagesh** in second root letter	הִתְקַטֵּל
Hifil	begins with הִ	יַקְטִיל
Hofal	begins with הָ	הָקְטַל

The Imperfect is a very common form in biblical Hebrew, and yet it can be one of the most difficult to identify or parse because the differences between the forms are more often differences in vowels than in consonants. The following table gives the clues to look for.

Stem	Description	Example
Qal	. vowel under prefix; ָ vowel under first root letter	יִקְטֹל
Nifal	. vowel under prefix; ָ vowel under first root letter	יִקָּטֵל
Piel	. vowel under prefix; _ vowel under first root letter	יְקַטֵּל
Pual	. vowel under prefix; ֻ vowel under first root letter	יְקֻטַּל
Hitpael	. vowel under prefix; _ vowel under first root letter	יִתְקַטֵּל
Hifil	_ vowel under prefix; ִ vowel under first root letter	יַקְטִיל
Hofal	ָ vowel under prefix; ָ vowel under first root letter	יָקְטַל

Although the tables are not necessarily reliable for weak verbs, once you know how to recognize verbs of the קָטַל type it will be easier to learn how and why the weak verbs deviate from the regular patterns.

OTHER STEMS

There are a few stems besides the seven we have learned. The first two are relatively common; the others are not.

Pilel/Polel: A version of Piel for reduplicated or hollow verbs, e.g. יְעוֹפֵף (Genesis 1:20) from עוּף

Pulal/Polal: A version of Pual for reduplicated or hollow verbs, e.g. חוֹלָלְתִּי (Proverbs 8:24) from חוּל

Pilpel: A version of Piel for reduplicated or hollow verbs, e.g. וַיְכַלְכֵּל (Genesis 47:12) from כּוּל

Hitpalel/Hitpolel: A version of Hithpael for reduplicated or hollow verbs, e.g. מִתְחוֹלֵל (Jeremiah 23:19) from חוּל; this example is a participle

Hitpalpel: Reflexive of Pilpel, e.g. יִשְׁתַּקְשְׁקוּן (Nahum 2:5 [Engl. 2:4]) from שָׁקַק; this example has a paragogic **nun** and exhibits metathesis because the root begins with a sibilant

Tifil: Very rare: תִּרְגַּלְתִּי (Hos 11:3) from רָגַל; probably causative

Hishtafel: Only used with the root חוה (see below: וְנִשְׁתַּחֲוֶה in Genesis 22:5), and apparently equivalent to Hitpalel, but this is debated. Other scholars say it is a metathesis of the Hitpalel of the root שׁחה

PRACTICE 3

Write out the principal parts of the following.

    a the Nifal of פָּקַד   **c** the Hifil of שָׁמַר

    b the Pual of קָטַל   **d** the Hofal of קָטַל

Reading

GENESIS 22:1–6

Points to look out for in this text:

▶ words we have already encountered

▶ verbs in causative stems.

1 וַיְהִי אַחַר הַדְּבָרִים הָאֵלֶּה וְהָאֱלֹהִים נִסָּה אֶת־אַבְרָהָם וַיֹּאמֶר אֵלָיו אַבְרָהָם
וַיֹּאמֶר הִנֵּנִי:

2 וַיֹּאמֶר קַח־נָא אֶת־בִּנְךָ אֶת־יְחִידְךָ אֲשֶׁר־אָהַבְתָּ אֶת־יִצְחָק וְלֶךְ־לְךָ אֶל־אֶרֶץ
הַמֹּרִיָּה וְהַעֲלֵהוּ שָׁם לְעֹלָה עַל אַחַד הֶהָרִים אֲשֶׁר אֹמַר אֵלֶיךָ:

3 וַיַּשְׁכֵּם אַבְרָהָם בַּבֹּקֶר וַיַּחֲבֹשׁ אֶת־חֲמֹרוֹ וַיִּקַּח אֶת־שְׁנֵי נְעָרָיו אִתּוֹ וְאֵת יִצְחָק בְּנוֹ
וַיְבַקַּע עֲצֵי עֹלָה וַיָּקָם וַיֵּלֶךְ אֶל־הַמָּקוֹם אֲשֶׁר־אָמַר־לוֹ הָאֱלֹהִים:

4 בַּיּוֹם הַשְּׁלִישִׁי וַיִּשָּׂא אַבְרָהָם אֶת־עֵינָיו וַיַּרְא אֶת־הַמָּקוֹם מֵרָחֹק:

5 וַיֹּאמֶר אַבְרָהָם אֶל־נְעָרָיו שְׁבוּ־לָכֶם פֹּה עִם־הַחֲמוֹר וַאֲנִי וְהַנַּעַר נֵלְכָה עַד־כֹּה
וְנִשְׁתַּחֲוֶה וְנָשׁוּבָה אֲלֵיכֶם:

6 וַיִּקַּח אַבְרָהָם אֶת־עֲצֵי הָעֹלָה וַיָּשֶׂם עַל־יִצְחָק בְּנוֹ וַיִּקַּח בְּיָדוֹ אֶת־הָאֵשׁ וְאֶת־
הַמַּאֲכֶלֶת וַיֵּלְכוּ שְׁנֵיהֶם יַחְדָּו:

💡 Language discovery

VERSE 1

וַיְהִי אַחַר הַדְּבָרִים הָאֵלֶּה

We saw the word וַיְהִי in Unit 8 and in Unit 17. Can you parse it? The construction הַדְּבָרִים הָאֵלֶּה should be familiar from Unit 6.

וְהָאֱלֹהִים נִסָּה אֶת־אַבְרָהָם

The subject comes before the verb here, which is often an indication of emphasis in biblical Hebrew. Can you identify the tense and stem of the verb?

וַיֹּאמֶר אֵלָיו אַבְרָהָם וַיֹּאמֶר הִנֵּנִי

The name אַבְרָהָם is the content of what is said: it is direct reported speech. The subject of the verb וַיֹּאמֶר is הָאֱלֹהִים. If Abraham were the subject we would expect to see his name directly after the verb, and if he were the object we would expect to see the object marker. However, in this context Abraham is being addressed by God. The word הִנֵּנִי is הִנֵּה with a pronominal suffix 1s. How would you translate it?

VERSE 2

וַיֹּאמֶר קַח־נָא אֶת־בִּנְךָ אֶת־יְחִידְךָ

The Imperative of לָקַח is קַח which is found here with the particle of entreaty נָא (the word for *please*). Why is the ל is absent in the Imperative of לָקַח? Which pronominal suffix do we find on בִּנְךָ and יָחִיד?

אֲשֶׁר־אָהַבְתָּ אֶת־יִצְחָק

Can you parse אָהַב? The relative pronoun אֲשֶׁר is probably best translated *whom*.

וְלֶךְ־לְךָ אֶל־אֶרֶץ הַמֹּרִיָּה וְהַעֲלֵהוּ שָׁם לְעֹלָה

The expression וְלֶךְ־לְךָ is similar to the phrase וַתֵּשֶׁב לָהּ which we saw in Genesis 21:16. לֵךְ is the Imperative of הָלַךְ, and the phrase means literally *go yourself*. Can you parse וְהַעֲלֵהוּ and identify the pronominal suffix? The noun עוֹלָה is related to the verb עָלָה, and with the preposition לְ it means *as a burnt offering*.

עַל אַחַד הֶהָרִים אֲשֶׁר אֹמַר אֵלֶיךָ

We have seen the number אֶחָד before. Here it is in construct form; can you identify it? We saw the word הַר in Unit 2 and הָרִים is the plural. Notice that the definite article is pointed with **segol** rather than with an *a* vowel as we might have expected. This is common when the definite article comes before a הָ sound. אֹמַר is the Imperfect 3ms of אָמַר; what does it mean? We are more used to seeing the VC Imperfect, which is slightly different in form.

VERSE 3

וַיַּשְׁכֵּם אַבְרָהָם בַּבֹּקֶר וַיַּחֲבֹשׁ אֶת־חֲמֹרוֹ

The first three words of this verse are identical to Genesis 21:14. Can you parse וַיַּשְׁכֵּם? The verb וַיַּחֲבֹשׁ is VC Imperfect 3ms from חָבַשׁ and the noun חֲמֹרוֹ has a pronominal suffix: can you identify it?

וַיִּקַּח אֶת־שְׁנֵי נְעָרָיו אִתּוֹ וְאֵת יִצְחָק בְּנוֹ

שְׁנֵי is the construct form of the dual word שְׁנַיִם meaning *two* (see Unit 8); what does it mean? אִתּוֹ is the preposition אֵת with a pronominal suffix and should not be confused with אֹתוֹ meaning *him*. The doubling of the ת in the preposition should help you to distinguish them (see Unit 9).

וַיְבַקַּע עֲצֵי עֹלָה

We saw the verb בָּקַע in Unit 17, where we translated it *to divide*, but it can also mean *to split*, as here where it refers to Abraham chopping the firewood. What stem is it? עֲצֵי is a plural construct form from עֵץ.

וַיָּקָם וַיֵּלֶךְ אֶל־הַמָּקוֹם אֲשֶׁר־אָמַר־לוֹ הָאֱלֹהִים

The first word is from קוּם and is VC Imperfect. Note that the last **qamets** is pronounced as a short **o**, so the whole word is pronounced **va-YĀ-kom**, although some accents do not distinguish between long **a** and short **o**. Do you remember what happens to hollow verbs in the VC Imperfect? The subject of אָמַר is הָאֱלֹהִים so the phrase means literally *which he said to him God*.

VERSE 4

בַּיּוֹם הַשְּׁלִישִׁי

The word הַשְּׁלִישִׁי means *third*. How would you translate the phrase?

וַיִּשָּׂא אַבְרָהָם אֶת־עֵינָיו

In Genesis 21 *Hagar lifted up her voice and wept*, which is an idiomatic expression in biblical Hebrew. Similarly, in biblical Hebrew people *lift their eyes and see*, which we could also understand as *looking up*.

וַיַּרְא אֶת־הַמָּקוֹם מֵרָחֹק

Can you parse וַיַּרְא?

VERSE 5

וַיֹּאמֶר אַבְרָהָם אֶל־נְעָרָיו

This phrase should be simple enough to translate. Remember that נְעָרָיו is a plural form with a pronominal suffix.

שְׁבוּ־לָכֶם פֹּה עִם־הַחֲמוֹר

This is direct speech. As you may have noticed, biblical Hebrew does not have punctuation equivalents to our quotation marks. The phrase שְׁבוּ־לָכֶם is very similar to וַתֵּשֶׁב לָהּ (Genesis 21:16) and לֶךְ־לְךָ (above, verse 2). שְׁבוּ is a masculine plural Imperative from יָשַׁב; we have looked mainly at masculine singular Imperatives but feminine and plural forms were addressed in Unit 14. However, since יָשַׁב is a weak verb the י drops out in the Imperative: it has an Imperative formed like קַח and לֵךְ, from לָקַח and הָלַךְ respectively. How would you translate this?

וַאֲנִי וְהַנַּעַר נֵלְכָה עַד־כֹּה

The verb נֵלְכָה is an Imperfect 1p from הָלַךְ. We might have expected נֵלֵךְ (since הָלַךְ behaves like a **pe yod** verb in the Imperfect). This word, however, has an extra ה (sometimes called a paragogic ה), which may have made it easier to pronounce before עַד־כֹּה.

וְנִשְׁתַּחֲוֶה וְנָשׁוּבָה אֲלֵיכֶם

These two verbs are Imperfects. The first verb, וְנִשְׁתַּחֲוֶה, is either a Hishtafel or a Hitpalel, depending on whose opinion you are more convinced by – but that decision may be deferred for now. If it is a Hitpael, it demonstrates metathesis. Here is another example of metathesis:

Qal Perfect 3ms		Hitpael Perfect 3ms	
שָׁמַר	he guarded	הִשְׁתַּמֵּר	he guarded himself
סָתַר	he hid (something)	הִסְתַּתֵּר	he hid himself

The second verb is Qal Impf 1p with an extra (paragogic) ה, from שׁוּב. Notice the pointing on each נ; it is a **sheva** rather than an *a* vowel. This means the verbs are not Vav Consecutive, so how would you translate them?

VERSE 6

וַיִּקַּח אַבְרָהָם אֶת־עֲצֵי הָעֹלָה

This phrase should be fairly simple to translate. The verb is VC Imperfect 3ms.

וַיָּשֶׂם עַל־יִצְחָק בְּנוֹ

The verb is VC Imperfect 3ms from שִׂים. The word עַל is a preposition and בְּנוֹ is the noun בֵּן with a pronominal suffix 3ms.

וַיִּקַּח בְּיָדוֹ אֶת־הָאֵשׁ וְאֶת־הַמַּאֲכֶלֶת

The subject of the verb is still Abraham. בְּיָדוֹ is the preposition בְּ, the noun יָד and the pronominal suffix 3ms. How would you translate this phrase?

וַיֵּלְכוּ שְׁנֵיהֶם יַחְדָּו

The verb is VC Imperfect 3mp. שְׁנֵיהֶם is the number שְׁנַיִם with a pronominal suffix 3mp and means *both*.

POSSIBLE TRANSLATION

And it came to pass (it happened) after these events (these things) God tested Abraham and he said to him, 'Abraham.' And he said, 'Behold me (Here I am).' And he said, 'Please take your only son Isaac, whom you love, and go to the land of Moriah and offer him up there as a burnt offering upon one of the mountains which I will tell you about.' And Abraham got up early in the morning and saddled his donkey and he took two of his young men with him, and Isaac his son. And he chopped wood for the sacrifice and he got up and went to the place about which God had told him. On the third day Abraham looked up and he saw the place in the distance. And Abraham said to his young men, 'Sit you down here (stay here) with the donkey and (whilst) I and the boy go further on that we might worship (lit. and we will worship) and we will return to you.' And Abraham took the wood for the burnt offering and he put it on Isaac his son but he himself carried the fire and the knife, and the two of them went on together.

Test yourself

1 Translate the following into English.

   a אָקִים

   b אָשִׁיב

   c יָבִיא

   d הֵבֵאתָ

   e הֻגַּד

2 Parse the following.

   a הִשְׁלַחְתָּ

   b מֵבִיא

   c הוּשַׁב

   d מֵשִׁיב

   e מוֹשִׁיב

SELF-CHECK

I CAN...

○ translate verbs in the Hifil and Hofal stems

○ identify stems according to their characteristics

○ read and translate Genesis 22:1–6

19

Dictionaries and lexicons, commentaries, and the Dead Sea Scrolls

In this unit you will learn about:
▶ how biblical Hebrew dictionaries and lexicons work
▶ ancient commentaries on biblical texts
▶ the Habakkuk **pesher** from the Dead Sea Scrolls

You will read:
▶ Genesis 22:7–12

Vocabulary builder

NOUNS

חֹק	*ordinance, law* (cstr. mp חֻקֵּי)
כַּשְׂדִּים	*Chaldeans (a nation)*
כִּתִּיִּים	*Kittim (a nation; there are various spellings of the Hebrew)*
מַאֲכֶלֶת	*knife* (f)
מִזְבֵּחַ	*altar*
מִלְחָמָה	*battle* (f)
מֶמְשֶׁלֶת	*dominion, reign* (f)
פֵּשֶׁר	*interpretation*

VERBS

אָבַד	*to die*; Piel *to destroy*
אָמַן	*to support*; Hif *to trust, rely on*
חָשַׂךְ	*to hold back, restrain, withhold*
יָרַשׁ	*to inherit, take possession*
לָחַם	*to fight*
מָהַר	*to be quick*

מָרַר	*to be bitter*
קוּם	*to arise*; Hif *to raise*
עָקַד	*to tie, bind*
עָרַךְ	*to arrange in order*
רָחַב	*to be wide*; Hif *to expand*
שָׁכַן	*to lie down, rest, inhabit*

OTHER

אַיֵּה	*where?* (interrogative adverb)
גִּבּוֹר	*strong, mighty* (adjective)
הִנְנִי, הִנֶּנִּי, הִנֵּנִי	הִנֵּה + suffix 1cs (demonstrative)
מְאוּמָה	*anything* (pronoun)
מַעַל	*above* (preposition)
מַר	*bitter* (adjective)
עַתָּה	*now* (adverb)

Grammar

DICTIONARIES AND LEXICONS

The work we have done on texts so far has included vocabulary lists, but of course when you come to read other passages in the Bible you will need to look up unknown words yourself. There are two kinds of books for looking up words in biblical Hebrew: lexicons and dictionaries. Anyone who wishes to read the biblical texts in Hebrew will need to be able to use a dictionary or lexicon. Since using a Hebrew–English dictionary is rather more complicated than using, say, a Spanish–English dictionary, we will look at some of the complexities.

Dictionaries tend to give definitions of words as well as examples of usage. Lexicons tend to offer grammatical analysis and sometimes definitions. For biblical Hebrew both are useful.

Problems faced by beginners include remembering the order of the alphabet, figuring out how the vowels fit into this order, and finding the exact combination of vowels and consonants that we are looking for.

Fortunately there are only a few words in biblical Hebrew that use exactly the same consonants as other words. And since vowels are used in dictionaries and lexicons of biblical Hebrew, there is an order to the vowels as well. So if you look up שְׁמֹר (Qal Impv ms or Qal Inf Cstr) you will find it somewhere between שָׁמֹר (Qal Inf Abs) and שֹׁמֵר (Qal Ptc ms). But if you look up אֶשְׁמֹר there will be no such problem because no other word in biblical Hebrew is spelled with the consonants אשמר. The majority of words in biblical Hebrew have unique consonantal spellings, so the task is simpler than we might have expected. So in a dictionary you might see the following list:

שֶׁמְּקָרֶה

שָׁמַּר

שָׁמַר

שָׁמֵר

שָׁמֹר

שְׁמֹר

שָׁמֵר

שֹׁמֵר

שָׁמְרָה

There are seven words in this list with the same consonants but different vowels. You are unlikely to encounter a set of consonants with more than seven vowel possibilities. If you are looking up שָׁמֹר you should be able to find it without problems. Can you find it in the list?

Although the order of the vowels in a lexicon is not usually a problem, it is important to remember that some vowels are written with consonants: יִ and יֵ and וֹ and וּ. In a dictionary or lexicon these consonants are treated as full consonants rather than as mere vowel-placers. For example, in words with a וֹ vowel (e.g. שָׁמוֹר), the Vav will be treated as a consonant, but where **holem** is written without Vav (e.g. שָׁמֹר) it will be treated as a vowel. This means that you will not find שָׁמוֹר next to שָׁמֹר even though they are essentially the same word: they are pronounced the same way and mean the same thing (they are both Qal Inf Abs from שָׁמַר). Instead you will find שָׁמוֹר between שְׁמוּעָה and שֵׁמוֹת, which are both spelled with וֹ:

שְׁמוּעָה

שָׁמוֹר

שֵׁמוֹת

Some dictionaries and lexicons have the majority of derivations listed after the root they come from. For example:

שָׁמַר

QAL Impf 3ms יִשְׁמֹר, Inf שְׁמֹר, Impv ms שְׁמֹר, Ptc שֹׁמֵר: *to hedge about, to guard, to watch, to keep*. NIFAL Perf נִשְׁמַר, Impf הִשָּׁמֵר: *to be kept*. PIEL Ptc מְשַׁמֵּר: *to worship, to honour*. HITPAEL הִשְׁתַּמֵּר: *to observe*.

This is a good basic indication of the meanings of שָׁמַר in the various verbal stems that we might encounter in biblical Hebrew. This is fine if we can work out which root a word comes from, and often it is straightforward enough. If we want to look up the word יִקְטֹל we can probably guess that it is an Imperfect from קָטַל and look up קָטַל to find the meaning.

But it might be less obvious in other cases.

PRACTICE 1

These words can be found in previous units of this course. Which roots do they come from?

a וַיִּשָּׂא

b וַיָּשֶׂם

c נָתַתִּי

d וַיַּעַשׂ

e קַח

A lexicon can help in these cases. In an analytical lexicon you will be able to look up any word in exactly the form in which it appears in the text. Note, however, that a great many words begin with the definite article הּ or the conjunction וּ, or even both. It is generally assumed that you can recognize these and that you do not need to look up הַמֶּלֶךְ under הּ or וַיִּשְׁמֹר under וּ. Look them up under מ and י respectively.

There are some disadvantages to using an analytical lexicon. Meanings are not usually given for each and every form; it usually points you to the root instead, so you may need to look up the root to understand the meaning.

For example

יִשְׁתַּמֵּר   Hit Impf 3ms שָׁמַר

The explanation means: Hitpael Imperfect 3rd person masculine singular from the root שָׁמַר.

If you look up שָׁמַר you will see that the Hitpael means *to observe*. Next, you need to determine how to translate Impf 3ms. 3ms is effectively *he*, and Imperfect is frequently translated with an English future tense. So the Hit Impf 3ms is likely to mean *he will observe*.

Look at the abbreviations on the first page of the lexicon to ensure you understand the analysis of the forms. Bear in mind that there can sometimes be grey areas. For example, some dictionaries might say that שֹׁמֵר is a noun; others might say it is a Qal participle. Participles are often used as nouns (see Unit 14), so in context it could be either.

In addition to listing all forms in alphabetical order, analytical lexicons will often list some of the most common forms under a main entry. Here is an example:

אֱנַשׁ	verb	*to be mortal*
אֲנָשִׁים	noun mp	*men*
אַנְשֵׁי	noun mp cstr	*men of*
אִשָּׁה	noun fs	*woman*
אֵשֶׁת	noun fs cstr	*woman of, wife of*
נָשִׁים	noun fp	*women*
נְשֵׁי	noun fp cstr	*women of*
אִשְׁתּוֹ	noun fs + suff 3ms	*his wife*

The words will usually be listed separately in alphabetical order, so that for example you could find נָשִׁים and נְשֵׁי under נ.

PRACTICE 2

Look up the following words in a lexicon and give the form, root and meaning, following the examples.

Examples:

Word	Form	Root	Meaning
דְּבָרֶיךָ	noun ms + suff 2ms	דָּבָר	*your words*
בַּדֶּרֶךְ	prep בְּ + noun ms	דֶּרֶךְ	*in the way/path*
וְהַמֶּלֶךְ	conj וֹ + def art + noun ms	מֶלֶךְ	*and the king*
פָּקַדְתִּי	Piel Perf 1s	פָּקַד	*I have mustered*
וַתִּשְׁלַח	Qal Impf 2ms	שָׁלַח	*and you sent/stretched out*

Word		Form	Root	Meaning
נוֹדַע	Unit 6			
וְהַנּוֹרָא	Unit 9			
מְבֹרָךְ	Unit 10			
וּתְנַחֲמֵנִי	Unit 12			
אֲסַפְּרָה	Unit 13			
נִפְלָאוֹתֶיךָ	Unit 13			
אֲזַמְּרָה	Unit 13			
יִכָּשְׁלוּ	Unit 13			
אִבַּדְתָּ	Unit 13			
כּוֹנֵן	Unit 13			
וְנִפְקְחוּ	Unit 14			
דִּבֶּר	Unit 15			
הַנּוֹלָד	Unit 15			
צִוָּה	Unit 15			
בְּהִוָּלֶד	Unit 15			
מִלֵּל	Unit 16			
גֵּרֵשׁ	Unit 16			

COMMENTARIES

Sometimes looking up words in a dictionary is not quite enough to grasp the sense of the text. There are points where the grammar seems unusual or the words do not appear to fit together coherently. Some passages have puzzled readers for centuries; other passages are sometimes seen as ambiguous and readers have debated their true meaning.

Commentaries are books that discuss the meaning of the biblical text. They often confine themselves to one or two books of the Bible: for example a commentary on Genesis or a commentary on Ezra and Nehemiah. There are some commentaries on the whole Bible, but they tend to be less detailed than commentaries on single books.

Interpreting the text is an ancient phenomenon. We can see this in one of the most significant archaeological finds of the 20th century: the Dead Sea Scrolls. Some of the scrolls are biblical texts; some are other writings, including interpretive scrolls known as **pesharim** (**pesher** means *interpretation*). It is widely believed that the scrolls were written about 2,000 years ago, and the story of their discovery is legendary. They were found by shepherds in 1947 in a cave near the Dead Sea, just as Palestine was on the verge of being partitioned prior to the decision to create the state of Israel. One of the first three scrolls found in the caves was a **pesher**, or commentary, on the biblical book of Habakkuk. Here is an example of the kind of commentary practised centuries ago.

First, the text of Habakkuk 1:6 as we find it in the Hebrew Bible:

כִּי־הִנְנִי מֵקִים אֶת־הַכַּשְׂדִּים הַגּוֹי הַמַּר וְהַנִּמְהָר לָמֶרְחֲבֵי־אֶרֶץ לָרֶשֶׁת מִשְׁכָּנוֹת לֹא־לוֹ:

Translation:

For behold, I am raising up the Chaldeans, the bitter and impetuous nation, to expand across the earth and to seize dwellings that do not belong to them.

Let's break it down.

כִּי־הִנְנִי מֵקִים אֶת־הַכַּשְׂדִּים

For behold, I am raising up the Chaldeans

According to Genesis 22:22, Kesed (כֶּשֶׂד) is a son of Nahor, Abraham's brother. He is the ancestor of the Chaldeans. The Chaldeans were the people who lived in Babylon.

הַגּוֹי הַמַּר וְהַנִּמְהָר

the nation the bitter and the impetuous.

The word מַר is an adjective from מָרַר. The word נִמְהָר is a Nif Ptc from מָהַר.

לָמֶרְחֲבֵי־אֶרֶץ

to expand (on) the earth

The word לָמֶרְחֲבֵי is the preposition לְ + Hif Inf Cstr from רָחַב.

לָרֶשֶׁת

Qal Inf Cstr from יָרַשׁ. Remember that infinitive constructs of I-י verbs are often monosyllabic: they lose the initial י.

מִשְׁכָּנוֹת

dwellings

noun fp from שָׁכַן. This noun often means *the temple* or *the sacred dwelling place of God*.

לֹא־לוֹ

not to him

The preposition לְ is used here to indicate possession. The suffix is 3ms rather than 3mp because it agrees grammatically with הַגּוֹי, which is ms. However, in English we would probably say *to them*.

From this vantage point we can look at the Habakkuk **pesher**. In column 2 we find:

line 10	יא הנני מקים את...
line 11	הר ... הכשדאים הגוי המ
line 12	פשרו על הכתיאים א... ה קלים וגבורים
line 13	במלחמה לאבד רכימ ... בממשלת
line 14	הכתיאים ירש...ת ולוא יאמינו
line 15	ל ... בְחוקי...

It looks rather daunting at first. There are no vowels, there seem to be chunks of text missing (indicated by dots above), and even when we spot words we think we recognize they appear to be spelled differently. But if we place the text of the Hebrew Bible alongside the **pesher**, we should be able to spot a few similarities. Words in square brackets indicate material that is absent in the scroll. The scrolls are ancient and have been damaged, and there are many gaps in the text. However, there is also much that is thoroughly legible.

line 10	יא הנני מקים את
Hab	כִּי־הִנְנִי מֵקִים אֶת־

There seems to be a כ missing at the beginning of line 10, and an extra א in the word כי. Sometimes when words are spelled with an extra א it indicates that the text has been influenced by Aramaic spellings. Otherwise, the words of the **pesher** seem to correspond to the biblical text.

line 11	הר ...... הכשדאים הגוי המ
Hab	הַכַּשְׂדִּים הַגּוֹי הַמַּר וְהַנִּמְהָר

There are some missing letters where the scroll is torn, but nevertheless the phrase seems to be identical to the Hebrew Bible, although notice another extra א in הכשדאים.

line 12	פשרו על הכתיאים א... ה קלים וגבורים

The quotation from Habakkuk has now finished, and the commentary begins. As there are no vowels, it is difficult for a beginner to read without help. But using the vocabulary at the beginning of the unit you may be able to make some sense of it.

As in כשדאים, there is also an extra א in Kittim. So we get:

Its interpretation is concerning the Kittim [...] fast and strong

line 13   במלחמה לאבד רכימ ... בממשלת

in battle to destroy [...], under the reign of

line 14   הכתיאים ירש ...ת ולוא יאמינו

the Kittim [...] and they will not trust

line 15   בחוקי ... ל

in the laws of [...]

There are quite a few gaps in our translation. So far our translation of the column reads:

[For] behold, I am raising up the Chaldeans, the [bitter and impetuous] nation. Its interpretation is concerning the Kittim [...] fast and strong in battle to destroy [...]; under the reign of the Kittim [...] and not trust in the laws of [...]

Some scholars have attempted to fill in some of the blanks, based on their knowledge of related texts and their ability to estimate how much space the missing words would have taken up. Based on their work, we can extrapolate that the text may have said something like the following:

[For] behold, I am raising up the Chaldeans, the [bitter and impetuous] nation. Its interpretation is concerning the Kittim [who are] fast and strong in battle to destroy [many people]. Under the reign of the Kittim [they will turn away from the way of the covenant] and not trust in the laws of [God.]

You will notice that the writer of the **pesher** interprets the prophecy about the Chaldeans as a reference to the Kittim. The next question, of course, is the identity of the Kittim. The name is used in biblical Hebrew to refer to peoples of the northern Mediterranean. Many scholars consider that the Kittim mentioned in the Habakkuk **pesher** are the Romans, based on the details of the comments and the dating of the scrolls. The interesting thing is that the **pesher** takes an old prophecy and gives it a fresh twist. Unfortunately, there is no space here to discuss the **pesher** at length, but this example at least demonstrates how ancient the tradition of biblical commentary is.

Modern commentaries usually fall into three categories. There are commentaries that seek to comment on devotional matters, commentaries that aim to comment on scholarly matters, and commentaries that try to do both. Some commentaries are written from a particular theological perspective and can be located within a particular tradition. For example, there are Catholic commentaries, Presbyterian commentaries and Jewish commentaries. Many people feel that it is important to look at commentaries from their own tradition, and readers in that position might like to consult a trusted community leader for suggestions and advice.

One aspect of commentary that is particularly useful for learners of Hebrew is a discussion of the grammar and translation of the text. Some commentaries do not discuss the Hebrew text at all. While such commentaries may be useful in many ways, they will not usually be very helpful in understanding the Hebrew. If you can find a commentary that discusses the meaning and interpretation of the Hebrew text you will find it easier to grasp what is at stake in contested, difficult or ambiguous passages.

PRACTICE 3

Look up unknown forms in a lexicon.

This is Genesis 22:7–9. Having looked up the words you did not recognize, check with the comments to see if you were right.

וַיֹּאמֶר יִצְחָק אֶל־אַבְרָהָם אָבִיו וַיֹּאמֶר אָבִי וַיֹּאמֶר הִנֶּנִּי בְנִי וַיֹּאמֶר הִנֵּה הָאֵשׁ וְהָעֵצִים
וְאַיֵּה הַשֶּׂה לְעֹלָה:

וַיֹּאמֶר אַבְרָהָם אֱלֹהִים יִרְאֶה־לּוֹ הַשֶּׂה לְעֹלָה בְּנִי וַיֵּלְכוּ שְׁנֵיהֶם יַחְדָּו:

וַיָּבֹאוּ אֶל־הַמָּקוֹם אֲשֶׁר אָמַר־לוֹ הָאֱלֹהִים וַיִּבֶן שָׁם אַבְרָהָם אֶת־הַמִּזְבֵּחַ וַיַּעֲרֹךְ אֶת־
הָעֵצִים וַיַּעֲקֹד אֶת־יִצְחָק בְּנוֹ וַיָּשֶׂם אֹתוֹ עַל־הַמִּזְבֵּחַ מִמַּעַל לָעֵצִים:

Reading

GENESIS 22:7–12

Points to look out for in this text:

▶ forms of weak verbs
▶ pronominal suffixes
▶ Jussive forms.

7   וַיֹּאמֶר יִצְחָק אֶל־אַבְרָהָם אָבִיו וַיֹּאמֶר אָבִי וַיֹּאמֶר הִנֶּנִּי בְנִי וַיֹּאמֶר הִנֵּה הָאֵשׁ
        וְהָעֵצִים וְאַיֵּה הַשֶּׂה לְעֹלָה:

8   וַיֹּאמֶר אַבְרָהָם אֱלֹהִים יִרְאֶה־לּוֹ הַשֶּׂה לְעֹלָה בְּנִי וַיֵּלְכוּ שְׁנֵיהֶם יַחְדָּו:

9   וַיָּבֹאוּ אֶל־הַמָּקוֹם אֲשֶׁר אָמַר־לוֹ הָאֱלֹהִים וַיִּבֶן שָׁם אַבְרָהָם אֶת־הַמִּזְבֵּחַ וַיַּעֲרֹךְ
        אֶת־הָעֵצִים וַיַּעֲקֹד אֶת־יִצְחָק בְּנוֹ וַיָּשֶׂם אֹתוֹ עַל־הַמִּזְבֵּחַ מִמַּעַל לָעֵצִים:

10   וַיִּשְׁלַח אַבְרָהָם אֶת־יָדוֹ וַיִּקַּח אֶת־הַמַּאֲכֶלֶת לִשְׁחֹט אֶת־בְּנוֹ:

11   וַיִּקְרָא אֵלָיו מַלְאַךְ יְהוָה מִן הַשָּׁמַיִם וַיֹּאמֶר אַבְרָהָם אַבְרָהָם וַיֹּאמֶר הִנֵּנִי:

12   וַיֹּאמֶר אַל־תִּשְׁלַח יָדְךָ אֶל־הַנַּעַר וְאַל־תַּעַשׂ לוֹ מְאוּמָה כִּי עַתָּה יָדַעְתִּי כִּי־יְרֵא
      אֱלֹהִים אַתָּה וְלֹא חָשַׂכְתָּ אֶת־בִּנְךָ אֶת־יְחִידְךָ מִמֶּנִּי:

💡 Language discovery

VERSE 7

וַיֹּאמֶר יִצְחָק אֶל־אַבְרָהָם אָבִיו וַיֹּאמֶר אָבִי

Most of this phrase should be familiar territory. אָבִיו is an irregular noun with a pronominal suffix 3ms; can you translate it? If in doubt, see Unit 4 where the plurals of irregular nouns are given.

וַיֹּאמֶר הִנֶּנִּי בְנִי

The word הִנֶּנִּי is הִנֵּה with pronominal suffix 1s and could be translated *behold me* but as in verse 1 it might be better translated *here I am* or even *yes*. Can you identify the suffix on בְנִי and translate the word?

וַיֹּאמֶר הִנֵּה הָאֵשׁ וְהָעֵצִים וְאַיֵּה הַשֶּׂה לְעֹלָה

This phrase should be fairly straightforward. Remember that וְ can mean *but*.

VERSE 8

אֱלֹהִים יִרְאֶה־לּוֹ הַשֶּׂה לְעֹלָה בְּנִי

The verb יִרְאֶה is Imperfect 3ms of רָאָה, which often means *to see* but can also mean *to provide*, as in this context. The use of the preposition לְ with a pronominal suffix is another construction like וַתֵּשֶׁב לָהּ in Genesis 21:16. Can you offer a translation of the phrase?

וַיֵּלְכוּ שְׁנֵיהֶם יַחְדָּו

This is the same as the last three words of verse 6.

VERSE 9

וַיָּבֹאוּ אֶל־הַמָּקוֹם אֲשֶׁר אָמַר־לוֹ הָאֱלֹהִים

The first verb is the VC Impf 3mp of בּוֹא. It is a weak verb; can you identify in what way it is weak? We could translate אֲשֶׁר as *about which* or *where*; the phrase is literally: *to the place which he said to him God*. How would you improve on this?

וַיִּבֶן שָׁם אַבְרָהָם אֶת־הַמִּזְבֵּחַ וַיַּעֲרֹךְ אֶת־הָעֵצִים

The verb וַיִּבֶן is VC Imperfect 3ms shortened (apocopated) from בָּנָה. Remember that many III-ה verbs lose the final ה in the VC 3ms form. The word שָׁם is an adverb; we saw it in Unit 10. וַיַּעֲרֹךְ is VC Impf 3ms from עָרַךְ.

וַיַּעֲקֹד אֶת־יִצְחָק בְּנוֹ

This story is sometimes known as the Aqedah or Akedah: the binding. The name comes from the verb עָקַד; can you identify the tense, person, gender and number of this verbal form? בְּנוֹ is the noun בֵּן with pronominal suffix 3ms.

וַיָּשֶׂם אֹתוֹ עַל־הַמִּזְבֵּחַ מִמַּעַל לָעֵצִים

The verb וַיָּשֶׂם is VC Impf 3ms from שִׂים. Can you explain the pattern of Imperfects of this kind of weak verb? The word אֹתוֹ is an object pronoun (see Unit 15). The phrase מִמַּעַל לָעֵצִים is literally: *above to the wood*. How would you improve on this?

VERSE 10

וַיִּשְׁלַח אַבְרָהָם אֶת־יָדוֹ

The verb שָׁלַח can mean *to send* or *to stretch out*. The second meaning is probably more appropriate here. Can you explain why this VC Impf 3ms has a **patach** instead of a **holem** under the middle root letter? Can you explain the word order in this clause? What kind of suffix does the noun יָד have here?

וַיִּקַּח אֶת־הַמַּאֲכֶלֶת לִשְׁחֹט אֶת־בְּנוֹ

The verb וַיִּקַּח is VC Impf 3ms from לָקַח; remember that לָקַח behaves like a I- י verb in the Imperfect. The word לִשְׁחֹט is the Infinitive Construct of שָׁחַט. How would you translate these verbs?

VERSE 11

וַיִּקְרָא אֵלָיו מַלְאַךְ יְהוָה מִן־הַשָּׁמַיִם

The verb וַיִּקְרָא is VC Impf 3ms from קָרָא. How would you translate the וֹ here? אֵלָיו is the preposition אֶל with a pronominal suffix; can you identify which one? If in doubt see Unit 9. On the basis that a construct noun's definiteness depends on the definiteness of the word with which it is in a construct relationship, how would you translate מַלְאַךְ יְהוָה?

וַיֹּאמֶר אַבְרָהָם אַבְרָהָם וַיֹּאמֶר הִנֵּנִי

At first glance it may be difficult to discern the subject of וַיֹּאמֶר. We are becoming used to seeing the verb וַיֹּאמֶר followed by the subject. However, it does not really make sense here for the subject of וַיֹּאמֶר to be אַבְרָהָם. The subject of the verb is more likely the angel, and the word וַיֹּאמֶר is followed by direct speech. How would you translate הִנֵּנִי?

VERSE 12

וַיֹּאמֶר אַל־תִּשְׁלַח יָדְךָ אֶל־הַנַּעַר

The subject of the verb is the angel again. He issues a prohibition: אַל־תִּשְׁלַח. What do we call this kind of second-person prohibition? How would you translate it? The preposition אֶל often means *to* but when used with שָׁלַח it can mean *against*. In biblical Hebrew, *to stretch out one's hand against* is an idiomatic way of saying *to injure* or *to harm*.

וְאַל־תַּעַשׂ לוֹ מְאוּמָה

This is another prohibition: תַּעַשׂ is 2ms from עָשָׂה and is often shortened: the final ה disappears. How would you translate אַל־תַּעַשׂ?

כִּי עַתָּה יָדַעְתִּי כִּי־יְרֵא אֱלֹהִים אַתָּה

The first כִּי here is used in the sense of *because*; the second כִּי means *that*. עַתָּה is the word for *now* and should not be confused with אַתָּה meaning *you* (also found in this phrase). יָדַעְתִּי is straightforward; can you parse it? The verb יְרֵא is a participle from יָרֵא. It is doubly weak because it is both I-י and III-א, and so does not have the characteristic vowel pattern of the Participle (see Unit 14). Literally it could mean *you are fearing God* or *you are a fearer of God* but neither phrase is ideal in English. How would you translate it?

וְלֹא חָשַׂכְתָּ אֶת־בִּנְךָ אֶת־יְחִידְךָ מִמֶּנִּי

The phrase וְלֹא חָשַׂכְתָּ might look like a Jussive after the Jussives earlier in this verse. However, it is not. Can you explain why not? The conjunction וֹ can sometimes mean *because*. The phrase אֶת־בִּנְךָ אֶת־יְחִידְךָ was found in verse 2. The word מִמֶּנִּי is a preposition מִן with a pronominal suffix; can you identify it?

POSSIBLE TRANSLATION

And Isaac said to Abraham his father, 'Father,' and he said, 'Yes, my son?' And he said 'I see the fire and the wood, but where is the lamb for the sacrifice?' And Abraham said, 'God himself will provide the lamb for the offering, my son.' So the two of them went on together. When they came to the place that God had told him, Abraham built the altar there and he laid the wood. He bound Isaac his son and placed him on the altar above the wood. Abraham stretched out his hand and took the knife to slaughter his son. But the angel of Yhwh spoke to him from heaven and he said, 'Abraham, Abraham.' And he said, 'Here I am.' And he said, 'Do not injure the boy, and do not do anything to him, for now I know that you fear God because you did not hold back your only son from me.'

Test yourself

1   List the following words in alphabetical order.

נֶעֱרְתָי נָסַבּוּ נֻפַּח נַעֲשֶׂה נַעֲשִׂים נַפְשֶׁךָ נַפְשִׁי נֶעֱבָד נְמֵרִים נָפוּץ

_____

2   Give an analysis for each word above: parse the verbs, determine the gender and number of the nouns, indicate wherever there is a pronominal suffix, etc. Use a lexicon to help with this task.

_____

_____

3   Now translate each of the words into English.

_____

_____

SELF-CHECK

I CAN...
understand the main uses of dictionaries and lexicons for biblical Hebrew
choose appropriate commentaries for use with biblical Hebrew
read and translate a portion of the Habakkuk **pesher**
read and translate Genesis 22:7–12

20 *Translations, scribal errors, accents and cantillation marks*

In this unit you will learn about:
▶ ancient translations of the biblical texts
▶ how scribes have addressed problems in the texts
▶ how accents and cantillation marks indicate the stress in Hebrew words

You will read:
▶ Genesis 22:13–20

Vocabulary builder

NOUNS

אֹיֵב	*enemy*
אַיִל	*ram*
אֲרִי	*lion*
בְּאֵר שֶׁבַע	*Beersheba* (name)
בַּר	*son* (Aramaic; equiv. of Hebrew בֵּן)
דֹּב	*bear*
זֶרַע	*seed, offspring, descendants*
חוֹל	*sand*
חֵמָה	*heat, anger* (f)
יְהוֹנָתָן	*Jonathan* (name)
כּוֹכָב	*star*
מִלְכָּה	*Milkah* (name)
מִסְתָּר	*secret place*
נְאֻם	*oracle*
נָחוֹר	*Nahor* (name)
סְבַךְ	*thicket, bush*

עוּלֵים	young man (Aramaic)
עֹנֶשׁ	punishment
קֶרֶן	horn
שָׂפָה	lip, shore
שַׁעַר	gate

VERBS

אָחַז	to grasp, take hold
אָרַב	to lie in wait
חוי	to show, tell (Aramaic Pael stem; Ptc מְחַוֵּי)
מוּת	to die Ptc מֵת dead
נָגַד	no Qal; Piel to show, tell Ptc מַגִּיד
רָבָה	to be many, great; Hif to increase, multiply
שָׁבַע	Qal only in passive; Nif to swear

OTHER

אַחַר	behind (adverb, preposition)
אֵיךְ	how? (interrogative adverb)
אֵיכְדֵין	how? (Aramaic)
איכן	how? (Syriac)
אֲרֵי	because, that (Aramaic)
גָּרָל	uncertain meaning (adjective)
ד	who, which (Aramaic)
יַעַן	because (preposition, conjunction)
עֵקֶב	because (conjunction)
שֵׁנִית	second (ordinal adjective)

Grammar

SOURCES AND VERSIONS

The text in a modern Hebrew Bible is not directly replicated from 2,500 year-old manuscripts, but has been transmitted through the centuries via copies of copies of copies. This copying was very careful because the texts were considered sacred, and yet inevitably some differences, and even errors, were introduced accidentally.

Today, most Hebrew Bibles that we can find are printed or online copies of the Masoretic Text (MT), which was compiled between the seventh and tenth centuries of the Common Era (CE). This was when the practice of writing vowels underneath the consonants became widespread; prior to the Masoretic Text, biblical Hebrew was written without vowels. The oldest manuscript we have of the Masoretic Text is about 1,100 years old, although some fragments of more ancient manuscripts have been preserved.

The Masoretes (scholars who produced the MT) also added cantillation marks: symbols that indicate how the texts should be read or sung. We have not looked at cantillation marks in this course because it is generally possible to understand the meaning of biblical Hebrew without knowing them. In other contexts it might be important to learn them.

There are some manuscripts of translations of the Hebrew Bible that are much older than extant Hebrew manuscripts. The Septuagint is an early Greek version, written LXX for short, which gets its name from the tradition that 70 translators arrived independently at identical versions. There are places where it differs from the Masoretic Text. We saw one example of this in Genesis 21:9 (Unit 16). The earliest manuscripts we have of the Septuagint date from the fourth century CE, though the translation itself is usually dated about six centuries earlier.

Other early translations are the Targumim. Targum (Tg) means *translation*, and the Targumim (plural: Tgg) are translations of the biblical texts into Aramaic, which was the language commonly spoken in the ancient Near East around 2,000 years ago. Some of the Targumim follow the Hebrew very closely; others seem to provide additional commentary on the text.

A little later, around the fourth century CE, the LXX, Targumim and Hebrew manuscripts were sources for a translation of the biblical texts into Syriac, a dialect of Aramaic, and the language spoken in much of the Middle East from about the second to seventh centuries CE. This translation is known as the Peshitta (P), which means *common* or *simple*, and is still used in some Middle Eastern Christian communities today.

And as we saw in Unit 19, since the discovery of the Dead Sea Scrolls we now have a further set of texts with which to work. The Dead Sea Scrolls are particularly interesting because the biblical texts sometimes agree with the LXX rather than the MT, as one might expect. They provide evidence of very early sources that differ somewhat from the tradition that led to the MT. They are also some of the earliest manuscripts we have of the biblical texts.

All of these, the MT, the LXX, the Tgg, the Peshitta and the Dead Sea Scrolls, are considered particularly valuable as sources that can be read alongside one another to help understand the meaning of the text. This is why in English translations some passages may follow the LXX rather than the MT.

It can be uncomfortable to deal with the idea of so many sources for the Bible. It might sound to some readers as if there are dozens of different Bibles going around; how can we know which is the correct one? Perhaps a more helpful way to look at it is to acknowledge that there are numerous texts that can help us to understand better what the biblical texts really mean.

Look at the following examples from manuscripts of 2 Samuel 1:5. They come from the Masoretic Text, Targum Jonathan, the Peshitta, a manuscript of Samuel from the Dead Sea Scrolls called 4QSama, and the Septuagint. It might be a good idea to read 2 Samuel 1 in English first, so that you have an idea of the context.

Syriac does not use the alphabet that we have learned for biblical Hebrew, but the Syriac of the Peshitta has been transliterated here into the familiar alphabet so that the similarities and differences can be seen. It was not possible to do the same with the Greek of the LXX, but it has been included for completeness, and for the sake of any readers who know some Greek.

The verses have been divided into columns to help you to compare the sections of the verse with the other versions.

PRACTICE 1

Translate the MT column of the following comparison, using a lexicon where necessary.

2 Samuel 1:5

	MT	TgJ	P	4QSamᵃ	LXX
a	וַיֹּאמֶר	ואמר	ואמר	ויאמר	καὶ εἶπεν
b	דָּוִד	דויד	דויד	דוד	Δαυιδ
c	אֶל־הַנַּעַר	לעולימא	לעלימא	אל־הנער	τῷ παιδαρίῳ
d	הַמַּגִּיד	דמחוי	חוני	המגיד	τῷ ἀπαγγέλλοντι
e	לוֹ	ליה		לו	αὐτῷ
f	אֵיךְ	איכדין	איכנא	איך	Πῶς
g	יָדַעְתָּ	ידעת		ידעת	οἶδας
h	כִּי־	ארי		כ־	ὅτι
i	מֵת	מית	מיתו	מת	τέθνηκεν
j	שָׁאוּל	שאול	שאול	שאול	Σαουλ
k	וִיהוֹנָתָן	ויהונתן	ויונתן	יהונתן	καὶ Ιωναθαν
l	בְּנוֹ׃	בריה׃	ברה׃	בנו	ὁ υἱὸς αὐτοῦ;

Here are some possible translations:

MT   *And David said to the young man* who told him, *'How do you know that Saul and his son Jonathan are dead?'*

TgJ   *And David said to the young man* who told him, *'How do you know that Saul and his son Jonathan are dead?'*

P   *And David said to the young man,* 'Tell me *how Saul and his son Jonathan died.'*

4QSam^a   *And David said to the young man* who told him, *'How do you know that Saul [and] his son Jonathan are dead?'*

LXX   *And David said to the boy* bringing the news, *'How do you know that Saul and his son Jonathan are dead?'*

The words in Roman typeface indicate where the manuscripts are at variance. The Peshitta is further from the MT than the other texts, although the meaning is not so different as to be confusing.

It can sometimes be helpful to look at other sources when the MT is difficult to understand. For example, in 2 Samuel 1:8 the Hebrew text of the MT may seem somewhat confused. The LXX is at variance with the MT, so we can see that (at least at one point in time) the text was understood slightly differently. (See below for a full discussion.) Many English translations of the Bible use the technique of comparing the MT with other versions such as the LXX when the text is difficult to understand.

KETIV AND QERE

Biblical manuscripts were copied by hand, and therefore it was possible for mistakes to be made in copying. When the Masoretes standardized the texts in about the ninth century, they did not want to edit the texts so instead they made a note in the margin to indicate places where a different word might be appropriate. The word in the text remained in the written text, but when the text was read aloud the reader was supposed to use the word in the margin instead. They called the word in the text **Ketiv** (כְּתָב *written*) and the word in the margin **Qere** (קְרָא *read*).

To help with this process, the Masoretes wrote the vowel sounds of the Qere word underneath the consonants of the Ketiv word in the text. For example, in 2 Sam 1:8, the young man who brings news of Saul's death to David recounts his conversation with the deceased king:

וַיֹּאמֶר לִי מִי־אָתָּה וָיאֹמַר אֵלָיו עֲמָלֵקִי אָנֹכִי

'He said to me, "Who are you?" and I said to him, "I am an Amalekite."'

The word וָיאֹמַר is the Ketiv. We might have expected to see it pointed וַיֹּאמֶר, but in the margin (or in a footnote) there is a note: ואומר ק׳.

If the biblical text were written without vowels, a reader seeing the word ויאמר would probably be inclined to pronounce it **va-YŌ-mer**. With the vowels that have been added it looks as if one is expected to pronounce וָיאֹמַר as **vā-YŌ-mar**. However, the note points us to the word ואומר which is pronounced **vā-ō-MAR**. And that is what the reader is expected to say out loud.

If we read the Ketiv instead of the Qere, the verse would read: 'He said to me, "Who are you?" and he said to him, "I am an Amalekite."' If we were to accept that reading, it would effectively indicate that the Amalekite was referring to himself as *he* rather than *I*, which would be unusual. And in fact, the LXX and the Peshitta both have a first-person verb in 2 Sam 1:8 instead of the MT's third-person verb.

The possibility of scribal errors is commonly given for the introduction of Qere readings, but in fact the situation may be more complicated than that. Some of the Qere words might testify to alternative manuscript traditions; others might indicate oral alternatives to the written text. Whatever the reason, the Qere words are now just as much a part of the received text as the Ketiv words.

In some cases, the vowels of the Qere reading are given without a marginal note. For example, we have seen that the divine name יהוה is written with the vowels of אֲדֹנָי and it is read **a-dōn-ī** or **ha-SHEM** (see Unit 3). There is no need for a marginal note indicating the Qere of יהוה because it is always the same. Similarly, the pronoun הִיא (*she*) is often written הוא with a ו instead of a י. In a text without vowels, it is therefore identical to הוא meaning *he*. In order to distinguish between the two pronouns, the feminine is pointed with the *i* vowel of הִיא but the middle ו remains unchanged, thus: הִוא. The reader should not pronounce this word **heev** although it looks as if it should be pronounced that way. Instead, the reader is expected to know that הִוא is an alternative spelling of הִיא and say **hee**. Since this word is very common in the biblical text there is no marginal note. These examples are known as Qere perpetuum: they are always pronounced with a variation from the written text and do not require to be highlighted.

Qere readings do not always significantly affect the meaning of the text. For example:

יָדַעְתָּ כִּי־כֹל תּוּכָל   Job 42:2a

Literally: *I know that all things you are able*; usually translated *I know that you can do all things*. The Ketiv is יָדַעְתָּ. The Qere is יָדַעְתִּי and the only difference is the final י, which is how we would expect יָדַעְתִּי to be spelled.

PRACTICE 2

Work out how to read the verse using the vowels of the Ketiv and the consonants of the Qere. How would you fill in the blanks in the translations? The words in brackets are Ketiv.

a שְׁמֹר (רַגְלְיךָ) כַּאֲשֶׁר תֵּלֵךְ אֶל־בֵּית הָאֱלֹהִים   Ecclesiastes 4:17

Guard _____ when you go to the house of God.

Qere   ק׳ רגלך

b וַיָּקֶם אֶת־(דְּבָרָיו) אֲשֶׁר־דִּבֶּר עָלֵינוּ   Daniel 9:12

And he has confirmed _____ which he has spoken against us.

Qere   ק׳ דברו

c דֹּב אֹרֵב הוּא לִי (אֲרִיה) בְּמִסְתָּרִים   Lamentations 3:10

To me he is a bear lying in wait; _____ in a hiding place.

Qere   ק׳ ארי

d (וַיֵּשְׁבִי) יְרוּשָׁלָם   2 Chronicles 34:9

And _____ returned to Jerusalem.

Qere   ק׳ וישבו

e (גְּרָל-) עֹנֶשׁ נֹשֵׂא חֵמָה   Proverbs 19:19

_____ anger will bear punishment.

Qere   ק׳ גדל-

(This last is very difficult to translate, so you are not expected to come up with a flawless translation. A suggestion will be sufficient.)

ACCENTS AND CANTILLATION MARKS

> **LANGUAGE INSIGHT**
>
> A syllable is a sound that is part of a word. A word can have any number of syllables, and one of these syllables is stressed. For example:
>
> | | | |
> |---|---|---|
> | one syllable | *pal* | **PAL** |
> | two syllables | *crystal* | **CRYS-tal** |
> | three syllables | *denial* | **de-NI-al** |
> | four syllables | *accidental* | **ac-ci-DEN-tal** |
> | five syllables | *editorial* | **ed-i-TO-ri-al** |
> | six syllables | *archaeological* | **ar-chae-o-LOG-i-cal** |
>
> In some languages (e.g. Hungarian) the stress is always on the first syllable of a word, but in English, as you can see, the stress can occur in almost any syllable, although it is often in the antepenultimate (third last) syllable. In Hebrew the stress is usually on the last syllable of a word (e.g. סוּסָה soo-SĀ), but there are exceptions, especially in the segolate nouns.

Learning cantillation marks and accents in the early stages can cause confusion and lead to discouragement. However, they are very useful once you begin to have a grasp of the language. Some (though not all) Hebrew Bibles contain not only vowels but also accents and cantillation marks. These indicate how the text is to be read or sung. There are a great many of them, but for the purposes of private reading it is not necessary to understand or distinguish the cantillation marks. However, it may be useful to know that they usually indicate where the stress comes in each word. For example Genesis 1:1:

without cantillation marks   בְּרֵאשִׁית בָּרָא אֱלֹהִים אֵת הַשָּׁמַיִם וְאֵת הָאָרֶץ:

with cantillation marks   בְּרֵאשִׁית בָּרָא אֱלֹהִים אֵת הַשָּׁמַיִם וְאֵת הָאָרֶץ:

As you can see, the marks indicate the places where the stress of each word can be found. In each of the first three words the stress is in the final syllable:

בְּרֵאשִׁית	bə-ray-SHEET
בָּרָא	bā-RĀ
אֱלֹהִים	elō-HEEM

The word אֵת does not have a stress: it is read as if it were part of the next word. In this case the next word is הַשָּׁמַיִם, with the stress on the second-to-last syllable.

אֵת הַשָּׁמַיִם	ayt ha-shā-MĪ-yim

That is the usual pattern for nouns with dual endings: the same is the true of יָדַיִם *hands*, רַגְלַיִם *feet*, מַיִם *water* and so on. They are pronounced **yā-DĪ-yim**, **rag-LĪ-yim** and **MĪ-yim** respectively.

This time there is a stress in אֶת, because it has the conjunction וְ in front of it. So the stress is on the second syllable of the word.

וְאֶת	və-AYT

The stress in הָאָרֶץ is on the second-to-last syllable because it is a segolate noun, like מֶלֶךְ (**ME-lech**) and נַעַר (**NA-ar**). These are outlined in Unit 16.

הָאָרֶץ	hā-ĀR-ets

Look again at the text of Genesis 1:1.

בְּרֵאשִׁית בָּרָא אֱלֹהִים אֵת הַשָּׁמַיִם וְאֵת הָאָרֶץ׃

Notice the wishbone-shaped mark under the ה of אֱלֹהִים. It is called **atnah** and it indicates that the reader should pause at this word, a little like the way a comma is used in English. You will usually see **atnah** underneath a word near the middle of a verse in the Bible.

The last word contains a small accent called **silluq**, which is the little line next to the second vowel in הָאָרֶץ. **Silluq** indicates that the reader should make a slightly longer pause than the pause at **atnah**. You will usually see **silluq** underneath the last word of a verse in the Bible. It functions a little like a full stop in English.

There is one other accent that is useful to know. It is called **meteg** and looks exactly like **silluq**. If you see it next to a **qamets**, it indicates that the vowel is to be pronounced as a long-*a* vowel, rather than a short-*o* vowel. For example:

פָּקְדָה	*she has visited*

This is pronounced **pā-kə-DĀH** and not **pok-DĀH**.

Of course, in some people's accents, these vowels are indistinguishable. Moreover, **meteg** is not found with every long *a*-vowel. It is only found where the structure of the word is such that an experienced reader might expect a short **o**-vowel instead of a long **a**-vowel. In general, it is best for beginners to assume that **qamets** is pronounced as a long **a**-vowel unless directed otherwise.

Knowing about these accents and about the cantillation marks can make it easier for us to read the biblical texts aloud, and can even help our understanding. If you incorrectly pronounce a word that you have seen before, you might have trouble recognizing it by its sound. If you pronounce it correctly, it should sound familiar.

PRACTICE 3

Mark each of the stressed syllables with a circle:

a   טֽוֹב־וְיָשָׁ֥ר יְהוָ֑ה עַל־כֵּ֤ן יוֹרֶ֬ה חַטָּאִ֣ים בַּדָּֽרֶךְ׃   Psalm 25:8

b   וַיֹּ֧אמֶר נָתָ֛ן אֶל־דָּוִ֖ד אַתָּ֣ה הָאִ֑ישׁ   2 Samuel 12:7a

c   נוֹדָ֣ע בִּֽיהוּדָ֣ה אֱלֹהִ֑ים בְּיִשְׂרָאֵ֗ל גָּד֥וֹל שְׁמֽוֹ׃   Psalm 76:2

d   אָ֣ז יָשִֽׁיר־מֹשֶׁה֩ וּבְנֵ֨י יִשְׂרָאֵ֜ל אֶת־הַשִּׁירָ֤ה הַזֹּאת֙ לַֽיהוָ֔ה   Exodus 15:1a

e   וַיְהִ֗י בִּימֵי֙ שְׁפֹ֣ט הַשֹּׁפְטִ֔ים וַיְהִ֥י רָעָ֖ב בָּאָ֑רֶץ וַיֵּ֨לֶךְ אִ֜ישׁ מִבֵּ֧ית   Ruth 1:1
        לֶ֣חֶם יְהוּדָ֗ה לָגוּר֙ בִּשְׂדֵ֣י מוֹאָ֔ב ה֥וּא וְאִשְׁתּ֖וֹ וּשְׁנֵ֥י בָנָֽיו׃

f   כִּ֚י יְהוָ֣ה אֱלֹֽהֵיכֶ֔ם ה֚וּא אֱלֹהֵ֣י הָֽאֱלֹהִ֔ים וַאֲדֹנֵ֖י הָאֲדֹנִ֑ים הָאֵ֨ל   Deuteronomy 10:17
        הַגָּדֹ֤ל הַגִּבֹּר֙ וְהַנּוֹרָ֔א אֲשֶׁר֙ לֹא־יִשָּׂ֣א פָנִ֔ים וְלֹ֥א יִקַּ֖ח שֹֽׁחַד׃

g   וַיֹּאמֶר֩ עָרֹ֨ם יָצָ֜תִי מִבֶּ֣טֶן אִמִּ֗י וְעָרֹם֙ אָשׁ֣וּב שָׁ֔מָּה יְהוָ֣ה נָתַ֔ן   Job 1:21
        וַיהוָ֖ה לָקָ֑ח יְהִ֛י שֵׁ֥ם יְהוָ֖ה מְבֹרָֽךְ׃

h   וְאָֽמַרְתָּ֙ בַּיּ֣וֹם הַה֔וּא אוֹדְךָ֣ יְהוָ֔ה כִּ֥י אָנַ֖פְתָּ בִּ֑י יָשֹׁ֥ב אַפְּךָ֖   Isaiah 12:1–2
        וּֽתְנַחֲמֵֽנִי׃ הִנֵּ֨ה אֵ֧ל יְשֽׁוּעָתִ֛י אֶבְטַ֖ח וְלֹ֣א אֶפְחָ֑ד כִּֽי־עָזִּ֤י
        וְזִמְרָת֙ יָ֣הּ יְהוָ֔ה וַֽיְהִי־לִ֖י לִֽישׁוּעָֽה׃

Reading

GENESIS 22:13–20

Points to look out for in this text:

▶ forms of weak verbs
▶ cantillation marks as indicators of the stress in each word
▶ examples of Qere perpetuum.

13   וַיִּשָּׂ֨א אַבְרָהָ֜ם אֶת־עֵינָ֗יו וַיַּרְא֙ וְהִנֵּה־אַ֔יִל אַחַ֕ר נֶאֱחַ֥ז בַּסְּבַ֖ךְ בְּקַרְנָ֑יו וַיֵּ֤לֶךְ אַבְרָהָם֙
    וַיִּקַּ֣ח אֶת־הָאַ֔יִל וַיַּעֲלֵ֥הוּ לְעֹלָ֖ה תַּ֥חַת בְּנֽוֹ׃

14   וַיִּקְרָ֧א אַבְרָהָ֛ם שֵֽׁם־הַמָּק֥וֹם הַה֖וּא יְהוָ֣ה יִרְאֶ֑ה אֲשֶׁר֙ יֵאָמֵ֣ר הַיּ֔וֹם בְּהַ֥ר יְהוָ֖ה יֵרָאֶֽה׃

15   וַיִּקְרָ֛א מַלְאַ֥ךְ יְהוָ֖ה אֶל־אַבְרָהָ֑ם שֵׁנִ֖ית מִן־הַשָּׁמָֽיִם׃

16   וַיֹּ֕אמֶר בִּ֥י נִשְׁבַּ֖עְתִּי נְאֻם־יְהוָ֑ה כִּ֗י יַ֚עַן אֲשֶׁ֤ר עָשִׂ֙יתָ֙ אֶת־הַדָּבָ֣ר הַזֶּ֔ה וְלֹ֥א חָשַׂ֖כְתָּ אֶת־
    בִּנְךָ֥ אֶת־יְחִידֶֽךָ׃

17 כִּי־בָרֵךְ אֲבָרֶכְךָ֗ וְהַרְבָּ֣ה אַרְבֶּ֤ה אֶֽת־זַרְעֲךָ֙ כְּכוֹכְבֵ֣י הַשָּׁמַ֔יִם וְכַח֕וֹל אֲשֶׁ֖ר עַל־שְׂפַ֣ת הַיָּ֑ם וְיִרַ֣שׁ זַרְעֲךָ֔ אֵ֖ת שַׁ֥עַר אֹיְבָֽיו׃

18 וְהִתְבָּרֲכ֣וּ בְזַרְעֲךָ֔ כֹּ֖ל גּוֹיֵ֣י הָאָ֑רֶץ עֵ֕קֶב אֲשֶׁ֥ר שָׁמַ֖עְתָּ בְּקֹלִֽי׃

19 וַיָּ֤שָׁב אַבְרָהָם֙ אֶל־נְעָרָ֔יו וַיָּקֻ֛מוּ וַיֵּלְכ֥וּ יַחְדָּ֖ו אֶל־בְּאֵ֣ר שָׁ֑בַע וַיֵּ֥שֶׁב אַבְרָהָ֖ם בִּבְאֵ֥ר שָֽׁבַע׃

20 וַיְהִ֗י אַחֲרֵי֙ הַדְּבָרִ֣ים הָאֵ֔לֶּה וַיֻּגַּ֥ד לְאַבְרָהָ֖ם לֵאמֹ֑ר הִ֠נֵּה יָלְדָ֨ה מִלְכָּ֥ה גַם־הִ֛וא בָּנִ֖ים לְנָח֥וֹר אָחִֽיךָ׃

💡 Language discovery

VERSE 13

The meaning of the word אַחַר is not very clear in this context. We would normally expect it to have a 3ms suffix. LXX and P have *one* (אֶחָד) instead of *behind*. Do you prefer to translate according to the MT or the LXX?

VERSE 14

The word רָאָה can mean *to see* or *to provide*, as we saw in verse 8. How would you translate the Nifal? The Nifal can also mean *to appear*. Which translation do you think is best, and why? Do you prefer to translate both the Qal and the Nifal of this verb with the same sense? The word הַיּוֹם can mean *today*.

VERSE 16

The Nifal of שָׁבַע means *to swear*; there is no need to make it passive in translation. The phrase נְאֻם־יְהוָה is common in prophetic literature, along with כֹּה אָמַר יְהוָה (*thus says Yhwh*).

VERSE 17

How are the infinitive absolutes used in this verse? The phrase *to possess the gate of the enemy* is often understood as a way of saying *to conquer the enemy*.

VERSE 18

The Hitpael here may have a reflexive sense, which is very common for Hitpael. However, many translations interpret this as a passive use of the Hitpael. Do you agree? How is the preposition בְּ used in this verse? The phrase *to listen to someone's voice* is often a way of saying *to obey*. Does that seem appropriate in this verse?

VERSE 19

Can you parse וַיָּשָׁב and וַיֵּשֶׁב? Which verbal roots are they from? What is the difference in meaning?

VERSE 20

The phrase גַם־הִוא is probably best translated *also* rather than *also she*; it is idiomatic.

POSSIBLE TRANSLATION

Abraham looked up and he noticed a ram behind him caught in a bush by its horns. So Abraham went and he took the ram and he sacrificed it instead of his son. And Abraham called the name of that place 'Yhwh will provide' so that it is said to this day 'On the mountain of Yhwh it will be provided.' The angel of Yhwh called to Abraham a second time from heaven and he said, 'By myself I have sworn,' says Yhwh, 'Because you have done this thing and because you did not keep back your only son, I will certainly bless you, and I will certainly multiply your offspring like the stars in the sky and the sand which is on the sea shore, and your offspring will possess the gate of his enemy. All the nations of the earth shall bless themselves through your offspring, because you have obeyed me.' Then Abraham returned to his young men and they got up and they went together to Beersheba, and Abraham settled in Beersheba. After these things Abraham was told, 'Behold, Milkah has also borne children to Nahor your brother.'

Test yourself

1 Describe the system of the verbal stems in Hebrew and give examples.

2 Give the principal parts of the Hitpael of פָּקַד (i.e. Perfect 3ms, Imperfect 3ms, Imperative 2ms, Infinitive Construct, Participle ms).

3 Explain first-second-and third-person commands (cohortative, imperative and jussive) in Hebrew and give examples.

4 Give Hebrew examples of singular and plural, masculine and feminine construct and absolute forms of nouns.

5 Give the Qal Vav Consecutive Imperfect 3ms of the following verbs: מָשַׁל הָלַךְ אָמַר קוּם.

SELF-CHECK

I CAN...

○ understand the use of early translations as sources for biblical texts

○ recognize scribal Qere readings when I encounter them

○ recognize accents and cantillation marks to stress the correct syllables

○ read and translate Genesis 22:13–20

Additional texts

Narrative texts

This section introduces several texts to read, with support for grammar and vocabulary. Most of these texts are fairly well known in faith communities and some are quite well known throughout Western culture. Try to translate as much as you can from your memory of vocabulary and verbal forms, but use the analysis underneath the text where necessary. Common and repeated words are usually omitted from the analysis.

There are also a few questions to answer on each passage to test your understanding of the grammatical features of biblical Hebrew. You should compare your translations with other translations, which you can find in printed Bibles or online. The first of these texts includes an example translation.

DEUTERONOMY 6:4–7 THE SHEMA

4 שְׁמַע יִשְׂרָאֵל יְהֹוָה אֱלֹהֵינוּ יְהֹוָה אֶחָד : 5 וְאָהַבְתָּ אֵת יְהֹוָה אֱלֹהֶיךָ בְּכָל־לְבָבְךָ וּבְכָל־נַפְשְׁךָ וּבְכָל־מְאֹדֶךָ : 6 וְהָיוּ הַדְּבָרִים הָאֵלֶּה אֲשֶׁר אָנֹכִי מְצַוְּךָ הַיּוֹם עַל־לְבָבֶךָ : 7 וְשִׁנַּנְתָּם לְבָנֶיךָ וְדִבַּרְתָּ בָּם בְּשִׁבְתְּךָ בְּבֵיתֶךָ וּבְלֶכְתְּךָ בַדֶּרֶךְ וּבְשָׁכְבְּךָ וּבְקוּמֶךָ :

4 שְׁמַע Qal Impv שָׁמַע *to hear.*

אֱלֹהֵינוּ noun m + suff 1cp אֱלֹהִים *(our God).*

אֶחָד numeral m אֶחָד *one, first.*

5 וְאָהַבְתָּ Qal VC Perf 2ms אָהַב *to love.*

אֱלֹהֶיךָ noun m + suff 2ms אֱלֹהִים.

בְּכָל prep בְּ + noun m cstr כֹּל *whole, entirety.*

לְבָבְךָ prep לְ + noun m + suff 2ms לֵבָב *heart, mind.*

וּבְכָל conj וְ + prep בְּ + noun m cstr כֹּל *(and with all).*

נַפְשְׁךָ noun f + suff 2ms נֶפֶשׁ *soul, life.*

וּבְכָל conj וְ + prep בְּ + noun m cstr כֹּל *and with all.*

מְאֹדֶךָ noun m + suff 2ms מְאֹד *power, strength.*

6 וְהָיוּ Qal VC Impf 3mp הָיָה *to be, become.*

הַדְּבָרִים def art + Qal Ptc דָּבָר *word, thing.*

הָאֵלֶּה def art + demonstrative m and f p אֵלֶּה *these.*

אֲשֶׁר rel pronoun *which.*

אָנֹכִי subj pronoun 1cs אָנֹכִי *I.*

מְצַוְּךָ Piel Ptc + suff 2ms צָוָה Piel *to appoint, command*.

הַיּוֹם def art + noun m יוֹם *day*.

עַל prep עַל *on, upon*.

7 וְשִׁנַּנְתָּם Piel VC Perf 2ms + suff 3mp שָׁנַן *to sharpen*; Piel *to teach*.

לְבָנֶיךָ prep לְ + noun mp + suff 2ms בֵּן *son*.

וְדִבַּרְתָּ Piel VC Perf 2ms דָּבַר Piel: *to speak*.

בָּם prep בְּ + suff 3mp בְּ (*about them, them*).

בְּשִׁבְתְּךָ prep בְּ + Qal Inf Cstr + suff 2ms יָשַׁב *to sit*.

בְּבֵיתֶךָ prep בְּ + noun m + suff 2ms בַּיִת *house*.

וּבְלֶכְתְּךָ conj וְ + prep בְּ + Qal Inf Cstr + suff 2ms הָלַךְ *to walk*.

בַדֶּרֶךְ prep בְּ + noun m דֶּרֶךְ *way, path, journey*.

וּבְשָׁכְבְּךָ conj וְ + prep בְּ + Qal Inf Cstr + suff 2ms שָׁכַב *to lie down*.

וּבְקוּמֶךָ conj וְ + prep בְּ + Qal Inf Cstr + suff 2ms קוּם *to get up*.

Questions

1 There are a number of possible translations of verse 4, which you can see if you compare translations. What feature of biblical Hebrew accounts for these differences?

2 In verse 7 there are several examples of the preposition בְּ used with the Infinitive Construct. What is the effect of this construction?

Example translation for comparison

Listen, Israel! The LORD our God, the LORD is one. And you will love the LORD your God with all your heart and with all your life and with all your strength. And these words that I command you today will be upon your heart, and you will teach them to your sons, and you will speak them when you sit in your house, and when you walk on the way, and when you lie down and when you get up.

ISAIAH 38:1–8 HEZEKIAH'S SUNDIAL

1 בַּיָּמִים הָהֵם חָלָה חִזְקִיָּהוּ לָמוּת וַיָּבוֹא אֵלָיו יְשַׁעְיָהוּ בֶן־אָמוֹץ הַנָּבִיא וַיֹּאמֶר אֵלָיו כֹּה־אָמַר יְהוָה צַו לְבֵיתֶךָ כִּי מֵת אַתָּה וְלֹא תִחְיֶה : 2 וַיַּסֵּב חִזְקִיָּהוּ פָּנָיו אֶל־הַקִּיר וַיִּתְפַּלֵּל אֶל־יְהוָה : 3 וַיֹּאמַר אָנָּה יְהוָה זְכָר־נָא אֵת אֲשֶׁר הִתְהַלַּכְתִּי לְפָנֶיךָ בֶּאֱמֶת וּבְלֵב שָׁלֵם וְהַטּוֹב בְּעֵינֶיךָ עָשִׂיתִי וַיֵּבְךְּ חִזְקִיָּהוּ בְּכִי גָדוֹל : 4 וַיְהִי דְּבַר־יְהוָה אֶל־יְשַׁעְיָהוּ לֵאמֹר : 5 הָלוֹךְ וְאָמַרְתָּ אֶל־חִזְקִיָּהוּ כֹּה־אָמַר יְהוָה אֱלֹהֵי דָּוִד אָבִיךָ שָׁמַעְתִּי אֶת־תְּפִלָּתֶךָ רָאִיתִי אֶת־דִּמְעָתֶךָ הִנְנִי יוֹסִף עַל־יָמֶיךָ חֲמֵשׁ עֶשְׂרֵה שָׁנָה : 6 וּמִכַּף מֶלֶךְ־אַשּׁוּר אַצִּילְךָ וְאֵת הָעִיר הַזֹּאת וְגַנּוֹתִי עַל־הָעִיר הַזֹּאת : 7 וְזֶה־לְּךָ הָאוֹת מֵאֵת יְהוָה אֲשֶׁר יַעֲשֶׂה יְהוָה אֶת־הַדָּבָר הַזֶּה אֲשֶׁר דִּבֵּר : 8 הִנְנִי מֵשִׁיב אֶת־צֵל הַמַּעֲלוֹת אֲשֶׁר יָרְדָה בְמַעֲלוֹת אָחָז בַּשֶּׁמֶשׁ אֲחֹרַנִּית עֶשֶׂר מַעֲלוֹת וַתָּשָׁב הַשֶּׁמֶשׁ עֶשֶׂר מַעֲלוֹת בַּמַּעֲלוֹת אֲשֶׁר יָרָדָה :

1 בַּיָּמִים prep בְּ + noun mp יוֹם (in the days).

הָהֵם def art + demonstr adj mp הֵם they, those.

חָלָה Qal Perf 3ms חָלָה to be weak, sick.

חִזְקִיָּהוּ proper noun Hezekiah.

לָמוּת prep לְ + Qal Inf Cstr מוּת to die.

וַיָּבוֹא Qal VC Impf 3ms בּוֹא to come; Hif to bring.

אֵלָיו prep + suff 3ms אֶל (to him).

יְשַׁעְיָהוּ proper noun Isaiah.

בֶּן noun ms cstr בֵּן (son of).

אָמוֹץ proper noun Amoz.

הַנָּבִיא def art + noun m נָבִיא prophet.

וַיֹּאמֶר Qal VC Impf 3ms אָמַר to say.

כֹּה adv thus, therefore.

אָמַר Qal Perf 3ms אָמַר to say.

צַו Piel Impv צָוָה no Qal; Piel to appoint, command (with בַּיִת to make a will).

לְבֵיתֶךָ prep לְ + noun m + suff 2ms בַּיִת house.

כִּי adv because, that, if.

מֵת Qal Perf 3ms מוּת to die.

אַתָּה subj pronoun 2ms (you).

וְלֹא conj וְ + negative particle לֹא (not, do not).

תִחְיֶה Qal Impf 2ms חָיָה to live.

2 וַיַּסֵּב Hif VC Impf 3ms סָבַב to turn; Hif to cause to turn.

פָּנָיו noun mp + suff 3ms פָּנִים face.

הַקִּיר def art + proper noun קִיר wall.

וַיִּתְפַּלֵּל Hitp VC Impf 3ms פָּלַל Hitp to intercede, pray.

3 אָנָּה interj of entreaty אָנָּה please.

זְכָר Qal Impv זָכַר to remember.

אֲשֶׁר rel pronoun.

הִתְהַלַּכְתִּי Hitp Perf 1cs הָלַךְ to walk; Hitp walk about, wander.

לְפָנֶיךָ prep לְ + noun mp + suff 2ms פָּנִים (before you).

בֶּאֱמֶת prep בְּ + noun f אֱמֶת truth, faithfulness, integrity.

וּבְלֵב conj וְ + prep בְּ + noun m לֵב heart, life.

שָׁלֵם adj m שָׁלֵם complete, perfect.

וְהַטּוֹב conj וְ + def art + noun m טוֹב good.

בְּעֵינֶיךָ prep בְּ + noun f dual + suff 2ms עַיִן eye.

עָשִׂיתִי Qal Perf 1cs עָשָׂה to *make, do*.

וַיֵּבְךְּ Qal VC Impf 3ms בָּכָה to *weep, grieve*.

בְּכִי noun m בְּכִי *weeping*.

גָּדוֹל adj m גָּדוֹל *big, large, great*.

4 וַיְהִי Qal VC Impf 3ms הָיָה (*and it came*).

דְּבַר noun ms cstr דָּבָר *word, thing, matter*.

לֵאמֹר prep לְ + Qal Inf Cstr אָמַר (*saying*).

5 הָלוֹךְ Qal Inf Abs הָלַךְ to *walk* (Inf standing for finite verb: *you will go*).

וְאָמַרְתָּ Qal VC Perf 2ms אָמַר to *say*.

כֹּה adv *thus, therefore*.

אֱלֹהֵי noun m cstr אֱלֹהִים.

דָּוִד proper noun (also דָּוִיד) *David*.

אָבִיךְ noun m + suff 2ms אָב.

שָׁמַעְתִּי Qal Perf 1cs שָׁמַע to *hear*.

תְּפִלָּתֶךְ noun f + suff 2ms תְּפִלָּה *prayer*.

רָאִיתִי Qal Perf 1cs רָאָה to *see*.

דִּמְעָתֶךְ noun f + suff 2ms דִּמְעָה *tear; collective tears*.

הִנְנִי interjection + suff 1s הִנֵּה (*behold I am*).

יוֹסִף Hif Ptc יָסַף to *increase, do again*; Hif as Qal.

עַל prep *on, upon*.

יָמֶיךְ noun mp + suff 2ms יוֹם *day your days*.

חֲמֵשׁ numeral f cstr חָמֵשׁ *five*.

עֶשְׂרֵה numeral f עֶשֶׂר *ten* (with above: *fifteen*).

שָׁנָה noun f *year* (often used in singular form with plural meaning).

6 וּמִכַּף conj וְ + prep מִן + noun f כַּף *palm of hand*.

אַשּׁוּר proper noun אַשּׁוּר *Assyria*.

אַצִּילְךְ Hif Impf 1cs + suff 2ms נָצַל Hif to *deprive, deliver*.

הָעִיר def art + noun f עִיר *city*.

הַזֹּאת def art + demonstr adj fs.

וְגַנּוֹתִי Qal VC Perf 1cs גָּנַן to *cover, defend*.

7 וְזֶה conj וְ + demonstr adj m זֶה *this*.

לְךְ prep לְ + suff 2ms לְ *to, at, for*.

הָאוֹת def art + noun f אוֹת *sign, ensign*.

מֵאֵת prep מִן + prep אֵת *with* (*from with*).

יַעֲשֶׂה Qal Impf 3ms עָשָׂה to *make, do*.

הַדָּבָר def art + noun m דָּבָר *word, thing, matter.*

דִּבֶּר Piel Perf 3ms דָּבַר Piel: *to speak.*

8 הִנְנִי interjection + suff 1s הִנֵּה *behold, look (behold I am).*

מֵשִׁיב Hif Ptc שׁוּב *to turn, return;* Hif *to restore, cause to turn.*

צֵל noun m צֵל *shadow, shade.*

הַמַּעֲלוֹת def art + noun fp מַעֲלָה *step, ascent, sundial, degree.*

יָרְדָה Qal Perf 3fs יָרַד *to go down.*

בְמַעֲלוֹת prep בְּ + noun fp cstr מַעֲלָה *(as above).*

אָחָז proper noun אָחָז *Ahaz.*

בַּשֶּׁמֶשׁ prep בְּ + noun m and f שֶׁמֶשׁ *sun.*

אֲחֹרַנִּית adv אֲחֹרַנִּית *backwards.*

עֶשֶׂר numeral f עֶשֶׂר *ten.*

מַעֲלוֹת noun fp מַעֲלָה *steps.*

וַתָּשָׁב Qal VC Impf 3fs שׁוּב *to turn, return;* Hif *to restore.*

הַשֶּׁמֶשׁ def art + noun m and f שֶׁמֶשׁ *sun.*

בַּמַּעֲלוֹת prep בְּ + noun fp cstr מַעֲלָה *(as above).*

יָרְדָה Qal Perf 3fs יָרַד *to go down;* Hif *to bring down.*

Questions

3 The phrase אֵת אֲשֶׁר is often translated *that which*, but this does not work in verse 3. How would you translate it in this context?

4 The word לֵאמֹר literally means *saying*. Is this an appropriate translation in this context? Explain why or why not.

5 In verse 8 the word מַעֲלוֹת is repeated several times. Which words in English will you use to translate it? The word order in Hebrew is a little confusing so it may take you a few attempts. Compare translations to see what others have made of it.

GENESIS 32:25–33 JACOB WRESTLES [ENGL. 32:24–32]

25 וַיִּוָּתֵר יַעֲקֹב לְבַדּוֹ וַיֵּאָבֵק אִישׁ עִמּוֹ עַד עֲלוֹת הַשָּׁחַר : 26 וַיַּרְא כִּי לֹא יָכֹל לוֹ וַיִּגַּע בְּכַף־יְרֵכוֹ וַתֵּקַע כַּף־יֶרֶךְ יַעֲקֹב בְּהֵאָבְקוֹ עִמּוֹ : 27 וַיֹּאמֶר שַׁלְּחֵנִי כִּי עָלָה הַשָּׁחַר וַיֹּאמֶר לֹא אֲשַׁלֵּחֲךָ כִּי אִם־בֵּרַכְתָּנִי : 28 וַיֹּאמֶר אֵלָיו מַה־שְּׁמֶךָ וַיֹּאמֶר יַעֲקֹב : 29 וַיֹּאמֶר לֹא יַעֲקֹב יֵאָמֵר עוֹד שִׁמְךָ כִּי אִם־יִשְׂרָאֵל כִּי־שָׂרִיתָ עִם־אֱלֹהִים וְעִם־אֲנָשִׁים וַתּוּכָל : 30 וַיִּשְׁאַל יַעֲקֹב וַיֹּאמֶר הַגִּידָה־נָּא שְׁמֶךָ וַיֹּאמֶר לָמָּה זֶּה תִּשְׁאַל לִשְׁמִי וַיְבָרֶךְ אֹתוֹ שָׁם : 31 וַיִּקְרָא יַעֲקֹב שֵׁם הַמָּקוֹם פְּנִיאֵל כִּי־רָאִיתִי אֱלֹהִים פָּנִים אֶל־פָּנִים וַתִּנָּצֵל נַפְשִׁי : 32 וַיִּזְרַח־לוֹ הַשֶּׁמֶשׁ כַּאֲשֶׁר עָבַר אֶת־פְּנוּאֵל וְהוּא צֹלֵעַ עַל־יְרֵכוֹ : 33 עַל־כֵּן לֹא־יֹאכְלוּ בְנֵי־יִשְׂרָאֵל אֶת־גִּיד הַנָּשֶׁה אֲשֶׁר עַל־כַּף הַיָּרֵךְ עַד הַיּוֹם הַזֶּה כִּי נָגַע בְּכַף־יֶרֶךְ יַעֲקֹב בְּגִיד הַנָּשֶׁה :

25 וַיִּוָּתֵר Nif VC Impf 3ms יָתַר Nif: *to be left.*

יַעֲקֹב proper noun יַעֲקֹב *Jacob.*

לְבַדּוֹ adv + suff 3ms לְבַד *only.*

וַיֵּאָבֵק Nif VC Impf 3ms אָבַק Nif *to wrestle.*

אִישׁ noun m *man.*

עִמּוֹ prep + suff 3ms עִם *with.*

עַד prep *until.*

עֲלוֹת Qal Inf Cstr עָלָה *to go up.*

הַשָּׁחַר def art + noun m שַׁחַר *dawn.*

26 וַיַּרְא Qal VC Impf 3ms apoc רָאָה *to see.*

כִּי adv *that.*

לֹא adv, negative particle לֹא *not.*

יָכֹל Qal Perf 3ms יָכֹל *to be able, prevail.*

לוֹ prep לְ + suff 3ms לְ *(over him).*

וַיִּגַּע Qal VC Impf 3ms נָגַע *to strike, touch, reach.*

בְּכַף prep בְּ + noun f כַּף *hollow of the hand, palm.*

יְרֵכוֹ noun m יָרֵךְ *thigh.*

וַתֵּקַע Qal VC Impf 3fs יָקַע *to be dislocated, alienated.*

יֶרֶךְ noun m יָרֵךְ *thigh.*

בְּהֵאָבְקוֹ prep בְּ + Nif Inf Cstr + suff 3ms אָבַק *(when he wrestled).*

עִמּוֹ prep עִם + suff 3ms עִם *with.*

27 שַׁלְּחֵנִי Piel Impv + suff 1cs שָׁלַח Piel *to let go, expel.*

עָלָה Qal Perf 3ms עָלָה *to go up.*

אֲשַׁלֵּחֲךָ Piel Impf 1cs + suff 2ms שָׁלַח Piel *to let go, expel.*

כִּי אִם adv *unless, but rather.*

בֵּרַכְתָּנִי Piel Perf 2ms + suff 1cs בָּרַךְ Piel *to praise, bless.*

28 אֵלָיו prep + suff 3ms אֶל *to.*

מַה pronoun מָה *what is.*

שְׁמֶךָ noun m + suff 2ms שֵׁם *name.*

29 יֵאָמֵר Nif Impf 3ms אָמַר *to say.*

עוֹד adv *any more.*

שָׂרִיתָ Qal Perf 2ms שָׂרָה *to fight, be a leader.*

עִם prep *with.*

אֱלֹהִים noun mp *God, gods.*

אֲנָשִׁים noun mp אִישׁ *man.*

וַתּוּכָל Qal VC Impf 2ms יָכֹל *to be able, prevail.*

30 וַיִּשְׁאַל Qal VC Impf 3ms שָׁאַל *to ask.*

הַגִּידָה Hif Impv 3ms + paragogic **he** נָגַד Hif *to tell*.

נָא particle of entreaty (*please*).

לָמָּה adv *why*.

זֶה demonstr ms זֶה *this*.

תִּשְׁאַל Qal Impf 2ms שָׁאַל *to ask*.

לִשְׁמִי prep לְ + noun m + suff 1cs שֵׁם *name*.

וַיְבָרֶךְ Piel VC Impf 3ms בָּרַךְ Piel *to praise, bless*.

אֹתוֹ object marker אֵת + suff 3ms (*him*).

שָׁם adv *there*.

31 וַיִּקְרָא Qal VC Impf 3ms קָרָא I *to call*; II *to meet*.

שֵׁם noun m שֵׁם *name*.

הַמָּקוֹם def art + noun m מָקוֹם *place*.

פְּנִיאֵל proper noun פְּנִיאֵל *Peniel* (also פְּנוּאֵל alt. spelling).

רָאִיתִי Qal Perf 1cs רָאָה *to see*.

פָּנִים noun mp פָּנִים *face*.

וַתִּנָּצֵל Nif VC Impf 3fs נָצַל Nif *to be delivered, saved*.

נַפְשִׁי noun f + suff 1cs נֶפֶשׁ *soul, life*.

32 וַיִּזְרַח Qal VC Impf 3ms זָרַח *to rise* (the sun).

הַשֶּׁמֶשׁ def art + noun m and f שֶׁמֶשׁ *sun*.

כַּאֲשֶׁר prep כְּ + rel pronoun אֲשֶׁר (*when*).

עָבַר Qal Perf 3ms עָבַר *to pass*.

פְּנוּאֵל proper noun פְּנוּאֵל *Penuel*.

וְהוּא conj וְ + subj pronoun 3ms הוּא *he, that*.

צֹלֵעַ Qal Ptc צָלַע *to limp*.

עַל prep עַל *upon*.

יְרֵכוֹ noun m יָרֵךְ *thigh*.

33 עַל־כֵּן prep עַל *therefore*.

יֹאכְלוּ Qal Impf 3mp אָכַל *to eat*.

בְנֵי noun mp cstr בֵּן *son*.

גִּיד noun m גִּיד *thread, tendon*.

הַנָּשֶׁה def art + noun m נָשֶׁה *nerve, tendon*.

אֲשֶׁר rel pronoun אֲשֶׁר (*which is*).

כַּף noun f כַּף *hollow of the hand, palm*.

הַיָּרֵךְ def art + noun f יָרֵךְ *thigh*.

נָגַע Qal Perf 3ms נָגַע *to strike, touch, reach*.

בְּכַף prep בְּ + noun f כַּף *hollow of the hand, palm.*

יָרֵךְ noun m יָרֵךְ *thigh.*

בְּגִיד prep בְּ + noun f גִּיד *thread, tendon.*

הַנָּשֶׁה def art + noun m נָשֶׁה *nerve, tendon.*

Questions

1 Give a literal translation of לֹא יַעֲקֹב יֵאָמֵר עוֹד שִׁמְךָ (verse 29). How would you express this in idiomatic English?

2 Do you prefer God or gods as a translation of אֱלֹהִים in verse 20? Why?

3 Why is וַתִּנָּצֵל in verse 31 feminine in form?

RUTH 1:11–19A RUTH MAKES A PLEDGE TO NAOMI

11 וַתֹּאמֶר נָעֳמִי שֹׁבְנָה בְנֹתַי לָמָּה תֵלַכְנָה עִמִּי הַעֽוֹד־לִי בָנִים בְּמֵעַי וְהָיוּ לָכֶם
לַאֲנָשִׁים׃ 12 שֹׁבְנָה בְנֹתַי לֵכְןָ כִּי זָקַנְתִּי מִהְיוֹת לְאִישׁ כִּי אָמַרְתִּי יֶשׁ־לִי תִקְוָה גַּם הָיִיתִי
הַלַּיְלָה לְאִישׁ וְגַם יָלַדְתִּי בָנִים׃ 13 הֲלָהֵן תְּשַׂבֵּרְנָה עַד אֲשֶׁר יִגְדָּלוּ הֲלָהֵן תֵּעָגֵנָה לְבִלְתִּי
הֱיוֹת לְאִישׁ אַל בְּנֹתַי כִּי־מַר־לִי מְאֹד מִכֶּם כִּי־יָצְאָה בִי יַד־יְהוָה׃ 14 וַתִּשֶּׂנָה קוֹלָן
וַתִּבְכֶּינָה עוֹד וַתִּשַּׁק עָרְפָּה לַחֲמוֹתָהּ וְרוּת דָּבְקָה בָּהּ׃ 15 וַתֹּאמֶר הִנֵּה שָׁבָה יְבִמְתֵּךְ אֶל־
עַמָּהּ וְאֶל־אֱלֹהֶיהָ שׁוּבִי אַחֲרֵי יְבִמְתֵּךְ׃ 16 וַתֹּאמֶר רוּת אַל־תִּפְגְּעִי־בִי לְעָזְבֵךְ לָשׁוּב
מֵאַחֲרָיִךְ כִּי אֶל־אֲשֶׁר תֵּלְכִי אֵלֵךְ וּבַאֲשֶׁר תָּלִינִי אָלִין עַמֵּךְ עַמִּי וֵאלֹהַיִךְ אֱלֹהָי׃ 17 בַּאֲשֶׁר
תָּמוּתִי אָמוּת וְשָׁם אֶקָּבֵר כֹּה יַעֲשֶׂה יְהוָה לִי וְכֹה יוֹסִיף כִּי הַמָּוֶת יַפְרִיד בֵּינִי וּבֵינֵךְ׃
18 וַתֵּרֶא כִּי־מִתְאַמֶּצֶת הִיא לָלֶכֶת אִתָּהּ וַתֶּחְדַּל לְדַבֵּר אֵלֶיהָ׃ 19 וַתֵּלַכְנָה שְׁתֵּיהֶם עַד־
בּוֹאָנָה בֵּית לָחֶם׃

11 וַתֹּאמֶר Qal VC Impf 3fs אָמַר *to say.*

נָעֳמִי proper noun נָעֳמִי *Naomi.*

שֹׁבְנָה Qal Impv fp שׁוּב *to turn, return;* Hif *to restore.*

בְנֹתַי noun fp + suff 1cs בַּת *daughter.*

לָמָּה adv לָמָּה *why.*

תֵלַכְנָה Qal VC Impf 2fp הָלַךְ *to walk, go.*

עִמִּי prep עִם + suff 1cs עִם *with.*

הַעֽוֹד interrog ה + adv עוֹד *again.*

לִי prep לְ + suff 1cs לְ *to, at, for.*

בָנִים noun mp בֵּן *son.*

בְּמֵעַי prep בְּ + noun m + suff 1cs מֵעֶה *intestines, womb.*

וְהָיוּ Qal VC Impf 3mp הָיָה *to be, become.*

לָכֶם prep לְ + suff 2mp לְ *to you.*

לַאֲנָשִׁים prep לְ + noun mp אִישׁ *for husbands.*

12 שֹׁבְנָה Qal Impv fp שׁוּב *to turn, return.*

לֵכְנָה Qal Impv fp הָלַךְ to walk, go.

זָקַנְתִּי Qal Perf 1cs זָקֵן to be old.

מִהְיוֹת prep מִן + Qal Inf Cstr הָיָה to be, become (I am too old to be).

לְאִישׁ prep לְ + noun m אִישׁ (to a man).

אָמַרְתִּי Qal Perf 1cs אָמַר to say (if I thought).

יֵשׁ noun m cstr יֵשׁ there is.

תִקְוָה noun f תִּקְוָה hope.

גַּם conj גַּם even, also.

הָיִיתִי Qal Perf 1cs הָיָה to be, become.

הַלַּיְלָה def art + noun m לַיְלָה (tonight).

וְגַם conj וְ + conj גַּם (and also).

יָלַדְתִּי Qal Perf 1cs יָלַד to give birth.

13 הֲלָהֵן interrog הַ + prep לְ + interj particle הֵן thus (would therefore).

תְּשַׂבֵּרְנָה Piel Impf 2fp שָׂבַר to look at; Piel to expect, wait.

יִגְדָּלוּ Qal Impf 3mp גָּדַל to be big, great; to grow.

תֵּעָגֵנָה Nif Impf 2fp עָגַן Nif: to be shut up, remain shut up.

לְבִלְתִּי prep לְ + adv בֵּלֶת not, without, except, unless.

הֱיוֹת Qal Inf Cstr הָיָה to be, become.

אַל negative particle אַל no, not, do not.

מַר Qal Perf 3ms מָרַר to flow, be bitter.

מְאֹד adv; noun; adj מְאֹד much; very; power.

מִכֶּם prep מִן + suff 2mp מִן from you (for you).

יָצְאָה Qal Perf 3fs יָצָא to go out.

בִי prep בְּ + suff 1s בְּ against me.

יַד noun fs cstr יָד hand.

14 וַתִּשֶּׂנָה Qal VC Impf 3fp נָשָׂא to lift up, to take, receive, accept.

קוֹלָן noun m + suff 3fs קוֹל voice.

וַתִּבְכֶּינָה Qal VC Impf 3fp בָּכָה to weep, grieve.

עוֹד adv again.

וַתִּשַּׁק Qal VC Impf 3fs נָשַׁק to kiss.

עָרְפָּה proper noun Orpah.

לַחֲמוֹתָהּ prep לְ + noun f + suff 3fs חֲמוֹת mother-in-law.

וְרוּת conj וְ + proper noun רוּת Ruth.

דָּבְקָה Qal Perf 3fs דָּבַק to adhere, attach to, cling.

בָּהּ prep בְּ + suff 3fs בְּ (to her).

15 **הִנֵּה** interjection **הִנֵּה** *look.*

שָׁבָה Qal Impf 3fs **שׁוּב** *to turn, return;* Hif *to restore.*

יְבִמְתֵּךְ noun f + suff 2fs **יְבֶמֶת** *sister-in-law.*

עַמָּהּ noun m + suff 3fs **עַם** *people.*

אֱלֹהֶיהָ noun mp + suff 3fs (*her gods*).

שׁוּבִי Qal Impv fs **שׁוּב** *to turn, return.*

אַחֲרֵי prep **אַחַר** *after.*

16 **אַל** noun used as adv, negative particle **אַל** *do not.*

תִּפְגְּעִי Qal Impf 2fs **פָּגַע** *to rush, urge.*

בִּי prep **בְּ** + suff 1s **בְּ** *in, with, by me.*

לְעָזְבֵךְ prep **לְ** + Qal Inf Cstr + suff 2fs **עָזַב** *to leave, desert.*

לָשׁוּב prep **לְ** + Qal Inf Cstr **שׁוּב** *to turn, return.*

מֵאַחֲרָיִךְ prep **מִן** + prep **אַחַר** *after, behind.*

אֲשֶׁר rel pronoun **אֲשֶׁר** *where.*

תֵּלְכִי Qal Impf 2fs **הָלַךְ** *to walk, go.*

אֵלֵךְ Qal Impf 1cs **הָלַךְ** *to walk, go.*

וּבַאֲשֶׁר conj **וְ** + prep **בְּ** + rel pronoun **אֲשֶׁר** (*and where*).

תָּלִינִי Qal Impf 2fs **לוּן** *to spend the night.*

אָלִין Qal Impf 1cs **לוּן** *to spend the night.*

17 **בַּאֲשֶׁר** prep **בְּ** + rel pronoun **אֲשֶׁר** *that, which, who, whom, whose, where.*

תָּמוּתִי Qal Impf 2fs **מוּת** *to die.*

אָמוּת Qal Impf 1cs **מוּת** *to die.*

וְשָׁם conj **וְ** + adv **שָׁם** *there.*

אֶקָּבֵר Nif Impf 1cs **קָבַר** *to bury;* Nif *to be buried.*

כֹּה adv **כֹּה** *thus.*

יַעֲשֶׂה Qal Impf 3ms **עָשָׂה** *to make, do* (Jussive).

וְכֹה conj **וְ** + adv **כֹּה** *thus.*

יוֹסִיף Hif Impf 3ms **יָסַף** *to increase, do again;* Hif as Qal (Jussive).

כִּי adv **כִּי** *if.*

הַמָּוֶת def art + noun m **מָוֶת** *death.*

יַפְרִיד Hif Impf 3ms **פָּרַד** *to break off;* Hif *to separate, disperse.*

בֵּינִי prep + suff 1cs **בֵּין** *between.*

וּבֵינֵךְ conj **וְ** + noun m + suff 2fs **בֵּין** *between.*

18 **וַתֵּרֶא** Qal VC Impf 3fs **רָאָה** *to see.*

מִתְאַמֶּצֶת Hitp Ptc fs **אָמַץ** *to support;* Hitp *to be of fixed mind* (*being of a fixed mind*).

לָלֶ֫כֶת prep לְ + Qal Inf Cstr הָלַךְ *to walk, go.*

אִתָּהּ object marker + suff 2fs אֵת *with.*

וַתֶּחְדַּל Qal VC Impf 3fs חָדַל *to cease, desist.*

לְדַבֵּר Piel Inf Cstr דָּבַר Piel: *to speak.*

אֵלֶ֫יהָ prep + suff 3fs אֶל *to.*

19 וַתֵּלַ֫כְנָה Qal VC Impf 3fp הָלַךְ *to walk, go.*

שְׁתֵּיהֶם numeral f + suff 3mp שְׁנַ֫יִם *two (both of them).*

בֹּאָ֫נָה Qal Inf Abs + suff 3fp בּוֹא *to come;* Hif *to bring.*

בֵּית לֶ֫חֶם proper noun *Bethlehem.*

Questions

1 Sometimes the conjunction ו has the sense of *so that* rather than simply *and*, such as in the word וְהָיוּ in verse 11. Can you make an idiomatic translation of this phrase?

2 In verse 13 the phrase הֲלָהֵן תֵּעָגֵ֫נָה לְבִלְתִּי הֱיוֹת לְאִישׁ means literally *would you therefore shut yourselves up, not being to a man.* Compare established translations and decide which you think is the best rendering.

3 The story of Ruth contains many feminine singular and plural forms that are encountered infrequently elsewhere. However, masculine grammatical forms are occasionally used. Can you find an example in verse 13?

1 SAMUEL 16:4–13 THE ANOINTING OF DAVID

4 וַיַּ֫עַשׂ שְׁמוּאֵל אֵת אֲשֶׁר דִּבֶּר יְהוָה וַיָּבֹא בֵּית לָ֑חֶם וַיֶּחֶרְדוּ זִקְנֵי הָעִיר לִקְרָאתוֹ
וַיֹּ֫אמֶר שָׁלֹם בּוֹאֶֽךָ׃ 5 וַיֹּ֫אמֶר שָׁלוֹם לִזְבֹּ֫חַ לַיהוָה בָּ֑אתִי הִֽתְקַדְּשׁוּ וּבָאתֶם אִתִּי בַּזָּ֑בַח
וַיְקַדֵּשׁ אֶת־יִשַׁי וְאֶת־בָּנָ֗יו וַיִּקְרָא לָהֶם לַזָּֽבַח׃ 6 וַיְהִי בְּבוֹאָם וַיַּ֫רְא אֶת־אֱלִיאָב וַיֹּ֫אמֶר אַךְ
נֶ֫גֶד יְהוָה מְשִׁיחֽוֹ׃ 7 וַיֹּ֫אמֶר יְהוָה אֶל־שְׁמוּאֵל אַל־תַּבֵּט אֶל־מַרְאֵ֫הוּ וְאֶל־גְּבֹ֫הַּ קוֹמָתוֹ כִּי
מְאַסְתִּ֑יהוּ כִּי לֹא אֲשֶׁר יִרְאֶה הָֽאָדָם כִּי הָֽאָדָם יִרְאֶה לַעֵינַ֫יִם וַיהוָה יִרְאֶה לַלֵּבָֽב׃
8 וַיִּקְרָא יִשַׁי אֶל־אֲבִינָדָב וַיַּֽעֲבִרֵ֫הוּ לִפְנֵי שְׁמוּאֵ֑ל וַיֹּ֫אמֶר גַּם־בָּזֶה לֹא־בָחַר יְהוָֽה׃
9 וַיַּֽעֲבֵר יִשַׁי שַׁמָּ֑ה וַיֹּ֫אמֶר גַּם־בָּזֶה לֹא־בָחַר יְהוָֽה׃ 10 וַיַּֽעֲבֵר יִשַׁי שִׁבְעַת בָּנָיו לִפְנֵי
שְׁמוּאֵ֑ל וַיֹּ֫אמֶר שְׁמוּאֵל אֶל־יִשַׁי לֹא־בָחַר יְהוָה בָּאֵֽלֶּה׃ 11 וַיֹּ֫אמֶר שְׁמוּאֵל אֶל־יִשַׁי הֲתַמּוּ
הַנְּעָרִים וַיֹּ֫אמֶר עוֹד שָׁאַר הַקָּטָן וְהִנֵּה רֹעֶה בַּצֹּ֑אן וַיֹּ֫אמֶר שְׁמוּאֵל אֶל־יִשַׁי שִׁלְחָה וְקָחֶ֫נּוּ כִּי
לֹא־נָסֹב עַד־בֹּאוֹ פֹֽה׃ 12 וַיִּשְׁלַח וַיְבִיאֵ֫הוּ וְהוּא אַדְמוֹנִי עִם־יְפֵה עֵינַ֫יִם וְטוֹב רֹ֑אִי וַיֹּ֫אמֶר
יְהוָה קוּם מְשָׁחֵ֫הוּ כִּי־זֶה הֽוּא׃ 13 וַיִּקַּח שְׁמוּאֵל אֶת־קֶ֫רֶן הַשֶּׁ֫מֶן וַיִּמְשַׁח אֹתוֹ בְּקֶ֫רֶב אֶחָ֑יו
וַתִּצְלַח רֽוּחַ־יְהוָה אֶל־דָּוִד מֵֽהַיּוֹם הַהוּא וָמָ֑עְלָה וַיָּ֫קָם שְׁמוּאֵל וַיֵּ֫לֶךְ הָרָמָֽתָה׃

4 וַיַּ֫עַשׂ Qal VC Impf 3ms apoc עָשָׂה *to make, do.*

שְׁמוּאֵל proper noun שְׁמוּאֵל *Samuel.*

דִּבֶּר Piel Perf 3ms דָּבַר Piel: *to speak.*

וַיָּבֹא Qal VC Impf 3ms בּוֹא *to come.*

וַיֶּחֶרְדוּ Qal Impf 3mp חָרַד *to be afraid, tremble.*

זִקְנֵי noun mp cstr זָקֵן *old man, elder.*

הָעִיר def art + noun f עִיר *city.*

לִקְרָאתוֹ prep לְ + Qal Inf Cstr+ suff 3mp קָרָא I *to call*; II *to meet.*

שָׁלוֹם noun m שָׁלוֹם *in peace.*

בּוֹאֲךָ Qal Inf Cstr + suff 2ms בּוֹא *to come* (*do you come?*).

5 לִזְבֹּחַ prep לְ + Qal Inf Cstr זָבַח *to sacrifice.*

לַיהוָה prep לְ + proper noun יְהוָה *to Yhwh.*

בָּאתִי Qal Perf 1cs בּוֹא *to come.*

הִתְקַדְּשׁוּ Hitp Impv mp קָדֵשׁ *to be holy*; Hitp *to consecrate oneself.*

וּבָאתֶם Qal VC Perf 2mp בּוֹא *to come.*

אִתִּי prep אֵת + suff 1cs אֵת *with.*

בַּזֶּבַח prep בְּ + noun m זֶבַח *sacrifice.*

וַיְקַדֵּשׁ Piel VC Impf 3ms קָדֵשׁ *to be holy*; Piel *to consecrate.*

יִשַׁי proper noun *Jesse.*

בָּנָיו noun mp + suff 3ms בֵּן *son.*

וַיִּקְרָא Qal VC Impf 3ms קָרָא I *to call*; II *to meet.*

לָהֶם prep לְ + suff 3mp לְ *to, at, for.*

לַזָּבַח prep לְ + noun m זֶבַח *sacrifice.*

6 בְּבוֹאָם prep בְּ + Qal Inf Cstr + suff 3mp בּוֹא *to come.*

וַיַּרְא Qal VC Impf 3ms apoc רָאָה *to see.*

אֱלִיאָב proper noun *Eliab.*

אַךְ adv אַךְ *certainly, surely.*

נֶגֶד prep *in front of.*

מְשִׁיחוֹ noun m + suff 3ms מָשִׁיחַ *his anointed.*

7 אַל negative particle אַל *do not.*

תַּבֵּט Hif Impf 2ms נָבַט no Qal; Hif *to look, see.*

מַרְאֵהוּ noun m + suff 3ms מַרְאֶה *appearance, vision.*

גְּבֹהַּ noun m גֹּבַהּ *height.*

קוֹמָתוֹ noun f קוֹמָה *stature.*

מְאַסְתִּיהוּ Qal Perf 1cs + suff 3ms מָאַס *to reject, despise.*

יִרְאֶה Qal Impf 3ms רָאָה *to see* (i.e. *the LORD sees*).

הָאָדָם def art + noun m אָדָם *earth, man.*

יִרְאֶה Qal Impf 3ms רָאָה *to see*; Nif *to appear, to be revealed.*

לַעֵינַיִם prep לְ + noun f dual cstr עַיִן *eye.*

וַיהוָה conj וְ + proper noun יְהוָה.

יִרְאֶה Qal Impf 3ms רָאָה *to see*.

לַלֵּבָב prep לְ + noun m לֵבָב *heart, mind, soul*.

8 וַיִּקְרָא Qal VC Impf 3ms קָרָא I *to call*; II *to meet*.

אֲבִינָדָב proper noun אֲבִינָדָב *Abinadab*.

וַיַּעֲבִרֵהוּ Hif VC Impf 3ms + suff 3ms עָבַר *to pass*; Hif *to cause to pass*.

לִפְנֵי prep לִפְנֵי *before, in front of*.

בָּזֶה prep בְּ + demonstr ms זֶה (also *this one*).

בָּחַר Qal Perf 3ms בָּחַר *to choose*, often used with בְּ to indicate the object.

9 וַיַּעֲבֵר Hif VC Impf 3ms עָבַר *to pass*; Hif *to cause to pass*.

שַׁמָּה proper noun *Shammah*.

10 וַיַּעֲבֵר Hif VC Impf 3ms עָבַר *to pass*; Hif *to cause to pass*.

שִׁבְעַת numeral m cstr שֶׁבַע *seven*.

לִפְנֵי prep לִפְנֵי *before, in front of*.

בָּאֵלֶּה prep בְּ + demonstrative אֵלֶּה *these*.

11 הֲתַמּוּ interrog הֲ + Qal Perf 3cp תָּמַם *to be finished* (*are they finished?*).

הַנְּעָרִים def art + noun mp נַעַר *young man, boy, servant*.

עוֹד adv עוֹד *again, further, yet, still*.

שָׁאַר Qal Perf 3ms שָׁאַר *to be left, remain*.

הַקָּטָן art + adj m קָטָן *little, small* (*the youngest*).

וְהִנֵּה conj וְ + interj הִנֵּה *behold, look*.

רֹעֶה Qal Ptc רָעָה *to feed, pasture*; noun: *a shepherd*.

בַּצֹּאן prep בְּ + noun f צֹאן *flock*.

שִׁלְחָה Qal Impv + paragogic ה שָׁלַח *to send, stretch out*.

וְקָחֶנּוּ conj וְ + Qal Impv + suff 3ms לָקַח *to take, receive*.

נָסֹב Qal Impf 1cp סָבַב *to turn, go around*; Hif *to cause to turn* (*we will not sit down*, i.e. around the table).

בֹאוֹ Qal Ptc + suff 3ms בּוֹא *to come*; Hif *to bring*.

פֹּה adv פֹּה *here*.

12 וַיִּשְׁלַח Qal VC Impf 3ms שָׁלַח *to send, stretch out*; Piel *to let go, expel*.

וַיְבִיאֵהוּ Hif VC Impf 3ms + suff 3ms בּוֹא *to come*; Hif *to bring*.

וְהוּא conj וְ + subj pronoun 3ms הוּא (*and he was*).

אַדְמוֹנִי adj m *red haired*.

עִם prep עִם *with*.

יְפֵה adj m cstr יָפֶה *beautiful*.

עֵינַיִם noun f dual עַיִן *eye*.

וְטוֹב **וְטוֹב** conj וְ + adj m טוֹב *good.*

רֹאִי **רֹאִי** noun m in pause רְאִי *vision, sight (good looking).*

קוּם **קוּם** Qal Impv קוּם *to get up.*

מְשָׁחֵהוּ **מְשָׁחֵהוּ** Qal Impv + suff 3ms מָשַׁח *to spread over, anoint.*

זֶה **זֶה** demonstr ms זֶה *this.*

הוּא **הוּא** subject pronoun 3ms הוּא *he, that.*

13 וַיִּקַּח **וַיִּקַּח** Qal VC Impf 3ms לָקַח *to take, receive.*

קֶרֶן **קֶרֶן** noun f קֶרֶן *horn, lightning.*

הַשֶּׁמֶן **הַשֶּׁמֶן** def art + noun m שֶׁמֶן *oil.*

וַיִּמְשַׁח **וַיִּמְשַׁח** Qal VC Impf 3ms מָשַׁח *to spread over, anoint.*

בְּקֶרֶב **בְּקֶרֶב** prep בְּ + noun m קֶרֶב *middle (among).*

אֶחָיו **אֶחָיו** noun mp + suff 3ms אָח *brother.*

וַתִּצְלַח **וַתִּצְלַח** Qal VC Impf 2fs צָלַח *to go through, attack, succeed.*

רוּחַ **רוּחַ** noun f רוּחַ *wind, spirit, breath.*

מֵהַיּוֹם **מֵהַיּוֹם** prep מִן + def art + noun m יוֹם *day.*

הַהוּא **הַהוּא** def art + demonstr adj ms הוּא *he, that.*

וָמַעְלָה **וָמַעְלָה** conj וְ + prep מַעַל *above, upward, onward (from that day forward).*

וַיָּקָם **וַיָּקָם** Qal VC Impf 3ms קוּם *to get up.*

וַיֵּלֶךְ **וַיֵּלֶךְ** Qal VC Impf 3ms הָלַךְ *to walk, go.*

הָרָמָתָה **הָרָמָתָה** def art + proper noun + ה *locale* רָמָה *Ramah (the* ה *locale indicates motion towards a place).*

Questions

1 In verse 7 most translations supply some additional words so that the sentence reads: *because the LORD does not see as men see.* How would this phrase look in Hebrew if it were written that way?

2 What English cognate have we taken from מָשִׁיחַ (verse 6)?

3 Why is Samuel impressed by Eliab's height? (Hint: compare 1 Samuel 9:2.)

2 SAMUEL 12:1–10 NATHAN'S PARABLE

1 וַיִּשְׁלַח יְהוָה אֶת־נָתָן אֶל־דָּוִד וַיָּבֹא אֵלָיו וַיֹּאמֶר לוֹ שְׁנֵי אֲנָשִׁים הָיוּ בְּעִיר אֶחָת אֶחָד עָשִׁיר וְאֶחָד רָאשׁ: 2 לֶעָשִׁיר הָיָה צֹאן וּבָקָר הַרְבֵּה מְאֹד: 3 וְלָרָשׁ אֵין־כֹּל כִּי אִם־כִּבְשָׂה אַחַת קְטַנָּה אֲשֶׁר קָנָה וַיְחַיֶּהָ וַתִּגְדַּל עִמּוֹ וְעִם־בָּנָיו יַחְדָּו מִפִּתּוֹ תֹאכַל וּמִכֹּסוֹ תִשְׁתֶּה וּבְחֵיקוֹ תִשְׁכָּב וַתְּהִי־לוֹ כְּבַת: 4 וַיָּבֹא הֵלֶךְ לְאִישׁ הֶעָשִׁיר וַיַּחְמֹל לָקַחַת מִצֹּאנוֹ וּמִבְּקָרוֹ לַעֲשׂוֹת לָאֹרֵחַ הַבָּא־לוֹ וַיִּקַּח אֶת־כִּבְשַׂת הָאִישׁ הָרָאשׁ וַיַּעֲשֶׂהָ לָאִישׁ הַבָּא אֵלָיו: 5 וַיִּחַר־אַף דָּוִד בָּאִישׁ מְאֹד וַיֹּאמֶר אֶל־נָתָן חַי־יְהוָה כִּי בֶן־מָוֶת הָאִישׁ הָעֹשֶׂה זֹאת: 6 וְאֶת־הַכִּבְשָׂה יְשַׁלֵּם אַרְבַּעְתָּיִם עֵקֶב אֲשֶׁר עָשָׂה אֶת־הַדָּבָר הַזֶּה וְעַל אֲשֶׁר לֹא־חָמָל: 7 וַיֹּאמֶר נָתָן אֶל־דָּוִד אַתָּה

הָאִישׁ כֹּה־אָמַר יְהֹוָה אֱלֹהֵי יִשְׂרָאֵל אָנֹכִי מְשַׁחְתִּיךָ לְמֶלֶךְ עַל־יִשְׂרָאֵל וְאָנֹכִי הִצַּלְתִּיךָ מִיַּד שָׁאוּל: 8 וָאֶתְּנָה לְךָ אֶת־בֵּית אֲדֹנֶיךָ וְאֶת־נְשֵׁי אֲדֹנֶיךָ בְּחֵיקֶךָ וָאֶתְּנָה לְךָ אֶת־בֵּית יִשְׂרָאֵל וִיהוּדָה וְאִם־מְעָט וְאֹסִפָה לְּךָ כָּהֵנָּה וְכָהֵנָּה: 9 מַדּוּעַ בָּזִיתָ אֶת־דְּבַר יְהֹוָה לַעֲשׂוֹת הָרַע בְּעֵינוֹ[1] אֵת אוּרִיָּה הַחִתִּי הִכִּיתָ בַחֶרֶב וְאֶת־אִשְׁתּוֹ לָקַחְתָּ לְּךָ לְאִשָּׁה וְאֹתוֹ הָרַגְתָּ בְּחֶרֶב בְּנֵי עַמּוֹן: 10 וְעַתָּה לֹא־תָסוּר חֶרֶב מִבֵּיתְךָ עַד־עוֹלָם עֵקֶב כִּי בְזִתַנִי וַתִּקַּח אֶת־אֵשֶׁת אוּרִיָּה הַחִתִּי לִהְיוֹת לְךָ לְאִשָּׁה:

1 וַיִּשְׁלַח Qal VC Impf 3ms שָׁלַח *to send, stretch out.*

נָתָן proper noun *Nathan.*

וַיָּבֹא Qal VC Impf 3ms בּוֹא *to come.*

שְׁנֵי numeral cstr שְׁנַיִם *two.*

הָיוּ Qal Perf 3cp הָיָה *to be, become.*

בְּעִיר prep בְּ + noun fs עִיר *city.*

אֶחָת numeral f (in pause) אֶחָד *one, first.*

עָשִׁיר adj, noun m עָשִׁיר *rich, noble.*

רָאשׁ Qal Ptc רוּשׁ *to be poor.*

2 לְעָשִׁיר prep לְ + noun m עָשִׁיר *to the rich one.*

הָיָה Qal Perf 3ms הָיָה *to be, become.*

צֹאן noun f צֹאן *flock.*

וּבָקָר conj וְ + noun m בָּקָר *herd, cattle.*

הַרְבֵּה Hif inf abs רָבָה *to be many; Hif to increase, multiply; inf abs used as adv: many.*

מְאֹד adverb; noun; adj מְאֹד *very.*

3 וְלָרָשׁ conj וְ + prep לְ + noun m רָשׁ *and to the poor one.*

אֵין noun m cstr (used as adv) אֵין *there was not.*

כֹּל noun ms *all, anything.*

כִּי־אִם adv כִּי *but, except.*

כִּבְשָׂה noun f כֶּבֶשׂ *lamb.*

אַחַת numeral f אֶחָד *one, first.*

קְטַנָּה adj f קָטָן *little, small.*

קָנָה Qal Perf 3ms קָנָה *to buy.*

וַיְחַיֶּהָ Piel VC Impf 3ms + suff 3fs חָיָה *to live; Piel to give life, nourish.*

וַתִּגְדַּל Qal VC Impf 3fs גָּדַל *to be big, great; to grow.*

עִמּוֹ prep עִם + suff 3ms עִם *with.*

יַחְדָּו adv יַחַד *together.*

---

[1] Qere בְּעֵינָי

226

מִפַּתּוֹ noun f פַּת food (from his food).

תֹּאכַל Qal Impf 3fs אָכַל to eat.

וּמִכֹּסוֹ conj וְ + noun f + suff 3ms כּוֹס receptacle, cup.

תִשְׁתֶּה Qal VC Impf 3fs שָׁתָה to drink.

וּבְחֵיקוֹ conj וְ + noun m + suff 3ms חֵיק chest, embrace.

תִשְׁכָּב Qal Impf 3fs שָׁכַב to lie down, rest.

וַתְּהִי Qal VC Impf 3fs הָיָה to be, become.

כְּבַת prep כְּ + noun f בַּת daughter.

4 וַיָּבֹא Qal VC Impf 3ms בּוֹא to come.

הֵלֶךְ noun m הֵלֶךְ journey, traveller.

וַיַּחְמֹל Qal VC Impf 3ms חָמַל to pity, spare.

לָקַחַת Qal Inf Cstr לָקַח to take, receive.

מִצֹּאנוֹ prep מִן + noun m + suff 3ms צֹאן flock.

וּמִבְּקָרוֹ conj וְ + prep מִן + noun m + suff 3ms בָּקָר herd, cattle.

לַעֲשׂוֹת Qal Inf Cstr עָשָׂה to make, do.

לָאֹרֵחַ Qal Ptc אֹרַח for the journeying man.

הַבָּא Qal Ptc בּוֹא the one who had come.

וַיִּקַּח Qal VC Impf 3ms לָקַח to take, receive.

כִּבְשַׂת noun f cstr כֶּבֶשׂ lamb.

וַיַּעֲשֶׂהָ Qal VC Impf 3ms עָשָׂה to make, do.

לָאִישׁ prep לְ + noun m אִישׁ man.

הַבָּא def art + Qal Ptc בּוֹא to come (the one who had come).

5 וַיִּחַר Qal Impf 3ms חָרָה to burn, be angry.

אַף noun m אַף nose, anger.

בָּאִישׁ prep בְּ + noun m אִישׁ against the man.

מְאֹד adv; noun; adj מְאֹד much; very; power.

חַי noun m חַי (by the) life of.

מָוֶת noun m מָוֶת death.

הָעֹשֶׂה Qal Ptc עָשָׂה the one doing.

זֹאת demonstr fs זֹאת this.

6 הַכִּבְשָׂה noun f כֶּבֶשׂ the ewe lamb.

יְשַׁלֵּם Piel Impf 3ms שָׁלֵם to be whole, completed; Piel to finish, recompense.

אַרְבַּעְתָּיִם adverb f dual אַרְבַּע four (fourfold).

עֵקֶב conj because.

עָשָׂה Qal Perf 3ms עָשָׂה to make, do.

הַדָּבָר def art + noun m דָּבָר *word, thing, matter.*

וְעַל conj וְ + prep עַל *on, upon, on account of.*

חָמַל Qal Perf 3ms חָמַל *to pity, have compassion.*

7 כֹה adv כֹה *thus, therefore.*

מְשַׁחְתִּיךָ Qal Perf 1s + suff 2ms מָשַׁח *to spread over, anoint.*

לְמֶלֶךְ prep לְ + noun m מֶלֶךְ *as king.*

עַל prep עַל *over.*

וְאָנֹכִי conj וְ + subj pronoun 1cs אָנֹכִי *I.*

הִצַּלְתִּיךָ Hif Perf 1cs + suff 2ms נָצַל no Qal; Hif *to deprive, deliver.*

מִיַּד prep מִן + noun f יָד *hand.*

שָׁאוּל proper noun שָׁאוּל *Saul.*

8 וָאֶתְּנָה Qal VC Impf 1s + paragogic ה נָתַן *to give, send, yield.*

בֵּית noun m cstr בַּיִת *house.*

אֲדֹנֶיךָ noun m + suff 2ms אָדוֹן *lord, master.*

נְשֵׁי noun fp cstr אִשָּׁה *woman.*

בְּחֵיקֶךָ noun m + suff 2ms חֵיק *chest, embrace.*

וִיהוּדָה conj וְ + proper noun יְהוּדָה *Judah.*

וְאִם conj וְ + conj אִם *and if.*

מְעָט substantive; adjective; adverb מְעָט *very little, a little.*

וְאֹסִפָה Hif VC Impf 1s + parag **he** יָסַף *to increase, do again;* Hif as Qal (*I would have increased;* Impf sometimes written with **alef**).

כָּהֵנָּה וְכָהֵנָּה subj pronoun 3fs הֵנָּה *those so much and more.*

9 מַדּוּעַ adv of interr מַה *what, how, why.*

בָּזִיתָ Qal Perf 2ms בָּזָה *to despise, neglect.*

לַעֲשׂוֹת prep לְ + Qal Inf Cstr עָשָׂה *to make, do.*

הָרַע def art + noun m רַע *evil, wickedness.*

בְּעֵינַי prep בְּ + noun f dual + suff 1s עַיִן *eye.*

אוּרִיָּה proper noun *Uriah.*

הַחִתִּי def art + gentilic noun חֵת *the Hittite.*

הִכִּיתָ Hif Perf 3ms נָכָה Hif: *to strike, kill.*

בַחֶרֶב prep בְּ + noun f חֶרֶב *sword.*

אִשְׁתּוֹ noun m + suff 3ms אִשָּׁה *woman.*

לָקַחְתָּ Qal Perf 2ms לָקַח *to take, receive.*

לְאִשָּׁה prep לְ + noun fs אִשָּׁה *as a wife.*

הָרַגְתָּ Qal Perf 2ms הָרַג *to kill.*

בְּנֵי noun mp cstr בֵּן *son.*

עַמּוֹן proper noun עַמּוֹן *Ammon.*

10 וְעַתָּה conj וְ + adv עַתָּה *now.*

תָּסוּר Qal Impf 3fs סוּר *to turn aside, depart.*

חֶרֶב noun f חֶרֶב *sword.*

מִבֵּיתְךָ prep מִן + noun m + suff 2ms בַּיִת *house.*

עוֹלָם noun m עוֹלָם *eternity.*

עֵקֶב conj עֵקֶב *because.*

בְזִתַנִי Qal Perf 2ms + suff 1s בָּזָה *to despise, neglect.*

וַתִּקַּח Qal Perf 2ms לָקַח *to take, receive.*

אֵשֶׁת noun fs cstr אִשָּׁה *woman.*

לִהְיוֹת prep לְ + Qal Inf Cstr הָיָה *to be, become: to be.*

Questions

1 Verse 1 contains two words for *one*. Which word refers to the city and which refers to the first man?

2 In verse 6 David describes the rich man as בֶּן־מָוֶת, an idiomatic phrase. What is its literal meaning, and how would you translate it?

3 Nathan tells David, 'You are the man.' What does he mean? Is the parable a good comparison with David's behaviour in 2 Samuel 11?

JONAH 3 THE REPENTANCE OF NINEVEH

1 וַיְהִי דְבַר־יְהוָה אֶל־יוֹנָה שֵׁנִית לֵאמֹר׃ 2 קוּם לֵךְ אֶל־נִינְוֵה הָעִיר הַגְּדוֹלָה וּקְרָא
אֵלֶיהָ אֶת־הַקְּרִיאָה אֲשֶׁר אָנֹכִי דֹּבֵר אֵלֶיךָ׃ 3 וַיָּקָם יוֹנָה וַיֵּלֶךְ אֶל־נִינְוֵה כִּדְבַר יְהוָה
וְנִינְוֵה הָיְתָה עִיר־גְּדוֹלָה לֵאלֹהִים מַהֲלַךְ שְׁלֹשֶׁת יָמִים׃ 4 וַיָּחֶל יוֹנָה לָבוֹא בָעִיר מַהֲלַךְ
יוֹם אֶחָד וַיִּקְרָא וַיֹּאמַר עוֹד אַרְבָּעִים יוֹם וְנִינְוֵה נֶהְפָּכֶת׃ 5 וַיַּאֲמִינוּ אַנְשֵׁי נִינְוֵה בֵּאלֹהִים
וַיִּקְרְאוּ־צוֹם וַיִּלְבְּשׁוּ שַׂקִּים מִגְּדוֹלָם וְעַד־קְטַנָּם׃ 6 וַיִּגַּע הַדָּבָר אֶל־מֶלֶךְ נִינְוֵה וַיָּקָם
מִכִּסְאוֹ וַיַּעֲבֵר אַדַּרְתּוֹ מֵעָלָיו וַיְכַס שַׂק וַיֵּשֶׁב עַל־הָאֵפֶר׃ 7 וַיַּזְעֵק וַיֹּאמֶר בְּנִינְוֵה מִטַּעַם
הַמֶּלֶךְ וּגְדֹלָיו לֵאמֹר הָאָדָם וְהַבְּהֵמָה הַבָּקָר וְהַצֹּאן אַל־יִטְעֲמוּ מְאוּמָה אַל־יִרְעוּ וּמַיִם
אַל־יִשְׁתּוּ׃ 8 וְיִתְכַּסּוּ שַׂקִּים הָאָדָם וְהַבְּהֵמָה וְיִקְרְאוּ אֶל־אֱלֹהִים בְּחָזְקָה וְיָשֻׁבוּ אִישׁ
מִדַּרְכּוֹ הָרָעָה וּמִן־הֶחָמָס אֲשֶׁר בְּכַפֵּיהֶם׃ 9 מִי־יוֹדֵעַ יָשׁוּב וְנִחַם הָאֱלֹהִים וְשָׁב מֵחֲרוֹן
אַפּוֹ וְלֹא נֹאבֵד׃ 10 וַיַּרְא הָאֱלֹהִים אֶת־מַעֲשֵׂיהֶם כִּי־שָׁבוּ מִדַּרְכָּם הָרָעָה וַיִּנָּחֶם הָאֱלֹהִים
עַל־הָרָעָה אֲשֶׁר־דִּבֶּר לַעֲשׂוֹת־לָהֶם וְלֹא עָשָׂה׃

1 יוֹנָה proper noun *Jonah.*

שֵׁנִית ordinal adj f שְׁנַיִם *two (second).*

לֵאמֹר prep לְ + Qal Inf Cstr אָמַר *saying.*

2 קוּם Qal Impv קוּם *to get up.*

לֵךְ Qal Impv הָלַךְ *to walk, go.*

נִינְוֵה proper noun נִינְוֵה *Nineveh.*

הַגְּדוֹלָה def art + adj f גָּדוֹל *big, large, great.*

וּקְרָא conj וְ + Qal Impv קָרָא *to call, proclaim.*

אֵלֶיהָ prep + suff 3fs אֶל *to.*

הַקְּרִיאָה def art + noun f קְרִיאָה *proclamation.*

דֹּבֵר Qal Ptc דָּבַר *to speak.*

אֵלֶיךָ prep + suff 2ms אֶל *to.*

3 וַיָּקָם Qal VC Impf 3ms קוּם *to get up.*

וַיֵּלֶךְ Qal VC Impf 3ms הָלַךְ *to walk, go.*

כִּדְבַר prep כְּ + noun m cstr דָּבָר *according to the word of.*

הָיְתָה Qal Perf 3fs הָיָה *to be, become.*

לֵאלֹהִים prep לְ + noun mp אֱלֹהִים *(superlative).*

מַהֲלַךְ noun m *journey.*

שְׁלֹשֶׁת noun m cstr שָׁלוֹשׁ *three.*

יָמִים noun mp יוֹם *day.*

4 וַיָּחֶל Hif VC Impf 3ms חָלַל *to perforate; Hif to begin.*

לָבוֹא prep לְ + Qal Inf Cstr בּוֹא *to come.*

וַיִּקְרָא Qal VC Impf 3ms קָרָא *to call, proclaim.*

עוֹד adv עוֹד *still, yet.*

אַרְבָּעִים numeral mp אַרְבַּע *four; plural 40.*

נֶהְפָּכֶת Nif Ptc הָפַךְ *to turn, overthrow; Nif to be overthrown.*

5 וַיַּאֲמִינוּ Hif VC Impf 3mp + suff 3ms אָמַן *to support; Hif to trust, believe.*

אַנְשֵׁי noun mp cstr אִישׁ *man.*

בֵּאלֹהִים prep בְּ + noun mp אֱלֹהִים.

וַיִּקְרְאוּ Qal VC Impf 3mp קָרָא *to call, proclaim.*

צוֹם noun m צוֹם *fast.*

וַיִּלְבְּשׁוּ Qal VC Impf 3mp לָבַשׁ *to put on (clothes).*

שַׂקִּים noun mp שַׂק *sackcloth.*

מִגְּדוֹלָם prep מִן + adj mp גָּדוֹל *big, large, great (from their greatest).*

וְעַד conj וְ + prep עַד *until, as far as.*

קְטַנָּם adj mp קָטָן *little, small (their smallest).*

6 וַיִּגַּע Qal VC Impf 3ms נָגַע *to strike, touch, reach.*

הַדָּבָר def art + noun m דָּבָר *word, thing, matter.*

וַיָּקָם Qal VC Impf 3ms **קוּם** *to get up* and *he got up.*

מִכִּסְאוֹ prep **מִן** + noun m + suff 3ms **כִּסֵּא** *seat, throne.*

וַיַּעֲבֵר Hif VC Impf 3ms **עָבַר** *to pass;* Hif *to cause to pass (and he removed).*

אַדַּרְתּוֹ noun f + suff 3ms **אַדֶּרֶת** *glory, cloak.*

מֵעָלָיו prep **מִן** + prep **עַל** + suff 3ms **עַל** *from upon him.*

וַיְכַס Piel VC Impf 3ms apoc **כָּסָה** *to cover.*

שַׂק noun m *sackcloth.*

וַיֵּשֶׁב Qal VC Impf 3ms **יָשַׁב** *to stay, sit, live.*

עַל prep **עַל** *on, upon.*

הָאֵפֶר def art + noun m **אֵפֶר** *ashes.*

7 **וַיַּזְעֵק** Hif VC Impf 3ms **זָעַק** *to call out, proclaim.*

מִטַּעַם prep **מִן** + noun m **טַעַם** *decree.*

וְהַבְּהֵמָה conj **וְ** + def art + noun f **בְּהֵמָה** *beast, cattle.*

הַבָּקָר def art + noun m **בָּקָר** *herd, cattle.*

וְהַצֹּאן conj **וְ** + def art + noun f **צֹאן** *flock.*

יִטְעֲמוּ Qal Impf 3ms **טָעַם** *to taste, try* (Jussive).

מְאוּמָה adv *anything, something.*

יִרְעוּ Qal Impf 3mp **רָעָה** *to feed, pasture* (Jussive).

וּמַיִם conj **וְ** + def art + noun m dual **מַיִם** *water.*

יִשְׁתּוּ Qal Impf 3mp **שָׁתָה** *to drink* (Jussive).

8 **וְיִתְכַּסּוּ** conj **וְ** + Hitp Impf 3mp **כָּסָה** *to cover* (Jussive).

וְיִקְרָאוּ Qal VC Impf 3mp **קָרָא** *to call, proclaim* (Jussive).

בְּחָזְקָה prep **בְּ** + noun f **חָזְקָה** *force, might, strength.*

וְיָשֻׁבוּ conj **וְ** + Qal Impf 3mp **שׁוּב** *to turn, return;* Hif *to restore* (Jussive).

מִדַּרְכּוֹ prep **מִן** + noun m + suff 3ms **דֶּרֶךְ** *way, path, journey.*

הָרָעָה def art + noun f **רָעָה** *evil, wickedness.*

הֶחָמָס def art + noun m **חָמָס** *violence, oppression.*

בְּכַפֵּיהֶם prep **בְּ** + noun fp + suff 3mp **כַּף** *palm of hand.*

9 **מִי** pronoun **מִי** *who.*

יוֹדֵעַ Qal Ptc **יָדַע** *to know;* Nif *to be known.*

יָשׁוּב Qal Impf 3ms **שׁוּב** *to turn, return.*

וְנִחַם Nif VC Perf 3ms **נָחַם** no Qal; Nif *to lament, repent.*

הָאֱלֹהִים def art + noun mp **אֱלֹהִים.**

וְשָׁב Qal VC Perf 3ms **שׁוּב** *to turn, return.*

מֵחֲרוֹן prep **מִן** + noun m **חָרוֹן** *heat, burning.*

אַפּוֹ noun m + suff 3ms **אַף** *nose, anger.*

נֹאבֵד Qal Impf 1cp **אָבַד** *to be lost, die.*

10 **וַיַּרְא** Qal Impf 3ms apoc **רָאָה** *to see.*

מַעֲשֵׂיהֶם noun m + suff 3mp **מַעֲשֶׂה** *deed, work.*

שָׁבוּ Qal Perf 3mp **שׁוּב** *to turn, return.*

מִדַּרְכָּם prep **מִן** + noun m + suff 2mp **דֶּרֶךְ** *way, path, journey.*

הָרָעָה def art + noun f **רָעָה** *evil, wickedness.*

וַיִּנָּחֶם Nif VC Impf 3ms **נָחַם** *no Qal; Nif to lament, repent.*

עַל prep **עַל** *at.*

דִּבֶּר Piel Perf 3ms **דָּבַר** *Piel: to speak: he had spoken.*

לַעֲשׂוֹת prep **לְ** + Qal Inf Cstr **עָשָׂה** *to make, do.*

עָשָׂה Qal Perf 3ms **עָשָׂה** *to make, do.*

Questions

1 This is the second time the word of the LORD has come to Jonah. What happened the first time? (Hint: see Jonah Chapters 1 and 2.)

2 How far has Jonah travelled inside the city of Nineveh when he begins to proclaim God's message?

3 How would you translate the Jussives in verses 7 and 8?

EXODUS 3:1–14 THE BURNING BUSH

1 וּמֹשֶׁה הָיָה רֹעֶה אֶת־צֹאן יִתְרוֹ חֹתְנוֹ כֹּהֵן מִדְיָן וַיִּנְהַג אֶת־הַצֹּאן אַחַר הַמִּדְבָּר וַיָּבֹא אֶל־הַר הָאֱלֹהִים חֹרֵבָה: 2 וַיֵּרָא מַלְאַךְ יְהוָה אֵלָיו בְּלַבַּת־אֵשׁ מִתּוֹךְ הַסְּנֶה וַיַּרְא וְהִנֵּה הַסְּנֶה בֹּעֵר בָּאֵשׁ וְהַסְּנֶה אֵינֶנּוּ אֻכָּל: 3 וַיֹּאמֶר מֹשֶׁה אָסֻרָה־נָּא וְאֶרְאֶה אֶת־הַמַּרְאֶה הַגָּדֹל הַזֶּה מַדּוּעַ לֹא־יִבְעַר הַסְּנֶה: 4 וַיַּרְא יְהוָה כִּי סָר לִרְאוֹת וַיִּקְרָא אֵלָיו אֱלֹהִים מִתּוֹךְ הַסְּנֶה וַיֹּאמֶר מֹשֶׁה מֹשֶׁה וַיֹּאמֶר הִנֵּנִי: 5 וַיֹּאמֶר אַל־תִּקְרַב הֲלֹם שַׁל־נְעָלֶיךָ מֵעַל רַגְלֶיךָ כִּי הַמָּקוֹם אֲשֶׁר אַתָּה עוֹמֵד עָלָיו אַדְמַת־קֹדֶשׁ הוּא: 6 וַיֹּאמֶר אָנֹכִי אֱלֹהֵי אָבִיךָ אֱלֹהֵי אַבְרָהָם אֱלֹהֵי יִצְחָק וֵאלֹהֵי יַעֲקֹב וַיַּסְתֵּר מֹשֶׁה פָּנָיו כִּי יָרֵא מֵהַבִּיט אֶל־הָאֱלֹהִים: 7 וַיֹּאמֶר יְהוָה רָאֹה רָאִיתִי אֶת־עֳנִי עַמִּי אֲשֶׁר בְּמִצְרָיִם וְאֶת־צַעֲקָתָם שָׁמַעְתִּי מִפְּנֵי נֹגְשָׂיו כִּי יָדַעְתִּי אֶת־מַכְאֹבָיו: 8 וָאֵרֵד לְהַצִּילוֹ מִיַּד מִצְרַיִם וּלְהַעֲלֹתוֹ מִן־הָאָרֶץ הַהִוא אֶל־אֶרֶץ טוֹבָה וּרְחָבָה אֶל־אֶרֶץ זָבַת חָלָב וּדְבָשׁ אֶל־מְקוֹם הַכְּנַעֲנִי וְהַחִתִּי וְהָאֱמֹרִי וְהַפְּרִזִּי וְהַחִוִּי וְהַיְבוּסִי: 9 וְעַתָּה הִנֵּה צַעֲקַת בְּנֵי־יִשְׂרָאֵל בָּאָה אֵלָי וְגַם־רָאִיתִי אֶת־הַלַּחַץ אֲשֶׁר מִצְרַיִם לֹחֲצִים אֹתָם: 10 וְעַתָּה לְכָה וְאֶשְׁלָחֲךָ אֶל־פַּרְעֹה וְהוֹצֵא אֶת־עַמִּי בְנֵי־יִשְׂרָאֵל מִמִּצְרָיִם: 11 וַיֹּאמֶר מֹשֶׁה אֶל־הָאֱלֹהִים מִי אָנֹכִי כִּי אֵלֵךְ אֶל־פַּרְעֹה וְכִי אוֹצִיא אֶת־בְּנֵי יִשְׂרָאֵל מִמִּצְרָיִם: 12 וַיֹּאמֶר כִּי־אֶהְיֶה עִמָּךְ וְזֶה־לְּךָ הָאוֹת כִּי אָנֹכִי שְׁלַחְתִּיךָ בְּהוֹצִיאֲךָ אֶת־הָעָם מִמִּצְרַיִם תַּעַבְדוּן אֶת־הָאֱלֹהִים עַל הָהָר הַזֶּה: 13 וַיֹּאמֶר מֹשֶׁה אֶל־הָאֱלֹהִים הִנֵּה אָנֹכִי בָא אֶל־בְּנֵי יִשְׂרָאֵל וְאָמַרְתִּי לָהֶם אֱלֹהֵי אֲבוֹתֵיכֶם שְׁלָחַנִי אֲלֵיכֶם וְאָמְרוּ־לִי מַה־שְּׁמוֹ מָה אֹמַר אֲלֵהֶם: 14 וַיֹּאמֶר אֱלֹהִים אֶל־מֹשֶׁה אֶהְיֶה אֲשֶׁר אֶהְיֶה וַיֹּאמֶר כֹּה תֹאמַר לִבְנֵי יִשְׂרָאֵל אֶהְיֶה שְׁלָחַנִי אֲלֵיכֶם:

1 וּמֹשֶׁה conj וְ + proper noun מֹשֶׁה *Moses.*

הָיָה Qal Perf 3ms הָיָה *to be, become.*

רֹעֶה Qal Ptc רָעָה *shepherd.*

אֶת prep *with.*

צֹאן noun f *flock.*

יִתְרוֹ proper noun *Jethro.*

חֹתְנוֹ noun m + suff 3ms חֹתֵן *father-in-law.*

כֹּהֵן noun m *priest.*

מִדְיָן proper noun *Midian.*

וַיִּנְהַג Qal VC Impf 3ms נָהַג *to drive, lead.*

אַחַר prep *after, behind.*

הַמִּדְבָּר def art + noun m *pasture, wilderness.*

וַיָּבֹא Qal VC Impf 3ms בּוֹא *to come.*

הַר noun m *mountain.*

חֹרֵבָה proper noun + ה locale חֹרֵב *Horeb.*

2 וַיֵּרָא Nif VC Impf 3ms רָאָה *to see;* Nif *to appear, to be revealed* (Qal would be וַיִּרְא).

מַלְאַךְ noun m *angel, messenger.*

בְּלַבַּת prep בְּ + noun f לַבָּה *flame, spear tip.*

אֵשׁ noun m/f *fire.*

מִתּוֹךְ prep מִן + noun m תּוֹךְ *middle.*

הַסְּנֶה def art + noun m סְנֶה *bush, thornbush.*

וַיַּרְא Qal VC Impf 3ms apoc רָאָה *to see.*

וְהִנֵּה conj וְ + interj *behold, look.*

בֹּעֵר Qal Ptc בָּעַר *to burn, consume.*

אֵינֶנּוּ adv + suff 3ms אֵין *it was not.*

אֻכָּל Pual Ptc אָכַל *to eat, consume.*

3 אָסֻרָה Qal Impf 1cs + paragogic **he** סוּר *to turn aside, depart* (cohortative: *let me turn aside*).

נָּא particle of entreaty *please.*

וְאֶרְאֶה conj וְ + Qal Impf 1cs רָאָה *to see.*

הַמַּרְאֶה def art + noun m *appearance, vision.*

מַדּוּעַ adv *why.*

יִבְעַר Qal Impf 3ms בָּעַר *to burn, consume, eat up.*

4 וַיַּרְא Qal VC Impf 3ms apoc רָאָה *to see.*

סָר Qal Perf 3ms סוּר *to turn aside, depart.*

לִרְאוֹת prep לְ + Qal Inf Cstr רָאָה *to see.*

וַיִּקְרָא Qal VC Impf 3ms קָרָא *to call.*

מִתּוֹךְ prep מִן + noun m תּוֹךְ *middle.*

הִנֵּנִי interjection + suff 1s (in pause) הִנֵּה *behold, look.*

5 תִּקְרַב Qal Impf 2ms קָרַב *to approach, come near* (Jussive).

הֲלֹם adv הֲלֹם *near, here.*

שַׁל Qal Impv ms נָשַׁל *to pull out, take off.*

נְעָלֶיךָ noun mp + suff 2ms נַעַל *shoe.*

מֵעַל prep מִן + prep עַל *on, upon.*

רַגְלֶיךָ noun f dual + suff 2ms רֶגֶל *foot.*

הַמָּקוֹם def art + noun m מָקוֹם *place.*

עוֹמֵד Qal Ptc עָמַד *to stand, remain.*

עָלָיו prep עַל + suff 3ms עַל *on, at, against, on account of.*

אַדְמַת noun f cstr אֲדָמָה *earth, ground.*

קֹדֶשׁ Qal Ptc קָדַשׁ *to be holy* (Ptc translated with adjective).

הוּא subject pronoun 3ms הוּא *he, that.*

6 יִצְחָק proper noun *Isaac.*

וַיַּסְתֵּר Hif VC Impf 3ms סָתַר *to hide;* Hif *to hide.*

פָּנָיו noun mp + suff 3ms פָּנִים *face.*

יָרֵא Qal Perf 3ms יָרֵא *to fear, revere.*

מֵהַבִּיט prep מִן + Hif Inf Cstr נָבַט no Qal; Hif *to look, see: of looking.*

7 רָאֹה Qal Inf Abs רָאָה *to see.*

רָאִיתִי Qal Perf 1cs רָאָה *to see.*

עֳנִי noun m עֳנִי *misery.*

עַמִּי noun m + suff 1cs עַם *people.*

אֲשֶׁר rel pronoun אֲשֶׁר *that, which, who, whom, whose.*

בְּמִצְרָיִם prep בְּ + proper noun *Egypt.*

צַעֲקָתָם noun f + suff 3mp צְעָקָה *cry, outcry.*

שָׁמַעְתִּי Qal Perf 1cs שָׁמַע *to hear.*

מִפְּנֵי prep מִן + noun mp cstr פָּנִים *(from before).*

נֹגְשָׂיו Qal Ptc mp + suff 3ms נָגַשׂ *taskmaster.*

יָדַעְתִּי Qal Perf 1cs יָדַע *to know.*

מַכְאֹבָיו noun mp + suff 3ms מַכְאוֹב *pain, sorrow, grief.*

8 וָאֵרֵד Qal VC Impf 1cs יָרַד *to go down.*

לְהַצִּילוֹ prep לְ + Hif Inf Cstr + suff 3ms נָצַל no Qal; Hif *to deprive, deliver.*

מִיַּד prep מִן + noun f cstr יָד *hand.*

מִצְרַיִם proper noun *Egypt*.

וּלְהַעֲלֹתוֹ conj וְ + prep לְ + Hif Inf Cstr + suff 3ms עָלָה *to go up*; Hif *to bring up, sacrifice*.

מִן prep *from*.

הָאָרֶץ def art + noun f אֶרֶץ *earth, land*.

הַהִוא def art + demonstr adj fs הִיא *she, that* (Qere perpetuum).

אֶרֶץ noun f אֶרֶץ *earth, land*.

טוֹבָה adj fs טוֹב *good*.

וּרְחָבָה conj וְ + adj f רָחָב *broad, wide, spacious*.

זָבַת Qal Ptc f cstr זוּב *to flow, flow away*.

חָלָב noun m חָלָב *milk*.

וּדְבַשׁ conj וְ + noun m דְּבַשׁ *honey*.

מְקוֹם noun m cstr מָקוֹם *place*.

הַכְּנַעֲנִי def art + gentilic noun כְּנַעַן *Canaanite* (usually translated with a plural).

וְהַחִתִּי conj וְ + gentilic noun m חֵת *Hittite*.

וְהָאֱמֹרִי conj וְ + gentilic noun m הָאֱמֹרִי *Amorite*.

וְהַפְּרִזִּי conj וְ + def art + gentilic adj פְּרִזִּי *Perrizite*.

וְהַחִוִּי conj וְ + gentilic noun m חִוִּי *Chivite*.

וְהַיְבוּסִי conj וְ + gentilic noun m יְבוּסִי *Jebusite*.

9 **וְעַתָּה** conj וְ + adv עַתָּה *now*.

הִנֵּה interjection *behold, look*.

צַעֲקַת noun f cstr צְעָקָה *cry, outcry*.

בָּאָה Qal Perf 3fs בּוֹא *to come*.

אֵלָי prep + suff 1cs אֶל *to*.

רָאִיתִי Qal Perf 1cs רָאָה *to see*.

הַלַּחַץ def art + noun m לַחַץ *oppression, distress*.

לֹחֲצִים Qal Ptc mp לָחַץ *to press, afflict*.

אֹתָם object pronoun 3mp אֵת *them*.

10 **לְכָה** Qal Impv ms הָלַךְ *to walk* (unusual spelling with paragogic **he**).

וְאֶשְׁלָחֲךָ conj וְ + Qal Impf 1cs + suff 2ms שָׁלַח *to send, stretch out*.

פַּרְעֹה noun m פַּרְעֹה *Pharaoh*.

וְהוֹצֵא conj וְ + Hif Impv יָצָא *to go out*; Hif *to bring out*.

עַמִּי noun m + suff 1cs עַם *people*.

מִמִּצְרָיִם prep מִן + proper noun מִצְרַיִם *Egypt*.

11 **מִי** pronoun מִי *who*.

אֵלֵךְ Qal Impf 1cs הָלַךְ *to walk*.

אוֹצִיא Hif Impf 1cs יָצָא to go out; Hif to bring out.

12 אֶהְיֶה Qal Impf 1cs הָיָה to be, become.

עִמָּךְ prep עִם + suff 2fs עִם with.

שְׁלַחְתִּיךָ Qal Perf 1cs + suff 2ms שָׁלַח to send, stretch out.

בְּהוֹצִיאֲךָ prep בְּ + Hif Inf Cstr + suff 2ms יָצָא to go out; Hif to bring out.

הָעָם def art + noun m עַם people.

תַּעַבְדוּן Qal Impf 2mp + paragogic **nun** עָבַד to work, serve.

עַל prep עַל on, upon.

הָהָר def art + noun m הַר mountain.

13 הִנֵּה interjection הִנֵּה behold, look.

בָא Qal Ptc בּוֹא to come; Hif to bring: when I come.

וְאָמַרְתִּי Qal VC Perf 1cs אָמַר to say.

אֲבוֹתֵיכֶם noun mp + suff 2mp אָב father.

שְׁלָחַנִי Qal Perf + suff 1cs שָׁלַח to send, stretch out; Piel to let go, expel.

אֲלֵיכֶם prep + suff 2mp אֶל to.

וְאָמְרוּ Qal VC Perf 3cp אָמַר to say.

מָה pronoun מָה what, how.

שְׁמוֹ noun m + suff 3ms שֵׁם name.

אֹמַר Qal Impf 1cs אָמַר to say.

אֲלֵהֶם prep + suff 3mp אֶל to.

14 כֹה adv כֹה thus, therefore.

תֹאמַר Qal Impf 2ms אָמַר to say.

לִבְנֵי prep לְ + noun mp cstr בֵּן son.

שְׁלָחַנִי Qal Perf 3ms + suff 1cs שָׁלַח to send, stretch out.

Questions

1 Why is שַׁל the imperative of נָשַׁל rather than the more usual imperative pattern of נְשֹׁל?

2 In verse 7 there is a Qal Infinitive Absolute of רָאָה followed by a Qal Perfect of רָאָה. What is the effect of this construction? How would you translate it?

3 The phrase אֶהְיֶה אֲשֶׁר אֶהְיֶה (verse 14) has several possible translations. How many can you think of?

EXODUS 20:1–13 THE TEN COMMANDMENTS

1 וַיְדַבֵּר אֱלֹהִים אֵת כָּל־הַדְּבָרִים הָאֵלֶּה לֵאמֹר : 2 אָנֹכִי יְהוָה אֱלֹהֶיךָ אֲשֶׁר הוֹצֵאתִיךָ מֵאֶרֶץ מִצְרַיִם מִבֵּית עֲבָדִים לֹא־יִהְיֶה לְךָ אֱלֹהִים אֲחֵרִים עַל־פָּנָי : 3 לֹא־תַעֲשֶׂה לְךָ פֶסֶל וְכָל־תְּמוּנָה אֲשֶׁר בַּשָּׁמַיִם מִמַּעַל וַאֲשֶׁר בָּאָרֶץ מִתָּחַת וַאֲשֶׁר בַּמַּיִם מִתַּחַת לָאָרֶץ :

4 לֹא־תִשְׁתַּחֲוֶה לָהֶם וְלֹא תָעָבְדֵם כִּי אָנֹכִי יְהוָה אֱלֹהֶיךָ אֵל קַנָּא פֹּקֵד עֲוֹן אָבֹת עַל־בָּנִים
עַל־שִׁלֵּשִׁים וְעַל־רִבֵּעִים לְשֹׂנְאָי׃ 5 וְעֹשֶׂה חֶסֶד לַאֲלָפִים לְאֹהֲבַי וּלְשֹׁמְרֵי מִצְוֹתָי׃
6 לֹא תִשָּׂא אֶת־שֵׁם־יְהוָה אֱלֹהֶיךָ לַשָּׁוְא כִּי לֹא יְנַקֶּה יְהוָה אֵת אֲשֶׁר־יִשָּׂא אֶת־שְׁמוֹ לַשָּׁוְא׃
7 זָכוֹר אֶת־יוֹם הַשַּׁבָּת לְקַדְּשׁוֹ׃ 8 שֵׁשֶׁת יָמִים תַּעֲבֹד וְעָשִׂיתָ כָּל־מְלַאכְתֶּךָ׃ 9 וְיוֹם הַשְּׁבִיעִי
שַׁבָּת לַיהוָה אֱלֹהֶיךָ לֹא תַעֲשֶׂה כָל־מְלָאכָה אַתָּה וּבִנְךָ וּבִתֶּךָ עַבְדְּךָ וַאֲמָתְךָ וּבְהֶמְתֶּךָ
וְגֵרְךָ אֲשֶׁר בִּשְׁעָרֶיךָ׃ 10 כִּי שֵׁשֶׁת־יָמִים עָשָׂה יְהוָה אֶת־הַשָּׁמַיִם וְאֶת־הָאָרֶץ אֶת־הַיָּם
וְאֶת־כָּל־אֲשֶׁר־בָּם וַיָּנַח בַּיּוֹם הַשְּׁבִיעִי עַל־כֵּן בֵּרַךְ יְהוָה אֶת־יוֹם הַשַּׁבָּת וַיְקַדְּשֵׁהוּ׃
11 כַּבֵּד אֶת־אָבִיךָ וְאֶת־אִמֶּךָ לְמַעַן יַאֲרִכוּן יָמֶיךָ עַל הָאֲדָמָה אֲשֶׁר־יְהוָה אֱלֹהֶיךָ נֹתֵן לָךְ׃
12 לֹא תִרְצָח לֹא תִנְאָף לֹא תִגְנֹב לֹא־תַעֲנֶה בְרֵעֲךָ עֵד שָׁקֶר׃ 13 לֹא תַחְמֹד בֵּית רֵעֶךָ לֹא־
תַחְמֹד אֵשֶׁת רֵעֶךָ וְעַבְדּוֹ וַאֲמָתוֹ וְשׁוֹרוֹ וַחֲמֹרוֹ וְכֹל אֲשֶׁר לְרֵעֶךָ׃

1 וַיְדַבֵּר Piel VC Impf 3ms דָּבַר Piel: *to speak*.

הַדְּבָרִים def art + noun mp דָּבָר *word, thing*.

לֵאמֹר prep לְ + Qal Inf Cstr אָמַר *saying*.

2 אָנֹכִי subj pronoun 1cs.

הוֹצֵאתִיךָ Hif Perf 1cs + suff 2ms יָצָא *to go out*; Hif *to lead out*.

מֵאֶרֶץ prep מִן + noun f אֶרֶץ *earth, land*.

מִצְרַיִם proper noun *Egypt*.

מִבֵּית prep מִן + noun m cstr בַּיִת *house*.

עֲבָדִים noun mp עֶבֶד *servant, slave (slavery)*.

לֹא neg particle *not, do not*.

יִהְיֶה Qal Impf 3ms הָיָה *to be, become*.

לְךָ prep לְ + suff 2ms *to, at, for*.

אֱלֹהִים noun mp *(gods)*.

אֲחֵרִים adj mp אַחֵר *following, other*.

עַל prep *on, above*.

פָּנַי noun mp + suff 1cs פָּנִים *face (before me)*.

3 תַעֲשֶׂה Qal Impf 2ms עָשָׂה *to make, do*.

פֶסֶל noun m פֶּסֶל *image, idol*.

וְכָל noun m כֹּל *whole, all, any*.

תְמוּנָה noun f תְּמוּנָה *appearance, form, image*.

בַּשָּׁמַיִם prep בְּ + noun m שָׁמַיִם *heaven*.

מִמַּעַל prep מִן + adv מַעַל *above*.

בָּאָרֶץ prep בְּ + noun fs אֶרֶץ *land, earth*.

מִתָּחַת prep מִן + prep תַּחַת *under, beneath: below*.

בַּמַּיִם prep בְּ + noun m dual מַיִם *water*.

4 תִשְׁתַּחֲוֶה Hitp Impf 2ms שָׁחָה *to bow down*; Hitpalel *to honour, worship*.

לָהֶם prep לְ + suff 3mp לְ *to, at, for: them.*

תַּעֲבְדֵם Qal Impf 2ms עָבַד *to work, serve.*

כִּי adv *because, that.*

אָנֹכִי subj pronoun 1cs *I.*

אֵל noun m אֵל *God, god.*

קַנָּא adj m *jealous.*

פֹּקֵד Qal Ptc פָּקַד *to visit, miss, punish.*

עֲוֹן noun m cstr עָוֹן *depravity, crime, sin.*

אָבֹת noun mp אָב *father.*

עַל prep עַל *on, upon.*

בָּנִים noun mp בֵּן *son.*

שִׁלֵּשִׁים noun mp שִׁלֵּשׁ *descendants of the third generation:* great-grandchildren.

רִבֵּעִים noun mp רִבֵּעַ *descendants of the fourth generation* great-great-grandchildren.

לְשֹׂנְאָי prep לְ + Qal Inf Cstr + suff 1cs שָׂנֵא *to hate, to be an enemy.*

5 וְעֹשֶׂה Qal Ptc עָשָׂה *to make, do.*

חֶסֶד noun m *love, kindness, mercy.*

לַאֲלָפִים prep לְ + numeral mp אֶלֶף *thousand (to the thousandth generation).*

לְאֹהֲבַי Qal Ptc + suff 1cs אָהַב *to love.*

וּלְשֹׁמְרֵי Qal Ptc mp cstr שָׁמַר *to keep, guard, observe.*

מִצְוֹתָי noun mp + suff 1cs מִצְוָה *commandment.*

6 תִשָּׂא Qal Impf 2ms נָשָׂא *to lift up, take, receive, accept.*

שֵׁם noun m *name.*

לַשָּׁוְא prep לְ + noun m שָׁוְא *evil, wickedness, emptiness.*

יְנַקֶּה Piel Impf 3ms נָקָה *to be pure; Piel to absolve, pardon.*

יִשָּׂא Qal Impf 3ms נָשָׂא *to lift up, to take, receive.*

שְׁמוֹ noun m + suff 3ms שֵׁם *name.*

לַשָּׁוְא prep לְ + noun m שָׁוְא *evil, wickedness, emptiness.*

7 זָכוֹר Qal Inf Abs זָכַר *to remember (Inf Abs used as Impv).*

הַשַּׁבָּת def art + noun m שַׁבָּת *sabbath, seventh day, week.*

לְקַדְּשׁוֹ prep לְ + Piel Inf Cstr + suff 3ms קָדַשׁ *to be holy; Piel to consecrate.*

8 שֵׁשֶׁת numeral f cstr שֵׁשׁ *six.*

יָמִים noun mp יוֹם *day.*

תַּעֲבֹד Qal Impf 2ms עָבַד *to work, serve.*

וְעָשִׂיתָ conj וְ + Qal Impf 2ms עָשָׂה *to make, do.*

מְלַאכְתֶּךָ noun f + suff 2ms מְלָאכָה *work, service.*

238

9 הַשְּׁבִיעִי def art + ordinal f שְׁבִיעִי *seventh*.

שַׁבָּת noun m שַׁבָּת *sabbath, seventh day, week*.

תַעֲשֶׂה Qal Impf 2ms עָשָׂה *to make, do: you will do*.

כָל noun m כֹּל *any*.

אַתָּה subj pronoun 2ms אַתָּה *you*.

וּבִנְךָ noun m + suff 2ms בֵּן *son*.

וּבִתֶּךָ noun f + suff 2ms בַּת *daughter*.

עַבְדְּךָ noun m + suff 2ms עֶבֶד *servant, slave*.

וַאֲמָתְךָ noun f + suff 2ms אָמָה *female servant*.

וּבְהֶמְתֶּךָ noun f + suff 2ms בְּהֵמָה *animal, cattle*.

וְגֵרְךָ noun m + suff 2ms גֵּר *foreigner*.

בִּשְׁעָרֶיךָ prep בְּ + noun mp + suff 2ms שַׁעַר *gate*.

10 שֵׁשֶׁת numeral f שֵׁשׁ *six*.

יָמִים noun mp יוֹם *day*.

עָשָׂה Qal Perf 3ms עָשָׂה *to make, do*.

הַיָּם noun m יָם *sea, river, west*.

בָּם prep בְּ + suff 3mp בְּ *in them*.

וַיָּנַח Qal VC Impf 3ms נוּחַ *to rest, finish*.

הַשְּׁבִיעִי def art + ordinal שְׁבִיעִי *seventh*.

עַל־כֵּן prep *therefore*.

בֵּרַךְ Piel Perf 3ms בָּרַךְ *kneel, bless*; Piel *to praise, bless*.

וַיְקַדְּשֵׁהוּ Piel VC Impf 3ms + suff 3ms קָדֵשׁ *to be holy*; Piel *to consecrate*.

11 כַּבֵּד Piel Impv כָּבֵד *to be heavy, serious*; Piel *to honour*.

אָבִיךָ noun m אָב *father*.

אִמֶּךָ noun f אֵם *mother*.

לְמַעַן prep לְ + prep subst מַעַן *so that*.

יַאֲרִכוּן Hif Impf 3mp + paragogic **nun** אָרַךְ *to stretch out*; Hif *to lengthen, be long*; *they will be long*.

יָמֶיךָ noun mp + suff 2ms יוֹם *day*.

הָאֲדָמָה def art + noun f אֲדָמָה *earth, ground*.

נֹתֵן Qal Ptc נָתַן *to give, was giving*.

לָךְ prep לְ + suff 2ms (in pause) לְ *to, at, for*.

12 תִּרְצָח Qal Impf 2ms רָצַח *to break in pieces, kill*.

תִּנְאָף Qal Impf 2ms נָאַף *to commit adultery, idolatry*.

תִּגְנֹב Qal Impf 2ms גָּנַב *to steal*.

עֲנֶה **תַּעֲנֶה** Qal Impf 2ms עָנָה *to answer, speak, testify.*

בְּרֵעֶךָ **בְּרֵעֶךָ** prep בְּ + noun m + suff 2ms רֵעַ *friend, neighbour: against your neighbour.*

עֵד **עֵד** noun m עֵד *witness.*

שָׁקֶר **שָׁקֶר** noun m שֶׁקֶר *lie, deception.*

13 תַחְמֹד **תַחְמֹד** Qal Impf 2ms חָמַד *to desire, delight in.*

בֵּית **בֵּית** noun ms cstr בַּיִת *house.*

רֵעֶךָ **רֵעֶךָ** noun m + suff 2ms רֵעַ *friend, neighbour.*

תַחְמֹד **תַחְמֹד** Qal Impf 2ms חָמַד *to desire, delight in.*

אֵשֶׁת **אֵשֶׁת** noun fs cstr אִשָּׁה *woman.*

וְעַבְדּוֹ **וְעַבְדּוֹ** conj וְ + noun m + suff 3ms עֶבֶד *servant, slave.*

וַאֲמָתוֹ **וַאֲמָתוֹ** conj וְ + noun f + suff 3ms אָמָה *female servant.*

וְשׁוֹרוֹ **וְשׁוֹרוֹ** conj וְ + noun m + suff 3ms שׁוֹר *ox, bull.*

וַחֲמֹרוֹ **וַחֲמֹרוֹ** conj וְ + noun m + suff 3ms חֲמוֹר *donkey.*

וְכֹל **וְכֹל** conj וְ + noun m כֹּל *whole, entirety: anything.*

לְרֵעֶךָ **לְרֵעֶךָ** prep לְ + noun m + suff 2ms רֵעַ *friend, neighbour (anything that belongs to your friend).*

Questions

1 This passage is generally known as the ten commandments. If you count them, do you find ten?

2 What is the term for constructions like לֹא תִגְנֹב and לֹא תִרְצָח? What is the difference between אַל תִּגְנֹב and לֹא תִגְנֹב?

3 This passage is often understood to be the foundation of legal systems. How many of these commandments are currently law in your jurisdiction?

GENESIS 3 THE TREE OF KNOWLEDGE OF GOOD AND EVIL

1 וְהַנָּחָשׁ הָיָה עָרוּם מִכֹּל חַיַּת הַשָּׂדֶה אֲשֶׁר עָשָׂה יְהוָה אֱלֹהִים וַיֹּאמֶר אֶל־הָאִשָּׁה אַף כִּי־
אָמַר אֱלֹהִים לֹא תֹאכְלוּ מִכֹּל עֵץ הַגָּן : 2 וַתֹּאמֶר הָאִשָּׁה אֶל־הַנָּחָשׁ מִפְּרִי עֵץ־הַגָּן נֹאכֵל :
3 וּמִפְּרִי הָעֵץ אֲשֶׁר בְּתוֹךְ־הַגָּן אָמַר אֱלֹהִים לֹא תֹאכְלוּ מִמֶּנּוּ וְלֹא תִגְּעוּ בּוֹ פֶּן־תְּמֻתוּן :
4 וַיֹּאמֶר הַנָּחָשׁ אֶל־הָאִשָּׁה לֹא־מוֹת תְּמֻתוּן : 5 כִּי יֹדֵעַ אֱלֹהִים כִּי בְּיוֹם אֲכָלְכֶם מִמֶּנּוּ
וְנִפְקְחוּ עֵינֵיכֶם וִהְיִיתֶם כֵּאלֹהִים יֹדְעֵי טוֹב וָרָע : 6 וַתֵּרֶא הָאִשָּׁה כִּי טוֹב הָעֵץ לְמַאֲכָל
וְכִי תַאֲוָה־הוּא לָעֵינַיִם וְנֶחְמָד הָעֵץ לְהַשְׂכִּיל וַתִּקַּח מִפִּרְיוֹ וַתֹּאכַל וַתִּתֵּן גַּם־לְאִישָׁהּ
עִמָּהּ וַיֹּאכַל : 7 וַתִּפָּקַחְנָה עֵינֵי שְׁנֵיהֶם וַיֵּדְעוּ כִּי עֵירֻמִּם הֵם וַיִּתְפְּרוּ עֲלֵה תְאֵנָה וַיַּעֲשׂוּ
לָהֶם חֲגֹרֹת : 8 וַיִּשְׁמְעוּ אֶת־קוֹל יְהוָה אֱלֹהִים מִתְהַלֵּךְ בַּגָּן לְרוּחַ הַיּוֹם וַיִּתְחַבֵּא הָאָדָם
וְאִשְׁתּוֹ מִפְּנֵי יְהוָה אֱלֹהִים בְּתוֹךְ עֵץ הַגָּן : 9 וַיִּקְרָא יְהוָה אֱלֹהִים אֶל־הָאָדָם וַיֹּאמֶר לוֹ
אַיֶּכָּה : 10 וַיֹּאמֶר אֶת־קֹלְךָ שָׁמַעְתִּי בַּגָּן וָאִירָא כִּי־עֵירֹם אָנֹכִי וָאֵחָבֵא : 11 וַיֹּאמֶר מִי
הִגִּיד לְךָ כִּי עֵירֹם אָתָּה הֲמִן־הָעֵץ אֲשֶׁר צִוִּיתִיךָ לְבִלְתִּי אֲכָל־מִמֶּנּוּ אָכָלְתָּ : 12 וַיֹּאמֶר
הָאָדָם הָאִשָּׁה אֲשֶׁר נָתַתָּה עִמָּדִי הִוא נָתְנָה־לִּי מִן־הָעֵץ וָאֹכֵל : 13 וַיֹּאמֶר יְהוָה אֱלֹהִים

לְאִשָּׁה מַה־זֹּאת עָשִׂית וַתֹּאמֶר הָאִשָּׁה הַנָּחָשׁ הִשִּׁיאַנִי וָאֹכֵל : 14 וַיֹּאמֶר יְהוָה אֱלֹהִים אֶל־הַנָּחָשׁ כִּי עָשִׂיתָ זֹּאת אָרוּר אַתָּה מִכָּל־הַבְּהֵמָה וּמִכֹּל חַיַּת הַשָּׂדֶה עַל־גְּחֹנְךָ תֵלֵךְ וְעָפָר תֹּאכַל כָּל־יְמֵי חַיֶּיךָ : 15 וְאֵיבָה אָשִׁית בֵּינְךָ וּבֵין הָאִשָּׁה וּבֵין זַרְעֲךָ וּבֵין זַרְעָהּ הוּא יְשׁוּפְךָ רֹאשׁ וְאַתָּה תְּשׁוּפֶנּוּ עָקֵב : 16 אֶל־הָאִשָּׁה אָמַר הַרְבָּה אַרְבֶּה עִצְּבוֹנֵךְ וְהֵרֹנֵךְ בְּעֶצֶב תֵּלְדִי בָנִים וְאֶל־אִישֵׁךְ תְּשׁוּקָתֵךְ וְהוּא יִמְשָׁל־בָּךְ : 17 וּלְאָדָם אָמַר כִּי־שָׁמַעְתָּ לְקוֹל אִשְׁתֶּךָ וַתֹּאכַל מִן־הָעֵץ אֲשֶׁר צִוִּיתִיךָ לֵאמֹר לֹא תֹאכַל מִמֶּנּוּ אֲרוּרָה הָאֲדָמָה בַּעֲבוּרֶךָ בְּעִצָּבוֹן תֹּאכֲלֶנָּה כֹּל יְמֵי חַיֶּיךָ : 18 וְקוֹץ וְדַרְדַּר תַּצְמִיחַ לָךְ וְאָכַלְתָּ אֶת־עֵשֶׂב הַשָּׂדֶה : 19 בְּזֵעַת אַפֶּיךָ תֹּאכַל לֶחֶם עַד שׁוּבְךָ אֶל־הָאֲדָמָה כִּי מִמֶּנָּה לֻקָּחְתָּ כִּי־עָפָר אַתָּה וְאֶל־עָפָר תָּשׁוּב : 20 וַיִּקְרָא הָאָדָם שֵׁם אִשְׁתּוֹ חַוָּה כִּי הִוא הָיְתָה אֵם כָּל־חָי : 21 וַיַּעַשׂ יְהוָה אֱלֹהִים לְאָדָם וּלְאִשְׁתּוֹ כָּתְנוֹת עוֹר וַיַּלְבִּשֵׁם : 22 וַיֹּאמֶר יְהוָה אֱלֹהִים הֵן הָאָדָם הָיָה כְּאַחַד מִמֶּנּוּ לָדַעַת טוֹב וָרָע וְעַתָּה פֶּן־יִשְׁלַח יָדוֹ וְלָקַח גַּם מֵעֵץ הַחַיִּים וְאָכַל וָחַי לְעֹלָם : 23 וַיְשַׁלְּחֵהוּ יְהוָה אֱלֹהִים מִגַּן־עֵדֶן לַעֲבֹד אֶת־הָאֲדָמָה אֲשֶׁר לֻקַּח מִשָּׁם : 24 וַיְגָרֶשׁ אֶת־הָאָדָם וַיַּשְׁכֵּן מִקֶּדֶם לְגַן־עֵדֶן אֶת־הַכְּרֻבִים וְאֵת לַהַט הַחֶרֶב הַמִּתְהַפֶּכֶת לִשְׁמֹר אֶת־דֶּרֶךְ עֵץ הַחַיִּים :

1 וְהַנָּחָשׁ conj וְ + def art + noun m נָחָשׁ *serpent, snake.*

עָרוּם adj mp *clever.*

מִכֹּל prep מִן + noun m כֹּל *(more than any).*

חַיַּת noun or adj f cstr חַי *alive, living; life, living thing.*

הַשָּׂדֶה def art + noun m שָׂדֶה *field.*

עָשָׂה Qal Perf 3ms עָשָׂה *to make, do.*

אַף adv, conj אַף *even, also;* with כִּי *is it true.*

תֹּאכְלוּ Qal Impf 2ms אָכַל *to eat.*

מִכֹּל prep מִן + noun m כֹּל *whole, all, any.*

עֵץ noun m *tree.*

הַגָּן def art + noun m גַּן *garden.*

2 הַנָּחָשׁ def art + noun m נָחָשׁ *serpent, snake.*

מִפְּרִי prep מִן + noun f פְּרִי *fruit.*

נֹאכֵל Qal Impf 1cp אָכַל *to eat.*

3 וּמִפְּרִי conj וְ + prep מִן + noun f פְּרִי *fruit.*

בְּתוֹךְ prep בְּ + noun m cstr תָּוֶךְ *middle.*

מִמֶּנּוּ prep מִן + suff 3ms מִן *from, more than.*

תִּגְּעוּ Qal Impf 2mp נָגַע *to strike, touch, reach.*

בּוֹ prep בְּ + suff 3ms בְּ *it.*

פֶּן conj פֶּן *lest, or else.*

תְּמֻתוּן Qal Impf 2mp + paragogic **nun** מוּת *to die.*

4 מוֹת Qal Inf Abs מוּת *to die.*

תְּמֻתוּן Qal Impf 2mp + paragogic **nun** מוּת *to die.*

5 יָדַע Qal Ptc יָדַע to know.

בְּיוֹם prep בְּ + noun m יוֹם day.

אֲכָלְכֶם Qal Inf Cstr + suff 2mp אָכַל to eat (your eating).

מִמֶּנּוּ prep מִן + suff 3ms מִן from.

וְנִפְקְחוּ Nif VC Impf 3mp פָּקַח to open; Nif to be opened.

עֵינֵיכֶם noun f dual + suff 2mp עַיִן eye.

וִהְיִיתֶם Qal VC Perf 2mp הָיָה to be, become.

כֵּאלֹהִים prep כְּ + noun mp אֱלֹהִים God, gods.

יֹדְעֵי Qal Ptc mp cstr יָדַע to know.

טוֹב adj m טוֹב good.

וָרָע conj וְ + noun m רַע evil.

6 וַתֵּרֶא Qal VC Impf 3fs רָאָה to see.

לְמַאֲכָל prep לְ + noun m מַאֲכָל food.

תַאֲוָה noun f תַאֲוָה desire, delight.

לָעֵינַיִם prep לְ + noun f dual cstr עַיִן eye.

וְנֶחְמָד conj וְ + Nif Ptc חָמַד to desire, covet, delight in; Nif to be desired (Ptc as adj: desirable).

לְהַשְׂכִּיל prep לְ + Hif Inf Cstr שָׂכַל to be prudent; Hif to contemplate, comprehend, give insight.

וַתִּקַּח Qal VC Impf 3fs לָקַח to take, receive.

מִפִּרְיוֹ prep מִן + noun f + suff 3ms פְּרִי fruit.

וַתֹּאכַל Qal VC Impf 3fs אָכַל to eat.

וַתִּתֵּן Qal VC Impf 3fs נָתַן to give.

גַּם conj גַּם even, also.

לְאִישָׁהּ prep לְ + noun m אִישׁ man.

עִמָּהּ prep עִם + suff 3fs עִם with.

וַיֹּאכַל Qal VC Impf 3ms אָכַל to eat.

7 וַתִּפָּקַחְנָה Nif VC Impf 3fp פָּקַח to open; Nif to be opened.

עֵינֵי noun f dual cstr עַיִן eye.

שְׁנֵיהֶם numeral m + suff 3mp שְׁנַיִם two.

וַיֵּדְעוּ Qal VC Impf 3mp יָדַע to know.

עֵירֻמִּם adj mp עֵירוֹם naked.

הֵם pronoun הֵם they, those.

וַיִּתְפְּרוּ Qal VC Impf 3mp תָּפַר to sew together.

עֲלֵה noun m cstr עָלֶה leaf, foliage.

תְאֵנָה noun f fig.

242

וַיַּעֲשׂוּ Qal VC Impf 3mp apoc עָשָׂה to make, do.

לָהֶם prep לְ + suff 3mp לְ to, at, for.

חֲגֹרֹת noun fp חֲגוֹרָה girdle, apron, clothing that is tied.

8 וַיִּשְׁמְעוּ Qal VC Impf 3mp שָׁמַע to hear.

קוֹל noun m קוֹל voice.

מִתְהַלֵּךְ Hitp Ptc הָלַךְ to walk; Hitp walk about, wander.

בַּגָּן prep בְּ + noun m גַּן garden.

לְרוּחַ prep לְ + noun f רוּחַ wind, spirit, breath (in the cool of).

וַיִּתְחַבֵּא Hitp VC Impf 3ms חָבָא to conceal; Nif to be concealed, conceal oneself; Hitp to hide oneself.

וְאִשְׁתּוֹ conj וְ + noun f + suff 3ms אִשָּׁה woman.

מִפְּנֵי prep מִן + noun mp cstr פָּנִים from before.

בְּתוֹךְ prep בְּ + noun m cstr תָּוֶךְ middle (among).

9 וַיִּקְרָא Qal VC Impf 3ms קָרָא to call.

אַיֶּכָּה adv + suff 2ms אַי where, how (less common form of the pronominal suffix).

10 קֹלְךָ noun m + suff 2ms קוֹל voice.

שָׁמַעְתִּי Qal Perf 1cs שָׁמַע to hear.

וָאִירָא Qal VC Impf 1cs יָרֵא to fear, revere.

עֵירֹם adj m עֵירֹם naked.

וָאֵחָבֵא Nif VC Impf 1cs חָבָא to conceal; Nif to be concealed, conceal oneself; Hitp to hide oneself.

11 מִי pronoun מִי who.

הִגִּיד Hif Perf 3ms נָגַד no Qal; Hif to tell.

עֵירֹם adj m naked.

הֲמִן interrog ה + prep מִן from.

צִוִּיתִיךָ Piel Perf 1cs + suff 2ms צָוָה no Qal; Piel to appoint, command.

לְבִלְתִּי prep לְ + adv בֶּלֶת not.

אֲכָל Qal Inf Cstr אָכַל to eat.

מִמֶּנּוּ prep מִן + suff 3ms מִן from, more than.

אָכָלְתָּ Qal Perf 2ms אָכַל to eat.

12 אֲשֶׁר rel pronoun אֲשֶׁר whom.

נָתַתָּה Qal Perf 2ms + paragogic **he** נָתַן to give.

עִמָּדִי prep עִם with.

הִוא subj pronoun 3fs הִיא she (Qere perpetuum).

נָתְנָה Qal Perf 3fs נָתַן to give.

וָאֹכֵל conj וְ + Qal Perf 1cs אָכַל *to eat.*

13 מַה pronoun *what, how.*

עָשִׂית Qal Perf 2fs עָשָׂה *to make, do.*

הִשִּׁיאַנִי Hif Perf 3ms + suff 1cs נָשָׁא no Qal; Hif *to seduce, corrupt.*

14 אָרוּר Qal Ptc passive אָרַר *to curse.*

מִכָּל prep מִן + noun m כֹּל *whole, all, any.*

הַבְּהֵמָה def art + noun f בְּהֵמָה *animal, cattle.*

עַל prep עַל *on, upon.*

גְּחֹנְךָ noun m + suff 2ms גָּחוֹן *belly of reptiles.*

תֵלֵךְ Qal Impf 2ms הָלַךְ *to walk, go.*

וְעָפָר conj וְ + noun m עָפָר *dust.*

תֹּאכַל Qal Impf 3fs אָכַל *to eat.*

יְמֵי noun mp cstr יוֹם *day.*

חַיֶּיךָ noun or adj m + suff 2ms חַי *alive, living; life, living thing.*

15 וְאֵיבָה conj וְ + noun f אֵיבָה *enmity, hostile mind.*

אָשִׁית Qal Impf 1cs שִׁית *to put, place, set.*

בֵּינְךָ prep + suff 2ms בֵּין *between.*

זַרְעֲךָ noun m + suff 2ms זֶרַע *seed, offspring.*

זַרְעָהּ noun m + suff 3fs זֶרַע *seed, offspring.*

יְשׁוּפְךָ Qal Impf 3ms + suff 2ms שׁוּף *to lie in wait, attack.*

רֹאשׁ noun m רֹאשׁ *head.*

וְאַתָּה conj וְ + subj pronoun 2ms אַתָּה *you.*

תְּשׁוּפֶנּוּ Qal Impf 2ms + suff 3ms שׁוּף *to lie in wait, attack.*

עָקֵב noun m עָקֵב *heel, hoof.*

16 הַרְבָּה Hif Inf Abs רָבָה *to be many; Hif to increase, multiply.*

אַרְבֶּה Hif Impf 1cs רָבָה *to be many; Hif to increase, multiply.*

עִצְּבוֹנֵךְ noun m + suff 2fs עִצָּבוֹן *hard work, pain, sorrow.*

וְהֵרֹנֵךְ conj וְ + noun m + suff 2fs הֵרָיוֹן *conception, pregnancy.*

בְּעֶצֶב prep בְּ + noun m עֶצֶב *pain, grief, hard work.*

תֵּלְדִי Qal Impf 2fs יָלַד *to give birth.*

אִישֵׁךְ noun m + suff 2fs אִישׁ *man.*

תְּשׁוּקָתֵךְ noun f + suff 2fs תְּשׁוּקָה *desire, longing.*

יִמְשָׁל Qal Impf 3ms מָשַׁל *to rule.*

בָּךְ prep בְּ + suff 2fs בְּ *over you.*

17 וּלְאָדָם conj וְ + prep לְ + noun אָדָם *earth, man, Adam.*

שָׁמַעְתָּ Qal Perf 2ms שָׁמַע *to hear.*

לְקוֹל prep לְ + noun m קוֹל *voice.*

אִשְׁתֶּךָ noun m + suff 2ms אִשָּׁה *woman.*

וַתֹּאכַל Qal VC Impf 3fs אָכַל *to eat.*

צִוִּיתִיךָ Piel Perf 1cs + suff 2ms צָוָה no Qal; Piel *to appoint, command.*

תֹאכַל Qal Impf 3fs אָכַל *to eat.*

מִמֶּנּוּ prep מִן + suff 3ms מִן *from.*

אֲרוּרָה Qal Ptc passive f אָרַר *to curse.*

הָאֲדָמָה def art + noun f אֲדָמָה *earth, ground.*

בַּעֲבוּרֶךָ prep בְּ + prep + suff 2ms עֲבוּר *because of.*

בְּעִצָּבוֹן prep בְּ + noun m עִצָּבוֹן *hard work, pain, sorrow.*

תֹּאכֲלֶנָּה Qal Impf + suff 3fs אָכַל *to eat.*

חַיֶּיךָ noun or adj m + suff 2ms חַי *alive, living; life, living thing.*

18 וְקוֹץ conj וְ + noun m קוֹץ *thorn, thorns.*

וְדַרְדַּר conj וְ + noun m דַּרְדַּר *weed, weeds.*

תַּצְמִיחַ Hif Impf 3fs צָמַח *to sprout;* Hif *to cause to sprout.*

וְאָכַלְתָּ Qal VC Pers 3fs אָכַל *to eat.*

עֵשֶׂב noun m עֵשֶׂב *green plant.*

19 בְּזֵעַת prep בְּ + noun f cstr זֵעָה *sweat.*

אַפֶּיךָ noun m + suff 3ms אַף *nose, anger.*

לֶחֶם noun m לֶחֶם *bread.*

עַד prep עַד *until.*

שׁוּבְךָ Qal Inf Cstr + suff 2ms שׁוּב *to turn, return.*

מִמֶּנָּה prep מִן + suff 3fs מִן *from.*

לֻקָּחְתָּ Pual Perf 2ms לָקַח *to take, receive.*

עָפָר noun m עָפָר *dust.*

תָּשׁוּב Qal Impf 2ms שׁוּב *to turn, return.*

20 וַיִּקְרָא Qal VC Impf 3ms קָרָא *to call.*

חַוָּה proper noun חַוָּה *Eve.*

הָיְתָה Qal Perf 3fs הָיָה *to be, become.*

אֵם noun f *mother.*

חָי noun or adj m חַי *alive, living; life, living thing.*

21 וַיַּעַשׂ Qal VC Impf 3ms apoc עָשָׂה *to make, do.*

לְאָדָם prep לְ + proper noun אָדָם *earth, man, Adam.*

וּלְאִשְׁתּוֹ conj וְ + prep לְ + noun f + suff 3ms אִשָּׁה *woman.*

כָּתְנֹת noun fp כְּתֹנֶת *tunic, shirt.*

עוֹר noun m עוֹר *skin, leather.*

וַיַּלְבִּשֵׁם Hif VC Impf 3mp + suff 3mp לָבַשׁ *to put on clothes;* Hif *to clothe.*

22 הֵן interjection הִנֵּה *look.*

הָיָה Qal Perf 3ms הָיָה *to be, become.*

אַחַד numeral m cstr אֶחָד *one, first.*

מִמֶּנּוּ prep מִן + suff 3ms מִן *of us.*

לָדַעַת prep לְ + Qal Inf Cstr יָדַע *to know;* Nif *to be known.*

טוֹב adj m טוֹב *good.*

וָרָע conj וְ + noun m רַע *evil.*

וְעַתָּה conj וְ + adv עַתָּה *now.*

פֶּן conj *lest.*

יִשְׁלַח Qal Impf 3ms שָׁלַח *to send, stretch out.*

יָדוֹ noun f + suff 3ms יָד *hand.*

וְלָקַח Qal VC Perf 3ms לָקַח *to take, receive.*

מֵעֵץ prep מִן + noun m עֵץ *tree.*

הַחַיִּים def art + noun mp חַיִּים *life.*

וְאָכַל Qal VC Perf 3ms אָכַל *to eat.*

וָחַי Qal VC Impf 3ms חָיָה *to live;* Piel *to give life, preserve.*

לְעֹלָם prep לְ + noun ms עוֹלָם *eternity.*

23 וַיְשַׁלְּחֵהוּ Piel VC Impf 3ms + suff 3ms שָׁלַח *to send, stretch out;* Piel *to let go, expel.*

מִגַּן prep מִן + noun m גַּן *garden.*

עֵדֶן proper noun *Eden.*

לַעֲבֹד prep בְּ + Qal Inf Cstr עָבַד *to work, serve.*

לֻקַּח Pual Perf 3ms לָקַח *to take, receive.*

מִשָּׁם prep מִן + adv שָׁם *there.*

24 וַיְגָרֶשׁ Piel VC Impf 3ms גָּרַשׁ *to drive out, expel;* Piel *to expel.*

וַיַּשְׁכֵּן Hif VC Impf 3ms שָׁכַן *to settle down;* Hif *to set, establish.*

מִקֶּדֶם prep מִן + noun m קֶדֶם *East.*

לְגַן prep לְ + noun m גַּן *garden.*

הַכְּרֻבִים def art + noun mp כְּרוּב *cherubim.*

לַהַט noun m לַהַט *flame.*

הַחֶרֶב def art + noun f חֶרֶב *sword.*

הַמִּתְהַפֶּכֶת def art + Hitp Ptc f הָפַךְ *to turn, overthrow;* Hitp *to turn, roll.*

לִשְׁמֹר prep לְ + Qal Inf Cstr שָׁמַר *to guard, keep.*

Questions

1 We looked at the first five verses in Unit 14, before we encountered the system of verbal stems. There are examples of six of the seven stems in this passage (there are no Hofal forms). Once you have worked through your translation, check the Nifal, Piel, Pual, Hitpael and Hifil forms: do you understand both forms and meanings? Some of these verbs are weak verbs and some have pronominal suffixes, which means understanding the forms may be more difficult. Check against the verb tables in the end of this course to see the verbal patterns.

2 Compare the wording of verse 16 with Genesis 4:7, in which the word תְּשׁוּקָה also occurs – you can look at the Hebrew, although comparing English translations might also work. Which translation of תְּשׁוּקָה might fit both contexts? How is מָשַׁל used in the two verses?

3 This chapter is probably one of the most well-known passages in the whole Bible. What do you think you have gained from being able to read it in the original Hebrew?

Poetic texts

This section introduces several poetic texts, with support for grammar and vocabulary. Like the narrative texts, most of these texts are fairly well known. Try to translate as much as you can from your memory of vocabulary and verbal forms, but use the analysis underneath the text where necessary. Common and repeated words are usually omitted from the analysis.

Many people find poetry more difficult to translate than prose because the syntax (grammatical structure) is unlike that of narrative, and the use of imagery introduces unfamiliar vocabulary. Therefore, translating may be very slow, although a slower speed can help to reinforce your understanding of verbal stems and pronominal suffixes. You may find it useful to compare your work with other translations as you go, to see what the options could be. There are also a few questions to answer on each passage to test your understanding.

SONG OF SONGS 8:4–7 THE POWER OF LOVE

4	בְּנוֹת יְרוּשָׁלָם	הִשְׁבַּעְתִּי אֶתְכֶם
	אֶת־הָאַהֲבָה עַד שֶׁתֶּחְפָּץ׃	מַה־תָּעִירוּ וּמַה־תְּעֹרְרוּ
5	מִתְרַפֶּקֶת עַל־דּוֹדָהּ	מִי זֹאת עֹלָה מִן־הַמִּדְבָּר
	שָׁמָּה חִבְּלַתְךָ אִמֶּךָ	תַּחַת הַתַּפּוּחַ עוֹרַרְתִּיךָ
		שָׁמָּה חִבְּלָה יְלָדַתְךָ׃
6	כַּחוֹתָם עַל־זְרוֹעֶךָ	שִׂימֵנִי כַחוֹתָם עַל־לִבֶּךָ
	קָשָׁה כִשְׁאוֹל קִנְאָה	כִּי־עַזָּה כַמָּוֶת אַהֲבָה
	שַׁלְהֶבֶתְיָה׃	רְשָׁפֶיהָ רִשְׁפֵּי אֵשׁ

מַיִם רַבִּים לֹא יוּכְלוּ
וּנְהָרוֹת לֹא יִשְׁטְפוּהָ
אִם־יִתֵּן אִישׁ

לְכַבּוֹת אֶת־הָאַהֲבָה

אֶת־כָּל־הוֹן בֵּיתוֹ בָּאַהֲבָה בּוֹז יָבוּזוּ לוֹ:

4 הִשְׁבַּעְתִּי Hif Perf 1cs שָׁבַע *to swear*; Hif *to urge, command*.

אֶתְכֶם object pronoun 2fp *you*.

בְּנוֹת noun fp בַּת *daughter*.

יְרוּשָׁלָםִ proper noun *Jerusalem*.

מַה pronoun מַה *what, how, do not* (very occasionally this pronoun has a negative sense).

תָּעִירוּ Hif Impf 2mp עוּר Hif *to awaken, rouse*.

תְּעֹרְרוּ Polel Impf 2mp עוּר Polel *to stir up, rouse, awaken*.

הָאַהֲבָה def art + noun f אַהֲבָה *love*.

עַד prep עַד *until, as far as, while*.

שֶׁתֶּחְפָּץ rel part שֶׁ + Impf 3fs חָפֵץ *to bend, to curve; to wish, to desire*. (The relative particle שֶׁ has the same meaning as אֲשֶׁר but is attached to a word, cf. inseparable prepositions.)

5 זֹאת demonst fs *this*.

עֹלָה Qal Ptc עָלָה *to go up*.

הַמִּדְבָּר def art + noun m *pasture, wilderness, desert*.

מִתְרַפֶּקֶת Hitp Ptc f רָפַק *to lean, rest upon*.

עַל prep עַל *on, upon, over*.

דּוֹדָהּ noun m + suff 3fs דּוֹד *love, lover*.

תַּחַת prep תַּחַת *under, beneath*.

הַתַּפּוּחַ def art + noun m *apple, apple tree*.

עוֹרַרְתִּיךָ Polel Perf 1cs + suff 2ms עוּר Polel *to stir up, rouse, awaken*.

שָׁמָּה adv + ה locale שָׁם *there: towards there*.

חִבְּלַתְךָ Piel Perf 3fs + suff 2ms חָבַל *to twist*; Piel *to writhe, bring forth (give birth)*.

אִמֶּךָ noun f + suff 2ms אֵם *mother*.

חִבְּלָה Piel Perf 3fs חָבַל *to twist*; Piel *to writhe, bring forth, give birth*.

יְלָדַתְךָ Qal Perf 3fs + suff 2ms יָלַד *to give birth*.

6 שִׂימֵנִי Qal Impv + suff 1cs שִׂים *to put, place, set, make*.

כַּחוֹתָם prep כְּ + noun m חוֹתָם *seal, seal ring*.

לִבֶּךָ noun m + suff 2ms לֵב *heart*.

זְרוֹעֶךָ noun f + suff 2ms זְרוֹעַ *arm, forearm*.

עַזָּה adj f עַז *strong*.

כַמָּוֶת prep כְּ + noun m מָוֶת *death*.

קָשָׁה adj f קָשָׁה *hard, difficult, harsh.*

כִּשְׁאוֹל prep כְּ + proper noun *Sheol, place of the dead.*

קִנְאָה noun f *jealousy, envy, passion, anger.*

רְשָׁפֶיהָ noun mp + suff 3fs רֶשֶׁף *flame, lightning.*

רִשְׁפֵּי noun mp cstr רֶשֶׁף *flame, lightning.*

אֵשׁ noun m and f אֵשׁ *fire.*

שַׁלְהֶבֶתְיָה Shafel Ptc f שַׁלְהֶבֶת *flame*; with יָה (for יהוה): *lightning.* (Scholars argue about whether this is really a Shafel stem; if not, it's simply a noun.)

7 מַיִם noun m מַיִם *water.*

רַבִּים adj mp רַב *many, much, great.*

יוּכְלוּ Hof Impf 3mp יָכֹל *to be able*; Hof as Qal.

לְכַבּוֹת prep לְ + Piel Inf Cstr כָּבָה *to be quenched*; Piel *to extinguish.*

וּנְהָרוֹת conj וְ + noun fp נָהָר *river, stream.*

יִשְׁטְפוּהָ Qal Impf 3mp + suff 3fs שָׁטַף *to gush, flow, drown.*

אִם conj, adv *if, surely.*

יִתֵּן Qal Impf 3ms נָתַן *to give, assign, set.*

הוֹן noun m הוֹן *wealth, substance.*

בֵּיתוֹ noun ms + suff 3ms בַּיִת *house.*

בּוֹז Qal Inf Abs בּוֹז *to despise.*

יָבוּזוּ Qal Impf 3mp בּוֹז *to despise.*

לוֹ prep לְ + suff 3ms לְ *him.*

Questions

1 What is the subject of שֶׁתֶּחְפָּץ (v. 4)?

2 How would you translate בּוֹז יָבוּזוּ לוֹ (v. 7) and why?

ISAIAH 41:8–13 GOD'S SERVANT

8	יַעֲקֹב אֲשֶׁר בְּחַרְתִּיךָ	וְאַתָּה יִשְׂרָאֵל עַבְדִּי
		זֶרַע אַבְרָהָם אֹהֲבִי׃
9	וּמֵאֲצִילֶיהָ קְרָאתִיךָ	אֲשֶׁר הֶחֱזַקְתִּיךָ מִקְצוֹת הָאָרֶץ
	בְּחַרְתִּיךָ וְלֹא מְאַסְתִּיךָ׃	וָאֹמַר לְךָ עַבְדִּי־אַתָּה
10	אַל־תִּשְׁתָּע כִּי־אֲנִי אֱלֹהֶיךָ	אַל־תִּירָא כִּי עִמְּךָ־אָנִי
	אַף־תְּמַכְתִּיךָ בִּימִין צִדְקִי׃	אִמַּצְתִּיךָ אַף־עֲזַרְתִּיךָ
11	כֹּל הַנֶּחֱרִים בָּךְ	הֵן יֵבֹשׁוּ וְיִכָּלְמוּ
	אַנְשֵׁי רִיבֶךָ׃	יִהְיוּ כְאַיִן וְיֹאבְדוּ

12	אַנְשֵׁי מַצֻּתֶךָ	תְּבַקְשֵׁם וְלֹא תִמְצָאֵם
13	אַנְשֵׁי מִלְחַמְתֶּךָ :	יִהְיוּ כְאַיִן וּכְאֶפֶס
	מַחֲזִיק יְמִינֶךָ	כִּי אֲנִי יְהוָה אֱלֹהֶיךָ
	אֲנִי עֲזַרְתִּיךָ :	הָאֹמֵר לְךָ אַל־תִּירָא

8 וְאַתָּה conj וְ + subj pronoun 2ms אַתָּה *you.*

עַבְדִּי noun m + suff 1cs עֶבֶד *servant.*

יַעֲקֹב proper noun יַעֲקֹב *Jacob.*

בְּחַרְתִּיךָ Qal Perf 1cs + suff 2ms בָּחַר *to choose, love.*

זֶרַע noun m זֶרַע *seed, descendant(s).*

אֹהֲבִי Qal Ptc + suff 1cs אָהַב *to love; as noun: my friend.*

9 הֶחֱזַקְתִּיךָ Hif Perf 1cs + suff 2ms חָזַק *to be strong; Hifil to take hold of, make strong.*

מִקְצוֹת prep מִן + noun m/f p cstr קָצָה *end, extremity, sum.*

וּמֵאֲצִילֶיהָ conj וְ + prep מִן + noun mp + suff 3fs אָצִיל *side.* קְרָאתִיךָ Qal Perf 1cs + suff 2ms קָרָא *to call, summon.*

וָאֹמַר Qal VC Impf 1cs אָמַר *to say.*

עַבְדִּי noun m + suff 1cs עֶבֶד *servant.*

מְאַסְתִּיךָ Qal Perf 1cs + suff 2ms מָאַס *to reject, despise, hold in contempt.*

10 אַל negative particle אַל *do not.*

תִּירָא Qal Impf 2ms יָרֵא *to fear, revere.*

עִמְּךָ prep עִם + suff 2ms עִם *with.*

אָנִי subj pronoun 1cs אֲנִי *I.*

תִּשְׁתָּע Hitp Impf שָׁעָה *to look, look away; Hitp to look around (e.g. in anxiety).*

אִמַּצְתִּיךָ Piel Perf 1cs + suff 2ms אָמַץ *to be strong; Piel to strengthen.*

אַף conj אַף *also, certainly.*

עֲזַרְתִּיךָ Qal Perf 1cs + suff 2ms עָזַר *to help, aid.*

תְּמַכְתִּיךָ Qal Perf 1cs + suff 2ms תָּמַךְ *to hold onto, support.*

בִּימִין prep בְּ + noun f יָמִין *right, right hand.*

צִדְקִי noun m + suff 1cs צֶדֶק *justice, righteousness.*

11 הֵן interjection הִנֵּה *behold, look.*

יֵבֹשׁוּ Qal Impf 3mp בּוּשׁ *to be ashamed, frustrated.*

וְיִכָּלְמוּ conj וְ + Nif Impf 3mp כָּלַם *Nif to be insulted, disgraced.*

הַנֶּחֱרִים def art + Nif Ptc mp חָרַר *to burn; Nif to be burned, to be angry.*

בָּךְ prep בְּ + suff 2ms in pause בְּ *in, with, by.*

יִהְיוּ Qal Impf 3mp הָיָה *to be, become*.

כְּאַיִן prep כְּ + noun m אַיִן *nothingness*.

וְיֹאבְדוּ conj וְ + Qal Impf 3mp אָבַד *to be lost, wander, die*.

אַנְשֵׁי noun mp cstr אִישׁ *man*.

רִיבֶךָ noun m + suff 2ms רִיב *contention, dispute*.

12 תְּבַקְשֵׁם Piel Impf 2ms + suff 3mp בָּקַשׁ Piel *to search, look for*.

תִמְצָאֵם Qal Impf 2ms + suff 3mp מָצָא *to find*.

מַצֻּתֶךָ noun f + suff 2ms מַצּוּת *strife, contention, dispute*.

יִהְיוּ Qal Impf 3mp הָיָה *to be, become*.

וּכְאֶפֶס conj וְ + prep כְּ + noun m; adv אֶפֶס *end, extremity* (in Isaiah this word sometimes means *nothing*).

מִלְחַמְתֶּךָ noun f + suff 2ms מִלְחָמָה *war, battle*.

13 מַחֲזִיק Hif Ptc חָזַק *to be strong*; Hif *to take hold of, make strong*.

יְמִינֶךָ noun f יָמִין *right, right hand*.

הָאֹמֵר def art + Qal Ptc אָמַר *to say*: *whoever says*.

תִּירָא Qal Impf 2ms יָרֵא *to fear, revere*; Nif *to be feared*.

עֲזַרְתִּיךָ Qal Perf 1cs + suff 2ms עָזַר *to help, aid*.

Questions

1 Can you explain how תִּשְׁתָּע (v. 10) is derived from שָׁעָה? Why are the letters of תִּשְׁתָּע different from the verbal root?

2 Can you give both a literal and an idiomatic translation of בִּימִין צִדְקִי (v. 10)?

3 The word אַנְשֵׁי is used idiomatically several times: אַנְשֵׁי רִיבֶךָ in v. 11 and אַנְשֵׁי מִלְחַמְתֶּךָ and מַצֻּתֶךָ in v. 12. Can you find an appropriate way to render it in English?

PSALM 23 THE LORD IS MY SHEPHERD

1	יְהוָה רֹעִי לֹא אֶחְסָר׃	מִזְמוֹר לְדָוִד
2	עַל־מֵי מְנֻחוֹת יְנַהֲלֵנִי׃	בִּנְאוֹת דֶּשֶׁא יַרְבִּיצֵנִי
3	יַנְחֵנִי בְמַעְגְּלֵי־צֶדֶק לְמַעַן שְׁמוֹ׃	נַפְשִׁי יְשׁוֹבֵב
4	לֹא־אִירָא רָע כִּי־אַתָּה עִמָּדִי	גַּם כִּי־אֵלֵךְ בְּגֵיא צַלְמָוֶת
	הֵמָּה יְנַחֲמֻנִי׃	שִׁבְטְךָ וּמִשְׁעַנְתֶּךָ
5	דִּשַּׁנְתָּ בַשֶּׁמֶן רֹאשִׁי כּוֹסִי רְוָיָה׃	תַּעֲרֹךְ לְפָנַי שֻׁלְחָן נֶגֶד צֹרְרָי
6	כָּל־יְמֵי חַיָּי	אַךְ טוֹב וָחֶסֶד יִרְדְּפוּנִי
	לְאֹרֶךְ יָמִים׃	וְשַׁבְתִּי בְּבֵית־יְהוָה

1 מִזְמוֹר noun m *psalm*.

לְדָוִד prep לְ + proper noun *David*.

רֹעִי Qal Ptc + suff 1cs רָעָה *to feed, pasture, associate with*.

אֶחְסָר Qal Impf 1cs חָסֵר *to be without, to lack*.

2 בִּנְאוֹת prep בְּ + noun f נָאָה *seat, dwelling, pasture*.

דֶּשֶׁא noun m *grass, herbs*.

יַרְבִּיצֵנִי Hif Impf 3ms + suff 1cs רָבַץ *to lie down*.

עַל prep עַל *on, upon, over, beside*.

מֵי noun m dual cstr מַיִם *water*.

מְנֻחוֹת noun f מְנוּחָה *rest, place of rest*.

יְנַהֲלֵנִי Piel Impf 3ms + suff 1cs נָהַל Piel *to lead, provide, sustain*.

3 נַפְשִׁי noun f + suff 1s נֶפֶשׁ *breath, soul, life*.

יְשׁוֹבֵב Polel Impf 3ms שׁוּב *to turn, return*; Polel *to restore*.

יַנְחֵנִי Hif Impf 3ms + suff 1cs נָחָה *to lead, lead back*; Hif as Qal.

בְמַעְגְּלֵי prep בְּ + noun m cstr מַעְגָּל *track, course of action*.

צֶדֶק noun m *justice, righteousness*.

לְמַעַן conj. *in order that, because of, for the sake of*.

שְׁמוֹ noun m + suff 3ms שֵׁם *name*.

4 גַּם conj *even, also*.

אֵלֵךְ Qal Impf 1cs הָלַךְ *to walk, go*.

בְּגֵיא prep בְּ + noun m or f גַּיְא *valley, plain, low or flat region*.

צַלְמָוֶת noun m literally 'shadow of death'; poetic: *thick darkness*.

אִירָא Qal Impf 1cs יָרֵא *to fear, revere*.

אַתָּה subj pronoun 2ms.

עִמָּדִי prep *with*.

שִׁבְטְךָ noun m + suff 2ms שֵׁבֶט *staff, sceptre, tribe*.

וּמִשְׁעַנְתֶּךָ conj וְ + noun f + suff 2ms מִשְׁעֶנָה *stick, rod*.

הֵמָּה pronoun mp *they, that, them*.

יְנַחֲמֻנִי Piel Impf 3ms + suff 1cs נָחַם Piel *to comfort*.

5 תַּעֲרֹךְ Qal Impf 2ms עָרַךְ *to set in order, prepare*.

לְפָנַי prep לְ + noun mp + suff 1cs פָּנִים *face* (before me).

שֻׁלְחָן noun m *table*.

נֶגֶד prep *opposite, in front of*.

צֹרְרָי Qal Ptc mp + suff 1cs צָרַר *to oppress, persecute*.

דִּשַּׁנְתָּ Piel Perf 2ms דָּשֵׁן *to be fat*; Piel *to make fat, anoint*.

בְּשֶׁמֶן prep בְּ + noun m or f שֶׁמֶן *fat, oil*.

רֹאשִׁי noun m + suff 1cs רֹאשׁ *head, supreme, top*.

כּוֹסִי noun f + suff 1cs כּוֹס *receptacle, cup*.

רְוָיָה noun f רְוָיָה *abundance*.

6 אַךְ adv *only, but, certainly*.

וָחֶסֶד conj וְ + noun m *love, kindness*.

יִרְדְּפוּנִי Qal Impf 3mp + suff 1cs רָדַף *to pursue, follow*.

יְמֵי noun mp cstr יוֹם *day*.

חַיָּי noun m + suff 1cs חַי plural חַיִּים *life, prosperity*.

וְשַׁבְתִּי Qal VC Perf 1cs יָשַׁב *to sit, live*.

בְּבֵית prep בְּ + noun m בַּיִת *house*.

לְאֹרֶךְ prep לְ + noun m אֹרֶךְ *length*.

יָמִים noun mp יוֹם *day*.

Questions

1 If the Qal of רָבַץ (v. 2) means *to lie down*, what does the Hifil mean?

2 The word יְשׁוֹבֵב is in the Polel stem, which is related to the Piel (there was an example in the passage from Song of Songs as well). The verbal root is שׁוּב. Can you explain why the stem is called Polel?

3 How would you translate לְאֹרֶךְ יָמִים (v. 6)?

PSALM 121 I WILL LIFT MY EYES TO THE HILLS

1	שִׁיר לַמַּעֲלוֹת
	אֶשָּׂא עֵינַי אֶל־הֶהָרִים מֵאַיִן יָבֹא עֶזְרִי׃
2	עֶזְרִי מֵעִם יְהוָה עֹשֵׂה שָׁמַיִם וָאָרֶץ׃
3	אַל־יִתֵּן לַמּוֹט רַגְלֶךָ אַל־יָנוּם שֹׁמְרֶךָ׃
4	הִנֵּה לֹא־יָנוּם וְלֹא יִישָׁן שׁוֹמֵר יִשְׂרָאֵל׃
5	יְהוָה שֹׁמְרֶךָ יְהוָה צִלְּךָ עַל־יַד יְמִינֶךָ׃
6	יוֹמָם הַשֶּׁמֶשׁ לֹא־יַכֶּכָּה וְיָרֵחַ בַּלָּיְלָה׃
7	יְהוָה יִשְׁמָרְךָ מִכָּל־רָע יִשְׁמֹר אֶת־נַפְשֶׁךָ׃
8	יְהוָה יִשְׁמָר־צֵאתְךָ וּבוֹאֶךָ מֵעַתָּה וְעַד־עוֹלָם׃

1 שִׁיר noun m *song*.

לַמַּעֲלוֹת prep לְ + noun fp מַעֲלָה *step, ascent*.

אֶשָּׂא Qal Impf 1s נָשָׂא *to lift up, receive*.

עֵינַי noun f dual + suff 1cs עַיִן *eye.*

הֶהָרִים noun mp הַר *mountain.*

מֵאַיִן prep מִן + adv אַי *where, how.*

יָבֹא Qal Impf 3ms בּוֹא *to come.*

עֶזְרִי noun m + suff 1cs עֵזֶר *help, aid.*

2 מֵעִם prep מִן + prep עִם *(from with).*

עֹשֵׂה Qal Ptc עָשָׂה *to make, do.*

3 אַל negative particle.

יִתֵּן Qal Impf 3ms נָתַן *to give, allow, set.*

לַמּוֹט prep לְ + noun m מוֹט *slipping, tottering, shaking.*

רַגְלֶךָ noun f + suff 2ms רֶגֶל *foot, leg.*

יָנוּם Qal Impf 3ms נוּם *to be drowsy, to sleep.*

שֹׁמְרֶךָ Qal Ptc + suff 2ms שָׁמַר *to keep, guard, observe.*

4 הִנֵּה interjection הִנֵּה *behold, look.*

יָנוּם Qal Impf 3ms נוּם *to be drowsy, to sleep.*

יִישָׁן Qal Impf 3ms יָשֵׁן *to fall asleep.*

5 שֹׁמְרֶךָ Qal Ptc + suff 2ms שָׁמַר *to keep, guard, notice, observe.*

צִלְּךָ noun m צֵל *shade, shadow.*

עַל prep עַל *on, upon, over.*

יַד noun fs cstr יָד *hand.*

יְמִינֶךָ noun f יָמִין *right, right hand.*

6 יוֹמָם adv יוֹם *by day.*

הַשֶּׁמֶשׁ def art + noun m and f שֶׁמֶשׁ *sun.*

יַכֶּכָּה Hif Impf 3ms + suff 2ms נָכָה Hif *to strike, attack, kill (the suffix is in a slightly unusual form).*

וְיָרֵחַ conj וְ + noun m יָרֵחַ *moon.*

בַּלָּיְלָה prep בְּ + noun m, in pause לַיְלָה *night.*

7 יִשְׁמָרְךָ Qal Impf 3ms + 2ms שָׁמַר *to keep, guard, observe.*

יִשְׁמֹר Qal Impf 3ms שָׁמַר *to keep, guard, notice, observe.*

נַפְשֶׁךָ noun f + suff 2ms נֶפֶשׁ *breath, soul, life.*

8 יִשְׁמָר Qal Impf 3ms שָׁמַר *to keep, guard, notice, observe.*

צֵאתְךָ Qal Ptc + suff 2ms יָצָא *to go out (e.g. to war), be born.*

וּבוֹאֶךָ conj וְ + Qal Ptc + suff 2ms בּוֹא *to come.*

מֵעַתָּה prep מִן + adv עַתָּה *now.*

וְעַד conj וְ + prep עַד *until, as far as, while.*

עוֹלָם noun m *ancient time, eternity.*

Questions

1 The word שֹׁמֵרֶךָ (v. 3) can be understood either as a participle or as a noun. What is the best translation?

2 The word יַכֶּכָה (v. 6) has a suffix which is 2ms, but the spelling is slightly unusual. How is this suffix usually spelled?

3 The word מִכָּל (v. 7) has a *dagesh* in the *kaf*. Can you explain why?

AMOS 8:1–7 A VISION

1   כֹּה הִרְאַנִי אֲדֹנָי יְהוִה וְהִנֵּה כְּלוּב קָיִץ׃

2   וַיֹּאמֶר מָה־אַתָּה רֹאֶה עָמוֹס וָאֹמַר כְּלוּב קָיִץ וַיֹּאמֶר יְהוָה אֵלַי

בָּא הַקֵּץ אֶל־עַמִּי יִשְׂרָאֵל   לֹא־אוֹסִיף עוֹד עֲבוֹר לוֹ׃

3 וְהֵילִילוּ שִׁירוֹת הֵיכָל

רַב הַפֶּגֶר   בְּכָל־מָקוֹם   הִשְׁלִיךְ הָס׃   בַּיּוֹם הַהוּא נְאֻם אֲדֹנָי יְהוִה

4 שִׁמְעוּ־זֹאת הַשֹּׁאֲפִים אֶבְיוֹן   וְלַשְׁבִּית עניו[2] אָרֶץ׃

5 לֵאמֹר מָתַי יַעֲבֹר הַחֹדֶשׁ וְנַשְׁבִּירָה שֶּׁבֶר

וְהַשַּׁבָּת וְנִפְתְּחָה־בָּר לְהַקְטִין אֵיפָה וּלְהַגְדִּיל שֶׁקֶל

וּלְעַוֵּת מֹאזְנֵי מִרְמָה׃

6 לִקְנוֹת בַּכֶּסֶף דַּלִּים וְאֶבְיוֹן בַּעֲבוּר נַעֲלָיִם

וּמַפַּל בַּר נַשְׁבִּיר׃

7 נִשְׁבַּע יְהוָה בִּגְאוֹן יַעֲקֹב

אִם־אֶשְׁכַּח לָנֶצַח כָּל־מַעֲשֵׂיהֶם

1 כֹּה adv *thus, therefore*.

הִרְאַנִי Hif Perf 3ms + suff 1cs רָאָה *to see*; Hif *to show*.

אֲדֹנָי noun mp + suff 1cs אָדוֹן *lord, master*: (*The LORD*, rather than *a lord*, because of **qamets** instead of **patach** under the **nun**).

וְהִנֵּה conj וְ + interj הִנֵּה *behold, look*.

כְּלוּב noun m כְּלוּב *wicker work, basket*.

קָיִץ noun m in pause קַיִץ *harvest, fruit, summer*.

2 וַיֹּאמֶר Qal VC Impf 3ms אָמַר *to say*.

מָה pronoun מַה *what, how*.

אַתָּה subj pronoun 2ms *you*.

---

2 Qere עֲנִיֵּי־

רֹאֶה Qal Ptc רָאָה *to see.*

עָמוֹס proper noun *Amos.*

וָאֹמַר Qal VC Impf 1cs אָמַר *to say.*

בָּא Qal Perf 3ms בּוֹא *to come.*

הַקֵּץ def art + noun m קֵץ *end, extremity, destruction.*

עַמִּי noun m + suff 1cs עַם *people.*

אוֹסִיף Hif Impf 1cs יָסַף *to add, do again;* Hif as Qal.

עוֹד adv עוֹד *again, further, yet, still.*

עֲבוֹר Qal Inf Cstr עָבַר *to pass, pass over, forgive.*

3 וְהֵילִילוּ Hif VC Perf 3cp יָלַל Hif *to wail, lament.*

שִׁירוֹת noun fp שִׁירָה *song.*

הֵיכָל noun m *temple, palace.*

בַּיּוֹם prep בְּ + noun m יוֹם *day.*

הַהוּא def art + demonst. adj m *he, that.*

נְאֻם Qal Ptc passive cstr נָאַם *to mutter, utter an oracle.*

רַב adj m רַב *many, much, great.*

הַפֶּגֶר def art + noun m פֶּגֶר *corpse, dead body.*

מָקוֹם noun m *place.*

הִשְׁלִיךְ Hif Perfect 3ms שָׁלַךְ Hif: *to throw, throw down.*

הָס adv in pause הַס *silently* (i.e. bodies will be disposed of in silence, in contrast to the wailing in the temple).

4 שִׁמְעוּ Qal Impv mp שָׁמַע *to hear, listen, obey.*

זֹאת demonst fs *this.*

הַשֹּׁאֲפִים def art + Qal Ptc mp שָׁאַף *to crush, trample; swallow.*

אֶבְיוֹן noun m *poor, needy.*

וְלַשְׁבִּית conj וְ + prep לְ + Hif Inf Cstr שָׁבַת *to sit, rest;* Hif *to interrupt, restrain, exterminate.*

עֲנִיֵּי adj mp cstr עָנִי *poor, afflicted, meek.*

5 לֵאמֹר prep לְ + Qal Inf Cstr אָמַר *saying.*

מָתַי adv מָתַי *when*

יַעֲבֹר Qal Impf 3ms עָבַר *to pass, pass over, forgive.*

הַחֹדֶשׁ def art + noun m חֹדֶשׁ *new moon, month.*

וְנַשְׁבִּירָה conj וְ + Hif Impf 1cp + paragogic ה שָׁבַר *to break;* Hif *to sell grain.*

שֶׁבֶר noun m שֶׁבֶר *corn, grain* (the **dagesh** in שׁ is euphonic: it occurs because the stress is on the first syllable of this word, which follows the unstressed **qamets-he** of the preceding word).

וְהַשַּׁבָּת conj וְ + def art + noun m שַׁבָּת *sabbath, seventh day, week.*

וְנִפְתְּחָה conj וְ + Qal Impf 1cp פָּתַח *to open.*

בַּר noun m בַּר *wheat, field, country (i.e. open the granaries to sell wheat).*

לְהַקְטִין prep לְ + Hif Inf Cstr קָטֹן *to be small, little; Hif to make small.*

אֵיפָה noun m אֵיפָה *measure of grain.*

וּלְהַגְדִּיל conj וְ + prep לְ + Hif Inf Cstr גָּדַל *to be big, great; Hif to make big or great.*

שֶׁקֶל noun m שֶׁקֶל *shekel, unit of currency.*

וּלְעַוֵּת conj וְ + prep לְ + Piel Inf Cstr עָוָה *to overturn, destroy; Piel to twist, distort.*

מֹאזְנֵי noun m dual cstr מֹאזְנַיִם *scales.*

מִרְמָה noun f מִרְמָה *fraud, deceit.*

6 **לִקְנוֹת** prep לְ + Qal Inf Cstr קָנָה *to acquire, buy.*

בַּכֶּסֶף prep בְּ + noun ms כֶּסֶף *silver.*

דַּלִּים adj mp דַּל *weak, powerless.*

בַּעֲבוּר prep בְּ + prep עֲבוּר *for.*

נַעֲלָיִם noun f dual (in pause) נַעַל *shoe.*

וּמַפַּל conj וְ + noun m מַפָּל *flake, husk.*

בַּר noun m בַּר *wheat, field, country.*

נַשְׁבִּיר Hif Impf 1cp שָׁבַר *to break; Hif to sell grain.*

7 **נִשְׁבַּע** Nif Perf 3ms שָׁבַע *to swear; Nif to swear.*

בִּגְאוֹן prep בְּ + noun m גָּאוֹן *glory, honour, pride.*

יַעֲקֹב proper noun *Jacob.*

אִם conj, adv אִם *if, surely, not.*

אֶשְׁכַּח Qal Impf 1cs שָׁכַח *to forget, leave.*

לָנֶצַח prep לְ + noun m נֶצַח *glory, sincerity, truth (adv: truly, surely).*

מַעֲשֵׂיהֶם noun mp + suff 3mp מַעֲשֶׂה *deed, work.*

Questions

1 The tetragrammaton in verse 1 is pointed with a *hiriq* where we might usually expect a *qamats*. Can you explain why? How might it be pronounced?

2 The word הִשְׁלִיךְ (v. 3) is in the Perfect tense, which is usually translated with an English past tense. However, most translations have an English future. Why?

3 The threats of destruction in Amos 8 and 9 give way to a note of hope by the end of the book, which might mitigate the apparent incongruity of a basket of fruit as the occasion of prophecies of doom. But there is also some Hebrew wordplay at work. Which two words in verses 1–2 sound almost the same?

PROVERBS 8:1–11 IN PRAISE OF WISDOM

#		
1	וּתְבוּנָה תִּתֵּן קוֹלָהּ׃	הֲלֹא־חָכְמָה תִקְרָא
2	בֵּית נְתִיבוֹת נִצָּבָה׃	בְּרֹאשׁ־מְרֹמִים עֲלֵי־דָרֶךְ
3	מְבוֹא פְתָחִים תָּרֹנָּה׃	לְיַד־שְׁעָרִים לְפִי־קָרֶת
4	וְקוֹלִי אֶל־בְּנֵי אָדָם׃	אֲלֵיכֶם אִישִׁים אֶקְרָא
5	וּכְסִילִים הָבִינוּ לֵב׃	הָבִינוּ פְתָאיִם עָרְמָה
6	וּמִפְתַּח שְׂפָתַי מֵישָׁרִים׃	שִׁמְעוּ כִּי־נְגִידִים אֲדַבֵּר
7	וְתוֹעֲבַת שְׂפָתַי רֶשַׁע׃	כִּי־אֱמֶת יֶהְגֶּה חִכִּי
8	אֵין בָּהֶם נִפְתָּל וְעִקֵּשׁ׃	בְּצֶדֶק כָּל־אִמְרֵי־פִי
9	וִישָׁרִים לְמֹצְאֵי דָעַת׃	כֻּלָּם נְכֹחִים לַמֵּבִין
10	וְדַעַת מֵחָרוּץ נִבְחָר׃	קְחוּ־מוּסָרִי וְאַל־כָּסֶף
11	וְכָל־חֲפָצִים לֹא יִשְׁווּ־בָהּ׃	כִּי־טוֹבָה חָכְמָה מִפְּנִינִים

1 הֲלֹא interrog ה + neg adv לֹא (*is not?*).

חָכְמָה noun f *wisdom*.

תִקְרָא Qal Impf 3fs קָרָא *to call, summon*.

וּתְבוּנָה noun f תָּבוּן *understanding*.

תִּתֵּן Qal Impf 2ms נָתַן *to give, assign, set*.

קוֹלָהּ noun m + suff 3fs קוֹל *voice*.

2 בְּרֹאשׁ prep בְּ + noun m רֹאשׁ *head, supreme, top*.

מְרֹמִים noun mp מָרוֹם *height, high place*.

עֲלֵי prep עַל *on, upon, over, beside* (poetic form).

דָרֶךְ noun m דֶּרֶךְ *way, path*.

בֵּית noun ms cstr בַּיִת *house, place*.

נְתִיבוֹת noun fp נָתִיב *trodden way, footpath*.

נִצָּבָה Nif Perf 3fs נָצַב *to set, put, place; Nif to be set, to stand*.

3 לְיַד prep לְ + noun f יָד *hand (next to)*.

שְׁעָרִים noun mp שַׁעַר *gate, measure*.

לְפִי prep לְ + noun f cstr פֶּה *mouth*.

קָרֶת noun f קָרֶת *city, town*.

מְבוֹא noun m מָבוֹא *entering, approach (at the entrance)*.

פְתָחִים noun mp פֶּתַח *opening, entrance, gate*.

תָּרֹנָּה Qal Impf 2fs רָנַן *to shout for joy, to sing*.

258

4 אֲלֵיכֶם prep + suff 2mp אֶל *to you.*

אִישִׁים noun mp אִישׁ *man.*

אֶקְרָא Qal Impf 1cs קָרָא *to call, summon.*

וְקוֹלִי conj וְ + noun m + suff 1cs קוֹל *voice.*

בְּנֵי noun mp cstr בֵּן *son.*

אָדָם noun m אָדָם *earth, man, Adam.*

5 הָבִינוּ Hif Impv mp בִּין *to distinguish;* Hif *to teach, understand.*

פְּתָאִים noun f פְּתִי *foolishness; foolish or gullible person.*

עָרְמָה noun f עָרְמָה *craftiness, prudence.*

וּכְסִילִים conj וְ + noun mp כְּסִיל *fool.*

הָבִינוּ Hif Impv mp בִּין *to distinguish;* Hif *to teach, understand.*

לֵב noun m לֵב *heart, mind, knowledge.*

6 שִׁמְעוּ Qal Impv שָׁמַע *to hear, listen, obey.*

נְגִידִים noun mp נָגִיד *leader, noble (noble things).*

אֲדַבֵּר Piel Impf 1cs דָּבַר Piel *to speak.*

וּמִפְתַּח conj וְ + noun m מִפְתָּח *opening, entrance.*

שְׂפָתַי noun f dual + suff 1cs שָׂפָה *lip, edge.*

מֵישָׁרִים noun mp מֵישָׁר *justice, sincerity (right things).*

7 אֱמֶת noun f אֱמֶת *truth.*

יֶהְגֶּה Qal Impf 3ms הָגָה *to mutter, speak.*

חִכִּי noun m + suff 1cs חֵךְ *palate, mouth.*

וְתוֹעֲבַת conj וְ + noun f cstr תּוֹעֵבָה *idolatry, immorality, abomination.*

שְׂפָתַי noun f dual + suff 1cs שָׂפָה *lip, edge.*

רֶשַׁע noun m רֶשַׁע *wickedness, fraud.*

8 בְּצֶדֶק prep בְּ + noun m צֶדֶק *justice, righteousness.*

אִמְרֵי noun mp cstr אֵמֶר *word, discourse, command.*

פִי noun m cstr פֶּה *mouth.*

אֵין noun m cstr (used as adv) אַיִן *there is not.*

בָּהֶם prep בְּ + suff 3mp בְּ *in, with, by.*

נִפְתָּל Nif Ptc פָּתַל Nif *to be twisted, to wrestle.*

וְעִקֵּשׁ conj וְ + adj m עִקֵּשׁ *distorted, deceitful, false.*

9 כֻּלָּם noun m + suff 3mp כֹּל *whole (all of them).*

נְכֹחִים adj mp נָכֹחַ *straight, right, just.*

לַמֵּבִין prep לְ + Hif Ptc בִּין *to distinguish;* Hif *to teach, understand (to the one who understands).*

וִישָׁרִים conj וְ + adj mp יָשָׁר *righteous, straight.*

לְמֹצְאֵי prep לְ + Qal Ptc mp cstr מָצָא *to find (to those who find).*

דָעַת noun f in pause דַּעַת *knowledge.*

קְחוּ 10 Qal Impv mp לָקַח *to take, receive.*

מוּסָרִי noun m + suff 1cs מוּסָר *correction, instruction.*

וְאַל conj וְ + negative particle אַל *nothing, not.*

כָּסֶף noun m (in pause) כֶּסֶף *silver.*

מֵחָרוּץ prep מִן + noun m חָרוּץ *judgment, gold (poetic).*

נִבְחָר Nif Ptc בָּחַר *to choose, love;* Nif *to be chosen: choice* (Nif Ptc used as adj).

טוֹבָה 11 adj fs טוֹב *good.*

חָכְמָה noun f *wisdom.*

מִפְּנִינִים prep מִן + noun mp פְּנִינִים *pearls; red gemstones.*

חֲפָצִים noun mp חֵפֶץ *desire, pleasure.*

יִשְׁווּ Qal Impf 3mp שָׁוָה *to be equal, suitable; to resemble* (this verb is not a hollow verb; the **vav** is a consonant rather than a vowel, so is followed by **shuruq** in the Impf 3mp).

בָהּ prep בְּ + suff 3fs בְּ *in, with, by.*

Questions

1 The word אִישִׁים in v. 4 is an unusual plural of אִישׁ. What is the usual plural?

2 The phrase וְתוֹעֲבַת שְׂפָתַי רֶשַׁע in v. 7 is difficult to render because of the construct form of תּוֹעֵבָה. Can you produce an idiomatic English translation?

3 How should you translate the combination of וְכֹל with the negative לֹא?

1 SAMUEL 2:1–10 HANNAH'S SONG

1
                          וַתִּתְפַּלֵּל חַנָּה וַתֹּאמַר

           רָמָה קַרְנִי בַּיהוָה   עָלַץ לִבִּי בַּיהוָה

          כִּי שָׂמַחְתִּי בִּישׁוּעָתֶךָ :   רָחַב פִּי עַל־אוֹיְבַי

2   וְאֵין צוּר כֵּאלֹהֵינוּ :   כִּי אֵין בִּלְתֶּךָ   אֵין־קָדוֹשׁ כַּיהוָה

3   יֵצֵא עָתָק מִפִּיכֶם   אַל־תַּרְבּוּ תְדַבְּרוּ גְּבֹהָה גְבֹהָה

          וְלֹא[3] נִתְכְּנוּ עֲלִלוֹת: כִּי אֵל דֵּעוֹת יְהוָה

4   וְנִכְשָׁלִים אָזְרוּ חָיִל: קֶשֶׁת גִּבֹּרִים חַתִּים

---

[3] Qere וְלוֹ

שְׂבֵעִים בַּלֶּחֶם נִשְׂכָּרוּ	5	וּרְעֵבִים חָדֵלּוּ עַד־
עֲקָרָה יָלְדָה שִׁבְעָה		וְרַבַּת בָּנִים אֻמְלָלָה׃
יְהוָה מֵמִית וּמְחַיֶּה	6	מוֹרִיד שְׁאוֹל וַיָּעַל׃
יְהוָה מוֹרִישׁ וּמַעֲשִׁיר	7	מַשְׁפִּיל אַף־מְרוֹמֵם׃
מֵקִים מֵעָפָר דָּל	8	מֵאַשְׁפֹּת יָרִים אֶבְיוֹן
לְהוֹשִׁיב עִם־נְדִיבִים		וְכִסֵּא כָבוֹד יַנְחִלֵם
כִּי לַיהוָה מְצֻקֵי אֶרֶץ		וַיָּשֶׁת עֲלֵיהֶם תֵּבֵל׃
רַגְלֵי חֲסִידָו⁴ יִשְׁמֹר	9	וּרְשָׁעִים בַּחֹשֶׁךְ יִדָּמּוּ
כִּי־לֹא בְכֹחַ יִגְבַּר־אִישׁ׃		
יְהוָה⁵ יֵחַתּוּ מְרִיבָו	10	עָלָו⁶ בַּשָּׁמַיִם יַרְעֵם
יְהוָה יָדִין אַפְסֵי־אָרֶץ		וְיִתֶּן־עֹז לְמַלְכּוֹ
וְיָרֵם קֶרֶן מְשִׁיחוֹ׃		

1 וַתִּתְפַּלֵּל Hitpael VC Impf 3fs פָּלַל Hitp *to intercede, pray*.

חַנָּה proper noun *Hannah*.

וַתֹּאמַר Qal VC Impf 3fs אָמַר *to say*.

עָלַץ Qal Perf 3ms עָלַץ *to rejoice*.

לִבִּי noun m + suff 1cs לֵב *heart, my heart*.

רָמָה Qal Perf 3fs רוּם *to rise, be high*.

קַרְנִי noun f suff 1cs קֶרֶן *horn*.

רָחַב Qal Perf 3ms רָחַב *to be or become wide, spacious*.

פִּי noun m + suff 1cs פֶּה *mouth*.

עַל prep עַל *on, upon, over*.

אוֹיְבַי noun mp + suff 1cs אֹיֵב *enemy*.

שָׂמַחְתִּי Qal Perf 1cs שָׂמַח *to rejoice, be glad*.

בִּישׁוּעָתֶךָ prep בְּ + noun m + suff 2ms יְשׁוּעָה *deliverance, help*.

2 אֵין noun m cstr (used as adv) אֵין *there is not*.

קָדוֹשׁ adj m קָדוֹשׁ *holy*.

בִּלְתֶּךָ adv + suff 2ms בִּלְתִּי *besides, except*.

צוּר noun m צוּר *rock, stone*.

---

4 Qere חֲסִידָיו

5 Qere מְרִיבָיו

6 Qere עָלָיו

כֵּאלֹהֵינוּ prep כְּ + noun m + suff 1cp אֱלֹהִים (*like our God*).

3 אַל negative particle אַל *do not*.

תַּרְבּוּ Hif Impf 2mp רָבָה Hif *to increase, multiply*.

תְּדַבְּרוּ Piel Impf 2mp דָּבַר Piel *to speak*.

גְּבֹהָה adj f גָּבֹהַּ *high, proud*.

יֵצֵא Qal Impf 3ms יָצָא *to go out, be born*.

עָתָק noun m עָתָק *arrogance*.

מִפִּיכֶם prep מִן + noun m + suff 3mp פֶּה *mouth*.

אֵל proper noun *God*.

דֵּעוֹת noun fp דֵּעָה *knowledge*.

וְלֹא conj וְ + negative particle (Ketiv; see below).

וְלוֹ prep לְ + suff 3ms לְ *to, at, for* (Qere).

נִתְכְּנוּ Nif Perf 3cp תָּכַן *to weigh*; Nif *to be levelled, be right, be measured*.

עֲלִלוֹת noun fp עֲלִילָה *deed, work*.

4 קֶשֶׁת noun f קֶשֶׁת *bow, rainbow*.

גִּבֹּרִים noun mp גִּבֹּר *strong man*.

חַתִּים adj mp חַת *broken*.

וְנִכְשָׁלִים conj וְ + Nif Ptc mp כָּשַׁל *to stumble, stagger*; Nif *to stagger, sink*.

אָזְרוּ Qal Perf 3cp אָזַר *to surround, strengthen*.

חָיִל noun m חַיִל *strength, integrity*.

5 שְׂבֵעִים Qal Ptc mp שָׂבַע *to be satisfied, satiated*.

בַּלֶּחֶם prep בְּ + noun m לֶחֶם *bread, food*.

נִשְׂכָּרוּ Nif Perf 3cp שָׂכַר *to hire, bribe* (Nif understood as reflexive here: *they hired themselves*).

וּרְעֵבִים conj וְ + adj mp רָעֵב *hungry*.

חָדֵלּוּ Qal Perf 3cp חָדַל *to cease, desist*.

עַד prep עַד *until, as far as, while*.

עֲקָרָה noun f עָקָר *infertile*.

יָלַדָה Qal Perf 3fs יָלַד *to give birth*.

שִׁבְעָה numeral m שֶׁבַע *seven*.

וְרַבַּת conj וְ + adj f cstr רַב *many, much, great*.

בָּנִים noun mp בֵּן *son*.

אֻמְלָלָה Pulal Perf 3fs אָמַל *to languish*; Pulal *to languish, be feeble* (this stem has the same range of meaning as Pual).

6 מֵמִית Hif Ptc מוּת *to die* (Hif used of death caused by God e.g. by plague, famine etc.).

וּמְחַיֶּה conj וְ + Piel Ptc חָיָה *to live*; Piel *to preserve, revive.*

מוֹרִיד Hif Ptc יָרַד *to go down.*

שְׁאוֹל proper noun *Sheol, place of the dead.*

וַיַּעַל Hif VC Impf 3ms apoc עָלָה *to go up*; Hif *to bring up, offer (a sacrifice).*

7 מוֹרִישׁ Hif Ptc יָרַשׁ *to inherit, dispossess*; Hif *to destroy, dispossess, reduce to poverty.*

וּמַעֲשִׁיר conj וְ + Hif Ptc עָשַׁר *to be straight*; Hif *to make rich.*

מַשְׁפִּיל Hif Ptc שָׁפֵל *be low*; Hif *bring low.*

אַף conj אַף *also, certainly also.*

מְרוֹמֵם Polel Ptc רוּם *to rise, be high*; Polel *to make high.*

8 מֵקִים Hif Ptc קוּם *to get up*; Hif *to raise up.*

מֵעָפָר prep מִן + noun m עָפָר *dust, dry earth.*

דָּל adj m דָּל *weak, powerless.*

מֵאַשְׁפֹּת prep מִן + noun m אַשְׁפֹּת *dung hill.*

יָרִים Hif Impf 3ms רוּם *to rise, be high*; Hif *to exalt.*

לְהוֹשִׁיב prep לְ + Hif Inf Cstr יָשַׁב *to sit, live*; Hif *to cause to live.*

עִם prep עִם *with.*

נְדִיבִים noun mp נָדִיב *prince, tyrant.*

וְכִסֵּא conj וְ + noun m כִּסֵּא *seat, throne.*

כָבוֹד noun m כָּבוֹד *honour, glory.*

יַנְחִלֵם Hif Impf 3ms + suff 3mp נָחַל *to receive, possess*; Hif *to distribute.*

לַיהוָה prep לְ + proper noun יְהוָה *Yhwh, to Yhwh.*

מְצֻקֵי noun mp cstr מָצוּק *column, pillar.*

וַיָּשֶׁת Qal VC Impf 3ms שִׁית *to put, place, set.*

עֲלֵיהֶם prep + suff 3mp עַל *on, upon, over, beside.*

תֵּבֵל noun f *world, earth.*

9 רַגְלֵי noun fp cstr רֶגֶל *foot, leg.*

חֲסִידָיו adj mp + suff 3ms חָסִיד *merciful, pious* (Qere).

יִשְׁמֹר Qal Impf 3ms שָׁמַר *to keep, guard, observe.*

וּרְשָׁעִים conj וְ + adj mp רָשָׁע *wicked.*

בַּחֹשֶׁךְ prep בְּ + noun m חֹשֶׁךְ *darkness.*

יִדָּמּוּ Nif Impf 3mp דָּמַם *to be silent*; Nif *to be silenced.*

בְּכֹחַ prep בְּ + noun m כֹּחַ *strength, power.*

יִגְבַּר Qal Impf 3ms גָּבַר *to be strong, prevail.*

10 יֵחַתּוּ Nif Impf 3mp חָתַת to break; Nif to be broken.

מְרִיבָיו Hif Ptc mp + suff 3ms רִיב to fight, to plead a cause; Hif Ptc enemy (Qere).

עָלָיו prep + suff 3ms עַל on, upon, over, against (Qere).

בַּשָּׁמַיִם prep בְּ + noun m שָׁמַיִם heaven.

יַרְעֵם Hif Impf 3ms רָעַם to rage, roar; Hif to thunder.

יָדִין Qal Impf 3ms דִּין to judge, rule.

אַפְסֵי noun mp cstr אֶפֶס end, extremity.

וְיִתֶּן conj וְ + Qal Impf 3ms נָתַן to give, assign, set.

עֹז noun m עֹז strength, power, glory.

לְמַלְכּוֹ prep לְ + noun m + suff 3ms מֶלֶךְ king.

וְיָרֵם conj וְ + Hif Impf 3ms רוּם to rise, be high; Hif to exalt.

קֶרֶן noun f קֶרֶן horn.

מְשִׁיחוֹ noun m + suff 3ms מָשִׁיחַ anointed.

Questions

1 The word מְרוֹמֵם (v. 7) is a Polel stem. What kind of verbs have a Polel instead of a Piel?

2 There are several Qere readings in this passage. Is there anything significant at stake in the differences between the Ketiv and the Qere?

3 The beginning of verse 10 is rather tricky to translate. Can you attempt two alternatives?

JOB 38:1–11 GOD SPEAKS FROM THE WHIRLWIND

1 וַיַּעַן יְהוָה אֶת־אִיּוֹב מנהסערה[7] וַיֹּאמַר:

2 מִי זֶה מַחְשִׁיךְ עֵצָה בְּמִלִּין בְּלִי־דָעַת:

3 אֱזָר־נָא כְגֶבֶר חֲלָצֶיךָ וְאֶשְׁאָלְךָ וְהוֹדִיעֵנִי:

4 אֵיפֹה הָיִיתָ בְּיָסְדִי־אָרֶץ הַגֵּד אִם־יָדַעְתָּ בִינָה:

5 מִי־שָׂם מְמַדֶּיהָ כִּי תֵדָע אוֹ מִי־נָטָה עָלֶיהָ קָּו:

6 עַל־מָה אֲדָנֶיהָ הָטְבָּעוּ אוֹ מִי־יָרָה אֶבֶן פִּנָּתָהּ:

7 בְּרָן־יַחַד כּוֹכְבֵי בֹקֶר וַיָּרִיעוּ כָּל־בְּנֵי אֱלֹהִים:

8 וַיָּסֶךְ בִּדְלָתַיִם יָם בְּגִיחוֹ מֵרֶחֶם יֵצֵא:

9 בְּשׂוּמִי עָנָן לְבֻשׁוֹ וַעֲרָפֶל חֲתֻלָּתוֹ:

10 וָאֶשְׁבֹּר עָלָיו חֻקִּי וָאָשִׂים בְּרִיחַ וּדְלָתָיִם:

11 וָאֹמַר עַד־פֹּה תָבוֹא וְלֹא תֹסִיף וּפֹא־יָשִׁית בִּגְאוֹן גַּלֶּיךָ:

---

[7] Qere מִן הַסְּעָרָה

264

1 וַיַּעַן Qal VC Impf 3ms apoc עָנָה *to answer*.

אִיּוֹב proper noun אִיּוֹב *Job*.

הַסְּעָרָה def art + noun f סַעַר *storm* (Qere).

וַיֹּאמַר Qal VC Impf 3ms אָמַר *to say*.

2 זֶה demonst ms *this*.

מַחְשִׁיךְ Hif Ptc חָשַׁךְ *to be dark, darkened*.

עֵצָה noun f עֵצָה *advice, wisdom*.

בְמִלִּין prep בְּ + noun fp מִלָּה *word* (Aramaic-style plural form).

בְּלִי prep *without*.

דָעַת noun f דַּעַת *knowledge*.

3 אֱזָר Qal Impv אָזַר *to surround, strengthen*.

נָא particle of entreaty.

כְגֶבֶר prep כְּ + noun m גֶּבֶר *strong man*.

חֲלָצֶיךָ noun m + suff 2ms חָלָץ *loin, hip*.

וְאֶשְׁאָלְךָ conj וְ + Qal Impf 1cs + suff 2ms שָׁאַל *to ask, search*.

וְהוֹדִיעֵנִי conj וְ + Hif Impv + suff 1cs יָדַע *to know*; Hif *to make known, declare*.

4 אֵיפֹה interrog adj אַי *where, how*.

הָיִיתָ Qal Perf 2ms הָיָה *to be, become*.

בְּיָסְדִי prep בְּ + Qal Inf Cstr + suff 1cs יָסַד *to place, set, establish*.

הַגֵּד Hif Impv נָגַד Hif *to show, tell, declare*.

אִם conj, adv אִם *if, surely, not if*.

יָדַעְתָּ Qal Perf 2ms יָדַע *to know*.

בִינָה noun f בִּינָה *understanding, discernment*.

5 שָׂם Qal Perf 3ms שִׂים *to put, place, set, make*.

מְמַדֶּיהָ noun m + suff 3fs מֵמַד *measurement*.

כִּי adv כִּי *if*.

תֵדָע Qal Impf 2ms יָדַע *to know*.

אוֹ conj אוֹ *or, and, either*.

נָטָה Qal Perf 3ms נָטָה *to stretch out, extend*.

עָלֶיהָ prep עַל + suff 3fs עַל *on, upon, over, beside*.

קָו noun m קָו *rope, measuring line*.

6 עַל prep עַל *on, upon, over*.

מָה pronoun מַה *what, how*.

אֲדָנֶיהָ noun mp + suff 3fs אֶדֶן *foundation, pillar*.

הָטְבָּעוּ Hof Perf 3cp טָבַע *to sink*.

אוֹ conj אוֹ *or, and, either.*

יָרָה Qal Perf 3ms יָרָה *to throw, lay foundations, sprinkle.*

אֶבֶן noun m אֶבֶן *stone.*

פִּנָּתָהּ noun f + suff 3fs פִּנָּה *corner.*

7 בְּרָן prep בְּ + Qal Inf Cstr רָנַן *to shout for joy, to sing.*

יַחַד adv: *together.*

כּוֹכְבֵי noun mp cstr כּוֹכָב *star.*

בֹּקֶר noun m בֹּקֶר *morning.*

וַיָּרִיעוּ Hif VC Impf 3mp רוּעַ *no Qal; Hif to cry aloud.*

בְּנֵי noun mp cstr בֵּן *son.*

8 וַיָּסֶךְ Hif VC Impf 3ms סָכַךְ *to hedge, fence about, shut in; Hif to screen, protect.*

בִּדְלָתַיִם prep בְּ + noun f dual דֶּלֶת *door.*

יָם noun m יָם *sea, river, west.*

בְּגִיחוֹ prep בְּ + Qal Inf Ctsr + suff 3ms גִּיחַ *to break out, burst forth.*

מֵרֶחֶם prep מִן + noun m רֶחֶם *uterus, womb, woman.*

יֵצֵא Qal Impf 3ms יָצָא *to go out, be born.*

9 בְּשׂוּמִי prep בְּ + Qal Inf Cstr + suff 1cs שִׂים *to put, set, make.*

עָנָן noun m עָנָן *cloud.*

לְבֻשׁוֹ noun m + suff 3ms לְבוּשׁ *garment, clothing.*

וַעֲרָפֶל conj וְ + noun m עֲרָפֶל *darkness of clouds, thick clouds.*

חֲתֻלָּתוֹ noun f חֲתֻלָּה *bandage, swaddling band.*

10 וָאֶשְׁבֹּר Qal VC Impf 1cs שָׁבַר *to break, buy or sell grain.*

עָלָיו prep עַל + suff 3ms עַל *on, upon, over.*

חֻקִּי noun m + suff 1cs חֹק *statute, law, limit.*

וָאָשִׂים Qal VC Impf 1cs שִׂים *to put, place, set, make.*

בְּרִיחַ noun m בְּרִיחַ *cross beam, bar, bars.*

וּדְלָתָיִם conj וְ + noun f dual דֶּלֶת *door.*

11 וָאֹמַר Qal VC Impf 1cs אָמַר *to say.*

עַד prep עַד *until, as far as, while.*

פֹּה adv פֹּה *here.*

תָבוֹא Qal Impf 3fs בּוֹא *to come.*

תֹּסִיף Hif Impf 2ms יָסַף *to add, do again; Hif as Qal (i.e. and no further).*

יָשִׁית Qal Impf 3ms שִׁית *to put, place, set.*

בִּגְאוֹן prep בְּ + noun m גָּאוֹן *glory, honour, pride.*

גַּלֶּיךָ noun m + suff 2ms גַּל *heap (of stones), wave.*

Questions

1. The word הָטְבְּעוּ (v. 6) is from the verb טָבַע which in Qal means *to sink*. What does the Hofal mean, and how would you translate the first half of this verse?

2. Who or what might the בְּנֵי אֱלֹהִים be (v. 7)? How would you translate this phrase?

3. The verb שָׁבַר usually means *to break*, but here it is difficult to discern what exactly is broken. Virtually all translators agree that the general idea is that God establishes decreed limits on the sea. How would you translate וָאֶשְׁבֹּר עָלָיו חֻקִּי?

ECCLESIASTES 12 REMEMBER YOUR CREATOR IN THE DAYS OF YOUR YOUTH

1 וּזְכֹר אֶת־בּוֹרְאֶיךָ בִּימֵי בְּחוּרֹתֶיךָ
עַד אֲשֶׁר לֹא־יָבֹאוּ יְמֵי הָרָעָה
וְהִגִּיעוּ שָׁנִים אֲשֶׁר תֹּאמַר אֵין־לִי בָהֶם חֵפֶץ׃

2 עַד אֲשֶׁר לֹא־תֶחְשַׁךְ הַשֶּׁמֶשׁ וְהָאוֹר וְהַיָּרֵחַ וְהַכּוֹכָבִים
וְשָׁבוּ הֶעָבִים אַחַר הַגָּשֶׁם׃

3 בַּיּוֹם שֶׁיָּזֻעוּ שֹׁמְרֵי הַבַּיִת וְהִתְעַוְּתוּ אַנְשֵׁי הֶחָיִל
וּבָטְלוּ הַטֹּחֲנוֹת כִּי מִעֵטוּ וְחָשְׁכוּ הָרֹאוֹת בָּאֲרֻבּוֹת׃

4 וְסֻגְּרוּ דְלָתַיִם בַּשּׁוּק בִּשְׁפַל קוֹל הַטַּחֲנָה
וְיָקוּם לְקוֹל הַצִּפּוֹר וְיִשַּׁחוּ כָּל־בְּנוֹת הַשִּׁיר׃

5 גַּם מִגָּבֹהַּ יִרָאוּ וְחַתְחַתִּים בַּדֶּרֶךְ
וְיָנֵאץ הַשָּׁקֵד וְיִסְתַּבֵּל הֶחָגָב וְתָפֵר הָאֲבִיּוֹנָה
כִּי־הֹלֵךְ הָאָדָם אֶל־בֵּית עוֹלָמוֹ וְסָבְבוּ בַשּׁוּק הַסֹּפְדִים׃

6 עַד אֲשֶׁר לֹא־ירחק[8] חֶבֶל הַכֶּסֶף וְתָרוּץ גֻּלַּת הַזָּהָב
וְתִשָּׁבֶר כַּד עַל־הַמַּבּוּעַ וְנָרֹץ הַגַּלְגַּל אֶל־הַבּוֹר׃

7 וְיָשֹׁב הֶעָפָר עַל־הָאָרֶץ כְּשֶׁהָיָה
וְהָרוּחַ תָּשׁוּב אֶל־הָאֱלֹהִים אֲשֶׁר נְתָנָהּ׃

8 הֲבֵל הֲבָלִים אָמַר הַקּוֹהֶלֶת הַכֹּל הָבֶל׃

9 וְיֹתֵר שֶׁהָיָה קֹהֶלֶת חָכָם עוֹד לִמַּד־דַּעַת אֶת־הָעָם
וְאִזֵּן וְחִקֵּר תִּקֵּן מְשָׁלִים הַרְבֵּה׃

10 בִּקֵּשׁ קֹהֶלֶת לִמְצֹא דִּבְרֵי־חֵפֶץ וְכָתוּב יֹשֶׁר דִּבְרֵי אֱמֶת׃

11 דִּבְרֵי חֲכָמִים כַּדָּרְבֹנוֹת וּכְמַשְׂמְרוֹת
נְטוּעִים בַּעֲלֵי אֲסֻפּוֹת נִתְּנוּ מֵרֹעֶה אֶחָד׃

___

[8] Qere יִרָתֵק

וְיֹתֵר מֵהֵמָּה   בְּנִי הִזָּהֵר

עֲשׂוֹת סְפָרִים הַרְבֵּה אֵין קֵץ   וְלַהַג הַרְבֵּה יְגִעַת בָּשָׂר :

סוֹף דָּבָר הַכֹּל נִשְׁמָע

אֶת־הָאֱלֹהִים יְרָא   וְאֶת־מִצְוֹתָיו שְׁמוֹר

כִּי־זֶה כָּל־הָאָדָם :

כִּי אֶת־כָּל־מַעֲשֶׂה הָאֱלֹהִים יָבָא בְמִשְׁפָּט

עַל כָּל־נֶעְלָם אִם־טוֹב וְאִם־רָע :

1 וּזְכֹר conj וְ + Qal Impv זָכַר *to remember.*

בּוֹרְאֶיךָ Qal Ptc + suff 2ms בָּרָא *to create.*

בִּימֵי prep בְּ + noun mp cstr יוֹם *day.*

בְּחוּרֹתֶיךָ noun fp + suff 2ms בְּחוּרוֹת *youth.*

עַד prep עַד *until, as far as, while.*

יָבֹאוּ Qal Impf 3mp בּוֹא *to come.*

הָרָעָה def art + noun f רָעָה *evil, wickedness, the evil.*

וְהִגִּיעוּ Hif VC Perf 3cp נָגַע *to touch, reach; Hif to reach, arrive.*

שָׁנִים noun fp שָׁנָה *year.*

תֹּאמַר Qal Impf 2ms אָמַר *to say.*

אֵין noun m cstr (used as adv) אֵין *there is not.*

בָהֶם prep בְּ + suff 3mp בְּ *in, with, by.*

חֵפֶץ noun m חֵפֶץ *desire, pleasure.*

2 עַד prep עַד *until, as far as, while.*

תֶּחְשַׁךְ Qal VC Perf 3fs חָשַׁךְ *to be dark, darkened.*

הַשֶּׁמֶשׁ def art + noun m and f שֶׁמֶשׁ *sun.*

וְהָאוֹר conj וְ + def art + noun m אוֹר *light.*

וְהַיָּרֵחַ conj וְ + noun m יָרֵחַ *moon.*

וְהַכּוֹכָבִים conj וְ + def art + noun mp כּוֹכָב *star.*

וְשָׁבוּ Qal VC Perf 3cp שׁוּב *to turn, return.*

הֶעָבִים def art + noun mp עָב *darkness, cloud.*

אַחַר prep אַחַר *after.*

הַגָּשֶׁם def art + noun m גֶּשֶׁם *rain.*

3 שֶׁיָּזֻעוּ rel part שֶׁ + Qal Impf 3mp זוּעַ *to move, tremble, shake: when they will tremble.*

שֹׁמְרֵי Qal Ptc mp cstr שָׁמַר *to keep, guard, notice, observe.*

הַבַּיִת def art + noun m בַּיִת *house.*

וְהִתְעַוְּתוּ Hitp VC Perf 3cp **עָוַת** Piel *to bend*; Hitp *to bend oneself*.

הֶחָיִל def art + noun m **חַיִל** *strength, integrity*.

וּבָטְלוּ Qal VC Perf 3cp **בָּטֵל** *be empty, cease; and they will cease*.

הַטֹּחֲנוֹת def art + Qal Ptc mp **טָחַן** *to grind, crush, mill*.

מִעֵטוּ Piel Perf 3cp **מָעַט** *to be little, few*; Piel as Qal.

וְחָשְׁכוּ conj **וְ** + Qal Perf 3cp **חָשַׁךְ** *to be dark, darkened*.

הָרֹאוֹת def art + Qal Ptc fp **רָאָה** *to see*.

בָּאֲרֻבּוֹת prep **בְּ** + noun fp **אֲרֻבָּה** *lattice, window*.

4 **וְסֻגְּרוּ** Pual VC Perf 3cp **סָגַר** *to shut, shut up*.

דְּלָתַיִם noun f dual **דֶּלֶת** *door*.

בַּשּׁוּק prep **בְּ** + noun m **שׁוּק** *street*.

בִּשְׁפַל prep **בְּ** + adj m **שָׁפָל** *low, depressed*.

קוֹל noun m **קוֹל** *voice, sound*.

הַטַּחֲנָה def art + noun f **טַחֲנָה** *mill*.

וְיָקוּם conj **וְ** + Qal Impf 3ms **קוּם** *to get up*.

לְקוֹל prep **לְ** + noun m **קוֹל** *voice, sound*.

הַצִּפּוֹר def art + noun f **צִפּוֹר** *bird, small bird, sparrow*.

וְיִשַּׁחוּ Nif VC Impf 3mp **שָׁחַח** *to crouch*; Nif *to be humbled*.

בְּנוֹת noun f cstr **בַּת** *daughter*.

הַשִּׁיר def art + noun m **שִׁיר** *song*.

5 **גַּם** conj **גַּם** *even, also*.

מִגָּבֹהַּ prep **מִן** + adj m **גָּבֹהַּ** *high, proud*.

יִרְאוּ Qal Impf 3mp **יָרֵא** *to be afraid*.

וְחַתְחַתִּים conj **וְ** + noun mp **חַתְחַת** *terror*.

בַּדֶּרֶךְ prep **בְּ** + noun m **דֶּרֶךְ** *way, path*.

וְיָנֵאץ conj **וְ** + Hif Impf 3ms **נָאַץ** *to despise, deride*; Hif *to be despised* (several versions translate it *shall bloom*, as if from **נָצֵץ**).

הַשָּׁקֵד def art + noun m **שָׁקֵד** *almond, almond tree*.

וְיִסְתַּבֵּל conj **וְ** + Hitp Impf 3ms **סָבַל** *to carry*; Hitpael *to become burdensome, drag oneself along*.

הֶחָגָב def art + noun m **חָגָב** *locust*.

וְתָפֵר conj **וְ** + Hif Impf 3fs **פָּרַר** *to break*; Hif *to bring to nothing, fail*.

הָאֲבִיּוֹנָה def art + noun f **אֲבִיּוֹנָה** *appetite, desire*.

הֹלֵךְ Qal Ptc **הָלַךְ** *to walk, go*.

הָאָדָם def art + noun m **אָדָם** *earth, man, Adam*.

בַּיִת noun ms cstr בַּיִת *house.*

עוֹלָמוֹ noun m + suff 3ms עוֹלָם *ancient time, eternity.*

וְסָבְבוּ Qal VC Perf 3cp סָבַב *to turn, go around, surround.*

בַּשׁוּק prep בְּ + noun m שׁוּק *street.*

הַסּוֹפְדִים def art + Qal Ptc mp סָפַד *to mourn, lament.*

6 עַד prep עַד *until, as far as, while.*

ירחק Qal Impf 3ms רָחַק *to go far away, recede, be distant* (Ketiv).

יֵרָתֵק Nif Impf 3ms רָתַק *no Qal; Nif to be untied* (Qere).

חֶבֶל noun m חֶבֶל *cord, rope.*

הַכֶּסֶף def art + noun m כֶּסֶף *silver.*

וְתָרוּץ conj וְ + Qal Impf 3fs רָצַץ *to break, crush, oppress.*

גֻּלַּת noun f cstr גֻּלָּה *fountain, bowl.*

הַזָּהָב def art + noun m זָהָב *gold.*

וְתִשָּׁבֶר conj וְ + Nif Impf 3fs שָׁבַר *to break; Nif to be broken.*

כַּד noun f כַּד *bucket, jar.*

עַל prep עַל *on, upon, over, beside.*

הַמַּבּוּעַ def art + noun m מַבּוּעַ *fountain.*

וְנָרֹץ Nif VC Perf 3ms רָצַץ *to break, crush, oppress.*

הַגַּלְגַּל def art + noun m גַּלְגַּל *wheel, whirlwind.*

הַבּוֹר def art + noun m בּוֹר *pit, cistern, grave.*

7 וְיָשֹׁב Qal VC Impf 3ms שׁוּב *to turn, return.*

הֶעָפָר def art + noun m עָפָר *dust.*

עַל prep עַל *on, upon, over, beside.*

כְּשֶׁהָיָה prep כְּ + rel part שֶׁ + Qal Perf 3ms הָיָה *to be, become.*

וְהָרוּחַ conj וְ + def art + noun f רוּחַ *wind, spirit, breath.*

תָּשׁוּב Qal Impf 3fs שׁוּב *to turn, return.*

נְתָנָהּ Qal Perf 3ms + suff 3fs נָתַן *to give, assign, set.*

8 הֲבֵל noun m הֶבֶל *breath, futility, vapour.*

אָמַר Qal Perf 3ms אָמַר *to say.*

הַקֹּהֶלֶת def art + proper noun קוֹהֶלֶת Qohelet (the name is a feminine participle from the verb קָהַל and means something like *she who assembles people*).

הַכֹּל def art + noun m כֹּל *whole: everything.*

9 וְיֹתֵר conj וְ + Qal Ptc יָתַר *to be redundant, abound; with rel part שֶׁ not only.*

שֶׁהָיָה rel part שֶׁ + Qal Impf 3mp הָיָה *to be, become.*

קֹהֶלֶת proper noun קֹהֶלֶת Qohelet.

חָכָם adj m חָכָם wise.

עוֹד adv עוֹד again, further, yet, still.

לְיַמֵּד prep לְ + Piel Inf Cstr לָמַד to chastise; Piel to train, teach.

דַעַת noun f דַּעַת knowledge.

הָעָם def art + noun m עַם people.

וְאִזֵּן conj וְ + Piel Perfect 3ms אָזַן; Piel to consider.

וְחִקֵּר conj וְ + Piel Perf 3ms חָקַר to search, investigate; Piel as Qal.

תִּקֵּן Piel Perf 3ms תָּקַן to be straight; Piel to make straight, set in order.

מְשָׁלִים noun mp מָשָׁל proverb, song, poem.

הַרְבֵּה Hif inf abs רָבָה Hif to increase, multiply: many (Inf Abs used as adv).

10 בִּקֵּשׁ Piel Perf 3ms בָּקַשׁ Piel to search, look for.

לִמְצֹא prep לְ + Qal Inf Cstr מָצָא to find.

דִּבְרֵי noun mp cstr דָּבָר word, thing, matter.

חֵפֶץ noun m חֵפֶץ desire, pleasure.

וְכָתוּב conj וְ + Qal Ptc passive כָּתַב to write.

יֹשֶׁר Qal Ptc יָשַׁר to be upright, straight, just.

דִּבְרֵי noun mp cstr דָּבָר word, thing, matter.

אֱמֶת noun f אֱמֶת truth.

11 דִּבְרֵי noun mp cstr דָּבָר word, thing, matter.

חֲכָמִים adj mp חָכָם wise.

כַּדָּרְבֹנוֹת prep כְּ + noun m דָּרְבוֹן goad.

וּכְמַשְׂמְרוֹת conj וְ + prep כְּ + noun fp מַשְׂמְרוֹת nails.

נְטוּעִים Qal Ptc passive mp נָטַע to plant, fasten, pitch a tent.

בַּעֲלֵי noun mp cstr בַּעַל lord, master, owner, husband.

אֲסֻפּוֹת noun fp אֲסֻפָּה congregation.

נִתְּנוּ Nif Perf 3cp נָתַן to give, assign, set.

מֵרֹעֶה prep מִן + noun m רֹעֶה shepherd.

אֶחָד numeral m אֶחָד one, first.

12 מֵהֵמָּה prep מִן + pronoun 3mp הֵם they, those (by those).

בְּנִי noun m + suff 1cs בֵּן son.

הִזָּהֵר Nif Impv זָהַר Nif to be taught, be admonished.

עֲשׂוֹת Qal Inf Cstr עָשָׂה to make, do.

סְפָרִים noun mp סֵפֶר book, writing.

הַרְבֵּה Hif inf abs רָבָה Hif to increase, multiply: many, much (Inf Abs used as adv).

קֵץ noun m קֵץ *end, extremity, destruction, event.*

וְלַהַג conj וְ + noun m לַהַג *study.*

הַרְבֵּה Hif inf abs רָבָה Hif *to increase, multiply: many, much* (Inf Abs used as adv).

יְגִעַת noun f cstr יְגִעָה *weariness, work.*

בָּשָׂר noun m בָּשָׂר *flesh.*

13 סוֹף noun m סוֹף *end.*

דָּבָר noun m דָּבָר *word, thing, matter.*

נִשְׁמָע Nif Perf 3ms שָׁמַע *to hear, understand, obey.*

יְרָא Qal Impv יָרֵא *to fear, revere.*

מִצְוֹתָיו noun mp + suff 3ms מִצְוָה *commandment.*

שְׁמוֹר Qal Impv שָׁמַר *to keep, guard, observe.*

זֶה demonst ms זֶה *this.*

הָאָדָם def art + noun m אָדָם *earth, man, Adam.*

14 מַעֲשֶׂה noun m מַעֲשֶׂה *deed, work.*

יָבֵא Hif Impf 3ms בּוֹא *to come;* Hif *to bring.*

בְמִשְׁפָּט prep בְּ + noun m מִשְׁפָּט *judgment.*

עַל prep עַל *on, upon, over, about.*

נֶעְלָם Nif Ptc עָלַם *to hide;* Nif *to be hidden.*

אִם conj, adv אִם *do not, if, whether.*

Questions

1 What is the word for the phenomenon you see in the spelling of וַיִּסְתַּבֵּל, the Hitpael Impf 3ms of סָבַל?

2 Verse 8 includes the phrase הֲבֵל הֲבָלִים – a frequent refrain in Ecclesiastes – and the meaning of הֲבֵל is particularly difficult to pin down. What do you think is the best translation in the current context?

3 What, in your view, is this chapter about?

EXODUS 15:1–19 THE SONG OF MOSES/THE SONG OF THE SEA

This text is often set out in columns that seem to represent the passing of the Israelites between the walls of water. The effect is clearer without verse numbers and sof pasuk (the two dots that mark the end of each verse).

אָז יָשִׁיר־מֹשֶׁה וּבְנֵי יִשְׂרָאֵל אֶת־הַשִּׁירָה הַזֹּאת לַיהוָה וַיֹּאמְרוּ

סוּס	אָשִׁירָה לַיהוָה כִּי־גָאֹה גָּאָה	לֵאמֹר
עָזִּי וְזִמְרָת יָהּ וַיְהִי־לִי		וְרֹכְבוֹ רָמָה בַיָּם
אֱלֹהִי	זֶה אֵלִי וְאַנְוֵהוּ	לִישׁוּעָה

אָבִי וַאֲרֹמְמֶנְהוּ

שְׁמוֹ

שָׁלִשָׁיו טֻבְּעוּ בְיַם־סוּף

אֶבֶן

יְהוָה תִּרְעַץ אוֹיֵב

קָמֶיךָ

אַפֶּיךָ נֶעֶרְמוּ מַיִם

נֹזְלִים

אוֹיֵב אֶרְדֹּף אַשִּׂיג

נַפְשִׁי

בְרוּחֲךָ כִּסָּמוֹ יָם

אַדִּירִים

כָּמֹכָה נֶאְדָּר בַּקֹּדֶשׁ

פֶּלֶא

בְחַסְדְּךָ עַם־זוּ גָּאָלְתָּ

קָדְשֶׁךָ

אָחַז יֹשְׁבֵי פְּלָשֶׁת

אֱדוֹם

כֹּל יֹשְׁבֵי כְנָעַן

וָפַחַד

יַעֲבֹר עַמְּךָ יְהוָה

קָנִיתָ

לְשִׁבְתְּךָ פָּעַלְתָּ יְהוָה

יָדֶיךָ

יְהוָה יִמְלֹךְ לְעֹלָם וָעֶד

בָּא סוּס פַּרְעֹה בְּרִכְבּוֹ וּבְפָרָשָׁיו בַּיָּם

מֵי הַיָּם

יְהוָה אִישׁ מִלְחָמָה יְהוָה

מַרְכְּבֹת פַּרְעֹה וְחֵילוֹ יָרָה בַיָּם

תְּהֹמֹת יְכַסְיֻמוּ יָרְדוּ בִמְצוֹלֹת כְּמוֹ

יְמִינְךָ יְהוָה נֶאְדָּרִי בַּכֹּחַ

תְּשַׁלַּח חֲרֹנְךָ יֹאכְלֵמוֹ כַּקַּשׁ

קָפְאוּ תְהֹמֹת בְּלֶב־יָם

אֲחַלֵּק שָׁלָל תִּמְלָאֵמוֹ

אָרִיק חַרְבִּי תּוֹרִישֵׁמוֹ יָדִי

מִי־כָמֹכָה בָּאֵלִם יְהוָה

נָטִיתָ יְמִינְךָ תִּבְלָעֵמוֹ אָרֶץ

שָׁמְעוּ עַמִּים יִרְגָּזוּן

אֵילֵי מוֹאָב יֹאחֲזֵמוֹ רָעַד

בִּגְדֹל זְרוֹעֲךָ יִדְּמוּ כָּאָבֶן

תְּבִאֵמוֹ וְתִטָּעֵמוֹ בְּהַר נַחֲלָתְךָ

וּבְנֵי יִשְׂרָאֵל הָלְכוּ בַיַּבָּשָׁה בְּתוֹךְ

וּמִבְחַר

יְמִינְךָ

תַּהֲרֹס

וּבְרוּחַ

נִצְּבוּ כְמוֹ־נֵד

אָמַר

נָשַׁפְתָּ

צָלֲלוּ כַּעוֹפֶרֶת בְּמַיִם

מִי

נֹרָא תְהִלֹּת עֹשֵׂה

נָחִיתָ

נֵהַלְתָּ בְעָזְּךָ אֶל־נְוֵה

חִיל

אָז נִבְהֲלוּ אַלּוּפֵי

נָמֹגוּ

תִּפֹּל עֲלֵיהֶם אֵימָתָה

עַד

עַד־יַעֲבֹר עַם־זוּ

מָכוֹן

מִקְּדָשׁ אֲדֹנָי כּוֹנְנוּ

כִּי

וַיָּשֶׁב יְהוָה עֲלֵהֶם אֶת הַיָּם

1 אָז adv אָז *then.*

יָשִׁיר Qal Impf 3ms שִׁיר *to sing.*

מֹשֶׁה proper noun מֹשֶׁה *Moses.*

וּבְנֵי conj וְ + noun mp cstr בֵּן *son.*

הַשִּׁירָה def art + noun f שִׁירָה *song.*

הַזֹּאת def art + demonst adj f זֹאת *this.*

וַיֹּאמְרוּ Qal VC Impf 3mp אָמַר *to say.*

לֵאמֹר prep לְ + Qal Inf Cstr אָמַר *saying.*

אָשִׁירָה Qal Impf 1cs שִׁיר *to sing.*

גָּאֹה Qal Inf Abs גָּאָה *to lift oneself up, be exalted.*

גָּאָה Qal Perf 3ms גָּאָה *to lift oneself up, be exalted.*

סוּס noun m סוּס *horse.*

וְרֹכְבוֹ conj וְ + Qal Ptc + suff 3ms רָכַב *to ride (on a horse; in a chariot).*

רָמָה Qal Perf 3ms רָמָה *to throw.*

בַיָּם prep בְּ + noun m יָם *sea, river, west.*

2 עָזִּי noun m + suff 1cs עֹז *strength, power, glory.*

וְזִמְרָת conj וְ + noun f זִמְרָת *song.*

יָהּ proper noun יְהוָה *Yhwh.*

וַיְהִי Qal VC Impf 3ms הָיָה *to be, become.*

לִישׁוּעָה prep לְ + noun f יְשׁוּעָה *deliverance, help.*

זֶה demonst ms *this.*

אֵלִי noun m + suff 1cs אֵל.

וְאַנְוֵהוּ conj וְ + Hif Impf 1cs + suff 3ms נָוָה *to sit down, rest; Hif to decorate, celebrate.*

אָבִי noun m + suff 1cs אָב *father.*

וַאֲרֹמְמֶנְהוּ conj וְ + Polel Impf 1cs + suff 3ms רוּם *to rise, be high; Polel to make high.*

3 מִלְחָמָה noun f מִלְחָמָה *war, battle.*

שְׁמוֹ noun m + suff 3ms שֵׁם *name.*

4 מַרְכְּבֹת noun fp מֶרְכָּבָה *chariot.*

פַּרְעֹה noun m פַּרְעֹה *Pharaoh.*

וְחֵילוֹ conj וְ + noun m + suff 3ms חַיִל *strength, army, integrity.*

יָרָה Qal Perf 3ms יָרָה *to throw, lay foundations, sprinkle.*

וּמִבְחַר conj וְ + noun m מִבְחַר *choice, best.*

שָׁלִשָׁיו noun mp + suff 3ms שָׁלוֹשׁ *three, triangle, charioteer.*

טֻבְּעוּ Pual Perf 3cp טָבַע *to sink; Pual and Hif as Qal.*

סוּף noun m סוּף *reed, rush, seaweed.*

5 תְּהֹמֹת noun m and f p תְּהוֹם *wave, ocean, abyss, deep.*

יְכַסְיֻמוּ Piel Impf 3mp + suff 3mp כָּסָה *to conceal*; Piel *to cover, conceal.*

יָרְדוּ Qal Perf 3cp יָרַד *to go down.*

בִמְצוֹלֹת prep בְּ + noun f מְצוֹלָה *depths (of the sea).*

כְּמוֹ prep כְּמוֹ *as, like.*

אָבֶן noun m (in pause) אֶבֶן *stone.*

6 יְמִינְךָ noun m + suff 2ms יָמִין *right, right hand.*

נֶאְדָּרִי Nif Ptc + paragogic י אָדַר Nif *to be made great.*

בַּכֹּחַ prep בְּ + noun m כֹּחַ *strength, power.*

יְמִינְךָ noun m + suff 2ms יָמִין *right, right hand.*

תִּרְעַץ Qal Impf 3fs רָעַץ *to break in pieces, oppress.*

אוֹיֵב noun m אֹיֵב *enemy.*

7 וּבְרֹב conj וְ + prep בְּ + adv רֹב *much, many.*

גְּאוֹנְךָ noun m + suff 2ms גָּאוֹן *glory, honour, pride.*

תַּהֲרֹס Qal Impf 2ms הָרַס *to pull down, destroy.*

קָמֶיךָ Qal Ptc 3mp + suff 2ms קוּם *to get up.*

תְּשַׁלַּח Piel Impf 2ms שָׁלַח *to send, stretch out*; Piel *to send, dismiss, expel.*

חֲרֹנְךָ noun m + suff 2ms חָרוֹן *anger, heat.*

יֹאכְלֵמוֹ Qal Impf 3ms + suff 3mp אָכַל *to eat, consume.*

כַּקַּשׁ prep כְּ + noun m קַשׁ *chaff, straw.*

8 וּבְרוּחַ conj וְ + prep בְּ + noun f רוּחַ *wind, spirit, breath.*

אַפֶּיךָ noun m + suff 2ms אַף *nose, anger.*

נֶעֶרְמוּ Nif Perf 3cp עָרַם Nif *to be heaped up.*

מַיִם noun m מַיִם *water.*

נִצְּבוּ Nif Perf 3cp נָצַב *to set, put, place*; Nif *to be set, to stand.*

כְּמוֹ prep כְּמוֹ *as, like.*

נֵד noun m נֵד *heap, pile.*

נֹזְלִים Qal Ptc mp נָזַל *to flow.*

קָפְאוּ Qal Perf 3cp קָפָא *to thicken, condense, congeal.*

תְּהֹמֹת noun m and f p תְּהוֹם *wave, ocean, abyss, deep.*

בְּלֶב prep בְּ + noun m לֵב *heart.*

9 אָמַר Qal Perf 3ms אָמַר *to say.*

אוֹיֵב noun m אֹיֵב *enemy.*

אֶרְדֹּף Qal Impf 1cs רָדַף *to pursue, follow.*

אַשִּׂיג Hif Impf 1cs נָשַׂג Hif *to reach, overtake.*

אֲחַלֵּק Piel Impf 1cs חָלַק *to divide;* Piel *to apportion, allot.*

שָׁלָל noun m שָׁלָל *spoil, prey, plunder.*

תִּמְלָאֵמוֹ Qal Impf 3fs + suff 3ms מָלֵא *to fill, be full.*

נַפְשִׁי noun f + suff 1cs נֶפֶשׁ *breath, soul, life.*

אָרִיק Hif Impf 1cs רִיק Hif *to pour out, to draw (a weapon).*

חַרְבִּי noun f + suff 1cs חֶרֶב *sword.*

תּוֹרִישֵׁמוֹ Hif Impf 3fs + suff 3ms יָרַשׁ *to inherit, dispossess;* Hif *to destroy.*

יָדִי noun f + suff 1cs יָד *hand.*

10 נָשַׁפְתָּ Qal Perf 2ms נָשַׁף *to blow.*

בְרוּחֲךָ prep בְּ + noun f + suff 2ms רוּחַ *wind, spirit, breath.*

כִּסָּמוֹ Piel Perf 3ms + suff 3ms כָּסָה *to conceal;* Piel *to cover, conceal.*

צָלֲלוּ Qal Perf 3cp צָלַל *to roll down, be rolled down.*

כַּעוֹפֶרֶת prep כְּ + noun m עוֹפֶרֶת *lead (lead has a whitish hue, like the colour of sand).*

בְּמַיִם prep בְּ + noun m מַיִם *water.*

אַדִּירִים adj mp אַדִּיר *large, great, powerful.*

11 כָמֹכָה prep כְּ + suff 2ms כְּ *as, like.*

בָּאֵלִם prep בְּ + noun mp אֵל *God, god, mighty.*

כָּמֹכָה prep כְּ + suff 2ms כְּ *as, like.*

נֶאְדָּר Nif Ptc אָדַר Nif *to be made great* (Nif Ptc used as adj: *powerful*).

בַּקֹּדֶשׁ prep בְּ + noun m קֹדֶשׁ *sacredness, holiness, sanctuary.*

נוֹרָא Nif Ptc יָרֵא *to fear, revere;* Nif *to be feared:* (Nif Ptc used as adj: *terrible*).

תְּהִלֹּת noun fp תְּהִלָּה *praise, hymn, glory, a person who is praised.*

עֹשֵׂה Qal Ptc עָשָׂה *to make, do.*

פֶלֶא noun m פֶּלֶא *miracle, wonder.*

12 נָטִיתָ Qal Perf 2ms נָטָה *to stretch out, extend.*

יְמִינְךָ noun m + suff 2ms יָמִין *right, right hand.*

תִּבְלָעֵמוֹ Qal Impf 3fs + suff 3mp בָּלַע *to swallow, engulf, devour.*

13 נָחִיתָ Qal Perf 2ms נָחָה *to lead, lead out, lead back.*

בְחַסְדְּךָ prep בְּ + noun m + suff 2ms חֶסֶד *desire, love, kindness.*

עַם noun m עַם *people.*

זוּ pronoun: demonstrative, relative זוּ *that, which, who, whose, whom.*

גָּאָלְתָּ Qal Perf 2ms גָּאַל *to redeem.*

נֵהַלְתָּ Piel Perf 2ms נָהַל Piel *to lead, guard, provide for, sustain.*

בְּעָזְּךָ prep בְּ + noun m + suff 2ms עֹז *strength, power, glory.*

נְוֵה noun m cstr נָוֶה *inhabiting, dwelling, seat, pasture.*

קׇדְשֶׁךָ noun m + suff 2ms קֹדֶשׁ *sacredness, holiness, sanctuary.*

14 שָׁמְעוּ Qal Perf 3cp שָׁמַע *to hear, understand, obey.*

עַמִּים noun mp עַם *people.*

יִרְגָּזוּן Qal Impf 3mp + paragogic ן רָגַז *to be moved, disturbed; to tremble, be afraid.*

חִיל noun m חִיל *pain (esp. childbirth), fear, trembling.*

אָחַז Qal Perf 3ms אָחַז *to seize, hold, take.*

יֹשְׁבֵי Qal Ptc mp cstr יָשַׁב *to sit, live.*

פְּלָשֶׁת proper noun פְּלָשֶׁת *Peleshet* (sometimes translated *Philistia*).

15 אָז adv אָז *then.*

נִבְהֲלוּ Nif Perf 3cp בָּהַל Nif *to tremble, be terrified.*

אַלּוּפֵי noun mp cstr אַלּוּף *leader, chief.*

אֱדוֹם proper noun *Edom.*

אֵילֵי noun mp cstr אַיִל *ram, leader.*

מוֹאָב proper noun *Moab.*

יֹאחֲזֵמוֹ Qal Impf 3mp + suff 3ms אָחַז *to seize, hold, take.*

רַעַד noun m רַעַד *trembling.*

נָמֹגוּ Nif Perf 3cp מוּג *to flow, dissolve, be dissolved;* Nif *to melt away.*

יֹשְׁבֵי Qal Ptc mp cstr יָשַׁב *to sit, live.*

כְּנָעַן proper noun כְּנַעַן *Canaan.*

16 תִּפֹּל Qal Impf 3fs נָפַל *to fall, prostate oneself, attack.*

עֲלֵיהֶם prep עַל + suff 3mp עַל *on, upon, over.*

אֵימָתָה noun f + paragogic ה אֵימָה *terror.*

וָפַחַד conj וְ + noun m פַּחַד *fear, terror.*

בִּגְדֹל prep בְּ + noun, adj m cstr גָּדוֹל *great, large,* pl. *great things.*

זְרוֹעֲךָ noun f + suff 2ms זְרוֹעַ *arm, forearm (i.e. your strength).*

יִדְּמוּ Qal Impf 3mp דָּמַם *to be silent;* Nif *to be silenced.*

כָּאָבֶן prep כְּ + noun m in pause אֶבֶן *stone.*

עַד prep עַד *until, as far as, while.*

יַעֲבֹר Qal Impf 3ms עָבַר *to pass, pass over, forgive.*

קָנִיתָ Qal Perf 2ms קָנָה *to acquire, buy.*

17 תְּבִאֵמוֹ Hif Impf 2ms + suff 3ms בּוֹא *to come;* Hif *to bring.*

וַתִּטָּעֵמוֹ conj וְ + Qal Impf 2ms + suff 3ms נָטַע *to plant, fasten, pitch a tent.*

בְּהַר prep בְּ + noun m הַר *mountain.*

נַחֲלָתְךָ noun f + suff 2ms נַחֲלָה *possession, inheritance.*

מָכוֹן noun m מָכוֹן *place, foundation.*

לְשִׁבְתְּךָ prep לְ + Qal Inf Cstr + suff 2ms יָשַׁב *to sit, live.*

פָּעַלְתָּ Qal Perf 2ms פָּעַל *to make, produce, undertake.*

מִקְדָּשׁ noun m מִקְדָּשׁ *holy thing, holy place, asylum.*

כּוֹנְנוּ Polel Perf 3cp כּוּן Polel *to confirm, establish.*

יָדֶיךָ noun fp + suff 2ms יָד *hand.*

18 יִמְלֹךְ Qal Impf 3ms מָלַךְ *to reign, to be king.*

לְעֹלָם prep לְ + noun m עוֹלָם *ancient time, eternity.*

וָעֶד conj וְ + noun m עַד *eternity.*

19 בָא Qal Ptc בּוֹא *to come.*

בְּרִכְבּוֹ prep בְּ + noun m + suff 3ms רֶכֶב *rider, chariot.*

וּבְפָרָשָׁיו conj וְ + prep בְּ + noun mp + suff 3ms פָּרָשׁ *horseman, horse.*

וַיָּשֶׁב Hif VC Impf 3ms שׁוּב *to turn, return.*

עֲלֵהֶם prep עַל + suff 3mp עַל *on, upon, over, beside.*

מֵי noun m dual cstr מַיִם *water.* וּבְנֵי conj וְ + noun mp cstr בֵּן *son.*

הָלְכוּ Qal Perf 3cp הָלַךְ *to walk, go.*

בַּיַּבָּשָׁה prep בְּ + noun f יַבָּשָׁה *dry land.*

בְּתוֹךְ prep בְּ + noun m cstr תָּוֶךְ *middle: in the middle of.*

Questions

1 The word בְּרִכְבּוֹ (v. 19, second last line) is a noun with a preposition and a pronominal suffix. What kind of noun is it, and what do you remember about this declension?

2 Verse 12 and verse 13 begin with the words נָטִיתָ and נָחִיתָ respectively. These are both weak verbs. What kind of weak verbs are they, and how can you tell from these two forms?

3 This passage may have been more difficult to follow with an unusual layout and without verse numbers. Nevertheless, there is usually a sense of accomplishment involved in reading Hebrew poetry, even when it is challenging. Reflecting on your progress so far, what do you think are the advantages of reading these ancient texts in their original languages?

Afterword

There is much that it was not possible to explain in an introductory course, but working through this course should give a learner a good grasp of the basics. It is hoped that any reader who has reached the end of this course will have the confidence to begin to explore the biblical texts with the help of a dictionary or lexicon and perhaps a few commentaries. A good Hebrew grammar will explain the details of the vowel changes in weak verbs, the many ways in which the 'tenses' and stems can be used, the peculiarities of biblical Hebrew syntax, and other advanced material.

Learning biblical Hebrew can be anything from a passing diversion to a lifetime's work. Whichever you wish to pursue, you should now have enough background to move forward. Your vocabulary extends to hundreds of words, and you will be able to work out many new forms in context. By now no doubt you have a very good grasp of the way biblical Hebrew works, and we hope that you have the confidence to learn new kinds of constructions as you encounter the text.

Answer key

Please note that answers to the questions in the Language discovery sections are not provided in this answer key. Producing an accurate translation will indicate that you have answered these questions correctly, and possible translations are provided in the units at the end of each Language discovery section.

UNIT 1

Test yourself

אבגדהוזחטיכלמנסעפצקרששת

UNIT 2

Practice 1

1 a הַר **j** אִישׁ **i** הִיא **h** הוּא **g** כֵּן **f** חֵר **e** עַל **d** עָם **c** רַע **b** טוֹב

2 a מַה *what* **b** עַד *until* **c** רַב *many* **d** שֶׂה *lamb* **e** עַז *strong* **f** פַּח *snare* **g** חַד *sharp* **h** קַל *light* **i** אֶל *to*

Practice 2

2

	Short vowels	Long vowels	Composite vowels
a	_ patach	ָ qamets	ֲ chatef patach
e	ֶ segol	ֵ tsere	ֱ chatef segol
i	ִ hireq	ִ hireq yod	--
o	ָ qamets chatuf	וֹ holem	ֳ chatef qamets chatuf
u	ֻ qibbuts	וּ shureq	--

Test yourself

It should sound something like this:

אֵת	הִים	לְ	אֶ	רָא	בָּ	שִׁית	רֵא	בְּ
ayt	heem	low	eh	rah	bah	sheet	ray	be

רֶץ	אָ	הָ	אֵת	וְ	יִם	מַ	שָׁ	הַ
rets	ah	ha	ayt	ve	yeem	ma	sha	ha

UNIT 3

Practice 1

אבגדהוזחטיכלמנסעפצקרששת

280

Practice 2

a father and mother **b** garden and tree **c** horse and lamb **d** sea and mountain **e** sister and brother **f** hand and palm **g** sharp and light **h** woman and man **i** land and people **j** heart and voice

Each of these could also be translated *A father and a mother* etc.

Test yourself

1 The following words begin with a **begadkefat** letter and take **dagesh**: בַּיִת גָּמָל דֶּלֶת פֶּה פֵּה תּוֹרָה

2 a אוֹר וְעַז **b** אֶרֶץ וְיָם **c** וְגָמָל סוּס **d** וּבַיִת שֵׁם **e** וְנָבִיא שָׂר

UNIT 4

Practice 1

1 b the daughter הַבַּת **c** the camel הַגָּמָל **d** the sand הַחוֹל **e** the hand הַיָּד **f** the heart הַלֵּבָב **g** the path הַדֶּרֶךְ **h** the voice הַקּוֹל **i** the land הָאָרֶץ **j** the light הָאוֹר **k** the prophet הַנָּבִיא

2 a the man and the woman **b** the father and the mother **c** the sand and the sea **d** the horse and the ox **e** the brother and the sister

Practice 2

1 c horses סוּסִים **d** eyes עֵנַיִם **e** the princes הַשָּׂרִים **f** the princesses הַשָּׂרוֹת **g** the voices הַקּוֹלִים **h** cows פָּרוֹת **i** the hands הַיָּדַיִם **j** feet רַגְלַיִם

2 a the hands and the feet **b** the horses and the mares **c** the mountains and the seas **d** the gardens and the paths

Practice 3

a a man אִישׁ the men הָאֲנָשִׁים **b** a daughter בַּת the daughters הַבָּנוֹת **c** the mother הָאֵם mothers אִמּוֹת **d** night לַיְלָה nights לֵילוֹת **e** the days and the nights הַיָּמִים וְהַלֵּילוֹת **f** cities and princes עָרִים וְשָׂרִים

Test yourself

a פָּרִים וּפָרוֹת; **e** הָעָם וְהָאָרֶץ; **d** הָעִיר וְהָהָר; **c** אֲחָיוֹת וְאַחִים; **b** הַיָּם וְהַשָּׁמַיִם; **f** הַבָּנִים וְהַבָּנוֹת; **j** הֶעָרִים וְהַיָּמִים; **i** הָאֲנָשִׁים וְהַנָּשִׁים; **h** אִמּוֹת וְאָבוֹת; **g** יָדַיִם וְרַגְלַיִם.

UNIT 5

Practice 1

he	הוּא	they (m)	הֵם or הֵמָּה
she	הִיא	they (f)	הֵנָּה
you (m)	אַתָּה	you (m)	אַתֶּם
you (f)	אַתְּ	you (f)	אַתֶּן
I	אֲנִי or אָנֹכִי	we	אֲנַחְנוּ

Practice 2

אֲנִי הַמֶּלֶךְ or אָנֹכִי הַמֶּלֶךְ e אַתְּ הַשָּׂרָה d אַתָּה הָאָח c הִיא הָאִשָּׁה b הוּא הַשָּׂר a
אַתֶּם הָאָבוֹת j הֵנָּה הַנָּשִׁים i הֵם הַבָּנִים or הֵמָּה הַבָּנִים h הִיא הָעִיר g הוּא הָהָר f
הֵנָּה הַפָּרוֹת n הֵם הַסּוּסִים or הֵמָּה הַסּוּסִים m אֲנַחְנוּ הַשָּׂרִים l אַתֶּן הַבָּנוֹת k

Test yourself

בגדכפת שׁ שׂ ר ק צ ע ס נ מ ל כ י ט ח ז ו ה ד ג ב א 2a ב ג ד כ פ ת 1
ב a ה ח ע ר 3 a ֻ ֹ c ַ ָ d b וֹ וּ יוֹ ָ ָ ֳ
הָהָר d לַיְלָה וְיוֹם c שָׂרָה וְשַׂר b אִישׁ וְאִשָּׁה a 4 הַיָּדַיִם d הָאֲנָשִׁים c הָאָרֶץ b הַמֶּלֶךְ a 5
הַגָּן וְהַיָּם f הַסּוּס וְהַסּוּסָה e וְהָעִיר 6 a *He is the man.* b *They are the princes.* c *We are the*
daughters. d *It is the city.* e *You are the women.* f *I am the sister.*

UNIT 6

Practice 1

1

3ms	קוֹלוֹ	*his voice*	3mp	קוֹלָם	*their voice*
3fs	קוֹלָהּ	*her voice*	3fp	קוֹלָן	*their voice*
2ms	קוֹלְךָ	*your voice*	2mp	קוֹלְכֶם	*your voice*
2fs	קוֹלֵךְ	*your voice*	2fp	קוֹלְכֶן	*your voice*
1cs	קוֹלִי	*my voice*	1cp	קוֹלֵנוּ	*our voice*

2

3ms	פָּרָתוֹ	*his cow*	3mp	פָּרָתָם	*their cow*
3fs	פָּרָתָהּ	*her cow*	3fp	פָּרָתָן	*their cow*
2ms	פָּרָתְךָ	*your cow*	2mp	פָּרַתְכֶם	*your cow*
2fs	פָּרָתֵךְ	*your cow*	2fp	פָּרַתְכֶן	*your cow*
1cs	פָּרָתִי	*my cow*	1cp	פָּרָתֵנוּ	*our cow*

3 a *my father* **b** *your hands* **c** *our God (or our gods, if referring to gods other than Yhwh)*
d *their kings* **e** *his mother*

Practice 2

a *The priest is small.* קָטֹן הַכֹּהֵן **b** *Swords are sharp.* חַדּוֹת הַחֲרָבוֹת **c** *The places are holy.*
קְדוֹשִׁים הַמְּקוֹמוֹת **d** *The prince is bad.* רַע הַשָּׂר **e** *The food is good.* טוֹבָה הָאָכְלָה **f** *The*
house is empty. רֵיק הַבַּיִת **g** *His love is beautiful.* יָפָה אַהֲבָתוֹ **h** *Our words are wise.* חֲכָמִים
דְּבָרֵינוּ **i** *My knowledge is great.* גְּדוֹלָה דַּעְתִּי **j** *Your blessings are new.* חֲדָשׁוֹת בִּרְכוֹתֵיכֶם

Practice 3

a *the sharp sword* **b** *the great city (or the large city)* **c** *the wise princesses* **d** *the holy words* **e** *the*
beautiful women

Test yourself

1 *his voice; your horse; our voice; our horse* **2** *their voices; her mares; our cows; your mares* **3 a** אָבִי
b שֵׁרַתוֹ **c** קוֹלֵינוּ **4** הַמֶּלֶךְ וְטוֹב רָעוֹת הֶעָרִים **5** *Our oxen are good but our cows are bad.*

UNIT 7

Practice 1

1 a *this name* **b** *this food* **c** *these words* **d** *these blessings* **e** *that house* **f** *that love* **g** *those places*
h *those swords*

2 a זֶה *This is the priest.* **b** הוּא *That is the heart.* **c** זֹאת *This is the land.* **d** אֵלֶּה *These are the*
nights. **e** הֵם *Those are the heavens* (or *That is heaven*). **f** אֵלֶּה *These are your mares.* **g** הִיא *That*
is his cow. **h** הֵנָּה *Those are the women.*

Practice 2

a *The priests of the LORD* (or *of HaShem/Yhwh*). **b** *The kings of the earth* (or *the land*). **c** *The love*
of the woman. **d** *The swords of David.* **e** *The God* (or *gods*) *of my father.*

Practice 3

1 a שֵׁם **g** עָרֵי יְהוּדָה **f** עֵינֵי הָעָם **e** בֶּן דָּוִד **d** מַלְכֵי יִשְׂרָאֵל **c** דְּבַר הַכֹּהֵן **b** אֵשֶׁת הָאִישׁ
h בֵּית אָבִי סוּסוֹ.

2 a *This is my father's wife.* **b** *These are your king's words.* **c** *That is his son's voice.* **d** *Those are our*
princess's lips.

Test yourself

1 זֶה ms; זֹאת fs; אֵלֶּה cs **2** הֵם mp; הֵנָּה fp **3 a** הָסּוּסוֹת הָהֵנָּה **b** הַסּוּסִים הָאֵלֶּה
4 *These are the wives of my father and those are his horses* **5** *These are the words of the priests*
of the kings of Israel **6 a** סוּסְךָ) זֶה סוּסִי וְהוּא סוּסְךָ *could be replaced by* סוּסְכֶם, סוּסְכֶן or
זֹאת אֵשֶׁת הַמֶּלֶךְ **c** גְּדוֹלִים הַסּוּסִים הָאֵלֶּה וּקְטַנָּה הַסּוּסָה הַהִיא (סוּסְכֶן **b**
d הוּא קוֹל שָׂרַת עִיר יְרוּשָׁלַיִם.

UNIT 8

Practice 1

1 a 4 **b** 8 **c** 5 **d** 1 **e** 7 **f** 2 **g** 6 **h** 3 **2 a** אָז יָשִׁיר דָּוִד לִפְנֵי הָעָם
b שָׁבַת הָאִישׁ בֵּין הָעִיר וּבֵין הָהָר **c** וַיֹּאמֶר מֹשֶׁה אֶל אִשְׁתּוֹ אַתָּה הַשָּׂרָה

Practice 2

a יֵשׁ־לְאִשָּׁה בַּת **f** פִּיהָ פְּתִחָה בְּדַעַת **e** מִן־הָעִיר הַזֹּאת **d** לַשָּׁמַיִם **c** כְּקוֹל **b** בַּלַּיְלָה
g סוּסֶיךָ (*instead of* סוּסֶיךָ, *you could use* גָּדוֹל סוּסִי מִכָּל־סוּסֶיךָ **h** אֵין־לָעָם מֶלֶךְ
סוּסֵיכֶם or סוּסֵיכֶן).

Practice 3

1 a *like an enemy* **b** *with a loud voice* **c** *from evening until morning* **d** *before the king* **e** *from*
this woman **2 a** *Love* (or *kindness*) *is better than knowledge.* **b** *The people are bad and there is*

no knowledge in them. **c** *You are in my hand.* **d** *She has a son.* **e** *We have these large (or great) horses.* OR: *These large horses are ours.*

Test yourself

1 a אֶל **b** עַל **c** תַּחַת **d** בֵּין **2** בֶּן יֶשׁ־לוֹ **3** *the king is greater than the men* **4 a** לִי; **b** בָּהּ ; **c** לָהֶם; **d** בָּנוּ. **5** *like my servant, in the city, to a young man.*

UNIT 9

Practice 1

a 4 *The brother (subject) loved the sisters (object).* **b** 5 *The man (subject) took the horses (object).* **c** 1 *The king (subject) lifted up the sword (object).* **d** 3 *The priest (subject) judged this city (object).* **e** 4 *David (subject) knew that song (object).*

Practice 2

1a

3ms	on him/it	עָלָיו	3mp	as far as them	עֲדֵיהֶם
3fs	to her/it	אֵלֶיהָ	3fp	on them	עֲלֵיהֶן
2ms	as far as you	עָדֶיךָ	2mp	to you	אֲלֵיכֶם
2fs	to you	אֵלַיִךְ	2fp	on you	עֲלֵיכֶן
1s	on me	עָלַי	1p	as far as us	עָדֵינוּ

b

3ms	after him/it	אַחֲרָיו	3mp	under them	תַּחְתֵּיהֶם
3fs	before her/it	לְפָנֶיהָ	3fp	after them	אַחֲרֵיהֶן
2ms	after you	אַחֲרֶיךָ	2mp	after you	אַחֲרֵיכֶם
2fs	under you	תַּחְתֶּיךָ	2fp	before you	לִפְנֵיכֶן
1s	before me	לְפָנַי	1p	under us	תַּחְתֵּינוּ

c

3ms	from him/it	מִמֶּנּוּ	3mp	from them	מֵהֶם
3fs	from her/it	מִמֶּנָּה	3fp	like them	כָּהֵן
2ms	like you	כָּמוֹךָ	2mp	from you	מִכֶּם
2fs	like you	כָּמוֹךְ	2fp	like you	כָּכֶן
1s	from me	מִמֶּנִּי	1p	from us	מִמֶּנּוּ

2 a *The king lifted up the sword with us* **b** *the man took the horses from them* **c** *the priest judged the city before him.*

284

Practice 3

a *And David was the youngest of his sons* **b** *and that man was greater than all the men of the city* **c** *you are the greatest king [king of kings] and I am your most humble servant [servant of servants]* **d** *this is the good and great king of Israel and I am his eldest daughter.*

Test yourself

1 אֶת, אֶת־ **2** *on you, from me, between them, like him* **3** *vanity of vanities* **4** *and Saul was stronger than the men* **5** *And Israel loved Joseph more than all his [other] sons.*

UNIT 10

Practice 1

	to visit פָּקַד	to write כָּתַב	to remember זָכַר
3ms	פָּקַד	כָּתַב	זָכַר
3fs	פָּקְדָה	כָּתְבָה	זָכְרָה
2ms	פָּקַדְתָּ	כָּתַבְתָּ	זָכַרְתָּ
2fs	פָּקַדְתְּ	כָּתַבְתְּ	זָכַרְתְּ
1s	פָּקַדְתִּי	כָּתַבְתִּי	זָכַרְתִּי
3p	פָּקְדוּ	כָּתְבוּ	זָכְרוּ
2mp	פְּקַדְתֶּם	כְּתַבְתֶּם	זְכַרְתֶּם
2fp	פְּקַדְתֶּן	כְּתַבְתֶּן	זְכַרְתֶּן
1p	פָּקַדְנוּ	כָּתַבְנוּ	זָכַרְנוּ

Practice 2

a 6 **b** 4 **c** 7 **d** 2 **e** 9 **f** 3 **g** 1 **h** 5 **i** 10 **j** 8

Practice 3

קָרָא	Perfect 3ms	קָרָא	*he has called*
קָטַלְתָּ	Perfect 2ms	קָטַל	*you have killed*
שָׁמַרְנוּ	Perfect 1cp	שָׁמַר	*we have guarded*
הֲלַכְתֶּן	Perfect 2fp	הָלַךְ	*you have walked*
זָכְרוּ	Perfect 3cp	זָכַר	*they have remembered*

Test yourself

a מָשַׁל אָכְלָה הָלַכְתִּי **b** קָטַל קָטְלָה קָטַלְתָּ קָטַלְתְּ קָטַלְתִּי קָטְלוּ קְטַלְתֶּם קְטַלְתֶּן קָטַלְנוּ **c** שָׁמְרוּ *She walked as far as the city.* **d** *David and Daniel ate the bread.* **e** *The king ruled over all the land of Judah: he and his sons.*

UNIT 11

Practice 1

	to visit פָּקַד	to write כָּתַב	to remember זָכַר
3ms	יִפְקֹד	יִכְתֹּב	יִזְכֹּר
3fs	תִּפְקֹד	תִּכְתֹּב	תִּזְכֹּר
2ms	תִּפְקֹד	תִּכְתֹּב	תִּזְכֹּר
2fs	תִּפְקְדִי	תִּכְתְּבִי	תִּזְכְּרִי
1s	אֶפְקֹד	אֶכְתֹּב	אֶזְכֹּר
3mp	יִפְקְדוּ	יִכְתְּבוּ	יִזְכְּרוּ
3fp	תִּפְקֹדְנָה	תִּכְתֹּבְנָה	תִּזְכֹּרְנָה
2mp	תִּפְקְדוּ	תִּכְתְּבוּ	תִּזְכְּרוּ
2fp	תִּפְקֹדְנָה	תִּכְתֹּבְנָה	תִּזְכֹּרְנָה
1p	נִפְקֹד	נִכְתֹּב	נִזְכֹּר

Practice 2

a 3 **b** 9 **c** 4 **d** 1 **e** 8 **f** 5 **g** 2 **h** 10 **i** 6 **j** 7

Practice 3

a one father **b** two women **c** three countries **d** four daughters **e** five cities **f** six mares **g** seven cows **h** eight princesses **i** nine swords **j** ten blessings

Test yourself

1 יִשְׁמֹר תִּשְׁמֹר תִּשְׁמֹר תִּשְׁמְרִי אֶשְׁמֹר יִשְׁמְרוּ תִּשְׁמֹרְנָה תִּשְׁמְרוּ 2 יִשְׁפֹּט; תִּמְשֹׁל; אֶקְטֹל; הַמֶּלֶךְ יַעֲמֹד; אֶקְטֹל; תִּמְשֹׁל; יִשְׁפֹּט נִשְׁמֹר תִּשְׁמֹרְנָה or תַּעֲמֹדְנָה 3 *He will kill the men.* 4 אֶשֶׁת אֶת תִּזְכֹּר 5 יְהוּדָה עָרֵי בְּכָל אֶמְשֹׁל

UNIT 12

Practice 1

3ms	יִשְׁמֹר	he will guard	וַיִּשְׁמֹר	and he guarded
3fs	תִּשְׁמֹר	she will guard	וַתִּשְׁמֹר	and she guarded
2ms	תִּשְׁמֹר	you will guard	וַתִּשְׁמֹר	and you guarded
2fs	תִּשְׁמְרִי	you will guard	וַתִּשְׁמְרִי	and you guarded
1s	אֶשְׁמֹר	I will guard	וָאֶשְׁמֹר	and I guarded
3mp	יִשְׁמְרוּ	they will guard	וַיִּשְׁמְרוּ	and they guarded
3fp	תִּשְׁמֹרְנָה	they will guard	וַתִּשְׁמֹרְנָה	and they guarded

2mp	תִּשְׁמְרוּ	you will guard	וַתִּשְׁמְרוּ	and you guarded
2fp	תִּשְׁמֹרְנָה	you will guard	וַתִּשְׁמֹרְנָה	and you guarded
1p	נִשְׁמֹר	we will guard	וַנִּשְׁמֹר	and we guarded

Practice 2

1 a *And he remembered your covenant.* **b** *And she (or you ms) wrote your words in a book.* **c** *And I ruled over them.* **d** *And they (or you fp) walked in the paths of righteousness.* **e** *And you (mp) ate the bread.* **f** *And they (mp) kept the law of Yhwh.* **g** *And she (or you ms) killed a man.* **h** *And he called the name of his son Solomon.* **i** *And he said, 'I will judge all the land of Judah.'* **j** *And they said, 'We will guard the king's house.'*

2

3ms	וְזָכַר	and he will remember
3fs	וְזָכְרָה	and she will remember
2ms	וְזָכַרְתָּ	and you will remember
2fs	וְזָכַרְתְּ	and you will remember
1s	וְזָכַרְתִּי	and I will remember
3p	וְזָכְרוּ	and they will remember
2mp	וּזְכַרְתֶּם	and you will remember
2fp	וּזְכַרְתֶּן	and you will remember
1p	וְזָכַרְנוּ	and we will remember

Test yourself

1 Past tense. **2 Patach**. **3** *And he went as far as Judah.* **4** *He was angry and he took his sword and I was afraid.* **5** Qal VC Imperfect 2fs of פָּקַד meaning *and you visited*.

UNIT 13

Practice 1

Verb		Meaning	Weakness(es)
	עָמַד	to stand	**pe** guttural
	שָׁלַח	to send, stretch out	**lamed** guttural
	שִׂים	to put, place	hollow
	רָאָה	to see	doubly weak: **ayin** guttural & **lamed he**
	שָׁמַע	to hear	**lamed** guttural
	שָׁתָה	to drink	**lamed he**

	עָלָה	to go up	doubly weak: **pe** guttural and **lamed he**
	בּוֹא	to come	doubly weak: hollow and **lamed alef**
	יָלַד	to give birth	**pe yod**
	יָצָא	to go out	doubly weak: **pe yod** and **lamed alef**
	יָרַד	to go down	**pe yod**
	מוּת	to die	hollow
	בָּנָה	to build	**lamed he**

Practice 2

a Perfect 3cp עָמַד we have stood **b** Perf 3fs שָׁלְחָה she has sent **c** Perf 3fs שִׂים she has put **d** Perf 1cp רָאָה we have seen **e** Perf 1cs שָׁמַע I have heard **f** Perf 2mp שָׁתָה you have drunk **g** Perf 3fs עָלָה she has gone up **h** Perf 3ms בּוֹא he has come **i** Perf 2fs יָלַד you have given birth **j** Perf 2fs יָצָא you have gone out **k** Perf 3cp יָרַד they have gone down **l** Perf 2fp מוּת you have died **m** Perf 3cp בָּנָה they have built

Practice 3

a The king will sit under the tree. **b** Deborah will get up and she will hear my voice. **c** You (ms) will not approach the city. **d** You (mp) will go around the mountain. **e** I will eat bread in the house. **f** They (f) will give horses to our sons.

Test yourself

1 The vowels change: **sheva** becomes composite **sheva** and in general gutturals attract a-type vowels (**patach** or **qamets**). **Cholem** is also found instead of **chireq** in the Imperfect. **2 Vav**; **yod**; **nun**; sometimes **he**; the third letter in a double **ayin** verb. **3** You found the king's horses. **4** And the woman gave birth to a son and she named him Abraham. **5** Qal VC Imperfect 3mp of שָׁמַע meaning and they heard.

UNIT 14

Practice 1

a Hear, O Israel, the Lord our God, the Lord is one. **b** Remember the Sabbath day to keep it holy **c** And they said, 'Call for Samson so that he will play/make sport for us.' **d** See, this is a new thing. **e** And Eli answered and said, 'Go in peace.' **f** Eat, friends, drink and get drunk with love. **g** Lift up your eyes to heaven. **h** And he said, 'Sit here,' and they sat.

Practice 2

Root	Participle	Meaning	Imperative	Meaning
אָכַל	אֹכֵל	eating	אֱכֹל	eat!
גָּלָה	גֹּלֶה	revealing	גְּלֵה	reveal!
יָרַד	יֹרֵד	going down	רֵד	go down!

יָשַׁב	יֹשֵׁב	*sitting*	שֵׁב	*sit!*
מוּת	מֵת	*dying*	מוּת	*die!*
מְצָא	מֹצֵא	*finding*	מְצָא	*find!*
נָגַשׁ	נֹגֵשׁ	*approaching*	גַּשׁ/גְּשָׁה	*approach!*
נָפַל	נֹפֵל	*falling*	נְפֹל	*fall!*
סָבַב	סוֹבֵב	*turning*	סֹב	*turn!*
עָמַד	עֹמֵד	*standing*	עֲמֹד	*stand!*
קוּם	קָם	*arising*	קוּם	*arise!*
קָטַל	קֹטֵל	*killing*	קְטֹל	*kill!*
שָׁחַט	שֹׁחֵט	*killing*	שְׁחֹט	*kill!*
שִׂים	שָׂם	*putting*	שִׂים	*put!*

Practice 3

A list of the Infinitive Constructs in Ecclesiastes 3:1–8.

לָלֶדֶת	יָלַד	*to be born*
לָמוּת	מוּת	*to die*
לָטַעַת	נָטַע	*to plant*
לַעֲקוֹר	עָקַר	*to pluck up*
לַהֲרֹג	הָרַג	*to kill*
לִרְפּוֹא	רָפָא	*to heal*
לִפְרֹץ	פָּרַץ	*to break*
לִבְנוֹת	בָּנָה	*to build*
לִבְכּוֹת	בָּכָה	*to weep*
לִשְׂחוֹק	שָׂחַק	*to laugh*
סְפוֹד	סָפַד	*to wail*
רְקוֹד	רָקַד	*to dance*
לְהַשְׁלִיךְ	שָׁלַךְ	*to throw (Hifil)*
כְּנוֹס	כָּנַס	*to gather*
לַחֲבוֹק	חָבַק	*to embrace*
לִרְחֹק	רָחַק	*to retreat*

לְבַקֵּשׁ		בָּקַשׁ	to search (Piel)
לְאַבֵּד		אָבַד	to destroy (Piel)
לִשְׁמוֹר		שָׁמַר	to keep
לְהַשְׁלִיךְ		שָׁלַךְ	to throw (Hifil)
לִקְרוֹעַ		קָרַע	to tear
לִתְפּוֹר		תָּפַר	to sew
לַחֲשׁוֹת		חָשָׁה	to be silent
לְדַבֵּר		דָּבַר	to speak (Piel)
לֶאֱהֹב		אָהַב	to love
לִשְׂנֹא		שָׂנֵא	to hate

Practice 4

a Imperative: שְׁמַע **b** Participle: עוֹמֵד **c** Infinitive Construct: לָדַעַת **d** Infinitive Absolute: עָשֹׂה or יָכֹל **e** Perfect: וְנָתַתִּי **f** Imperfect: תַּעֲשֶׂה or תּוּכַל

Test yourself

1 *Write books* **2** The root שָׁלַח is III-guttural and so its Participle form contains a **patach** furtive. **3** *And Daniel answered me saying, 'Please sit and eat.'* **4** It is used with a finite verb, e.g. מוֹת תָּמוּת literally *dying you will die* or *you will certainly die.* **5** וַיֹּאמֶר שְׁמֹר אַתָּה וְזֶה עֵת לִשְׁמֹר אֶת־סוּסִי פֶּן־מוֹת תָּמוּת

UNIT 15

Practice 1

a (אֹתְךָ אֹתָךְ אֶתְכֶם) יִירָא הַמֶּלֶךְ אֹתְךָ **b** יִבְרָא יהוה אֹתָם (the pronoun could be any of (אֹתָךְ אֹתָךְ אֶתְכֶם) **c** (אֶתְכֶן) לֹא יִבְחַן דָּוִד אֹתִי (the pronoun could be אֹתָן or אֶתְכֶן) **d** תִּרְאֶה אִמִּי אֹתָם (the pronoun could be אֹתָם or אֶתְכֶן) **e** נִבְלַע אֹתָהּ (אֹתְךָ אֹתָךְ אֶתְכֶם אֶתְכֶן אֹתָךְ) (the pronoun could be any of **f** תִּכְרֹת הַחֶרֶב אֹתְכֶן (the pronoun could be אֹתוֹ or אֹתָהּ (אֹתָה) **g** תִּקְחֶנָה הַנָּשִׁים אֶתְכֶם (the pronoun could be any of יִמְצָא גִּדְעוֹן (אֹתָן) i (the pronoun could be אֹתוֹ or אֹתוֹ **h** אֶשְׁלַח אֹתָהּ (אֹתְךָ אֹתָךְ אֶתְכֶם אֶתְכֶן (the pronoun could be any of יַעֲנֶה אֶתְכֶן אֶתְכֶן **j** אֹתָה (אֹתְךָ אֹתָךְ אֶתְכֶם אֶתְכֶן).

Practice 2

אֲשֶׁר אֲשֶׁר אֵי אֲשֶׁר מִי לָמָּה מָה

David came to the house which is between the mountains. And he saw the servant who guards the house. And he said to him, 'Where is the woman whose father lives in this house?' And the servant said, 'Who are you?' And David answered, 'I am the king.' And the servant said, 'Why have you come?' And David said, 'I have come to visit Sarah. What is your name?'

Practice 3

Verb	Participle		Infinitive Construct	
בָּלַע	בֹּלֵעַ	swallowing	בְּלֹעַ	to swallow
נָטַע	נֹטֵעַ	planting	נְטֹעַ	to plant
קָרַע	קֹרֵעַ	tearing	קְרֹעַ	to tear
פָּקַח	פֹּקֵחַ	opening	פְּקֹחַ	to open

Practice 4

Singular absolute	Meaning	Singular construct	Meaning
חֶרֶב	sword	חֶרֶב	sword of
גּוֹאֵל	redeemer	גּוֹאֵל	redeemer of
רָעָב	famine	רְעָב	famine of
נָחָשׁ	snake	נְחַשׁ	snake of
יָשָׁר	just	יְשַׁר	just of

Test yourself

1 *Why?* לָמָה or לָמֶה *What?* מַה or מֶה *Who?* מִי 2 *Whose* (These are the men whose voices will sing songs). 3 Participle שֹׁמֵעַ; Infinitive Construct שְׁמֹעַ; Infinitive Absolute שָׁמוֹעַ 4 Eight years old. 5 יִירָא אֹתִי דָּוִד וְכָל־הַנֹּגֵעַ אֶת סוּסִי יִצְחָק

UNIT 16
Practice 1

Nifal Perfect	שָׁמַר	מָשַׁל	פָּקַד
3ms	נִשְׁמַר	נִמְשַׁל	נִפְקַד
3fs	נִשְׁמְרָה	נִמְשְׁלָה	נִפְקְדָה
2ms	נִשְׁמַרְתָּ	נִמְשַׁלְתָּ	נִפְקַדְתָּ
2fs	נִשְׁמַרְתְּ	נִמְשַׁלְתְּ	נִפְקַדְתְּ
1cs	נִשְׁמַרְתִּי	נִמְשַׁלְתִּי	נִפְקַדְתִּי
3cp	נִשְׁמְרוּ	נִמְשְׁלוּ	נִפְקְדוּ
2mp	נִשְׁמַרְתֶּם	נִמְשַׁלְתֶּם	נִפְקַדְתֶּם
2fp	נִשְׁמַרְתֶּן	נִמְשַׁלְתֶּן	נִפְקַדְתֶּן
1p	נִשְׁמַרְנוּ	נִמְשַׁלְנוּ	נִפְקַדְנוּ

Nifal Imperfect	שָׁמַר	פָּקַד	זָכַר
3ms	יִשָּׁמֵר	יִפָּקֵד	יִזָּכֵר
3fs	תִּשָּׁמֵר	תִּפָּקֵד	תִּזָּכֵר
2ms	תִּשָּׁמֵר	תִּפָּקֵד	תִּזָּכֵר
2fs	תִּשָּׁמְרִי	תִּפָּקְדִי	תִּזָּכְרִי
1cs	אֶשָּׁמֵר	אֶפָּקֵד	אֶזָּכֵר
3mp	יִשָּׁמְרוּ	יִפָּקְדוּ	יִזָּכְרוּ
3fp	תִּשָּׁמַרְנָה	תִּפָּקַדְנָה	תִּזָּכַרְנָה
2mp	תִּשָּׁמְרוּ	תִּפָּקְדוּ	תִּזָּכְרוּ
2fp	תִּשָּׁמַרְנָה	תִּפָּקַדְנָה	תִּזָּכַרְנָה
1p	נִשָּׁמֵר	נִפָּקֵד	נִזָּכֵר

Practice 2

1 *Do not murder; do not commit adultery/idolatry; do not steal; do not bear false witness against your neighbour. Do not desire your neighbour's house; do not desire your neighbour's wife, or his servant, or his female servant, or his ox or his donkey, or anything that is his.*

2 a *Please live in my land.* אֶרֶץ like מֶלֶךְ **b** *Do not kill the guards.* שָׁמֵר like אֹיֵב **c** *Let the heart of Moses be full.* לֵבָב like דָּבָר **d** *You must not touch my nose.* אַף like יָם **e** *Remember the righteousness of Solomon.* יְדָקָה like דָּבָר **f** *Let the judges of Israel rejoice.* שֹׁפֵט like אֹיֵב **g** *You must not destroy the sanctuaries of Judah.* קֹדֶשׁ like מֶלֶךְ **h** *Let my redeemer visit me.* גּוֹאֵל like אֹיֵב **i** *Do not forget the mothers of the children (or sons) of Israel.* אֵם like יָם **j** *Do not fear my knowledge.* דַּעַת like מֶלֶךְ

Test yourself

1 a *it was written* **b** *they were eaten* **c** *it/she will be remembered* **2 a** *Moab* **b** *Egypt* **c** *Israel* **3** *let him remember* יִזְכֹּר; *let them be remembered* **4** יִזְכְּרוּ **a** *He was visited in the morning:* נִפְקַד בַּבֹּקֶר **b** *The law of the king was remembered in Israel:* נִזְכַּר תֹּרַת הַמֶּלֶךְ בְּיִשְׂרָאֵל **c** *And the words of the prophets of Israel were written in the books of the priests:* יִכָּתְבוּ דִּבְרֵי נְבִיאֵי יִשְׂרָאֵל בְּסִפְרֵי הַכֹּהֲנִים

UNIT 17

Practice 1

a 7 **b** 8 **c** 2 **d** 1 **e** 3 **f** 4 **g** 5 **h** 6

Practice 2

a *And he said, 'Let me come to my wife.'* **b** *And she said, 'Let me find grace in your eyes.'* (Or *in your sight.*) **c** *Come, and let us walk in the light of the LORD.* **d** *And let us take corn and let us eat.* **e** *And let us shut the doors of the temple.*

Practice 3

	Perf. 3ms	Perf. 1s	Perf. 3mp	Impf. 3ms	Impv.
Qal	קָדֵשׁ	פָּקַדְתִּי	בָּקְעוּ	—	פְּקֹד
Meaning	he is holy	I have visited	they have divided	—	visit
Piel	קִדֵּשׁ	פִּקַּדְתִּי	בִּקְּעוּ	יְצַוֶּה	פַּקֵּד
Meaning	he has consecrated	I have mustered	they have torn in pieces	he will command	muster
Pual	קֻדַּשׁ	פֻּקַּדְתִּי	בֻּקְּעוּ	יְצֻוֶּה	—
Meaning	he has been consecrated	I have been mustered	they have been torn in pieces	he will be commanded	—
Hitpael	הִתְקַדֵּשׁ	הִתְפַּקַּדְתִּי	הִתְבַּקְּעוּ	—	הִתְפַּקֵּד
Meaning	he has consecrated himself	I have mustered	they have been torn	—	muster

	Impf. 1p	Impf. 3mp	Impv.	Part.	Inf. Cstr.
Qal	נִבְקַע	יַאַסְפוּ	קְדַשׁ	אֹסֵף	בְּקֹעַ
Meaning	we will divide	they will gather	be holy	gathering	to divide
Piel	נְבַקַּע	יְאַסְּפוּ	קַדֵּשׁ	מְאַסֵּף	בַּקֵּעַ
Meaning	we will tear in pieces	they will gather	consecrate	gathering	to tear in pieces
Pual	נְבֻקַּע	יְאֻסְּפוּ	—	מְאֻסָּף	בֻּקַּע
Meaning	we will be torn in pieces	they will be gathered	—	being gathered	to be torn in pieces
Hitpael	נִתְבַּקַּע	יִתְאַסְּפוּ	הִתְקַדֵּשׁ	מִתְאַסֵּף	הִתְבַּקֵּעַ
Meaning	we will be torn	they will be gathered together	consecrate yourself	being gathered together	to be torn

Test yourself

1 a Piel VC Impf 3ms + suff 3mp בָּרַךְ *and he blessed them* b Qal Perf 2ms + suff 1cs אָהַב *you love me* c Qal Impf 3ms + suff 2ms שָׁמַר *he will guard/keep you* 2 בָּקַשׁ 3 a אֶדְרְשָׁה b דָּבַר c לָקַח d בָּרַךְ

UNIT 18

Practice 1

a וַתַּשְׁלֵךְ אֶת־הַיֶּלֶד c וַיַּשְׁכֵּם אַבְרָהָם בַּבֹּקֶר b מִי מִלֵּל לְאַבְרָהָם הֵינִיקָה בָנִים שָׂרָה
וַתְּמַלֵּא אֶת־הַחֵמֶת מַיִם וַתַּשְׁקְ אֶת־הַנַּעַר d תַּחַת אַחַד הַשִּׂיחִם

כֹּה הִרְאַנִי אֲדֹנָי יְהוִה g וּמִכַּף מֶלֶךְ־אַשּׁוּר אַצִּילְךָ f מִי הִגִּיד לְךָ כִּי עֵירֹם אָתָּה e
אֲבִיאֲךָ אֶל־בֵּית אִמִּי j וַיִּזְעַק וַיֹּאמֶר בְּנִינְוֵה מִטַּעַם הַמֶּלֶךְ i בִּנְאוֹת דֶּשֶׁא יַרְבִּיצֵנִי h

Practice 2

a *you have saved us* **b** *I will praise/thank you* **c** *she will nurse* **d** *and hold* **e** *and she gave a drink*

Practice 3

a the Nifal of פָּקַד

Perfect 3ms	נִפְקַד
Imperfect 3ms	יִפָּקֵד
Imperative ms	הִפָּקֵד
Infinitive	הִפָּקֵד
Participle	נִפְקָד

b the Pual of קָטַל

Perfect 3ms	קֻטַּל
Imperfect 3ms	יְקֻטַּל
Imperative ms	--
Infinitive	קֻטַּל
Participle	מְקֻטָּל

c the Hifil of שָׁמַר

Perfect 3ms	הִשְׁמִיר
Imperfect 3ms	יַשְׁמִיר
Imperative ms	הַשְׁמֵר
Infinitive	הַשְׁמִיר
Participle	מַשְׁמִיר

d the Hofal of קָטַל

Perfect 3ms	הָקְטַל
Imperfect 3ms	יָקְטַל
Imperative ms	--
Infinitive	הָקְטַל
Participle	מָקְטָל

Test yourself

1 a *I will raise* **b** *I will restore/cause to return* **c** *He will bring* **d** *You have brought* **e** *He was told*

2 a Hif Perf 2ms שָׁלַח *you dismissed/expelled* **b** Hif Ptc בּוֹא *bringing* **c** Hif Impv ms יָשַׁב *cause [someone] to live* **d** Hif Ptc שׁוּב *causing to turn* **e** Hif Ptc יָשַׁב *causing [someone] to live*

UNIT 19

Practice 1

a Qal VC Impf 3ms נָשָׂא **b** Qal VC Impf 3ms שִׂים **c** Qal Perf 1s נָתַן **d** Qal VC Impf apoc עָשָׂה **e** Qal Impv 2ms לְקַח

Practice 2

Word		Form	Root	Meaning
נוֹדַע	Unit 6	Nif Ptc ms	יָדַע	*being known*
וְהַנּוֹרָא	Unit 9	VC Nif Ptc ms	יָרֵא	*being afraid*
מְבֹרָךְ	Unit 10	Pual Ptc ms	בָּרַךְ	*being blessed*
וַתְּנַחֲמֵנִי	Unit 12	VC Piel Impf 2ms + suff 1cs	נָחַם	*and you comforted me*
אֲסַפְּרָה	Unit 13	Piel Impf 1s	סָפַר	*I will count, tell*
נִפְלְאוֹתֶיךָ	Unit 13	Nif Ptc mp + suff 2ms	פלא	*your great things*
אֲזַמְּרָה	Unit 13	Piel Impf 1s + parag ה	זמר	*I will sing praises to*
יִכָּשְׁלוּ	Unit 13	Nif Impf 3mp	כשל	*they will stumble*
אִבַּדְתָּ	Unit 13	Piel Perf 2ms	אבד	*you have destroyed*
כּוֹנֵן	Unit 13	Pilel Perf 3ms	כון	*he has established*
וְנִפְקְחוּ	Unit 14	VC Nif Perf 3mp	פָּקַח	*and they will be opened*
דִּבֶּר	Unit 15	Piel Perf 3ms	דָּבַר	*he has said, he has promised*
הַנּוֹלָד	Unit 15	Nif Perf 3ms	יָלַד	*being born*
צִוָּה	Unit 15	Piel Perf 3ms	צָוָה	*he has commanded*
בְּהִוָּלֶד	Unit 15	Prep בְּ + Nif Inf cstr	יָלַד	*in being born*
מִלֵּל	Unit 16	Piel Perf 3ms	מָלַל	*he said, he spoke*
גָּרֵשׁ	Unit 16	Piel Impv ms	גָּרַשׁ	*expel, drive away*

Practice 3

אַיֵּה	Interrogative אֵי + paragogic ה	*where?*
יִרְאֶה	Qal Impf 3ms רָאָה	*he will provide* (the verb רָאָה *to see* also has this meaning)
וַיֵּלְכוּ	Qal VC Impf 3mp הָלַךְ	*and they went*
שְׁנֵיהֶם	Numeral m + suff 3mp שְׁנַיִם	*both of them*
יַחְדָּו	Adverb יַחַד	*together* (literally *they together*)
וַיִּבֶן	Qal VC Impf 3ms בָּנָה	*and he built*
מִזְבֵּחַ	Noun ms	*altar*
וַיַּעֲרֹךְ	Qal Impf 3ms עָרַךְ	*and he arranged, laid out*
וַיַּעֲקֹד	Qal Impf 3ms עָקַד	*and he tied up, bound*
וַיָּשֶׂם	Qal VC Impf 3ms שִׂים	*and he placed*
מִמַּעַל	Prep מִן + prep מַעַל	*above*

Test yourself

1

Word (in order)	Analysis	Meaning
נְמֵרִים	noun mp נָמֵר	*leopards*
נָסַבּוּ	Nif Perf 3mp סָבַב	*they turned around, surrounded*
נֶעֱבָד	Nif Perf 3ms עָבַד	*he is/was served*
נַעֲרֹתַי	noun fp + suff 1cs נַעֲרָה	*my female servants*
נַעֲשֶׂה	Qal Impf 1cs עָשָׂה	*we will do*
נַעֲשִׂים	Nif Ptc mp עָשָׂה	*being done*
נָפוּץ	Qal Ptc (passive) נָפַץ	*broken*
נֹפֵחַ	Qal Ptc נָפַח	*blowing*
נַפְשִׁי	noun f + suff 1cs נֶפֶשׁ	*my soul, life*
נַפְשְׁךָ	noun f + suff 2ms נֶפֶשׁ	*your soul, life*

UNIT 20

Practice 1

a *and he said* **b** *David* **c** *to the servant* **d** *the one telling* **e** *to him* **f** *how* **g** *you know* **h** *that* **i** *dead* **j** *Saul* **k** *and Jonathan* **l** *his son*

Practice 2

a *Guard your foot when you go to the house of God.* Meaning: either *your feet* (K) or *your foot* (Q). **b** *And he has confirmed his word which he has spoken against us.* Meaning: either *his words* (K) or *his word* (Q). **c** *To me he is a bear lying in wait; a lion in a hiding place.* Meaning: *a lion* (Q). The Ketiv has no meaning. **d** *And they returned to Jerusalem.* Meaning: *they returned* (Q); The Ketiv does not make sense. The **dagesh** in the final י of וַיָּשֻׁבִי (K) represents the **dagesh** in the וּ of וַיָּשֻׁבוּ (Q). **e** *Great anger will bear punishment.* Meaning: *angry* (K) or *great* (Q). Neither meaning is easy to understand in the context. The LXX has *a malicious man will be severely punished* and most English translations follow this reading.

Practice 3

a : וַיֹּאמֶר נָתָן אֶל־דָּוִד אַתָּה הָאִישׁ **b** טוֹב־וְיָשָׁר יְהוָה עַל־כֵּן יוֹרֶה חַטָּאִים בַּדָּרֶךְ
c : אָז יָשִׁיר־מֹשֶׁה וּבְנֵי יִשְׂרָאֵל אֶת־הַשִּׁירָה **d** נוֹדָע בִּיהוּדָה אֱלֹהִים בְּיִשְׂרָאֵל גָּדוֹל שְׁמוֹ
וַיְהִי בִּימֵי שְׁפֹט הַשֹּׁפְטִים וַיְהִי רָעָב בָּאָרֶץ וַיֵּלֶךְ אִישׁ מִבֵּית לֶחֶם יְהוּדָה **e** הַזֹּאת לַיהוָה
כִּי יְהוָה אֱלֹהֵיכֶם הוּא אֱלֹהֵי הָאֱלֹהִים וַאֲדֹנֵי **f** לָגוּר בִּשְׂדֵי מוֹאָב הוּא וְאִשְׁתּוֹ וּשְׁנֵי בָנָיו :
וַיֹּאמֶר עֵרֹם **g** הָאֲדֹנִים הָאֵל הַגָּדֹל הַגִּבֹּר וְהַנּוֹרָא אֲשֶׁר לֹא־יִשָּׂא פָנִים וְלֹא יִקַּח שֹׁחַד :
וְאָמַרְתָּ **h** יָצָתִי מִבֶּטֶן אִמִּי וְעָרֹם אָשׁוּב שָׁמָּה יְהוָה נָתַן וַיהוָה לָקָח יְהִי שֵׁם יְהוָה מְבֹרָךְ :
בַּיּוֹם הַהוּא אוֹדְךָ יְהוָה כִּי אָנַפְתָּ בִּי יָשֹׁב אַפְּךָ וּתְנַחֲמֵנִי : הִנֵּה אֵל יְשׁוּעָתִי אֶבְטַח וְלֹא
אֶפְחָד כִּי־עָזִּי וְזִמְרָת יָהּ יְהוָה וַיְהִי־לִי לִישׁוּעָה :

Most of these should have been where you expected them to be on the basis of the cantillation marks, with only a few exceptions.

Test yourself

The examples are my own; you may be using different verbs or nouns as examples. Make sure that the form is correct even if you are using different words.

1 There are seven main verbal stems or **binyanim**. They modify the verbal root to convey meanings such as passive, factitive or causative. Most verbs are found in one or two stems, although some are found in all seven stems. There are a few less common stems that seem to overlap in meaning with the more common stems. Examples:

Stem	Example	Meaning
Qal (light)	פָּקַד	*to go to* (to visit; attack)
Nifal (passive)	נִפְקַד	*to be missing, to be punished*
Piel (intensive)	פִּקֵּד	*to muster* (an army – intensively visiting to attack)
Pual (intensive passive)	פֻּקַד	*to be mustered*
Hitpael (intensive reflexive)	הִתְפַּקֵּד	*to be counted* (e.g. in a census; not really reflexive in meaning)
Hifil (causative)	הִפְקִיד	*to put someone in charge of something* (i.e. causing someone to visit someone else)
Hofal (causative passive)	הָפְקַד	*to be put in charge of something*

Perfect 3ms	הִתְפַּקֵּד
Imperfect 3ms	יִתְפַּקֵּד
Imperative ms	הִתְפַּקֵּד
Infinitive	הִתְפַּקֵּד
Participle	מִתְפַּקֵּד

3 First-person commands use the cohortative, e.g.: אֶשְׁמְרָה *let me guard*; Second-person commands use the imperative, e.g.: שְׁמֹר *guard!* Third-person commands use the Jussive (usually identical to the imperfect), e.g.: יִשְׁמֹר *let him guard*.

4

	Masculine Absolute	Masculine Construct	Feminine Absolute	Feminine Construct
Singular	סוּס	סוּס	סוּסָה	סוּסַת
Plural	סוּסִים	סוּסֵי	סוּסוֹת	סוּסוֹת

5

Verb		Qal VC Impf 3ms
	מָשַׁל	וַיִּמְשֹׁל
	הָלַךְ	וַיֵּלֶךְ
	אָמַר	וַיֹּאמֶר
	קוּם	וַיָּקָם

Additional texts

Translations of the narrative and poetic texts are available either in printed Bibles or online.

NARRATIVE TEXTS

Deuteronomy 6:4–7 The Shema

1 Verbless clauses where the verb *to be* is implied rather than written.

2 It has a temporal sense, e.g. *when you sit, when you walk*, etc.

Isaiah 38:1–8 Hezekiah's sundial

1 Most translations render אֵת אֲשֶׁר הִתְהַלַּכְתִּי with *how I walked* or *that I walked* or a freer translation such as *how I served you*.

2 Some translations include *saying* but many leave it out. A reason to include it might be that it introduces God's speech in the next verse. A reason to leave it out might be that English syntax is better without it.

3 If you compare translations you will see that the phrase מַעֲלוֹת אָחָז is sometimes translated *the sundial of Ahaz* and sometimes *the steps of Ahaz*. The word is also used to mean a sundial and the degrees by which the sun moves through the sky above the horizon.

Genesis 32:25–33 Jacob wrestles

1 Literal: *Not Jacob it will be called any more your name*. Idiomatic: *Your name will no longer be Jacob* or *You will no longer be called Jacob*.

2 A reason to prefer *God*: Jacob names the place Peniel, which means *the face of God*, whom he says he has seen face to face. Jacob's wrestling has often been understood in a metaphorical sense, placing him in a tradition with Abraham and Moses in which biblical characters argue with God. A reason to prefer *gods*: in the history of interpretation the figure who wrestles with Jacob is understood to be an angel, even though the text does not use the word מַלְאָךְ (but see Hosea 12:4), and the word אֱלֹהִים can be understood to mean other divine or 'supernatural' beings (see e.g. 1 Samuel 28:13).

3 Because it qualifies the noun נֶפֶשׁ which is feminine.

Ruth 1:11–19a Ruth makes a pledge to Naomi

1 *'Will I have sons in my womb again so that they can become your husbands?'*

2 There is a choice to be made between ideas that the women would *refrain from having husbands* and that they would *refrain from marrying*. The Hebrew seems to convey an idea of *belonging to a husband*, rather than *having a husband*. Whether this seems like the same idea might depend on your theological or social perspective. See Genesis 20:3 for a similar construction in which a woman *has a husband* or *is a man's wife* in English translations that mediate a difficult Hebrew phrase.

3 The word מִכֶּם has a masculine suffix: we would expect מִכֶּן. There is a similar example with לָכֶם in verse 11 and שְׁתֵּיהֶם in verse 19.

1 Samuel 16:4–13 The anointing of David

1 כִּי לֹא יִרְאֶה יְהוָה אֲשֶׁר יִרְאֶה הָאָדָם

2 Messiah.

3 Saul is taller than everyone else (9:2), and Eliab also seems to be tall (16:7), but David's height is clearly contrasted: he is the youngest (הַקָּטָן: the smallest).

2 Samuel 12:1–10 Nathan's parable

1 The word for *city* is feminine: בְּעִיר אֶחָת *in one city*. The word for man is masculine: אִישׁ אֶחָד *one man*.

2 *A son of death*. Most translations have something like *he deserves to die*. Some have other nuances, such as *he will certainly die* or *he is demonic*.

3 David's many wives are compared with the rich man's flocks and herds: he is a polygamous king. In other respects the parable does not provide a direct comparison: Uriah is killed rather than Bathsheba (assuming she's the lamb). However, Nathan may be comparing David's moral corruption with that of the rich man.

Jonah 3 The repentance of Nineveh

1 Jonah ran away to sea and was swallowed by a large fish in which he prayed to God. This is the most well-known part of the story and it seems quite unusual in comparison with other stories of prophets in the Bible.

2 The narrator tells the reader that Nineveh is so big it takes three days to journey across it. Jonah travels one day and begins to speak, so he is approximately a third of the way into the city.

3 *Let them not taste; let them not feed; let them not drink; let them cover themselves; let them call; let them turn.*

Exodus 3:1–14 The burning bush

1 Because נָשַׁל is a weak verb of the I-**nun** type and this type forms monosyllabic imperatives.

2 The use of the Infinitive Absolute in this construction intensifies the verbal idea. Translation: *I have certainly seen.*

3 *I am who I am; I am what I am; I will be what I will be; Let me be what I will be.* There may be other possibilities but these are the most common. Which do you prefer, and why?

Exodus 20:1–13 The ten commandments

1 It's easy to count 11 or 14 or arrive at other totals that are not 10. Different traditions have different ways of numbering them, which you can find in a good commentary on Exodus.

2 These are prohibitions and are expressed with a negative particle and the Jussive. The imperative is not used for prohibitions. Strong prohibitions are expressed with לֹא and weaker prohibitions are expressed with אַל. So לֹא תִגְנֹב means something like *never, ever steal*, whereas אַל תִגְנֹב would mean something like *you probably shouldn't steal*. The distinction in my example here may be slightly exaggerated for effect.

3 Where I live, only three of these are illegal: murder, stealing and bearing false witness. Adultery is grounds for divorce but is not illegal. Taking God's name in vain may invite disapproval but there are no penalties. Keeping the Sabbath day holy (understood as Sunday) is culturally and spiritually important in parts of my country, and Sunday trading laws differ from legislation governing the rest of the week. The verb חָמַד probably means something stronger than simply desiring: it probably indicates an intention to deprive your neighbour of his property. This appears to imply *mens rea* without an *actus reus*, which would be difficult to prosecute where I live.

Genesis 3: The tree of knowledge of good and evil

1 Particularly difficult forms are: נֶחְמָד (verse 6), הַגִּיד (verse 11), צִוִּיתִיךָ (verse 11 and verse 17), הִשִּׁיאַנִי (verse 13), תַּצְמִיחַ (verse 18), וַיַּלְבִּשֵׁם (verse 21), וַיְשַׁלְּחֵהוּ (verse 23) and הַמִּתְהַפֶּכֶת (verse 23). These are more difficult because most of them are weak verbs, and some of them have suffixes.

2 The word תְּשׁוּקָה can be translated *desire*, *longing*, or even *hunger*. It also occurs in Song of Songs 7:11 (Engl. 7:10), although without the idea of ruling over anything or anyone. In

Genesis 3:16 the woman desires her partner but he will rule over her. In Genesis 4, sin desires Cain but he will rule over it. Most English translations present this as an instruction: *you must rule over it*, although it could also be translated with a future: *you will rule over it*.

3 There are no 'obvious' answers to this question, but there are particular themes that regularly come up when people discuss this. Some people find that reading the story in Hebrew allows them to see aspects of the narrative in an entirely new way, especially compared to the way the story is usually represented in art and literature. It is much slower to read in a new language than to read in your native language, and slowing down can also help us develop new understandings. For others, the repeated vocabulary takes on a new resonance. Occasionally people feel aggrieved at the perception that the punishment is unfair and does not fit the crime of eating fruit, even from a prohibited tree. But whatever our responses to the material, it can be quite compelling to discover a new angle on an ancient narrative.

POETIC TEXTS

Song of Songs 8:4–7 The power of love

1 The subject is הָאַהֲבָה since שֶׁתֶּחְפָּץ is feminine singular and the other potential subjects are plural. Notice that the imperatives are masculine plural rather than feminine plural, even though the people being addressed are the daughters of Jerusalem. This phenomenon is not unusual in biblical Hebrew and can also be seen in the book of Ruth.

2 Literally this phrase means *despising they will despise him* but your translation should reflect the idiomatic use of the Infinitive Absolute. Most translations also prefer a passive in English: *he [or it] would be completely despised*. One question is whether the man giving his wealth for love is despised, or whether the offer of wealth itself is despised. Translations are divided on this.

Isaiah 41:8–13 God's servant

1 The word תִּשְׁתָּע is derived from a verb that begins with a sibilant (an **s**-sound). It is a Hitpael form and therefore exhibits metathesis, where letters change places. This form is a second-person imperfect so begins with תִּת, where the second **tav** is exchanged with the **shin** of שָׁעַה. The verb is also III-**he** and has lost its final **he** via apocopation.

2 Literal: *with the right hand of my righteousness*. Idiomatic: *with my righteous right hand*.

3 Most translations have something like *those who fight you*, *those who make war against you*, etc.

Psalm 23 The LORD is my shepherd

1 The Hifil is *to cause to lie down*. Most translations have either *he makes me lie down* or *he lets me lie down*.

2 Just as Piel takes its name from the modifications to the verb פעל, so Polel describes the modifications to the verb פעל. The last letter of the verbal root is repeated and the vowels are **holem** and **tsere**. This stem has the same function as Piel but is used for hollow verbs, and the doubled final letter and **holem** probably occur because the middle **vav** or **yod** is really a vowel and therefore cannot take the **dagesh** which is characteristic of the 'intensive' stems.

3 The phrase is literally *for the length of days* but it is better rendered as *forever* or *as long as I live*.

Psalm 121 I will lift my eyes to the hills

1 Most translations have something like *the one who watches you* or *your guardian*.

2 The second-person masculine singular suffix is usually ךָ.

3 The **dagesh** represents the assimilated **nun** of מִן.

Amos 8:1–7 A vision

1 The tetragrammaton is pointed to be pronounced as אֲדֹנָי which is the preceding word in v. 1. In this situation it is pronounced אֱלֹהִים and pointed with the corresponding vowels. Note that both אֲדֹנָי and אֱלֹהִים take a composite **sheva** as their first vowel; they each begin with a guttural. The tetragrammaton does not begin with a guttural and thus takes a simple **sheva**.

2 Amos is generally understood to be foretelling the future, so that could be a reason. However, there is also a grammatical reason: the Vav Consecutive Perfect at the beginning of the verse conveys a future sense and the second half of the verse seems to be continuing the prediction of future disaster. Hebrew tenses do not map easily onto English tenses.

3 The words קָיִץ and קֵץ. The use of this kind of word play in prophecy is quite common in the Hebrew Bible and it has been suggested that it might have a theological significance.

Proverbs 8:1–11 In praise of wisdom

1 The usual plural of אִישׁ is אֲנָשִׁים.

2 The phrase is literally *an idolatry of my lips is wickedness*. Most translations have something like *wickedness is an abomination to my lips*. The word *abomination* is rare in everyday English, and so some translations have a version of *my lips hate wickedness*.

3 Perhaps *no desire resembles it* (i.e. wisdom is incomparable). Most translations have something like *nothing you desire compares with it* or *nothing desirable can be compared to it*.

1 Samuel 2:1–10 Hannah's song

1 Hollow verbs, also known as II-**yod** and II-**vav** verbs.

2 The Qere readings introduce some differences in meaning. Verse 3: K ולא means *and not*; Q וְלוֹ means *and by him*. Most translations follow the Qere because it seems to make more sense. Verse 9: K חסידו means *his pious one*; Q חֲסִידָיו means *his pious ones*. Similarly in verse 10 K מריבו means *his enemy* and Q מְרִיבָיו means *his enemies*. Translations accept the plural (Qere) forms: in the case of מְרִיבָיו the verb is plural indicating plural enemies. Also in verse 10 we find עלו for עָלָיו which has no alternative meaning. Some examples of Ketiv/Qere elicit considerable discussion among scholars, but these examples are probably less significant.

3 Two likely translations: either *The LORD! His enemies will be broken; he will thunder against them in heaven* or *The enemies of the LORD will be shattered; he thunders against them in heaven*. Translations differ in how they handle the tetragrammaton as well as the tenses.

Job 38:1–11 God speaks from the whirlwind

1 The Hofal is causative passive, so it means *to be sunk*. A translation might be *on what were its pillars sunk?*

2 Literally it means *the sons of God*. Some traditions and translations understand these to be members of the heavenly court or angels. Other traditions reject this interpretation. This phrase occurs elsewhere in the Hebrew Bible, notably in Genesis 6:1–4 but also in Job 1–2.

3 If you prefer to follow the traditional reading, perhaps *And I established my decree upon it*. Otherwise you might use some poetic licence: *And I broke up the land where I wished to limit it.*

Ecclesiastes 12 Remember your creator in the days of your youth

1 Metathesis, because סָבַל begins with a sibilant.

2 The word is often translated *vanity* which might not be ideal since the word is now primarily used to indicate conceitedness. The sense of futility or meaninglessness seems important, and *absurdity* might also be a useful translation, but it is difficult to find a single English word that conveys the range of הֶבֶל. Perhaps it is הֶבֶל to attempt to translate הֶבֶל.

3 There are a number of ways of looking at this chapter. You can read it as a warning about old age, or a metaphor for political upheaval. Some scholars interpret it as an allegory for the end of the world.

Exodus 15:1–19 The song of Moses/The song of the sea

1 A segolate noun. They are the same in the construct singular as the absolute singular but they follow the דָּבָר pattern in the plural.

2 These verbs are III-**he** which is clear from their form because they have the suffixes of the Perfect 2ms and the **he** has been replaced by **yod**. They are also I-**nun** but this does not affect their form in the Perfect.

3 There is no obvious answer to this question, although it is to be hoped that the insights gained from wrestling with the text will be useful in determining which texts to approach next as the reader continues to develop familiarity with the language and the biblical world.

Glossary of grammatical terms

absolute   In Hebrew, the form of a noun or adjective found in a dictionary.

Absolute: דָּבָר   Plural: דְּבָרִים   Construct: דְּבַר
Some nouns do not change in the construct (e.g. מֶלֶךְ).

accent   A mark that indicates how a letter or word is supposed to be read. Accents are sometimes called diacritical marks. There are a number of types of accent in Hebrew, and the following have their own entries in this glossary: **atnah**, **dagesh**, **mappiq**, **maqqef**, **meeg**, **silluq**.

active voice   A verb whose subject is doing something is said to be in the active voice. A verb whose subject is having something done to it is said to be in the **passive** voice.

Examples:

Active: יָלְדָה שָׂרָה בֵּן   *Sarah has borne a son*

Passive: נוֹלַד לְשָׂרָה בֵּן   *A son has been born to Sarah*

adjective   A word that qualifies a noun: the *good* king, *big* horses. In Hebrew, an adjective used in this way comes after the noun it qualifies, and agrees with the noun in person, gender, number and definiteness.

Examples in Hebrew:

הַמֶּלֶךְ הַטּוֹב   *the good king*   סוּסִים גְּדוֹלִים   *big horses*

Adjectives can be used in Hebrew with the verb *to be* implied. In this case the adjective comes before the noun it qualifies, and agrees with the noun in person, gender and number but **not** definiteness.

Examples:

טוֹב הַמֶּלֶךְ   *the king is good*   גְּדוֹלִים סוּסִים   *horses are big*

An adjectival construction is a phrase containing at least one noun qualified by at least one adjective.

adverb   Adverbs can qualify several kinds of words. Qualifying a verb: I read *slowly*. Qualifying an adjective: Your work is *very* good. Qualifying another adverb: It all happened *quite* quickly.

Examples in Hebrew:

יָשַׁב שָׁם   *He lived there* (qualifying a verb)

טוֹב מְאֹד הַמֶּלֶךְ   *The king is very good* (qualifying an adjective)

הָלַךְ אָבִי בִּמְהֵרָה מְאֹד   *My father walked very quickly*

agreement   A change in a word's spelling so that it matches the words it is connected with. Examples:

גְּדוֹלִים וְרָעִים הָאַחִים   *The brothers are big and bad*

טוֹבוֹת וַחֲכָמוֹת הָאִמּוֹת   *The mothers are good and wise*

apocopation   Shortening of a word; very common in VC Imperfect forms of roots that end in הּ. Example:

Root עָשָׂה *to make, do* (weak verb)   Impf 3ms full form יַעֲשֶׂה   VC Impf 3ms apoc וַיַּעַשׂ

article   An article indicates definiteness. In English, there are two articles, the definite article: *the*, and the indefinite article: *a/an*. In Hebrew, the definite article is the letter הּ vocalized with an *a* vowel or an *e* vowel and eliciting a **dagesh** in the first letter of the word (unless that letter is a guttural or רּ). Example:

הָאִישׁ וְהַמֶּלֶךְ הֶחָכָם   *The man and the wise king*

Hebrew has no indefinite article. Examples:

שָׁפְטָה אִשָּׁה אֶת־יִשְׂרָאֵל   *A woman has judged Israel*

אָכַל מֶלֶךְ עִם עֶבֶד   *A king has eaten with a servant*

שָׁמְרוּ כֹהֲנִים אֶת־הַתּוֹרָה   *Priests have kept the law*

assimilation   When a letter 'disappears' from a word and is represented in the next letter of the word by a **dagesh**. Example:

Root נָתַן *to give* (weak)   *I have given* נָתַתִּי (instead of נָתַנְתִּי)

atnah   An accent, often found around the middle of a verse, and functioning a little like a comma.

ayin **guttural verb**   A verb with a guttural as the middle letter of its root form. Example: שָׁחַט. See verb tables for conjugations.

ayin yod or *ayin vav* **verb**   A verb with יּ or וּ as the middle letter of its root form. Example: קוּם. See verb tables for conjugations.

clause   A sentence, or part of a sentence, that contains a verbal idea. English examples:
I saw that the sun had set in the west. In this example, *that the sun had set* is a clause but *in the west* is not, because it has no verb.

In Hebrew, a clause usually has a verb. However, certain verbless clauses have only an implied verb: the verb *to be*. Example: טוֹב הַמֶּלֶךְ *the king is good*.

cohortative   A way of expressing commands to oneself, or expressing an intention. For example:

אֶזְכְּרָה דְּבָרֶיךָ   *Let me remember your words*

נִכְרְתָה בְּרִית   *Let us make a covenant*

comparative   A form that makes a comparison, in English often by adding the suffix *-er*: *The sun is brighter than the moon.* Comparatives can also be expressed by using *more … than …* : *I am more extrovert than my sister.*

In Hebrew, comparisons are made using the preposition מִן. For example:

| גָּדוֹל סוּס מִן שֶׂה | A horse is bigger than a sheep |
| חָכָם אַתָּה מִדָּנִאֵל | You are wiser than Daniel |

conjugation   All the forms of a verb. In English, for example, the verb *remember* is conjugated:

Present:	I, you, we, they	remember
	he, she, it	remembers
Present participle		remembering
Past		remembered
Past participle		remembered

English Infinitives and Imperatives are the same as the Present.

Hebrew conjugation tables list all the forms of the Perfect and Imperfect, and usually the Imperative, Infinitive and Participle for the Qal and for all the other stems (Nifal, Piel, Pual, Hifil, Hofal and Hitpael) of a verb.

conjunction   A word that connects two other words or phrases. Examples include *and, but, or*. In Hebrew, the sense of *and* and *but* is provided by the particle וֹ, usually vocalized with **sheva**.

Examples in Hebrew:

רַע וְטוֹב	bad and good
בַּת וּבֵן	daughter and son
דָּנִאֵל וּדְבוֹרָה	Daniel and Deborah

consonant   The alphabet we use to write English is made up of 5 vowels (*AEIOU*) and 21 consonants (all the rest of the letters). The Hebrew alphabet is composed entirely of consonants, although two of them are silent.

construct   One way of indicating possession in Hebrew is to use the construct (the other is the use of the preposition לְ). A word can be in *construct relationship* to another word, which involves placing it in front of the word it is in relationship to: סוּס הָאִישׁ *the man's horse*. Some words change their spelling when they are in construct relationship, and they are said to be in *construct state*:

| דָּבָר | a word | דְּבַר אֱלֹהִים | God's word |

Other words do not change spelling when they are in construct relationship:

| מֶלֶךְ | a king | מֶלֶךְ יִשְׂרָאֵל | the king of Israel |

Words in construct relationship never take the definite article in Hebrew. However, when translating into English they must agree in definiteness with the word they are in relationship to:

קוֹל אִשָּׁה   *a voice of a woman*   קוֹל הָאִשָּׁה   *the woman's voice*

Any number of nouns can be placed in a construct chain:

דִּבְרֵי בְּנוֹת נְבִיאֵי בֵּית אֱלֹהִים   *The words of the daughters of the prophets of the house of God*

dagesh   A dot in a letter that signifies any of the following:

doubling of the letter	example: סַבּוֹתִי	Qal Perf 1s of סָבַב
assimilation of a letter	example: יִפֹּל	Nif Impf 3ms of נָפַל
the definite article	example: הַמֶּלֶךְ	

declension   A way of dividing nouns (and adjectives) into categories according to their spelling or the way they change in different contexts. The main declensions in Hebrew are:

Nouns with long-*a* type vowels	Example: דָּבָר	*word*
Nouns with short-*e* type vowels (these are also known as segolate nouns)	Example: מֶלֶךְ	*king*
Nouns with Participle-pattern vowels	Example: שֹׁמֵר	*guard*
Consonant-doubling (**dagesh**) nouns	Example: יָם, plural יַמִּים	*sea/seas*

definiteness   A way of expressing whether something can be identified. If we refer to *a blue house* the house cannot be identified: it could be any one of all the blue houses in the world. But if we refer to *the blue house* we are talking about a specific blue house and we can identify exactly which blue house we mean. In Hebrew, nouns are indefinite unless they take the definite article:

Indefinite: בַּיִת   *a house*   Definite: הַבַּיִת   *the house*

However, proper nouns are definite:

יִשְׂרָאֵל   *Israel*   דָּוִד   *David*

Nouns can also be considered definite if they are in construct relationship to a definite noun.

demonstrative   A word that singles out a particular thing (or things) for attention. In English, demonstratives are *this, these, that, those*. Demonstratives can be used as adjectives or as pronouns.

Without demonstrative	הַבַּיִת	*the house*
With demonstrative	הַבַּיִת הַזֶּה	*this house*
Demonstrative adjective	גָּדוֹל הַבַּיִת הַזֶּה	*this house is big*
Demonstrative pronoun	זֶה הַבַּיִת הַגָּדוֹל	*this is the big house*

direct speech   Speech that is quoted directly, as opposed to indirect speech, which is reported indirectly. Examples:

Direct	וַיֹּאמֶר אָכַלְתִּי אֶת־הַפְּרִי	And he said, 'I have eaten the fruit.'
Indirect	וַיֹּאמֶר כִּי־אָכַל אֶת־הַפְּרִי	And he said that he had eaten the fruit.

Direct speech is often introduced with the Infinitive Construct of the verb אָמַר, which is לֵאמֹר:

וַיַּעַן לֵאמֹר אָכַלְתִּי אֶת־הַפְּרִי	And he answered saying, 'I have eaten the fruit.'

double *ayin* verb   A verb in which the second and third root letters are identical. Example: סָבַב. See verb tables for conjugations.

geminate verb   See **double *ayin*** verb

gender   A division of nouns, and words that qualify nouns, into different kinds. The different kinds of nouns in Hebrew are known as *masculine* and *feminine*. Sometimes this reflects gender that is considered inherent:

masculine	אִישׁ	man
feminine	אִשָּׁה	woman

However, nouns that might not be considered inherently gendered nevertheless are described as masculine or feminine:

masculine	יוֹם	day
feminine	יָד	hand

Some languages have a neuter gender, but Hebrew does not. However, some words in Hebrew are of common gender, which means that they can be either masculine or feminine. Example: שֶׁמֶשׁ *sun*.

gentilic adjective/noun   A word describing a person or people by their place of origin, such as Glaswegian, Scottish, European. Hebrew examples are:

מוֹאָבִי	*Moabite*	מִצְרִי	*Egyptian*

guttural   Any of the letters א, ה, ח or ע. The term *guttural* refers to how they are, or were, pronounced. They have certain properties that separate them from other consonants, except the letter ר, which often behaves like a guttural: they cannot take **dagesh**; they usually take a composite **sheva** instead of a simple **sheva**; they attract *a* vowels; they cause changes in the vowel patterns of weak verbs.

Hifil   One of the Hebrew verb stems. It represents a change to the form of a verb to indicate a causative effect:

Root בוֹא Qal *to come*, Hif *to bring* (i.e. *to cause to come*) (weak verb)

Qal Perf 3ms	בָּא	*he came*
Hifil Perf 3ms	הֵבִיא	*he brought*

Hitpael One of the Hebrew verb stems. It is an intensive form related to the Piel, and it represents a change to the form of the verb to indicate a reflexive effect:

Root קָדַשׁ Qal *to be holy*, Hitp *to consecrate oneself*

| Qal | קָדַשׁ | *he is holy* |
| Hitpael | הִתְקַדֵּשׁ | *he has consecrated himself* |

Hofal One of the Hebrew verb stems. A passive form of the Hifil.

Root בּוֹא Qal *to come*, Hif *to bring* (i.e. *to cause to come*) (weak verb)

Qal Perf 3ms	בָּא	*he came*
Hifil Perf 3ms	הֵבִיא	*he brought* (e.g. a present)
Hofal Perf 3ms	הוּבָא	*he was brought* (e.g. by guards)

hollow verb See *ayin vav* or *ayin yod* **verb**

idiom A form of expression that is characteristic of a language and that does not make literal sense. Examples:

| English | *He has two left feet* (he finds dancing a challenge) |
| Hebrew | גָּדוֹל יהוה מִכָּל־הָאֱלֹהִים *Yhwh is great from all the gods*, meaning *Yhwh is greater than all the gods* |

However, some Hebrew idioms have made their way into English via translations of the Bible. Examples:

| *to pour out one's heart* | שִׁפְכוּ־לְפָנָיו לְבַבְכֶם (Ps 62:9 [Engl. 62:8]) *Pour out your heart before him* |
| *the skin of one's teeth* | וָאֶתְמַלְּטָה בְּעוֹר שִׁנָּי (Job 19:20) *I have escaped by the skin of my teeth* |

imperative A verbal form that indicates the giving of orders or instructions.

Root הָלַךְ *to go* (weak verb)

| Imperfect | תֵּלֵךְ | *you will go* |
| Imperative | לֵךְ | *go!* |

imperfect A verbal form that expresses an idea of incomplete action. Often translated with an English future tense, but can be translated with English past or present tenses. Forms include all persons, genders and numbers. Example:

Root זָכַר *to remember* (strong verb)

יִזְכֹּר	3ms	יִזְכְּרוּ	3mp
תִּזְכֹּר	3fs	תִּזְכֹּרְנָה	3fp
תִּזְכֹּר	2ms	תִּזְכְּרוּ	2mp

תִּזְכְּרִי	2fs	תִּזְכֹּרְנָה	2fp
אֶזְכֹּר	1cs	נִזְכֹּר	1cp

infinitive   A verb form that has no finite parts. In English, infinitives are usually expressed with the preposition *to*: *to go, to sleep, to think*. There are two kinds of infinitive in Hebrew.

The Infinitive Construct is frequently used in the same way as the English infinitive, with the preposition לְ:

לִזְכֹּר   *to remember*   לִפְקֹד   *to visit*

The Infinitive Absolute is frequently used with a finite form of the same verb to indicate emphasis:

בָּרֵךְ אֲבָרֶכְךָ   *I will certainly bless you*

לֹא־מוֹת תְּמֻתוּן   *you certainly will not die*

interjection   A word that conveys emotion without having much grammatical function in the sentence. Examples in English are words like *hurray* and *ouch*. A common example in Hebrew is הִנֵּה *behold*.

interrogative   A word that asks a question. In Hebrew the most common are:

מִי	*Who … ?*	אֵי or אַיֵּ	*Where … ?*
מֶה or מַה	*What … ?*	מָתַי	*When … ?*
לְמֶה or לָמָּה	*Why … ?*	אֵיךְ	*How … ?*

Jussive   A means of giving commands or instructions in the 2nd or 3rd person. Usually, but not always, identical in form to the Imperfect. Also used for prohibitions in the 3rd person. Examples:

יִקְטֹל אוֹתָם	*he will kill them*	Imperfect 3ms
יִקְטֹל אוֹתָם	*let him kill them*	Jussive 3ms
קְטֹל אוֹתָם	*kill them*	Imperative 2ms
אַל תִּקְטֹל אוֹתָם	*do not kill them*	Jussive 2ms + negative particle אַל
לֹא תִקְטֹל אוֹתָם	*you absolutely must not kill them*	Jussive 2ms + negative particle לֹא

lamed alef verb   A verb with א as the final letter of its root form. Example: מָצָא. See verb tables for conjugations.

lamed guttural verb   A verb with a guttural as the final letter of its root form. Example: שָׁלַח. See verb tables for conjugations.

Ketiv   A word in the written text of the Hebrew Bible that is substituted when the text is read aloud. The word read instead is called the Qere.

mappiq   A dot in the letter הּ to indicate that it is to be pronounced as a consonant (roughly similar to the pronunciation of ח). Frequently found in 3fs pronominal suffixes:

לָהּ   *to her*   סוּסָהּ   *her horse*

maqqef   A line like a hyphen that joins two words so that they are pronounced as if they were one word. For example: כָּל־אֶרֶץ יִשְׂרָאֵל *all the land of Israel*.

meteg   An accent that is used to mark occasions where ָ is to be pronounced ā rather than o. In fact ָ is almost always pronounced ā, but in closed unstressed syllables it is generally pronounced as a short-o vowel. Therefore, in syllables where it needs to be pronounced as an a vowel, the **meteg** reminds the reader of the pronunciation. For example:

זָכְרָה   *she has remembered*

Nifal   One of the Hebrew verb stems. Often translated as a passive form of the Qal, but can sometimes be reflexive.

Root פָּקַד Qal *to visit*, Nif *to be visited*

Qal Perf 3ms	פָּקַד	*he has visited*
Nifal Perf 3ms	נִפְקַד	*he has been visited*

noun   The name of a thing, a person or a place. Examples:

בַּיִת   *house*   אַבְרָהָם   *Abraham*   מִצְרַיִם   *Egypt*

number   Forms of a word that indicate how many of something there are. In English we have two possibilities: singular and plural. In Hebrew, there is a third option: dual. Example:

Singular	יָד	*hand*
Plural	יָדוֹת	*hands* (non-human, e.g. the arms of a chair)
Dual	יָדַיִם	*hands* (human)

Hebrew verbs also have singular and plural forms:

Singular	שָׁמַרְתִּי	*I have guarded*
Plural	שָׁמַרְנוּ	*we have guarded*

object   Put simply, the thing that something happens to. The subject of a sentence does something, the verb indicates what is being done, and the object indicates who or what it is being done to. Example:

Sentence: אָהֲבָה מִיכַל דָּוִד   *Michal loved David*

Subject: מִיכַל *Michal*   Verb: אָהֲבָה *loved*   Object: דָּוִד *David*

object marker   A Hebrew particle (אֵת or אֶת־) that identifies the object(s) of a verb. There is no English word that translates it. Example:

צִוָּה יוֹסֵף אֶת־מֹשֶׁה לֶאֱכֹל אֶת־הַלֶּחֶם   *Joseph commanded Moses to eat the bread*

paragogic   An extra letter usually added to the end of a word for various reasons. In Hebrew we commonly find paragogic ה and paragogic ן. Examples:

Usual form	תְּמוּתוּ	*you will die*	(Qal Impf 2mp from מוּת)
With paragogic ן	תְּמֻתוּן	*you will die*	
Usual form	נֵלֵךְ	*we will go*	(Qal Impf 1p from הָלַךְ)
With paragogic ה	נֵלְכָה	*we will go*	

participle   A form of the verb that works like an adjective, adverb or noun. Examples:

הוּא שֹׁפֵט אֶת־עַם הָאָרֶץ	*He was judging the people of the land*
הוּא הַשֹּׁפֵט	*He is the judge*

particle   A word that has a grammatical function but does not change form. An example in English is the word *to* used as part of the infinitive, e.g. *to sing* or *to dance*. Hebrew has numerous particles. Some words that are described as particles may also be described in other ways: for example, the particle גַּם is sometimes known as the conjunction גַּם.

passive   A verb whose subject is having something done to it is said to be in the **passive** voice. See **active** for examples.

patach **furtive**   An *a* vowel (called **patach**) that looks as if it is creeping into a word because it is pronounced before, rather than after, the final consonant (this is more noticeable if the final consonant is ח than if it is ע). Common under the last letter of **lamed** guttural verbs in certain forms. Examples:

Ptc	שֹׁמֵעַ	*hearing*	Inf cstr	שְׂמֹחַ	*to rejoice*

pause   There are usually two places in a verse of biblical Hebrew where the reader is required to pause: at the points indicated by **atnah** and **silluq**. Some words take a longer vowel when they are in pause. However, the meaning does not change. Example:

Usual form	בַּדֶּרֶךְ	*in the path*
Pausal form	בַּדָּרֶךְ	*in the path*

pe alef **verb**   A verb with an א as the first letter of its root form. Example: אָכַל. See verb tables for conjugations.

pe **guttural verb**   A verb with a guttural as the first letter of its root form. Example: עָמַד. See verb tables for conjugations.

pe nun **verb**   A verb with an נ as the first letter of its root form. Example: נָגַשׁ. See verb tables for conjugations.

pe vav **or** *pe yod* **verbs**   A verb with a ו or י as the first letter of its root form. Example: יָשַׁב. See verb tables for conjugations.

perfect A verbal form that expresses an idea of incomplete action. Often translated with an English past tense, but can be translated with English future or present tenses. Forms include all persons, genders and numbers. Example:

Root כָּתַב *to write* (strong verb)

כָּתַב	3ms	כָּתְבוּ	3cp
כָּתְבָה	3fs		
כָּתַבְתָּ	2ms	כְּתַבְתֶּם	2mp
כָּתַבְתְּ	2fs	כְּתַבְתֶּן	2fp
כָּתַבְתִּי	1cs	כָּתַבְנוּ	1cp

Piel One of the Hebrew verb stems. It represents a change to the form of a verb to indicate an intensive effect, or a variety of other effects such as factitive or resultative.

Root שָׁבַר Qal *to break*, Pi *to shatter*

Qal Perf 3ms	שָׁבַר	*it broke*
Pi Perf 3ms	שִׁבֵּר	*it shattered*

pointing Another word for the vowels added to the consonantal Hebrew text. Also known as vocalization.

prefix A letter or letters that are added to the beginning of a word to indicate its meaning. Examples:

Imperfect forms	יִקְטֹל	*he has killed*	prefix יִ
Inseparable prepositions	לַיהוָה	*to Yhwh*	prefix לְ

preposition A word that indicates a relationship between a noun or pronoun and other words in the sentence. Example:

עָמַד הַמַּלְאָךְ תַּחַת הָעֵץ	*The angel stood under the tree*

The word *under* describes where the angel is in relation to the tree.

pronominal suffixes A letter or letters that are added to the end of a word to indicate which person is involved. Each suffix represents a pronoun. A pronominal suffix can be added to a noun to indicate possession, to a verb to indicate its object, or to prepositions to indicate the relationship between the subject and the object, expressed by a pronoun. Even interjections in Hebrew can take pronominal suffixes. Examples:

pronoun A word that stands in place of a noun. In English, for example, we could say: *My sister has visited me; Deborah has visited me; A woman has visited me.* Or we could simply say *She has visited me*, with *she* (pronoun) standing in place of *my sister*, *Deborah* or *the woman*. The word *me* is also a pronoun.

noun	סוּסוֹ	*his horse*
verb	אֲהַבְתִּךָ	*I love you*

| preposition | לָהֶם | to them |
| interjection | הִנְנִי | (Literally *Behold me*), *here I am* |

proper noun   The name of a person or place. Examples:

| גִּדְעוֹן | Gideon | בֵּית לֶחֶם | Bethlehem |

Pual   One of the Hebrew verb stems. A passive form of the Piel.

Root שָׁבַר Qal *to break*, Piel *to shatter*

Qal Perf 3ms	שָׁבַר	it broke
Piel Perf 3ms	שִׁבֵּר	it shattered
Pual Perf 3ms	שֻׁבַּר	it was shattered

Qal   One of the Hebrew verb stems. This stem is known as the 'light' form because it is the basic form of the verb, without the additions of the other stems (such as the נ prefix of the Nifal, the **dagesh** in the middle root letter of the Piel, or the ה prefix of the Hifil).

Qere   A word in the margins beside the text of the Hebrew Bible. It is intended to be read aloud as a substitute for one of the written words, and its pointing is given within the word it replaces. See also **Ketiv**. Some Ketiv words are not given marginal Qere readings; instead the vowels of the Qere are simply written into the Ketiv without an accompanying note. These words are always read as Qere and are called Qere perpetuum. Example: the name of God is read **a-dō-NĪ** and is written with the vowels of אֲדֹנָי, thus: יְהֹוָה.

reduplicated verbs   See **double *ayin*** verbs.

reflexive   A means of referring to oneself. In English, reflexive ideas are frequently expressed with words like *myself* or *yourselves*. Example: *He opened the oven and burned himself*. In Hebrew, the reflexive is generally expressed by the Hitpael stem although sometimes the Nifal has a reflexive sense.

relative pronoun   A word that expresses a relationship between a clause and its context in the sentence. In English we distinguish between *who*, *which* and *that*. In Hebrew they are all represented by אֲשֶׁר. Example:

| הַמָּקוֹם אֲשֶׁר אַתָּה עוֹמֵד עָלָיו אַדְמַת־קֹדֶשׁ הוּא | *The place that you are standing on is holy ground* |

root   The word that forms the basis of a Hebrew verb. Most roots have three letters, though roots such as קוּם are sometimes described as biliteral (having two letters). In this case, and others like it, the letter ו is considered to be a vowel rather than a consonant.

silluq   An accent that is identical in form to **meteg** but has an entirely different function. It marks the pause at the end of a verse, functioning a little like a full stop.

stem   One of the building blocks of Hebrew verbs. Each stem has distinctive features and each stem has a distinctive range of meanings. The seven principal stems are: Qal, Nifal, Piel, Pual, Hitpael, Hifil and Hofal. Verbs can be conjugated within each of the stems. However, not all verbs are found in all stems in biblical Hebrew. There are additional stems that are found less frequently.

stress   The point where a word is emphasized. Examples:

English	the *hap* in *happy*
Hebrew	the בֵּר in דָּבֵר

strong verb   A verb that follows the קָטַל pattern and has no vowels (י or ו), no gutturals, and no ן in its root. Neither should it begin with נ or be reduplicated.

subject   The part of a sentence that indicates who or what is doing something. In the following sentence, *the king* (הַמֶּלֶךְ) is the subject: נָתַן הַמֶּלֶךְ לִי סוּסוֹ *The king gave his horse to me.*

suffix   A letter or letters that are added to the end of a word to indicate its meaning. Examples:

Perfect forms	קָטַלְתִּי	*I have killed*	suffix תִּי
Pronominal suffixes	יְהַלְלָהּ	*he will praise her*	suffix הָ

superlative   A word used to indicate that something transcends others of its type. In English, this is done by adding the ending -*est*; examples: *tallest*, *fastest*. It can also be done by using the term *the most*: *She is the most talkative child in her class.* In Hebrew, superlatives can be expressed in a number of ways. One of the most common is by means of the construct relationship. Examples:

קְטֹן בָּנָיו	*the youngest of his sons*
קֹדֶשׁ הַקֳּדָשִׁים	*the holiest place* (literally *the holy of holies*)

syllable   One of the sounds in a word. In the word מַאֲכֶלֶת there are four syllables: מַ and אֲ and כֶ and לֶת.

Vav Consecutive   The means by which Hebrew verbs use the conjunction ו to link a series of verbs. In English, this often requires changing the translating tense from future to past (for VC Imperfect) or from past to future (for VC Perfect). Example:

יִשְׁמֹר	*He will guard*	וַיִּשְׁמֹר	*And he guarded*

verb   A word that denotes some kind of activity.

vocalization   See **pointing**.

vowel   In English, the letters *AEIO* and *U* (and sometimes *Y*) represent vowel sounds. However, the Hebrew alphabet is made up entirely of consonants. Vowel sounds are represented by dots and dashes underneath the consonants, although the long-*o* vowel is written above the consonant.

weak verb   A verb that contains a letter that cannot take **dagesh** (the gutturals and ן), or is prone to disappearing at the beginning of a word (נ), or otherwise causes the verb to depart from the קָטַל strong-verb pattern, is known as a weak verb.

Lexicon

Abbreviations

1	first person
2	second person
3	third person
abs	absolute
adj	adjective
adv	adverb
cohort	Cohortative
conj	conjunction
cstr	construct
f	feminine
gent	gentilic
Hif	Hifil
Hitp	Hitpael
Hof	Hofal
Impf	Imperfect
Impv	Imperative
Inf	Infinitive
m	masculine
Nif	Nifal
p	plural
parag	paragogic (extra)
pass	passive
Perf	Perfect
Pi	Piel
pr noun	proper noun
prep	preposition
Ptc	Participle
s	singular
suff	suffix
VC	Vav Consecutive

Entry	Related words	Form	Meaning/Look up Hebrew word
אָב		noun ms	*father*
	אָבוֹת	noun mp	*fathers*
	אָבוֹת	noun mp cstr	*fathers of*
	אָבִיו	noun ms + suff 3ms	*his father*
	אַבְרָהָם	pr noun	*Abraham*
אָבֹאָה		Qal Impf 1s + parag ה	בּוֹא
אָבַד		verb	*to be lost, to wander, to perish; Pi to destroy*
אִבַּדְתָּ		Pi Perf 2ms	אָבַד
אֲבוֹת		noun mp cstr	אָב
אָבוֹת		noun mp	אָב
אֶבְטַח		Qal Impf 1s	בָּטַח
אָבִי		noun ms + suff 1s	אָב
אֲבִיאֲךָ		Hif Impf 1s + suff 2ms	בּוֹא
אָבִיו		noun ms + suff 3ms	אָב
אֶבֶן		noun m	*stone*
אַבְרָהָם		pr noun	אָב
אֲבָרֶכְךָ		Pi Impf 1s + suff 2ms	בָּרַךְ
אֶגְלֶה		Qal Impf 1s	גָּלָה
אֶגַּשׁ		Qal Impf 1s	נָגַשׁ
אֲדָמָה		noun fs	*earth, land*
אַדְמַת		noun fs cstr	אֲדָמָה
אָדוֹן		noun ms	*lord*
אֲדֹנָי		noun ms	דוֹן
אֲדֹנָי		noun ms	אָדוֹן
אֲדֹנִים		noun mp	דוֹן
אֵדַע		Qal Impf 1s	יָדַע
אָהַב		verb	*to love*
	אַהֲבָה	noun fs	*love*
אַהֲבָה		noun fs	אָהַב
אָהַבְתָּ		Qal Perf 2ms	אָהַב
אוֹדֶה		Hif Impf 1s	יָדָה

אוֹדְךָ		Hif Impf 1s + suff 2mp	יָדָה
אוֹיְבַי		noun mp + suff 1s	אָיַב
אוֹר		noun m	*light*
אָז		adv	*then, therefore*
אֶזְכֹּר		Qal Impf 1s	זָכַר
אֶזְכְּרָה		cohort 1p	זָכַר
אֲזַמְּרָה		Pi Impf 1s + parag ה	זָמַר
אֹזֶן		noun fs	*ear*
	אָזְנַיִם	noun f dual	*ears*
אָזְנַיִם		noun f dual	אֹזֶן
אַח		noun ms	*brother*
	אֲחִי	noun ms cstr	*brother of*
	אֲחֵי	noun mp cstr	*brothers of*
	אַחִים	noun mp	*brothers*
	אָחֹת	noun fs	*sister*
	אֲחָיוֹת	noun fp	*sisters*
אֶחָד		numeral	*one*
אַחַד		numeral cstr	*one of*
אָחַז		verb	*to seize, catch; Nif to be caught*
אֲחִי		noun ms cstr	אַח
אֲחֵי		noun mp cstr	אַח
אֲחָיוֹת		noun fp	אַח
אָחִיךָ		noun ms + suff 2ms	אַח
אַחִים		noun mp	אַח
אַחַר		prep	אָחַר
אָחַר		verb	*to stay; Pi to linger*
	אָחוֹר	noun ms (also adv)	*back part, west (adv: back)*
	אַחַר	prep	*after*
	אַחֲרֵי	prep	*after*
	אַחֲרָיו	prep + suff 3ms	*after him (or it)*
אַחֲרֵי		prep	אָחַר
אַחֲרַי		prep + suff 1s	אָחַר

אַחֲרֶיהָ		prep + suff 3fs	אָחַר
אַחֲרֵיהֶם		prep + suff 3mp	אָחַר
אַחֲרֵיהֶן		prep + suff 3fp	אָחַר
אַחֲרָיו		prep + suff 3ms	אָחַר
אַחֲרֶיךָ		prep + suff 2ms	אָחַר
אַחֲרַיִךְ		prep + suff 2fs	אָחַר
אַחֲרֵיכֶם		prep + suff 2mp	אָחַר
אַחֲרֵיכֶן		prep + suff 2fp	אָחַר
אַחֲרֵינוּ		prep + suff 1p	אָחַר
אַחַת		noun fs	אָח
אֵי		interrog pronoun	*where … ?*
	אֵי	interrog pronoun	*where … ?*
	אֵיךְ	interrog pronoun	*how … ?*
אָיַב		verb	*to hate, to be an enemy*
	אֹיֵב	noun ms	*enemy*
	אֹיְבִים	noun mp	*enemies*
אֹיֵב		noun ms	אָיַב
אֹיְבִי		noun ms + suff 1s	אָיַב
אֹיְבֵי		noun mp cstr	אָיַב
אֹיְבָיו		noun ms + suff 3ms	אָיַב
אֹיְבִים		noun mp	אָיַב
אַיֵּה		interrog pronoun	*where … ?*
אֵיךְ		interrog pronoun	אֵי
אֵיכְדֵין		adv (Aramaic)	*how?*
אִיכֵן		adv (Syriac)	*how?*
אַיִל		noun ms	*ram*
אֵין		adv cstr	*there is not, there are not;* abs is אַיִן
אִישׁ		noun ms	*man*
אַךְ		adv	*only, but*
אָכוֹל		Qal Inf abs	אָכַל
אֱכֹל		Qal Inf cstr	אָכַל
אֱכֹל		Qal Impv ms	אָכַל

אָכַל		verb	to eat
	אָכְלָה	noun fs	food
	מַאֲכֶלֶת	noun fs	knife
אֹכֵל		Qal Ptc	אָכַל
אֹכַל		Qal Impf 1s	אָכַל
אָכְלָה		Qal Perf 3fs	אָכַל
אָכְלָה		noun fs	אָכַל
אָכְלוּ		Qal Perf 3p	אָכַל
אֲכַלְכֶם		Qal Perf 2mp	אָכַל
אֲכַלְנוּ		Qal Perf 1p	אָכַל
אָכַלְתְּ		Qal Perf 2fs	אָכַל
אָכַלְתָּ		Qal Perf 2ms	אָכַל
אָכַלְתִּי		Qal Perf 1s	אָכַל
אֲכַלְתֶּם		Qal Perf 2mp	אָכַל
אֲכַלְתֶּן		Qal Perf 2fp	אָכַל
אֶכְתֹּב		Qal Impf 1s	כָּתַב
אֶכְתְּבָה		cohort 1p	כָּתַב
אֵל		noun ms	God, god
	אֱלֹהִים	noun ms, mp	God, gods
	אֱלֹהֵי	pr noun cstr	God of
	כֵּאלֹהִים	prep כְּ + noun ms, mp	like God
אֶל		prep	to
	אֵלָיו	prep + suff 3ms	to him, to it
אַל		negative particle	not
אֵלֶּה		pronoun mp and fp	these
אֱלֹהֵי		pr noun cstr	אֵל
אֱלֹהִים		pr noun; noun ms or mp	אֵל
אֱלֹהֵינוּ		noun m + suff 1p	אֱלֹהִים
אֱלוֹהַּ		noun m	אֱלֹהִים
אֵלַי		prep + suff 1s	אֶל
אֵלֶיהָ		prep + suff 3fs	אֶל
אֲלֵיהֶם		prep + suff 3mp	אֶל
אֲלֵיהֶן		prep + suff 3fp	אֶל

אֵלָיו		prep + suff 3ms	אֶל
אֵלָיו		prep + suff 3ms	אֶל
אֵלֶיךָ		prep + suff 2ms	אֶל
אֵלַיִךְ		prep + suff 2fs	אֶל
אֲלֵיכֶם		prep + suff 2mp	אֶל
אֲלֵיכֶן		prep + suff 2fp	אֶל
אֵלֵינוּ		prep + suff 1p	אֶל
אֵלֵךְ		Qal Impf 1s	הָלַךְ
אֵם		noun fs	mother
	אִמּוֹת	noun fp	mothers
	אִמּוֹ	noun fs + suff 3ms	his mother
אָמָה		noun fs	handmaid
אִמּוֹ		noun fs + suff 3ms	אֵם
אִמּוֹת		noun fp	אֵם
אִמִּי		noun fs + suff 1s	אֵם
אָמַן		verb	אָמַן
אֶמְצָא		Qal Impf 1s	מָצָא
אָמַר		verb	to say
	וַיֹּאמֶר	Qal VC Impf 3ms	and he said
	וַיֹּאמְרוּ	Qal VC Impf 3mp	and they said
אֹמַר		Qal Impf 1s	אָמַר
אָמְרָה		Qal Perf 3fs	אָמַר
אָמַרְתָּ		Qal Perf 3fs	אָמַר
אָמַרְתָּ		Qal Perf 2ms	אָמַר
אֲמַרְתֶּן		Qal Perf 2fp	אָמַר
אֶמְשֹׁל		Qal Impf 1s	מָשַׁל
אֲנַחְנוּ		pronoun 1p	we
אֲנִי		pronoun 1s	I
אָנֹכִי		pronoun 1s	I
אָנַף		verb	to be angry
	אַף	noun ms	nose, anger
אָנַפְתָּ		Qal Perf 2ms	אָנַף
אָנַשׁ		verb	to be mortal

	אֲנָשִׁים	noun mp	men	
	אַנְשֵׁי	noun mp cstr	men of	
	אִשָּׁה	noun fs	woman	
	אֵשֶׁת	noun fs cstr	woman of, wife of	
	נָשִׁים	noun fp	women	
	נְשֵׁי	noun fp cstr	women of	
	אִשְׁתּוֹ	noun fs + suff 3ms	his wife	
אֲנְשֵׁי		noun mp cstr		אֱנָשׁ
אֲנָשִׁים		noun mp		אֱנָשׁ
אָסֹב		Qal Impf 1s		סָבַב
אֲסַפְּרָה		Pi Impf 1s		סָפַר
אֶעֱבֹר		Qal Impf 1s		עָבַר
אֶעֶלְצָה		Qal Impf 1s + parag ה		עָלַץ
אֶעֱמֹד		Qal Impf 1s		עָמַד
אַף		conj	also, moreover, indeed; אַף כִּי is it so that … ?	
אַף		noun ms		אָנַף
אֶפְחָד		Qal Impf 1s		פָּחַד
אַפְּךָ		noun ms + suff 2ms		אָנַף
אֶפֹּל		Qal Impf 1s		נָפַל
אֲפַקֵּד		Pi Impf 1s		פָּקַד
אֶפְקֹד		Qal Impf 1s		פָּקַד
אֶפְקְדָה		cohort 1p		פָּקַד
אַפְקִיד		Hif Impf 1s		פָּקַד
אַצִּילְךָ		Hif Impf 1s + suff 2ms		נָצַל
אָקוּם		Qal Impf 1s		קוּם
אֶקְטֹל		Qal Impf 1s		קָטַל
אֶקָּטֵל		Nif Impf 1s		קָטַל
אֶרְאָה		Qal Impf 1s		רָאָה
אָרַב		verb		אָרַב
אַרְבַּע		numeral f	four	
אֲרֵי		conj (Aramaic)	because, that	
אֲרִי		noun m	lion	

אֶרֶץ		noun fs	*land*
	אֲרָצוֹת	noun fp	*lands*
	אַרְצוֹת	noun fp cstr	*lands of*
אֲרָצוֹת		noun fp	אֶרֶץ
אַרְצוֹת		noun fp cstr	אֶרֶץ
אֵשׁ		noun ms and fs	*fire*
אֵשֵׁב		Qal Impf 1s	יָשַׁב
אֵשֵׁב		Qal Impf 1s	יָשַׁב
אִשָּׁה		noun fs	אָנַשׁ
אָשׁוּב		Qal Impf 1s	שׁוּב
אֶשְׁחַט		Qal Impf 1s	שָׁחַט
אֲשִׂימֶנּוּ		Qal Impf 1s	שִׂים
אֶשְׁלַח		Qal Impf 1s	שָׁלַח
אֶשְׂמְחָה		Qal Impf 1s + parag ה	שָׂמַח
אֶשְׁמֹר		Qal Impf 1s	שָׁמַר
אֶשְׁפֹּט		Qal Impf 1s	שָׁפַט
אֲשֶׁר		relative pronoun	*that, which, who*
	כַּאֲשֶׁר	prep כְּ + pronoun	*as, when*
אֶשֶׁר		noun ms	*happiness*
אַשְׁרֵי		noun mp cstr	אֶשֶׁר
אֵשֶׁת		noun fs cstr	אָנַשׁ
אִשְׁתּוֹ		noun fs + suff 3ms	אָנַשׁ
אִשְׁתּוֹ		noun fs + suff 3fs	אָנַשׁ
אַתְּ		pronoun 2fs	*you*
אֵת (1)		particle	*object marker (no English word translates it)*
	אֹתוֹ	pronoun 3ms	*him*
	אֹתָם	pronoun 3mp	*them*
אֵת (2)		prep	*with*
	אִתּוֹ	prep + suff 3ms	*with him (or it)*
	אִתָּם	prep + suff 3mp	*with them*
אִתָּהּ		prep + suff 3fs	אֵת (2)
אַתָּה		pronoun 2ms	*you*

אֹתָהּ		pronoun 3fs	אֵת (1)
אִתּוֹ		prep + suff 3ms	אֵת (2)
אֹתוֹ		pronoun 3ms	אֵת (1)
אִתִּי		prep + suff 1s	אֵת (2)
אֹתִי		pronoun 1s	אֵת (1)
אִתְּךָ		prep + suff 2ms	אֵת (2)
אִתָּךְ		prep + suff 2fs	אֵת (2)
אֹתְךָ		pronoun 2ms	אֵת (1)
אֹתָךְ		pronoun 2fs	אֵת (1)
אִתְּכֶם		prep + suff 2mp	אֵת (2)
אֶתְכֶם		pronoun 2mp	אֵת (1)
אִתְּכֶן		prep + suff 2fp	אֵת (2)
אֶתְכֶן		pronoun 2fp	אֵת (1)
אִתָּם		prep + suff 3mp	אֵת (2)
אַתֶּם		pronoun 2mp	*you*
אֹתָם		pronoun 3mp	אֵת (1)
אִתָּן		prep + suff 3fp	אֵת (2)
אֶתֵּן		Qal Impf 1s	נָתַן
אַתֵּן		pronoun 2fp	*you*
אֹתָן		pronoun 3fp	אֵת (1)
אִתָּנוּ		prep + suff 1p	אֵת (2)
אֹתָנוּ		pronoun 1p	אֵת (1)
אֶתְקַדֵּשׁ		Hitp Impf 1s	קָדַשׁ
בְּ		prep	*in, with*
	בּוֹ	prep + suff 3ms	*in/with him (or it)*
בָּא		Qal Perf 3ms	בּוֹא
בֹּאוּ		Qal Impv mp	בּוֹא
בָּאַר		verb	Pi *to engrave*
	בְּאֵר	noun fs	*well*
	בְּאֵר שֶׁבַע	pr noun	*Beersheba*
בְּאֵר שֶׁבַע		pr noun	*Beersheba*
בָּאָרֶץ		prep בְּ + noun fs	אֶרֶץ
בְּאֶרֶץ		prep בְּ + noun fs cstr	אֶרֶץ

בְּאַרְצִי		prep בְּ + noun fs + suff 1s	אֶרֶץ
בַּבֹּקֶר		prep בְּ + noun ms	בֹּקֶר
בַּגָּן		prep בְּ + noun ms	גַּן
בַּדֶּרֶךְ		prep בְּ + noun ms	דֶּרֶךְ
בְּדַרְכֵי		noun mp cstr	דֶּרֶךְ
בָּהּ		prep + suff 3fs	בְּ
בְּהִוָּלֵד		prep בְּ + Nif Inf cstr	יָלַד
בָּהֶם		prep + suff 3mp	בְּ
בָּהֶן		prep + suff 3fp	בְּ
בָּהָר		prep בְּ + noun ms	הַר
בּוֹ		prep + suff 3ms	בְּ
בּוֹא		verb	Qal *to come*; Hif *to bring*; Hof *to be brought*
בּוֹאָנָה		Qal Inf abs + suff 3fp	בּוֹא
בְּזָכְרֵנוּ		prep בְּ + Qal Inf Cstr	זָכַר
בְּזַרְעֶךָ		prep בְּ + noun ms + suff 2ms	זֶרַע
בְּחָכְמָה		prep בְּ + noun fs	חָכַם
בָּחַן		verb	*to try, test*
בָּטַח		verb	*to cling to, trust, rely on*
בֶּטֶן		noun fs	*belly, womb*
בִּי		prep + suff 1s	בְּ
בְּיָדוֹ		prep בְּ + noun fs + suff 3ms	יָד
בִּיהוּדָה		prep בְּ + pr noun	יָדָה
בַּיּוֹם		prep בְּ + noun ms	יוֹם
בִּימֵי		prep בְּ + noun mp cstr	יוֹם
בִּין		verb	*to discern, distinguish*
	בֵּין	prep	*between*
	בֵּינוֹ	prep + suff 3ms	*between him* (or it)
בֵּין		prep	בִּין
בִּינָהּ		prep + suff 3fs	בִּין
בֵּינוֹ		prep + suff 3ms	בִּין
בֵּינִי		prep + suff 1s	בִּין
בֵּינֵיהֶם		prep + suff 3mp	בִּין

בֵּינֵיהֶן		prep + suff 3fp	בֵּין
בֵּינֵיכֶם		prep + suff 2mp	בֵּין
בֵּינֵיכֶן		prep + suff 2fp	בֵּין
בֵּינֵינוּ		prep + suff 1p	בֵּין
בֵּינְךָ		prep + suff 2ms	בֵּין
בֵּינֵךְ		prep + suff 2fs	בֵּין
בְּיִצְחָק		prep בְּ + pr noun	צָחַק
בְּיִשְׂרָאֵל		prep בְּ + pr noun	שָׂרָה
בֵּית		noun ms cstr	בָּנָה
בֵּית		noun ms	בָּנָה
בֵּית לֶחֶם		pr noun	בָּנָה
בְּךָ		prep + suff 2ms	בְּ
בָּךְ		prep + suff 2fs	בְּ
בָּכָה		verb	to weep, lament
בָּכֶם		prep + suff 2mp	בְּ
בָּכֶן		prep + suff 2fp	בְּ
בָּלָה		verb	to swallow
בַּמִּדְבָּר		prep בְּ + noun ms	דָּבַר
בְּמוֹת		prep בְּ + noun ms cstr	מוּת
בְּמֵישָׁרִים		prep בְּ + noun mp (also an adverb)	יָשָׁר
בִּמְעֵי		prep בְּ + noun ms cstr	מֵעֶה
בֵּן		noun ms	בָּנָה
בֵּן		noun ms cstr	בָּנָה
בִּנְאוֹת		prep בְּ + noun fp	נָאָה
בָּנָה		verb	to build
	בֵּית	noun ms cstr	house of
	בַּיִת	noun ms	house
	בֵּית לֶחֶם	pr noun	Bethlehem
	בֵּן	noun ms	son
	בֶּן	noun ms cstr	son of
	בְּנוֹ	noun ms + suff 3ms	his son
	בָּנִים	noun mp	sons

		בַּת	noun fs	*daughter*
		בָּתִּים	noun mp	*houses*
בְּנוֹ			noun ms + suff 3ms	בָּנָה
בָּנוּ			prep + suff 1p	בְּ
בְּנוֹת			noun fp cstr	בָּנָה
בָּנוֹת			noun fp	בָּנָה
בְּנִי			noun ms + suff 1s	בָּנָה
בְּנֵי			noun mp cstr	בָּנָה
בָּנָיו			noun mp + suff 3ms	בָּנָה
בָּנִים			noun mp	בָּנָה
בְּנִינְוֵה			prep בְּ + pr noun	נִינְוֵה
בָּנֶךָ			noun ms + suff 2ms (in pause for בִּנְךָ)	בָּנָה
בִּנְךָ			noun ms + suff 2ms	בָּנָה
בַּסְּבַךְ			prep בְּ + noun ms	סְבַךְ
בַּסָּךְ			prep בְּ + noun ms	סָךְ
בְּסִפְרַיִךְ			prep בְּ + noun ms + suff 2fs	סֵפֶר
בְּעֵינֶיךָ			prep בְּ + noun mp + suff 2ms	עַיִן
בָּעִיר			prep בְּ + noun fs	עִיר
בְּקוֹל			prep בְּ + noun ms	קוֹל
בְּקֹלָהּ			prep בְּ + noun ms + suff 3fs	קוֹל
בְּקֹלִי			prep בְּ + noun ms + suff 1s	קוֹל
בָּקַע			verb	Pi *to divide, split*
בָּקַר			verb	Pi *to search, observe*
		בֹּקֶר	noun ms	*morning*
		בָּקְרִי	noun ms + suff 1s	*my morning*
		בָּקְרֵי	noun mp cstr	*mornings of*
		בְּקָרִים	noun mp	*mornings*
בָּקָר			noun ms	בָּקָר
בְּקָרִי			noun ms + suff 1s	בָּקָר
בְּקָרֵי			noun mp cstr	בָּקָר
בְּקָרִים			noun mp	בָּקָר
בְּקַרְנָיו			prep בְּ + noun fs + suff 3ms	קֶרֶן

בַּר		noun m (Aramaic; equiv. of Hebrew בֵּן)	son
בָּרָא		verb	to create, form, make
בְּרֵאשִׁית		prep בְּ + noun fs	רֹאשׁ
בָּרָאתָ		Qal Perf 2ms	בָּרָא
בָּרָה		verb	to cut
	בְּרִית	noun fs	covenant
בְּרִית		noun fs	בָּרָה
בְּרִיתִי		noun m + suff 1s	בָּרָה
בְּרִיתְכֶם		noun m + suff 2mp	בְּרִית
בֶּרֶךְ		noun ms	בָּרַךְ
בָּרֵךְ		Pi Inf abs	בָּרַךְ
בָּרַךְ		verb	to kneel; Pi to bless, give thanks
	בֶּרֶךְ	noun fs	knee
	בְּרָכָה	noun fs	blessing
בְּרָכָה		noun fs	בָּרַךְ
בְּרָכוֹת		noun fp	בָּרַךְ
בִּרְכַּיִם		noun f dual	בָּרַךְ
בֵּרַכְנוּכֶם		Pi Perf 1p + suff 2mp	בָּרַךְ
בְּרִנְנָה		prep בְּ + noun fs	רְנָנָה
בְּשָׂדֶה		prep בְּ + noun ms	שָׂדֶה
בִּשְׂדֵי		prep בְּ + noun mp cstr	שָׂדֶה
בְּשׁוּב		prep בְּ + Qal Inf cstr	שׁוּב
בְּשִׂמְחָה		prep בְּ + noun fs	שִׂמְחָה
בַּת		noun fs	בָּנָה
בַּת		noun fs	בָּנָה
בִּתּוֹ		noun fs + suff 3ms	בַּת
בְּתוֹךְ		prep בְּ + noun ms	in the middle
בָּתֵּי		noun mp cstr	בָּנָה
בָּתִּים		noun mp	בָּנָה
גְּאוּלִים		Qal Ptc mp	גָּאַל
גָּאַל		verb	to redeem
	גּוֹאֵל	noun ms	redeemer

גֹּאֲלִי		noun m + suff 1s	גָּאַל
גִּבּוֹר		adj ms	*strong, mighty*
גָּבַר		verb	*to be strong*
	גִּבֹּר	adj ms	*strong*
גִּבֹּר		adj ms	*strong, mighty*
גֶּבֶר		noun m	*man*
גָּדוֹל		adj ms	גָּדַל
גָּדַל		verb	*to be great, grow*
	גָּדוֹל	adj ms	*great, large*
גָּדַע		verb	*to cut off*
גִּדְעוֹן		pr noun	*Gideon*
גּוֹאֵל		noun ms	גָּאַל
גּוֹי		noun ms	*nation*
	גּוֹיִם	noun mp	*nations*
גּוֹיֵי		noun mp cstr	גּוֹי
גּוּר		verb	*to live (temporarily)*
גְּלֵה		Qal Impv ms	גָּלָה
גָּלָה		verb	*to uncover, reveal; Pi to uncover, reveal*
גָּלֹה		Qal Inf abs	גָּלָה
גֹּלֶה		Qal Ptc	גָּלָה
גָּלוּ		Qal Perf 3mp	גָּלָה
גְּלוֹת		Qal Inf cstr	גָּלָה
גָּלִינוּ		Qal Perf 1p	גָּלָה
גָּלִית		Qal Perf 2fs	גָּלָה
גָּלִיתָ		Qal Perf 2ms	גָּלָה
גָּלִיתִי		Qal Perf 1s	גָּלָה
גְּלִיתֶם		Qal Perf 2mp	גָּלָה
גְּלִיתֶן		Qal Perf 2fp	גָּלָה
גָּלְתָה		Qal Perf 3fs	גָּלָה
גַּם		conj, adv	*also, even*
גָּמַל		verb	*to wean*
גָּמָל		noun m	*camel*

גַּן		noun ms and fs	גָּנַן
גָּנַב		verb	to steal
גָּנַן		verb	to protect
	גַּן	noun ms and fs	garden
גָּעַר		verb	to rebuke
גָּעַר		Qal Perf 2ms	גָּעַר
גָּרָל		adj ms	uncertain meaning
גָּרֵשׁ		Pi Impv ms	גָּרַשׁ
גָּרַשׁ		verb	to drive away, expel
גַּשׁ		Qal Impv ms	נָגַשׁ
גְּשָׁה		Qal Impv ms	נָגַשׁ
גֶּשֶׁת		Qal Inf cstr	נָגַשׁ
ד		relative particle (Aramaic)	who, which
דֹּב		noun m	bear
דְּבַר		noun ms cstr	דָּבָר
דִּבֶּר		Pi Perf 3ms	דָּבַר
דָּבַר		verb	Pi to speak, promise
	דְּבַר	noun ms cstr	word of
	דָּבָר	noun ms	word, thing
	דְּבָרִים	noun mp	words
	מִדְבָּר	noun ms	desert
דְּבָר		noun ms	דָּבָר
דְּבָרִי		noun ms + suff 1s	דָּבָר
דְּבָרֵי		noun mp cstr	דָּבָר
דְּבָרֶיךָ		noun mp + suff 2ms	דָּבָר
דִּבְרֵיכֶם		noun mp + suff 2mp	דָּבָר
דְּבָרִים		noun mp	דָּבָר
דָּג		noun m	fish
דָּגָן		noun m	corn, grain
דּוֹד		noun ms	beloved
דָּוִד		pr noun	David
דּוֹדִי		noun m + suff 1s	דּוֹד
דּוּן		verb	to govern, judge

	דִּין	noun ms	*judgement, cause*	
	דָּנִאֵל	pr noun	*Daniel*	
	מִדְיָן	pr noun	*Midian*	
דִּין		noun ms		דּוּן
דִּינִי		noun ms + suff 1s		דּוּן
דֶּלֶת		noun fs	*door*	
דַּלְתוֹת		noun fp		דֶּלֶת
דָּנִאֵל		pr noun		דּוּן
דַּעַת		Qal Inf cstr		יָדַע
דַּעַת		noun fs		יָדַע
דָּרַךְ		verb	*to tread*	
	דֶּרֶךְ	noun ms	*way, path*	
דֶּשֶׁא		noun m	*sprout, grass*	
הֶבֶל		noun m	*vanity*	
הֲבָלִים		noun mp		הֶבֶל
הִגִּיד		Hif Perf 3ms		נָגַד
הִגָּמֵל		Nif Inf cstr		גָּמַל
הָגָר		pr noun	*Hagar*	
הוּא		pronoun 3ms	*he, that*	
	הוּא	pronoun 3fs	*she, that*	
	הִיא	pronoun 3fs	*she, that*	
הוֹשַׁעְתָּנוּ		Hif Perf 2ms + suff 1p		יָשַׁע
הַחֲזִיקִי		Hif Impv fs		חָזַק
הִיא		pronoun 3fs		הוּא
הָיָה		verb	*to be*	
	וַיְהִי	Qal VC Impf 3ms	*and it was*	
הֱיִיתֶם		Qal Perf 2mp		הָיָה
הֵיכָל		noun m	*temple, palace*	
הֵינִיקָה		Hif Perf 3fs		יָנַק
הָלוֹךְ		Qal Inf abs		הָלַךְ
הָלַךְ		verb	*Qal to go, walk; Pi to go, walk*	
	יֵלֵךְ	Qal Impf 3ms		

	לֵךְ	Qal Impv ms	
הָלְכָה		Qal Perf 3fs	הָלַךְ
הָלְכוּ		Qal Perf 3p	הָלַךְ
הָלַכְנוּ		Qal Perf 1p	הָלַךְ
הָלַכְתְּ		Qal Perf 2fs	הָלַךְ
הָלַכְתָּ		Qal Perf 2ms	הָלַךְ
הָלַכְתִּי		Qal Perf 1s	הָלַךְ
הֲלַכְתֶּם		Qal Perf 2mp	הָלַךְ
הֲלַכְתֶּן		Qal Perf 2fp	הָלַךְ
הָלַל		verb	Pi *to praise*
הֵם		pronoun 3mp	*they, those*
הֵמָּה		pronoun 3mp	*they, those*
הֵן		interj	*behold*
	הִנֵּה	interj	*behold*
	הִנֵּנִי	interj הִנֵּה + suff 1s	*here I am*
הֵנָּה		interj	הֵן
הֵנָּה		pronoun 3fs	*they*
הַנּוֹלַד		Nif Perf 3ms	יָלַד
הִנְנִי		interj הִנֵּה + suff 1s	הֵן
הִנְנִי		interj + suff 1s	הֵן
הַעֲלֵהוּ		Hif Impv ms + suff 3ms	עָלָה
הַפְקֵד		Hif Impv ms	פָּקַד
הַפְקֵד		Hif Inf abs	פָּקַד
הִפְקַדְנוּ		Hif Perf 1p	פָּקַד
הִפְקַדְתָּ		Hif Perf 2ms	פָּקַד
הִפְקַדְתִּי		Hif Perf 1s	פָּקַד
הִפְקַדְתֶּם		Hif Perf 2mp	פָּקַד
הִפְקַדְתֶּן		Hif Perf 2fp	פָּקַד
הִפְקִיד		Hif Perf 3ms	פָּקַד
הַפְקִיד		Hif Inf cstr	פָּקַד
הִפְקִידָה		Hif Perf 3fs	פָּקַד
הִפְקִידוּ		Hif Perf 3fp	פָּקַד
הִפְקִידְתְּ		Hif Perf 2fs	פָּקַד

הִקְטִיל		Hif Perf 3ms	קָטַל
הַקְטִיל		Hif Inf cstr	קָטַל
הַקְטֵל		Hif Impv 2ms	קָטַל
הַקְטֵל		Hif Impv 2ms	קָטַל
הָקְטַל		Hof Inf cstr	קָטַל
הָקְטַל		Hof Perf 3ms	קָטַל
הַר		noun ms	*mountain*
	הָרִים	noun mp	*mountains*
הִרְאַנִי		Hif Perf 3ms + suff 1s	רָאָה
הָרָה		verb	*to conceive, be pregnant*
הַרְחֵק		Hif Inf abs	רָחַק
הָרִים		noun mp	הַר
הִתְבָּרֲכוּ		Hitp Perf 3p	בָּרַךְ
הִתְפַּקֵּד		Hitp Perf 3ms	פָּקַד
הִתְקַדֵּשׁ		Hitp Perf 3ms	קָדַשׁ
הִתְקַטֵּל		Hitp Impv 2ms	קָטַל
הִתְקַטֵּל		Hitp Inf cstr	קָטַל
הִתְקַטֵּל		Hitp Perf 3ms	קָטַל
וּ		particle (conj)	*and, but*
וַיְהִי		Qal VC Impf 3ms	הָיָה
וַיְשַׂחֵק		Pi VC Impf 3ms	שָׂחַק
זֹאת		pronoun fs	זֶה
זָבַח		verb	*to slaughter for sacrifice*
	מִזְבֵּחַ	noun ms	*altar*
זֶה		pronoun ms	*this*
	זֹאת	pronoun fs	*this*
זוּלָתִי		noun fs + paragogic י	*besides*
זְכוֹר		Qal Impv ms	זָכַר
זָקֵן		verb	*to be old*
	זְקֻנִים	noun mp	*old age*
זָכַר		verb	*to remember*
	זֵכֶר	noun ms	*remembrance, memory*
זָכְרָה		Qal Perf 3fs	זָכַר

זִכְרָם		noun ms + suff 3mp	זָכַר
זָכַרְתִּי		Qal Perf 1s	זָכַר
זְמָן		noun m	time
זָמַר		verb	to sing praises
	זִמְרָה	noun fs	song, praise, music
זִמְרָת		noun fs cstr	זָמַר
זִקְנָה		noun fs	old age
זְקֵנִים		noun mp	זָקֵן
זְקֻנִים		noun mp	old age
זָרַע		verb	to scatter
	זֶרַע	noun ms	seed, progeny, family
זַרְעֲךָ		noun ms + suff 2ms	זֶרַע
חָבַשׁ		verb	to bind, saddle (an animal)
חָג		noun m	feast
חַד		adj ms	חָדַד
חָדַד		verb	to be sharp
חָדַשׁ		verb	Pi to make new
	חָדָשׁ	adj ms	new
חָדָשׁ		adj ms	חָדָשׁ
חוי		verb	חוי
חוּל		verb	to dance; Hif to shake
	חוֹל	noun ms	sand
חוּר		verb	to be white
חָזַק		verb	to be strong; Hif with בְּ to hold
	חָזָק	adj ms	strong, powerful
חָזָק		adj ms	חָזַק
חֲזָקִים		adj mp	חָזַק
חָטָא		verb	to miss, sin
	חַטָּא	noun ms	sinner
	חַטָּאת	noun fs	sin
חַטָּאִים		noun mp	חָטָא
חַטָּאת		noun fs	חָטָא

חַטָּאתֶיךָ		noun fp + suff 2ms	חָטָא
חָי		noun ms	חָיַי
חַיָּה		noun fs	חָיַי
חָיָה		verb	to live
חָיִי		verb	to live
	חָי	noun ms	living thing
	חַיָּה	noun fs	living thing
חַיִּים		noun m	living thing, life
חַיַּת		noun fp cstr	חָיַי
חָכַם		verb	to be wise
	חָכְמָה	noun fs	wisdom
	חָכָם	adj ms	wise
חָכָם		adj ms	חָכַם
חָכְמָה		noun fs	חָכַם
חֲלוֹם		noun ms	חָלַם
חָלַם		verb	to dream
	חֲלוֹם	noun ms	dream
חָמַד		verb	to desire
חֵמָה		noun fs	heat, anger
חֲמוֹר		noun ms	חָמַר
חָמַר		verb	to be red
	חֲמוֹר	noun ms and fs	donkey
חֲמֹרוֹ		noun ms + suff 3ms	חָמַר
חָמֵשׁ		numeral f	five
חֵמֶת		noun ms	container
חֲמַת		noun fs cstr	חֵמֶת
חָסַד		verb	Hitp to show oneself kind
	חֶסֶד	noun ms	love, kindness
חֵפֶץ		noun m	pleasure, matter
חֵץ		noun m	arrow
חֹק		noun m	ordinance, law (cstr. mp חֻקֵּי)
חֹר		noun ms	חוּר

חָרֵב		noun fs	חָרַב
חָרַב		verb	*to destroy*
	חֶרֶב	noun fs	*sword*
	חָרְבָּה	noun fs	*desolation, ruin*
חָרְבָּה		noun fs	חָרַב
חֲרָבוֹת		noun fp	חָרַב
חָשַׂךְ		verb	*to hold back, restrain*
חֹשֶׁךְ		noun ms	*darkness*
חָשַׂכְתָּ		Qal Perf 2ms	חָשַׂךְ
טוֹב		adj ms	*good*
טוֹבָה		adj fs	טוֹב
טוֹבוֹת		adj fp	טוֹב
טוֹבִים		adj mp	טוֹב
טָחָה		verb	*to shoot*
טַעַם		noun ms	*taste, decree*
טַעֲמוּ		Qal Impv mp	טָעַם
יֹאבְדוּ		Qal Impf 3mp	אָבַד
יֶאֱהָבֵהוּ		Qal Impf 3ms + suff 3ms	אָהַב
יֹאכַל		Qal Impf 3ms	אָכַל
יֹאכְלוּ		Qal Impf 3mp	אָכַל
יֵאָמֵר		Nif Impf 3ms	אָמַר
יֹאמַר		Qal Impf 3ms	אָמַר
יֹאמְרוּ		Qal Impf 3mp	אָמַר
יָבֹאוּ		Qal Impf 3mp	בּוֹא
יָבֵל		noun fs	*world, earth*
יִבֶן		Qal Impf 3ms apoc	בָּנָה
יְבַקַּע		Pi Impf 3ms	בָּקַע
יַבָּשָׁה		noun fs	*dry land*
יַגֵּד		Hif Impf 3ms	נָגַד
יֻגַּד		Hof Impf 3ms	נָגַד
יִגְדַּל		Qal Impf 3ms	גָּדַל
יִגְלֶה		Qal Impf 3ms	גָּלָה
יִגְלוּ		Qal Impf 3mp	גָּלָה

יִגָּמֵל		Nif Impf 3ms	גָּמַל
יִגַּשׁ		Qal Impf 3ms	נָגַשׁ
יִגְּשׁוּ		Qal Impf 3mp	נָגַשׁ
יָד		noun fs	hand
	יָדוֹ	noun fs + suff 3ms	his hand
	יָדַיִם	noun f dual	יָד
יָדָה		verb	to throw; Hif to thank, praise
	יְהוּדָה	pr noun	Judah
יָדוֹ		noun fs + suff 3ms	יָד
יָדוֹעַ		Qal Inf abs	יָדַע
יָדַיִם		noun f dual	יָד
יָדִין		Qal Impf 3ms	דוּן
יָדְךָ		noun fs + suff 2ms	יָד
יָדֵךְ		noun fs + suff 2fs	יָד
יֵדַע		Qal Impf 3ms	יָדַע
יֵדַע		Qal Impf 3ms	יָדַע
	דַּעַת	noun fs	knowledge
יָדַע		verb	to know
יֹדֵעַ		Qal Ptc	יָדַע
יֵדְעוּ		Qal Impf 3mp	יָדַע
יֹדְעֵי		Qal Ptc mp cstr	יָדַע
יָדַעְתִּי		Qal Perf 1s	יָדַע
יְדַעְתָּם		Qal Perf 2ms + suff 3mp	יָדַע
יָהּ		pr noun	יְהֹוָה
יְהוּדָה		pr noun	יָדָה
יְהֹוָה		pr noun	name of God
	יָהּ	pr noun	abbreviation of יְהֹוָה
יְהוֹנָתָן		pr noun	Jonathan
יְהוֹשֻׁעַ		pr noun	יָשַׁע
יְהִי		Qal Impf 3ms	הָיָה
יוֹדֵעַ		Qal Ptc	יָדַע
יוֹם		noun ms	day

	יְמֵי	noun mp cstr	days of	
	יָמִים	noun mp	days	
יוֹנָה		pr noun	Jonah	
יוֹסֵף		pr noun		יָסַף
יוֹסִפוּ		Hif Impf 3mp		יָסַף
יוֹרֶה		Qal Ptc		יָרָה
יִזְכְּרֶךָ		Qal Impf 3ms + suff 2fs		זָכַר
יַזְעֵק		Hif Impf 3ms		זָעַק
יַחֲבֹשׁ		Qal Impf 3ms		חָבַשׁ
יָחַד		verb	to be united, be one	
	יַחְדָּו	adv	together	
	יָחִיד	adj ms	only	
יַחְדָּו		adv		יָחַד
יָחִיד		adj ms		יָחַד
יְחִידְךָ		adj ms + suff 2ms		יָחַד
יַחֲלֹם		Qal Impf 3ms		חָלַם
יֶחֱסֶה		Qal Impf 3ms		חָסָה
יִירַשׁ		Qal Impf 3ms		יָרַשׁ
יָכֹל		Qal Inf abs		יָכֹל
יִכְלוּ		Qal Impf 3mp apoc		כָּלָה
יִכָּשְׁלוּ		Nif Impf 3mp		כָּשַׁל
יֶלֶד		noun ms		יֶלֶד
יָלַד		verb	Qal to give birth; Hif to beget; Hof to be born	
	יֶלֶד	noun ms	child	
יָלְדָה		Qal Perf 3fs		יָלַד
יָלַדְתְּ		Qal Perf 2fs		יָלַד
יֵלֵךְ		Qal Impf 3ms		הָלַךְ
יֵלֶךְ		Qal Impf 3ms		הָלַךְ
יֵלְכוּ		Qal Impf 3mp		הָלַךְ
יֵלְכוּ		Qal Impf 3mp		הָלַךְ
יַם		noun ms cstr		יָם
יָם		noun ms	sea	
	יַם	noun ms cstr	sea of	

		יַמִּים	noun mp	*seas*
יְמֵי			noun mp cstr	יוֹם
יָמִי			noun ms + suff 1s	יָם
יַמֵּי			noun mp cstr	יָם
יַמִּים			noun mp	יָם
יְמִים			noun mp	יוֹם
יְמַן			Pi Impf 3ms	מָנָה
יִמְצָא			Qal Impf 3ms	מָצָא
יִמְצְאוּ			Qal Impf 3mp	מָצָא
יִמְשֹׁל			Qal Impf 3ms	מָשַׁל
יִמְשְׁלוּ			Qal Impf 3mp	מָשַׁל
יָנַק			verb	*to suck; Hif to breastfeed*
יָסֹב			Qal Impf 3ms	סָבַב
יָסֹבּוּ			Qal Impf 3mp	סָבַב
יָסַף			verb	*to add, increase*
		יוֹסֵף	pr noun	*Joseph*
יָעַד			verb	*to appoint*
		מוֹעֵד	noun ms	*time*
יַעֲלֵהוּ			Qal Impf 3ms + suff 3ms	עָלָה
יַעֲמֹד			Qal Impf 3ms	עָמַד
יַעַמְדוּ			Qal Impf 3mp	עָמַד
יַעַן			prep; conj	*because*
יַעֲנֵנִי			Qal Impf 3ms + suff 1s	עָנָה
יַעֲקֹד			Qal Impf 3ms	עָקַד
יַעֲרֹךְ			Qal Impf 3ms	עָרַךְ
יַעַשׂ			Qal Impf 3ms apoc	עָשָׂה
יַעַשׂ			Qal Impf 3ms apoc	עָשָׂה
יָפֶה			adj ms	יָפֶה
יָפָה			verb	*to be beautiful*
		יָפֶה	adj ms	*beautiful*
		יָפָה	adj fs	יָפֶה
יִפֹּל			Qal Impf 3ms	נָפַל
יִפְּלוּ			Qal Impf 3mp	נָפַל

יִפָּקֵד		Pi Impf 3ms	פָּקַד
יִפָּקֵד		Nif Impf 3ms	פָּקַד
יִפַּקְדוּ		Pi Impf 3mp	פָּקַד
יִפְקְדוּ		Qal Impf 3mp	פָּקַד
יִפְקְדוּהוּ		Qal Impf 3mp + suff 3ms	פָּקַד
יִפְקְדֵנִי		Qal Impf 3ms + suff 1s	פָּקַד
יִפְקוֹד		Qal Impf 3ms	פָּקַד
יִפְקַח		Qal Impf 3ms	פָּקַח
יִפְקַח		Qal Impf 3ms	פָּקַח
יַפְקִיד		Hif Impf 3ms	פָּקַד
יַפְקִידוּ		Hif Impf 3mp	פָּקַד
יָצָא		verb	*to go out, be born*
יָצָאת		Qal Perf 2fs	יָצָא
יִצְחָק		Qal Impf 3ms	צָחַק
יִצְחָק		pr noun	צָחַק
יָצָתִי		Qal Perf 1s for יָצָאתִי	יָצָא
יָקֵא		Hif Impf 3ms	קוֹא
יָקוּם		Qal Impf 3ms	קוּם
יָקוּמוּ		Qal Impf 3mp	קוּם
יִקַּח		Qal Impf 3ms	לָקַח
יִקַּח		Qal Impf 3ms	לָקַח
יִקָּחוּם		Qal Impf 3ms + suff 3mp	לָקַח
יַקְטִיל		Hif Impf 3ms	קָטַל
יְקֻטַּל		Pual Impf 3ms	קָטַל
יִקְטֹל		Qal Impf 3ms	קָטַל
יִקָּטֵל		Nif Impf 3ms	קָטַל
יָקְטַל		Hof Impf 3ms	קָטַל
יִקְטְלוּ		Qal Impf 3mp	קָטַל
יִקָּטְלוּ		Nif Impf 3mp	קָטַל
יָקָם		with prefix וַ : VC Qal Impf 3ms	קוּם
יָקֻמוּ		Qal Impf 3mp	קוּם
יִקְרָא		Qal Impf 3ms	קָרָא

יִקְרָא		Qal Impf 3ms	קָרָא
יִקָּרֵא		Nif Impf 3ms	קָרָא
יָרֵא		adj ms	*fearing*
יַרְא		Qal Impf 3ms apoc	רָאָה
יָרֵא		verb	*to be afraid, fear*
יִרְאֶה		Qal Impf 3ms	רָאָה
יֵרָאֶה		Nif Impf 3ms	רָאָה
יַרְבִּיצֵנִי		Hif Impf 3ms + suff 1s	רָבַץ
יָרַד		verb	*to go down (e.g. to Egypt)*
יָרְדוּ		Qal Perf 3p	יָרַד
יָרָה		verb	*to show, teach, instruct, shoot*
	תּוֹרָה	noun fs	*law, instruction*
יְרוּשָׁלַיִם		pr noun	*Jerusalem*
יִרַע		Qal Impf 3ms	רָעַע
יָרַע		Qal Impf 3ms	רָעַע
יִרַשׁ		Qal Impf 3ms	יָרַשׁ
יָרַשׁ		verb	*to inherit, possess*
יֵשׁ		adv	*there is, there are*
יֶשׁ־		adv	*there is, there are*
יִשָּׂא		Qal Impf 3ms	נָשָׂא
יֹשֵׁב		Qal Ptc	יָשַׁב
יֵשֶׁב		Qal Impf 3ms	יָשַׁב
יֵשֵׁב		Qal Impf 3ms	יָשַׁב
יֵשֶׁב		Qal Impf 3ms	יָשַׁב
יָשַׁב		verb	*to sit, live*
יֵשֶׁב		with prefix וְ : VC Qal Impf 3ms	שׁוּב
יָשֹׁב		Qal Impf 3ms apoc	שׁוּב
יָשְׁבָה		Qal Perf 3fs	יָשַׁב
יֵשְׁבוּ		Qal Impf 3mp	יָשַׁב
יָשְׁבוּ		Qal Perf 3p	יָשַׁב
יָשֻׁבוּ		Qal Impf 3mp	שׁוּב
יָשַׁבְנוּ		Qal Perf 1p	יָשַׁב

יָשַׁבְתָּ		Qal Perf 2ms	יָשַׁב
יָשַׁבְתְּ		Qal Perf 2fs	יָשַׁב
יָשַׁבְתִּי		Qal Perf 1s	יָשַׁב
יְשַׁבְתֶּם		Qal Perf 2mp	יָשַׁב
יְשַׁבְתֶּן		Qal Perf 2fp	יָשַׁב
יָשׁוֹב		Qal Inf abs	יָשַׁב
יְשׁוּעָה		noun fs	יָשַׁע
יְשׁוּעָתִי		noun fs + suff 1s	יָשַׁע
יִשְׁחַט		Qal Impf 3ms	שָׁחַט
יִשְׁחֲטוּ		Qal Impf 3mp	שָׁחַט
יַשְׁכֵּם		Hif Impf 3ms	שָׁכַם
יַשְׁכֵּם		Hif Impf 3ms	שָׁכַם
יִשְׁלַח		Qal Impf 3ms	שָׁלַח
יְשַׁלְחֶהָ		Pi Impf 3ms + suff 3fs	שָׁלַח
יִשְׁלְחוּ		Qal Impf 3mp	שָׁלַח
יָשֶׂם		with prefix וַ : VC Qal Impf 3ms	שִׂים
יִשְׁמַע		Qal Impf 3ms	שָׁמַע
יִשְׁמַע		Qal Impf 3ms	שָׁמַע
יִשְׁמְעוּ		Qal Impf 3mp	שָׁמַע
יִשְׁמֹר		Qal Impf 3ms	שָׁמַר
יִשְׁמְרוּ		Qal Impf 3mp	שָׁמַר
יִשְׁמָרְךָ		Qal Impf 3ms + suff 2ms	שָׁמַר
יָשַׁע		verb	Hif *to save, deliver*
	יְהוֹשֻׁעַ	pr noun	*Joshua*
	יְשׁוּעָה	noun fs	*help, salvation*
יִשְׁפֹּט		Qal Impf 3ms	שָׁפַט
יָשַׁר		verb	*to be right, straight, upright*
	יָשָׁר	adj ms	*right, upright, honest*
	מֵישָׁר	noun ms	*righteousness, justice, equity*
יָשָׁר		adj ms	יָשַׁר
יִשְׂרָאֵל		pr noun	שָׂרָה
יִתֵּן		Qal Impf 3ms	נָתַן

342

יִתְּנוּ		Qal Impf 3mp		נָתַן
יִתְפַּלֵּל		Hitp Impf 3ms		פָּלַל
יִתְקַדֵּשׁ		Hitp Impf 3ms		קָדַשׁ
יִתְקַדְּשׁוּ		Hitp Impf 3mp		קָדַשׁ
יִתְקַטֵּל		Hitp Impf 3ms		קָטַל
כְּ		prep	as, like	
	כָּמוֹהוּ	prep + suff 3ms	like him (or it)	
כְּאֹיֵב		prep כְּ + noun ms		אֹיֵב
כֵּאלֹהִים		prep כְּ + noun ms		אֵל
כַּאֲשֶׁר		prep כְּ + pronoun		אֲשֶׁר
כָּבֵד		verb	to be heavy, difficult	
	כָּבֵד	adj ms	heavy, difficult	
כְּבוֹאָנָה		prep כְּ + Qal Inf Abs + suff 3fp		בּוֹא
כָּהֶם		prep + suff 3mp		כְּ
כָּהֵן		prep + suff 3fp		כְּ
כָּהֵן		verb	Pi to prepare, act as a priest	
	כֹּהֵן	noun ms	priest	
	כֹּהֲנִים	noun mp	priests	
כֹּהֲנִי		noun ms + suff 1s		כָּהֵן
כֹּהֲנֵי		noun mp cstr		כָּהֵן
כֹּהֲנִים		noun mp		כָּהֵן
כּוֹכָב		noun ms	star	
כּוּן		verb	to establish	
	כֵּן	adv	therefore	
כּוֹנֵן		Pilel Perf 3ms		כּוּן
כִּזְכֹר		prep כְּ + Qal Inf Cstr		זָכַר
כַּחוֹל		prep כְּ + noun ms		חוֹל
כֹּחִי		noun m + suff 1s	strength, power	
כִּי		adv	because, that, if	
כְּכוֹכְבֵי		prep כְּ + noun mp cstr		כּוֹכָב
כִּכְלוֹת		prep כְּ + Qal Inf Cstr		כָּלָה
כָּכֶם		prep + suff 2mp		כְּ

כָּכֶן		prep + suff 2fp	כְּ
כְּלָל		noun ms	כָּלָל
כְּלָל-		noun ms (cstr)	כָּלָל
כָּלָה		verb	to be finished
כָּלַל		verb	to complete
	כֹּל	noun ms	all, entirety, the whole
	כָּל-	noun ms (cstr)	all, entirety, the whole
	כּוֹל	noun m	all (totality)
כָּמוֹהָ		prep + suff 3fs	כְּ
כָּמוֹהוּ		prep + suff 3ms	כְּ
כָּמוֹךְ		prep + suff 2fs	כְּ
כָּמוֹךָ		prep + suff 2ms	כְּ
כָּמוֹנוּ		prep + suff 1p	כְּ
כָּמוֹנִי		prep + suff 1s	כְּ
כַּמָּוֶת		prep כְּ + noun ms	מָוֶת
כִּמְטַחֲוֵי		prep כְּ + Pilel Ptc mp cstr	טָחָה
כֵּן		adv	כּוּן
כָּנָף		noun fs	wing, skirt (of a robe)
כִּסֵּא		noun ms	seat, throne
כִּסְאוֹ		noun ms + suff 3ms	כִּסֵּא
כַּעֲבְדִי		prep כְּ + noun ms + suff 1s	עֶבֶד
כַּף		noun fs	כָּפַף
כָּפַף		verb	to bend, bow down
	כַּף	noun fs	palm (of hand)
כָּרַת		verb	to cut
כַּשְׂדִּים		gentilic noun mp	Chaldeans (a nation)
כָּשַׁל		verb	to stumble
כְּתֹב		Qal Impv ms	כָּתַב
כָּתַב		verb	to write
כִּתְבוּ		Qal Impv fs	כָּתַב
כִּתְבִי		Qal Impv mp	כָּתַב
כְּתֹבְנָה		Qal Impv fp	כָּתַב

כִּתִּיִּים		gentilic noun mp	*Kittim* (a nation; there are various spellings of the Hebrew)
לְ		prep	*to, at, for*
	לוֹ	prep + suff 3ms	*to/at/for him (or it)*
לֹא		adv	*not*
לְאַבְרָהָם		prep לְ + pr noun	אָב
לְאֶחָיו		prep לְ + noun mp + suff 3ms	אָח
לְאֹם		noun ms	*people, nation*
לְאֻמִּים		noun mp	לְאֹם
לֵב		noun m	*heart*
לֵבָב		noun ms	*heart*
	לֵב	noun ms	*heart*
לִבִּי		noun ms + suff 1s	לֵבָב
לִבְכּוֹת		prep לְ + Qal Inf cstr	בָּכָה
לִבְלֹעַ		prep לְ + Qal Inf cstr	בָּלַע
לִבְנִי		prep לְ + noun m + suff 1s	בֵּן
לְגוֹי		prep לְ + noun ms	גְּוָה
לָגוּר		prep לְ + Inf cstr	גוּר
לָדַעַת		prep לְ + noun f	דַּעַת
לָהּ		prep + suff 3fs	לְ
לָהֶם		prep + suff 3mp	לְ
לָהֶן		prep + suff 3fp	לְ
לוֹ		prep + suff 3ms	לְ
לִזְקֵנָיו		prep לְ + noun ms + suff ms	זָקֵן
לֶחֶם		noun ms	*bread*
לָחַם		verb	לָחַם
לַחְמִי		noun m + suff 1s	לֶחֶם
לַחֹשֶׁךְ		prep לְ + noun m	חֹשֶׁךְ
לִי		prep + suff 1s	לְ
לַיהוָה		prep לְ + pr noun	יהוה
לַיְלָה		noun ms	*night*
	לֵילוֹת	noun mp	*nights*
לֵילוֹת		noun mp	לַיְלָה

לִישׁוּעָה		prep לְ + noun fs	יֵשַׁע
לְךָ		prep + suff 2ms	לְ
לֵךְ		Qal Impv ms	הָלַךְ
לָךְ		prep + suff 2fs	לְ
לְכוּ		Qal Impv mp	הָלַךְ
לָכֶם		prep + suff 2mp	לְ
לָכֶן		prep + suff 2fp	לְ
לְכִסֵּא		prep לְ noun ms	כִּסֵּא
לָמַד		verb	Pi *to teach*
לָמֶה		interrog pronoun	מָה
לָמָה		interrog pronoun	*why … ?*
לָמָּה		interrog pronoun	מָה
לְמוֹעֵד		prep לְ + noun ms	יָעַד
לְמֶרְחֲבֵי		prep לְ + noun mp cstr	מֶרְחָב
לִמְשֹׁל		Qal Inf cstr	מָשַׁל
לְמִשְׁפָּט		prep לְ + noun ms	שָׁפַט
לָנוּ		prep + suff 1p	לְ
לְנָחוֹר		prep לְ + pr noun	נָחוֹר
לְנַעַר		prep לְ + noun m	נַעַר
לָנֶצַח		adv	נָצַח
לְעוֹלָם		prep לְ noun ms	עָלַם
לְעֹלָה		prep לְ + noun fs	עָלָה
לַעֲמֹד		Qal Inf cstr	עָמַד
לְעֵצִים		prep לְ + noun mp	עֵצָה
לְעֵת		prep לְ + noun f	עֵת
לִפְנֵי		prep	פָּנָה
לִפְנֵי		prep	*before*
לְפָנָיו		prep לְ + noun m + suff 3ms	פָּנִים
לְקָדְשׁוֹ		prep לְ + Pi Inf cstr + suff 3ms	קָדַשׁ
לָקַח		verb	*to take*
	יִקַּח	Qal Impf 3ms	
	קַח	Qal Impv ms	
לָקֹחַ		Qal Inf abs	לָקַח

346

לֹקֵחַ		Qal Ptc	לָקַח
לָקְחָה		Qal Perf 3fs	לָקַח
לָקְחוּ		Qal Perf 3p	לָקַח
לָקַחְנוּ		Qal Perf 1p	לָקַח
לָקַחְתָּ		Qal Perf 2ms	לָקַח
לָקַחְתְּ		Qal Perf 2fs	לָקַח
לָקַחְתִּי		Qal Perf 1s	לָקַח
לְקַחְתֶּם		Qal Perf 2mp	לָקַח
לְקַחְתֶּן		Qal Perf 2fp	לָקַח
לִקְטֹל		Qal Inf cstr	קָטַל
לָרֶשֶׁת		prep לְ + Qal Inf cstr	יָרַשׁ
לִשְׂחוֹק		prep לְ + Qal Inf cstr	שָׂחַק
לִשְׁחֹט		prep לְ + Qal Inf cstr	שָׁחַט
לִשְׁמֹר		Qal Inf cstr	שָׁמַר
לְשָׂרָה		prep לְ + pr noun	שָׂרַר
מְאֹד		adv	*very*
מֵאָה		numeral	*one hundred*
	מְאַת	numeral cstr	
מְאוּמָה		pronoun	מַה
מַאֲכֶלֶת		noun fs	אָכַל
מֵאֶרֶץ		prep מִן + noun fs cstr	אֶרֶץ
מְאַת		numeral cstr	מֵאָה
מִבֶּטֶן		prep מִן + noun ms	בֶּטֶן
מִבֵּית		prep מִן + noun ms cstr	בָּנָה
מִבַּיִת		prep מִן + noun ms	בַּיִת
מִבַּלְעֲדֵי		adv	*except*
מְבֹרָךְ		Pual Ptc ms	בָּרַךְ
מִבֵּתוֹ		prep מִן + noun ms + suff 1s	בַּיִת
מִדְבַּר		noun ms	דָּבַר
מִדְיָן		pr noun	דּוּן
מִדָּנִאֵל		prep מִן + pr noun	דָּנִאֵל
מִדַּעַת		prep מִן + noun f	דַּעַת
מַה		pronoun ms	*what . . . ?*

	מְאוּמָה	pronoun	anything	
	מָה	interrog pronoun	what … ?	
	מִי	interrog pronoun	who … ?	
מֵהֶם		prep + suff 3mp		מִן
מֵהֶן		prep + suff 3fp		מִן
מִהַר		verb		מָהַר
מוֹאָב		pr noun	Moab	
	מוֹאָבִי	gent noun ms	Moabite	
	מוֹאָבִית	gent noun fs	Moabite	
מוֹאָבִי		gent noun ms	Moabite	
מוֹאֲבִיּוֹת		gent noun fp		מוֹאָב
מוֹאֲבִים		gent noun mp		מוֹאָב
מוֹאָבִית		gent noun fs		מוֹאָב
מוּל		verb	to cut off, circumcise	
מוֹעֵד		noun ms		יָעַד
מוֹת		Qal Inf cstr		מוּת
מוּת		verb	to die	
	מָוֶת	noun ms	death	
מָוֶת		noun ms		מוּת
מִזְבֵּחַ		noun ms		זָבַח
מָחָה		verb	to destroy	
מָחִיתָ		Qal Perf 2ms		מָחָה
מִטַּעַם		prep מִן + noun ms		טַעַם
מִי		pronoun	who … ?	
מִי		interrog pronoun	who … ?	
מִיַּד		prep מִן + noun fs cstr		יָד
מִיהוּדָה		prep מִן + pr noun		יָדָה
מִיכַל		pr noun	Michal	
מַיִם		noun m dual	water	
מֵישָׁר		noun ms		יָשַׁר
מִכָּל		prep מִן + noun ms		כָּלַל
מִכֶּם		prep + suff 2mp		מִן
מִכֶּן		prep + suff 2fp		מִן

מִכַּף		prep מִן + noun f	כַּף
מָלֵא		verb	to be full; Pi to fill
מַלְאָךְ		noun ms	angel, messenger
מִלְחָמָה		noun fs	war, battle
מָלַךְ		verb	to reign, be king
	מֶלֶךְ	noun ms	king
	מִלְכָּה	pr noun	Milcah
	מְלָכִים	noun mp	kings
מִלְכָּה		pr noun	Milcah
מַלְכִּי		noun ms + suff 1s	מֶלֶךְ
מַלְכֵי		noun mp cstr	מֶלֶךְ
מְלָכִים		noun mp	מֶלֶךְ
מִלֵּל		Pi Perf 3ms	מָלַל
מָלַל		verb	to say, speak
מִמְּךָ		prep + suff 2ms	מִן
מִמֵּךְ		prep + suff 2fs	מִן
מִמֶּלֶךְ		prep מִן + noun ms	מֶלֶךְ
מִמֶּנָּה		prep + suff 3fs	מִן
מִמֶּנּוּ		prep + suff 1p or prep + suff 3ms	מִן
מִמֶּנִּי		prep + suff 1s	מִן
מִמַּעַל		adv	עָלָה
מֶמְשֶׁלֶת		noun fs	dominion, reign (f)
מִן		prep	from
	מִמֶּנּוּ	prep + suff 3ms	from him (or it)
מָנָה		verb	to assign, appoint
מִסְתָּר		noun m	secret place
מֵעֶה		noun m	intestines, belly, womb, heart
מֵעִירְךָ		prep מִן + noun ms + suff 2ms	עוּר
מֵעַל		prep מִן + prep	עַל
מַעַל		prep	above
מֵעֶרֶב		prep מִן + noun ms	עֶרֶב

מִפָּנֶיךָ		noun mp + suff 2ms	פָּנָה
מְפַקֵּד		Pi Ptc	פָּקַד
מַפְקִיד		Hif Ptc	פָּקַד
מִפְּרִי		prep מִן + noun ms	פָּרָה
מְצָא		Qal Impv ms	מָצָא
מָצָא		verb	*to find*
מֹצֵא		Qal Ptc	מָצָא
מָצְאָה		Qal Perf 3fs	מָצָא
מָצְאוּ		Qal Perf 3p	מָצָא
מָצָאנוּ		Qal Perf 1p	מָצָא
מָצָאת		Qal Perf 2fs	מָצָא
מָצָאתָ		Qal Perf 2ms	מָצָא
מָצָאתִי		Qal Perf 1s	מָצָא
מְצָאתֶם		Qal Perf 2mp	מָצָא
מְצָאתֶן		Qal Perf 2fp	מָצָא
מָצוֹא		Qal Inf abs	מָצָא
מְצַחֵק		Pi Ptc	צָחַק
מִצְרִי		gent noun ms	מִצְרַיִם
מִצְרִיּוֹת		gent noun fp	מִצְרַיִם
מִצְרִים		gent noun mp	מִצְרַיִם
מִצְרַיִם		pr noun	*Egypt*
	מִצְרִי	gent noun ms	*Egyptian*
	מִצְרִית	gent noun fs	*Egyptian*
מִצְרִית		gent noun fs	*Egyptian (fs)*
מִקֶּדֶם		noun ms	קָדַם
מָקוֹם		noun ms	קוּם
מְקוֹמוֹת		noun mp	קוּם
מַקְטִיל		Hif Ptc	קָטַל
מְקֻטָּל		Pual Ptc	קָטַל
מָקְטָל		Hof Ptc	קָטַל
מֵקִים		Hif Ptc	קוּם
מַר		adj ms	*bitter*
מֶרְחָב		noun ms	*breadth*

מֶרָחֹק		adv	רָחַק
מֹרִיָּה		pr noun	*Moriah*
מָרַר		verb	מָרַר
מֹשֶׁה		pr noun	*Moses*
מִשְׁכָּנוֹת		noun mp	*dwelling place, tent*
מְשֹׁל		Qal Inf cstr or Impv ms	מָשַׁל
מְשֹׁל		Qal Inf cstr	מָשַׁל
מָשֵׁל		verb	*to rule*
מָשְׁלָה		Qal Perf 3fs	מָשַׁל
מָשְׁלוּ		Qal Perf 3p	מָשַׁל
מָשַׁלְנוּ		Qal Perf 1p	מָשַׁל
מָשַׁלְתְּ		Qal Perf 2fs	מָשַׁל
מָשַׁלְתָּ		Qal Perf 2ms	מָשַׁל
מָשַׁלְתִּי		Qal Perf 1s	מָשַׁל
מְשַׁלְתֶּם		Qal Perf 2mp	מָשַׁל
מְשַׁלְתֶּן		Qal Perf 2fp	מָשַׁל
מִשְׁמָר		noun ms	שָׁמַר
מִשְׁמֶרֶת		noun fs	שָׁמַר
מִשְׁפָּט		noun ms	שָׁפַט
מִשְׁפָּטִי		noun ms + suff 1s	שָׁפַט
מִשְׁתֶּה		noun ms	שָׁתָה
מָתַי		adv	*when … ?*
מַתֶּן		Qal Perf 2fp	מוּת
מִתְקַקֵּל		Hitp Ptc	קָטַל
נָא		particle	*please*
נָאָה		noun fs	*pasture*
נֶאֱחָז		Nif Ptc ms	אָחַז
נֹאכֵל		Qal Impf 1p	אָכַל
נֹאכַל		Qal Impf 1p	אָכַל
נֹאכְלָה		Qal Impf 1p + parag ה	אָכַל
נָאַם		verb	*to speak, declare*
	נְאֻם	noun (Qal Ptc pass) ms cstr	*oracle, declaration*

נָאַף		verb	*to commit adultery, commit idolatry*
נָבָא		verb	Nif *to prophesy*
	נָבִיא	noun ms	*prophet*
נְבִיא		noun ms cstr	נָבָא
נָבִיא		noun ms	נָבָא
נְבִיאִי		noun ms + suff 1s	נָבָא
נְבִיאֵי		noun mp cstr	נָבָא
נְבִיאִים		noun mp	נָבָא
נֶגֶד		prep	*in front of, opposite*
נָגַד		verb	Hif *to tell, declare; to praise*
נָגוֹעַ		Qal Inf abs	נָגַע
נָגוֹשׁ		Qal Inf abs	נָגַשׁ
נִגְלֶה		Qal Impf 1p	גָּלָה
נְגֹעַ		Qal Inf cstr	נָגַע
נָגַע		verb	*to touch*
נִגַּשׁ		Qal Impf 1p	נָגַשׁ
נָגַשׁ		verb	*to approach*
נֹגֵשׁ		Qal Ptc	נָגַשׁ
נָגְשָׁה		Qal Perf 3fs	נָגַשׁ
נָגְשׁוּ		Qal Perf 3p	נָגַשׁ
נָגַשְׁנוּ		Qal Perf 1p	נָגַשׁ
נָגַשְׁתְּ		Qal Perf 2fs	נָגַשׁ
נָגַשְׁתָּ		Qal Perf 2ms	נָגַשׁ
נָגַשְׁתִּי		Qal Perf 1s	נָגַשׁ
נְגַשְׁתֶּם		Qal Perf 2mp	נָגַשׁ
נְגַשְׁתֶּן		Qal Perf 2fp	נָגַשׁ
נֵדַע		Qal Impf 1p	יָדַע
נוֹגֵעַ		Qal Ptc	נָגַע
נוֹדָע		Nif Ptc ms	יָדַע
נוֹלַד		Nif Perf 3ms	יָלַד
נוֹרָא		Nif Ptc ms	יָרֵא
נִזְכֹּר		Qal Impf 1p	זָכַר

נִזְכְּרָה		cohort 1p	זָכַר
נָחוֹר		pr noun	Nahor
נָחַם		verb	Pi to comfort, console
נָחָשׁ		noun ms	serpent, snake
נִינְוֵה		pr noun	Nineveh
נִכְתֹּב		Qal Impf 1p	כָּתַב
נִכְתְּבָה		cohort 1p	כָּתַב
נֵלֵךְ		Qal Impf 1p	הָלַךְ
נֵלְכָה		Qal Impf 1p + parag ה	הָלַךְ
נִמְהָר		Nif Ptc	מָהַר
נִמְצָא		Qal Impf 1p	מָצָא
נְמֵרִים		noun mp	leopards
נִמְשֹׁל		Qal Impf 1p	מָשַׁל
נָסֹב		Qal Impf 1p	סָבַב
נָסַבּוּ		Nif Perf 3mp	סָבַב
נִסְגְּרָה		Qal Impf 1p + parag ה	סָגַר
נִסָּה		Pi Perf 3ms	נָסָה
נָסָה		verb	Pi to test, try
נֶעֱבַד		Nif Perf 3ms	עָבַד
נַעֲמֹד		Qal Impf 1p	עָמַד
נָעֳמִי		pr noun	Naomi
נַעַר		noun ms	young man, servant
נַעֲרִי		noun ms + suff 1s	נַעַר
נַעֲרֵי		noun mp cstr	נַעַר
נְעָרָיו		noun mp + suff 3ms	נַעַר
נְעָרִים		noun mp	נַעַר
נַעֲרֹתַי		noun fp + suff 1s	נַעַר
נַעֲשֶׂה		Qal Impf 1s	עָשָׂה
נָפוֹל		Qal Inf abs	נָפַל
נְפֹל		Qal Inf cstr or Impv ms	נָפַל
נִפֹּל		Qal Impf 1p	נָפַל
נָפַל		verb	to fall
נֹפֵל		Qal Ptc	נָפַל

נִפְלָאוֹת		noun (Nif Ptc) fp	פָּלָא
נִפְלְאוֹתֶיךָ		Nif Ptc fp + suff 2ms	פָּלָא
נִפַקֵּד		Pi Impf 1p	פָּקַד
נִפְקֹד		Qal Impf 1p	פָּקַד
נִפְקְדָה		cohort 1p	פָּקַד
נִפְקַדְתָּ		Nif Perf 2ms	פָּקַד
נִפְקְחוּ		Nif Perf 3p	פָּקַח
נִפְקְחוּ		Nif Perf 3mp	פָּקַח
נַפְקִיל		Hif Impf 1p	פָּקַד
נֶפֶשׁ		noun fs	soul, life
נַפְשִׁי		noun fs + suff 1s	נֶפֶשׁ
נָצַח		verb	Pi to excel; Nif to be perfect, complete
	לָנֶצַח	adv	forever
נָקוּם		Qal Impf 1p	קוּם
נִקְחָה		Qal Impf 1p + parag ה	לָקַח
נִקְטַל		Nif Perf 3ms	קָטַל
נִקְטֹל		Qal Impf 1p	קָטַל
נִקָּטֵל		Nif Impf 1p	קָטַל
נִקְטְלָה		Nif Perf 3fs	קָטַל
נִקְטְלוּ		Nif Perf 3p	קָטַל
נִקְטַלְנוּ		Nif Perf 1p	קָטַל
נִקְטַלְתָּ		Nif Perf 2ms	קָטַל
נִקְטַלְתְּ		Nif Perf 2fs	קָטַל
נִקְטַלְתִּי		Nif Perf 1s	קָטַל
נִקְטַלְתֶּם		Nif Perf 2mp	קָטַל
נִקְטַלְתֶּן		Nif Perf 2fp	קָטַל
נָשָׂא		verb	to lift, carry
נֵשֵׁב		Qal Impf 1p	יָשַׁב
נִשְׁבַּעְתִּי		Nif Perf 1s	שָׁבַע
נָשׁוּבָה		Qal Impf 1p + parag ה	שׁוּב
נִשְׁחַט		Qal Impf 1p	שָׁחַט
נְשֵׁי		noun fp cstr	אָנַשׁ

נָשִׂיא		noun m	prince
נָשִׁים		noun fp	אֱנָשׁ
נִשְׁלַח		Qal Impf 1p	שָׁלַח
נִשְׁמֹר		Qal Impf 1p	שָׁמַר
נִשְׁפֹּט		Qal Impf 1p	שָׁפַט
נִשְׁתַּחֲוֶה		Hitp Impf 1p	שָׁחָה
נִתֵּן		Qal Impf 1p	נָתַן
נָתַן		verb	*to give*
	יִתֵּן	Qal Impf 3ms	*he gave*
	נָתָן	pr noun	*Nathan*
	נָתַתִּי	Qal Perf 1s	*I have given*
נָתְנָה		Qal Perf 3fs	נָתַן
נָתְנוּ		Qal Perf 3p	נָתַן
נָתַנּוּ		Qal Perf 1p	נָתַן
נָתַק		verb	*to pull off, tear away; Pi to tear apart, tear to pieces*
נִתְקַדֵּשׁ		Hitp Impf 1p	קָדֵשׁ
נָתַשׁ		verb	*to tear, destroy*
נָתַשְׁתָּ		Qal Perf 2ms	נָתַשׁ
נָתַתְּ		Qal Perf 2fs	נָתַן
נָתַתָּ		Qal Perf 2ms	נָתַן
נָתַתִּי		Qal Perf 1s	נָתַן
נְתַתֶּם		Qal Perf 2mp	נָתַן
נְתַתֶּן		Qal Perf 2fp	נָתַן
סֹב		Qal Inf cstr or Impv ms	סָבַב
סָבַב		verb	*to turn*
סָבְכָה		Qal Perf 3fs	סָבַב
סָבְבוּ		Qal Perf 3p	סָבַב
סָבוֹב		Qal Inf abs	סָבַב
סַבּוֹנוּ		Qal Perf 1p	סָבַב
סַבּוֹת		Qal Perf 2fs	סָבַב
סַבּוֹתָ		Qal Perf 2ms	סָבַב
סַבּוֹתִי		Qal Perf 1s	סָבַב

סַבּוֹתֶם		Qal Perf 2mp	סָבַב
סַבּוֹתֶן		Qal Perf 2fp	סָבַב
סָבַךְ		verb	*to entwine*
	סְבָךְ	noun ms	*thicket*
סָגַר		verb	*to shut, close up*
סוֹבֵב		Qal Ptc	סָבַב
סוּס		noun ms	*horse*
	סוּסָה	noun fs	*mare*
	סוּסוֹ	noun ms + suff 3ms	*his horse*
סוּסָה		noun fs	סוּס
סוּסָהּ		noun ms + suff 3fs	סוּס
סוּסוֹ		noun ms + suff 3ms	סוּס
סוּסוֹת		noun fp	סוּס
סוּסוֹתַי		noun fp + suff 1s	סוּס
סוּסוֹתֶיהָ		noun fp + suff 3fs	סוּס
סוּסוֹתֵיהֶם		noun fp + suff 3mp	סוּס
סוּסוֹתֵיהֶן		noun fp + suff 3fp	סוּס
סוּסוֹתָיו		noun fp + suff 3ms	סוּס
סוּסוֹתֶיךָ		noun fp + suff 2ms	סוּס
סוּסוֹתַיִךְ		noun fp + suff 2fs	סוּס
סוּסוֹתֵיכֶם		noun fp + suff 2mp	סוּס
סוּסוֹתֵיכֶן		noun fp + suff 2fp	סוּס
סוּסוֹתֵינוּ		noun fp + suff 1p	סוּס
סוּסִי		noun ms + suff 1s	סוּס
סוּסַי		noun mp + suff 1s	סוּס
סוּסֶיהָ		noun mp + suff 3fs	סוּס
סוּסֵיהֶם		noun mp + suff 3mp	סוּס
סוּסֵיהֶן		noun mp + suff 3fp	סוּס
סוּסָיו		noun mp + suff 3ms	סוּס
סוּסֶיךָ		noun mp + suff 2ms	סוּס
סוּסַיִךְ		noun mp + suff 2fs	סוּס
סוּסֵיכֶם		noun mp + suff 2mp	סוּס
סוּסֵיכֶן		noun mp + suff 2fp	סוּס

סוּסִים		noun mp	סוּס
סוּסֵינוּ		noun mp + suff 1p	סוּס
סוּסְךָ		noun ms + suff 2ms	סוּס
סוּסֵךְ		noun ms + suff 2fs	סוּס
סוּסְכֶם		noun ms + suff 2mp	סוּס
סוּסְכֶן		noun ms + suff 2fp	סוּס
סוּסָם		noun ms + suff 3mp	סוּס
סוּסָן		noun ms + suff 3fp	סוּס
סוּסֵנוּ		noun ms + suff 1p	סוּס
סוּסָתָהּ		noun fs + suff 3fs	סוּס
סוּסָתוֹ		noun fs + suff 3ms	סוּס
סוּסָתִי		noun fs + suff 1s	סוּס
סוּסָתְךָ		noun fs + suff 2ms	סוּס
סוּסָתֵךְ		noun fs + suff 2fs	סוּס
סוּסַתְכֶם		noun fs + suff 2mp	סוּס
סוּסַתְכֶן		noun fs + suff 2fp	סוּס
סוּסָתָם		noun fs + suff 3mp	סוּס
סוּסָתָן		noun fs + suff 3fp	סוּס
סוּסָתֵנוּ		noun fs + suff 1p	סוּס
סוּר		verb	to turn, depart
סָךְ		noun ms	סְכָךְ
סָכַךְ		verb	to cover
	סָךְ	noun ms	crowd
סָפַד		verb	to mourn
סְפוֹד		Qal Inf cstr	סָפַד
סָפַר		verb	to count; Pi to tell
	סֵפֶר	noun ms	book
	סְפָרִים	noun mp	books
סִפְרִי		noun ms + suff 1s	סֵפֶר
סִפְרֵי		noun mp cstr	סֵפֶר
סְפָרִים		noun mp	סֵפֶר
עָבַד		verb	to work
	עֶבֶד	noun ms	servant

עִבְדוּ		Qal Impv mp	עָבַד
עֲבָדָיו		noun mp + suff 3ms	עֶבֶד
עֲבָדִים		noun mp	עֶבֶד
עָבַר		verb	*to pass over, go* (used with בְּ)
עֵד		noun m	*testimony, witness*
עֵד		noun ms	עֵדָה
עַד		prep	עֵדָה
עַד־כֹּה		adv	עֵדָה
עָדָה		verb	*to pass by*
	עַד	prep	*until, as far as*
	עֵד	noun ms	*eternity*
	עָדָיו	prep + suff 3ms	*as far as him* (or *it*)
	עֵת	noun fs	*time*
	עַתָּה	adv	*now*
עָדַי		prep + suff 1s	עֵדָה
עָדֶיהָ		prep + suff 3fs	עֵדָה
עֲדֵיהֶם		prep + suff 3mp	עֵדָה
עֲדֵיהֶן		prep + suff 3fp	עֵדָה
עָדָיו		prep + suff 3ms	עֵדָה
עָדֶיךָ		prep + suff 2ms	עֵדָה
עָדַיִךְ		prep + suff 2fs	עֵדָה
עֲדֵיכֶם		prep + suff 2mp	עֵדָה
עֲדֵיכֶן		prep + suff 2fp	עֵדָה
עָדֵינוּ		prep + suff 1p	עֵדָה
עוֹד		adv	*still, again*
עוֹלָה		noun fs	עָלָה
עוּלִים		noun m (Aramaic)	*young man*
עוֹלָם		noun ms	עָלַם
עוֹמֵד		Qal Ptc	עָמַד
עוּר		verb	*to wake up, watch*
	עִיר	noun fs	*city*
	עָרִים	noun fp	*cities*

עַז		adj ms	עָזַז
עַז		noun ms	עָזַז
עָזַב		verb	*to abandon, forsake*
עֲזַבְתָּנִי		Qal Perf 2ms + suff 1s	עָזַב
עַזָּה		adj fs	עָזַז
עָזַז		verb	*to be strong, make strong*
	עַז	adj ms	*strong*
	עַזָּה	adj fs	*strong*
עֻזִּי		noun ms + suff 1s	עָזַז
עַיִן		noun fs	*eye*
	עֵין	noun fs cstr	*eye of*
	עֵינַיִם	noun f dual	עַיִן
עֵינֵי		noun fp cstr	עַיִן
עֵינֶיהָ		noun f dual + suff 3fs	עַיִן
עֵינָיו		noun f dual + suff 3ms	עַיִן
עֵינֵיכֶם		noun f dual + suff 2mp	עַיִן
עֵינַיִם		noun f dual	עַיִן
עִיר		noun fs	עוּר
עֵירֹם		adj ms	*naked*
עַל		prep	עָלָה
עַל אֹדֹת		adv	*on account of, because of*
עַל־כֵּן		adv	עָלָה
עָלָה		verb	Qal *to go up*; Hif *to offer*
	עַל אֹדֹת	adv	*on account of, because of*
	עֹלָה	noun fs	*burnt offering*
	עוֹלָה	noun fs	*burnt offering*
	עַל	prep	*on, upon, against*
	מִמַּעַל	adv	*above*
	עַל־כֵּן	adv	*therefore*
	עָלָיו	prep + suff 3ms	*on him (or it)*
עֹלָה		noun fs	עָלָה
עָלַי		prep + suff 1s	עָלָה
עָלֶיהָ		prep + suff 3fs	עָלָה

עֲלֵיהֶם		prep + suff 3mp	עָלָה
עֲלֵיהֶן		prep + suff 3fp	עָלָה
עָלָיו		prep + suff 3ms	עָלָה
עֶלְיוֹן		adj ms	עָלָה
עָלֶיךָ		prep + suff 2ms	עָלָה
עָלַיִךְ		prep + suff 2fs	עָלָה
עֲלֵיכֶם		prep + suff 2mp	עָלָה
עֲלֵיכֶן		prep + suff 2fp	עָלָה
עָלֵינוּ		prep + suff 1p	עָלָה
עָלַם		verb	*to hide, conceal*
	עוֹלָם	noun ms	*hidden time, unlimited time, ancient times*
עָלַץ		verb	*to rejoice; + בְּ = rejoice in*
עָלְתָה		Qal Perf 3fs	עָלָה
עִם		prep	עָמַם
עַם		noun ms	עָמַם
עֲמֹד		Qal Inf cstr or Impv ms	עָמַד
עָמַד		verb	*to stand*
עֹמֵד		Qal Ptc	עָמַד
עָמַדְנוּ		Qal Perf 3p	עָמַד
עָמַדְתִּי		Qal Perf 1s	עָמַד
עִמָּהּ		prep + suff 3fs	עָמַם
עִמּוֹ		prep + suff 3ms	עָמַם
עָמוֹד		Qal Inf abs	עָמַד
עִמִּי		prep + suff 1s	עָמַם
עַמִּי		noun ms + suff 1s	עָמַם
עַמֵּי		noun mp cstr	עָמַם
עַמִּים		noun mp	עָמַם
עִמְּךָ		prep + suff 2ms	עָמַם
עִמָּךְ		prep + suff 2fs	עָמַם
עִמָּכֶם		prep + suff 2mp	עָמַם
עִמָּכֶן		prep + suff 2fp	עָמַם
עִמָּם		prep + suff 3mp	עָמַם

עָמַם		verb	to associate	
	עַם	noun ms	people	
	עִם	prep	with	
	עִמּוֹ	prep + suff 3ms	with him (or it)	
	עַמִּים	noun mp	peoples	
עִמָּן		prep + suff 3fp		עָמַם
עִמָּנוּ		prep + suff 1p		עָמַם
עָנָה		verb	to answer	
עֵנַיִם		noun f dual		עַיִן
עֹנֶשׁ		noun m	punishment	
עֵץ		noun ms		עֵצָה
עָצָה		verb	to close (the eyes); Arabic to be hard	
	עֵץ	noun ms	tree	
עֲצֵי		noun mp cstr		עֵצָה
עֵצִים		noun mp		עֵץ
עֵקֶב		conj	because	
עָקַב		verb	to take by the heel	
	עֵקֶב	adv	because	
	עֵקֶב אֲשֶׁר	adv	because	
עָקַד		verb	to bind	
עֶרֶב		noun m	evening	
עָרַג		verb	to long for (used with אֶל)	
עָרוֹם		adj ms		עָרַם
עָרֵי		noun fp cstr		עוּר
עָרִים		noun fp		עוּר
עָרִים		noun fp		עִיר
עָרַךְ		verb	to lay in rows	
עָרַם		verb	to be cunning	
	עָרֹם	adj ms	naked	
	עָרוּם	adj ms	clever, cunning, prudent	
עָשָׂה		verb	to do, make, accomplish	
	יַעַשׂ	Qal Impf 3ms apoc	he made	

עָשִׂיתָ		Qal Perf 2ms	עָשָׂה
עָשִׂיתִי		Qal Perf 1s	עָשָׂה
עֶשֶׂר		numeral f	*ten*
עֵת		noun fs	עָדָה
עַתָּה		adv	עָדָה
פָּאָה		verb	Hif *to blow*
	פֶּה	noun ms	*mouth*
פָּארָן		pr noun	*Paran*
פֵּאָה		noun ms	פָּאָה
פֹּה		adv	*here*
פַּח		noun ms	פָּחַח
פָּחַד		verb	*to tremble, be afraid*
פָּחַח		verb	Hif *to ensnare*
	פַּח	noun ms	*snare*
פִּיהָ		noun m + suff 3fs	פֶּה
פָּלָא		verb	Nif *to be extraordinary*
	נִפְלָאוֹת	noun (Nif Ptc) fp	*great deeds, greatness*
פָּלַל		verb	*to intercede, pray*
פֶּן		conj	פָּנָה
פָּנֶה		noun ms	פָּנָה
פָּנָה		verb	*to turn, turn oneself*
	לִפְנֵי	prep	*in front of*
	פֶּן	conj	*lest*
	פָּנֶה	noun ms	*face*
	פָּנִים	noun mp	*face(s)*
פָּנִים		noun mp	פָּנָה
פָּקֵד		Pi Perf 3ms	פָּקַד
פַּקֵּד		Pi Impv ms	פָּקַד
פַּקֵּד		Pi Inf cstr	פָּקַד
פַּקֹּד		Pi Inf abs	פָּקַד
פָּקַד		verb	*to visit;* Pi *to muster;* Hif *to appoint;* Hof *to be appointed*
פֻּקַּד		Pual Perf 3ms	פָּקַד

פָּקְדָה		Pi Perf 3fs	פָּקַד
פָּקְדוּ		Pi Perf 3p	פָּקַד
פָּקְדוּ		Qal Perf 3p	פָּקַד
פָּקְדוּ		Pi Perf 3mp	פָּקַד
פָּקְדוּ		Qal Perf 3mp	פָּקַד
פְּקָדוּהוּ		Qal Impf 3mp + suff 3ms	פָּקַד
פְּקַדְנוּ		Pi Perf 2fp	פָּקַד
פְּקָדַנִי		Qal Impf 3ms + suff 1s	פָּקַד
פָּקַדְתְּ		Pi Perf 2fs	פָּקַד
פָּקַדְתָּ		Pi Perf 2ms	פָּקַד
פָּקַדְתִּי		Pi Perf 1s	פָּקַד
פָּקַדְתֶּם		Pi Perf 3p	פָּקַד
פָּקַדְתֶּן		Pi Perf 2mp	פָּקַד
פָּקַח		verb	to open (eyes)
פַּר		noun ms	פָּרַר
פָּרָה		verb	to be fertile, fruitful
	פְּרִי	noun ms	fruit
פָּרָה		noun fs	פָּרַר
פָּרוֹת		noun fp	פָּרָה
פְּרִי		noun ms	פָּרָה
פָּרִים		noun mp	פָּרַר
פָּרַר		verb	to break in pieces
	פַּר	noun ms	ox, bull
	פָּרָה	noun fs	cow
פָּשַׁע		verb	to turn away, sin
פֵּשֶׁר		noun m	interpretation
פָּתַח		verb	to open
פָּתְחָה		Qal Impf 3fs	פָּתַח
צָדַק		verb	to be righteous, just
	צֶדֶק	noun ms	justice
	צְדָקָה	noun fs	righteousness
צְדָקָה		noun fs	צָדַק
צִוָּה		Pi Perf 3ms	צָוָה

צַוָּה		verb	Pi *to appoint, to command*	
	צִיּוֹן	pr noun	*Zion*	
צוּר		noun m	*rock*	
צָחַק		verb	*to laugh, mock*	
	צְחֹק	noun ms	*laughter, ridicule*	
	יִצְחָק	pr noun	*Isaac*	
צִיּוֹן		pr noun		צַוָּה
צָרָה		noun fs	*distress*	
קָדוֹשׁ		adj ms		קָדַשׁ
קָדַם		verb	*to precede*	
	מִקֶּדֶם	noun ms	*olden time, of old; east; formerly*	
קִדַּשׁ		Pi Perf 3ms		קָדַשׁ
קָדַשׁ		verb	Qal *to be holy*; Pi *to sanctify, consecrate*	
	קָדוֹשׁ	adj ms	*holy*	
קֹדֶשׁ		noun ms		קָדַשׁ
קַדֵּשׁ		Pi Impf 3ms		קָדַשׁ
קֳדָשִׁים		noun mp		קָדַשׁ
קוֹא		verb	*to vomit*	
קוֹל		noun ms	*voice*	
קוֹם		Qal Inf abs		קוּם
קוּם		verb	*to arise*	
	יָּקָם	with prefix וַ : VC Qal Impf 3ms	*and he arose*	
	מָקוֹם	noun ms	*place*	
	קָם	Qal Perf 3ms	*he has arisen*	
קוּם		Qal Inf cstr or Impv ms		קוּם
קוּמִי		Qal Impv fs		קוּם
קוֹשׁ		verb	*to lay snares*	
	קֶשֶׁת	noun fs	*bow (weapon)*	
קַח		Qal Impv ms		לָקַח
קַחַת		Qal Inf cstr		לָקַח
קָטוֹל		Qal Inf abs		קָטַל

קְטֹל		Qal Inf cstr or Impv ms	קָטַל
קָטֵל		verb	*to kill*
קֹטֵל		Qal Ptc	קָטַל
קֻטַּל		Pual Impv 2ms	קָטַל
קֻטַּל		Pual Perf 3ms	קָטַל
קָטְלָה		Qal Perf 3fs	קָטַל
קָטְלוּ		Qal Perf 3p	קָטַל
קָטַלְנוּ		Qal Perf 1p	קָטַל
קָטַלְתְּ		Qal Perf 2fs	קָטַל
קָטַלְתָּ		Qal Perf 2ms	קָטַל
קָטַלְתִּי		Qal Perf 1s	קָטַל
קְטַלְתֶּם		Qal Perf 2mp	קָטַל
קְטַלְתֶּן		Qal Perf 2fp	קָטַל
קָטֹן		adj ms	*small*
קְטַנָּה		adj fs	קָטֹן
קַל		adj ms	קָלַל
קֹלָהּ		noun ms + suff 3fs	קוֹל
קָלַל		verb	*to be light, to be fast*
	קַל	adj ms	*light*
קָם		Qal Perf 3ms or Ptc	קוּם
קָמָה		Qal Perf 3fs	קוּם
קָמוּ		Qal Perf 3p	קוּם
קַמְנוּ		Qal Perf 1p	קוּם
קַמְתְּ		Qal Perf 2fs	קוּם
קַמְתָּ		Qal Perf 2ms	קוּם
קַמְתִּי		Qal Perf 1s	קוּם
קַמְתֶּם		Qal Perf 2mp	קוּם
קַמְתֶּן		Qal Perf 2fp	קוּם
קָרָא		verb	*to call*
קֶרֶן		noun fs	*horn of animal*
קֶשֶׁת		noun fs	קוֹשׁ
רָאָה		verb	*to see*
רָאָה		Qal Perf 3fs	רָאָה

רְאוּ		Qal Impv mp	רָאָה
רָאִינוּ		Qal Perf 1p	רָאָה
רֹאשׁ		noun ms	head
	רֵאשִׁית	noun fs	beginning, former time
רֵאשִׁית		noun fs	רֹאשׁ
רָאֲתָה		Qal Perf 3fs	רָאָה
רַב		adj ms	רָבַב
רָבַב		verb	to be many, become many
	רַב	adj ms	many
רָבָה		verb	to shoot
רֹבֶה		Qal Ptc	רָבָה
רֶגֶל		noun fs	foot
	רַגְלַיִם	noun f dual	רֶגֶל
רַגְלַיִם		noun f dual	רֶגֶל
רוּם		verb	to be high; Hif to raise, exalt; Hof to be exalted
רוּק		verb	Hif to empty
	רֵיק	adj ms	empty
רָחַק		verb	to be distant
	הַרְחֵק	Hif Inf abs	far away
	מֵרָחֹק	adv	in the distance
רֵיק		adj ms	רוּק
רְנָנָה		noun fs	shouting with joy
רֵעַ		noun m	friend
רַע		adj ms	רָעַע
רַע		adj ms	bad, evil
רָעֵב		verb	to be hungry
	רָעָב	noun ms	famine
רָעוֹת		adj fp	רָעַע
רָעִים		adj mp	רָעַע
רָעַע		verb	to break in pieces, to be evil
	רַע	adj ms	evil, bad
רָצַח		verb	to kill, murder

366

רָקַד		verb	to leap, dance
רְקוֹד		Qal Inf cstr	רָקַד
רְשַׁע		adj ms cstr	wicked
רָשַׁע		verb	to be wicked
רָשָׁע		adj ms	wicked
	רְשַׁע	adj ms cstr	wicked
רִשְׁעֵי		adj mp cstr	רָשָׁע
רְשָׁעִים		adj mp	רָשָׁע
שְׁאוֹל		pr noun	Sheol
שְׂאִי		Qal Impv fs	נָשָׂא
שֵׁב		Qal Impv ms	יָשַׁב
שְׁבוּ		Qal Impv mp	יָשַׁב
שִׁבֳּלִים		noun fp	שִׁבֹּלֶת
שִׁבֹּלֶת		noun fs	ear of corn
שֶׁבַע		numeral f	seven
שָׁבַע		verb	to swear; with בְּ or with לְ to swear to (something)
שָׁבַר		verb	Qal to break; Pi to shatter
שֶׁבֶת		Qal Inf cstr	יָשַׁב
שַׁבָּת		noun ms and fs	Sabbath
שָׁבַת		verb	to rest
שָׁבַתְנוּ		Qal Perf 1p	שָׁבַת
שָׂדֶה		noun ms	field
שֶׂה		noun ms	lamb, sheep, goat
שָׁחֲטָה		Qal Perf 3fs	שָׁחַט
שָׁחֲטוּ		Qal Perf 3p	שָׁחַט
שׁוֹב		Qal Inf abs	שׁוּב
שׁוּב		verb	to return; Hif to restore; Hof to be restored
שָׁוַע		verb	to implore, ask for help
שִׁוַּעְתִּי		Pi Perf 1s	שָׁוַע
שׁוֹפֵט		Qal Ptc	שָׁפַט
שׁוֹר		noun m	ox, bull
שָׁחַד		verb	to give presents, bribe

	שֹׁחַד	noun ms	present, bribe
שָׁחָה		verb	to bow down, Hit to worship
שָׁחוֹט		Qal Inf abs	שָׁחַט
שְׁחֹט		Qal Inf cstr or Impv ms	שָׁחַט
שְׁחֹט		Qal Impv ms	שָׁחַט
שָׁחַט		verb	to kill, slaughter
שֹׁחֵט		Qal Ptc	שָׁחַט
שֹׁחֵט		Qal Ptc	שָׁחַט
שָׁחַטְנוּ		Qal Perf 1p	שָׁחַט
שָׁחַטְתְּ		Qal Perf 2fs	שָׁחַט
שָׁחַטְתָּ		Qal Perf 2ms	שָׁחַט
שָׁחַטְתִּי		Qal Perf 1s	שָׁחַט
שְׁחַטְתֶּם		Qal Perf 2mp	שָׁחַט
שְׁחַטְתֶּן		Qal Perf 2fp	שָׁחַט
שָׂחַק		verb	to laugh
שִׂיחַ		noun ms	shrub
שִׂיחִם		noun mp	שִׂיחַ
שִׂים		verb	to put, place
שִׁיר		verb	to sing
	שִׁירָה	noun fs	song
שִׁירָה		noun fs	song
שִׁירִים		noun mp	שִׁיר
שָׁכוֹחַ		Qal Inf abs	שָׁכַח
שְׁכֹחַ		Qal Inf cstr	שָׁכַח
שָׁכַח		verb	to forget
שֹׁכֵחַ		Qal Ptc	שָׁכַח
שָׁכַם		verb	to get up early
	שְׁכֶם	noun ms	shoulder
שִׁכְמָה		noun ms + suff 3fs	שְׁכֶם
שָׁכַן		verb	שָׁכַן
שָׁכַר		verb	to get drunk
שָׁלוֹחַ		Qal Inf abs	שָׁלַח

שָׁלוֹם		noun m	שָׁלֵם
שָׁלוֹשׁ		numeral	*three*
	שְׁלִישִׁי	ordinal adj	*third*
שְׁלַח		Qal Impv ms	שָׁלַח
שְׁלֹחַ		Qal Inf cstr	שָׁלַח
שָׁלַח		verb	*to stretch out, send*
שֹׁלֵחַ		Qal Ptc	שָׁלַח
שָׁלְחָה		Qal Perf 3fs	שָׁלַח
שָׁלְחוּ		Qal Perf 3p	שָׁלַח
שָׁלַחְנוּ		Qal Perf 1p	שָׁלַח
שָׁלַחְתְּ		Qal Perf 2fs	שָׁלַח
שָׁלַחְתָּ		Qal Perf 2ms	שָׁלַח
שָׁלַחְתִּי		Qal Perf 1s	שָׁלַח
שְׁלַחְתֶּם		Qal Perf 2mp	שָׁלַח
שְׁלַחְתֶּן		Qal Perf 2fp	שָׁלַח
שְׁלִישִׁי		ordinal adj	שָׁלוֹשׁ
שָׁלַךְ		verb	*to throw*
שָׁלֵם		verb	*to be whole, to be complete, to be at peace*
	שָׁלוֹם	noun m	*safety, peace*
	שְׁלֹמֹה	pr noun	*Solomon*
שְׁלֹמֹה		pr noun	*Solomon*
שֵׁם		noun ms	*name*
	שְׁמוֹ	noun ms + suff 3ms	*his name*
שָׂם		Qal Perf 3ms or Ptc	שִׂים
שָׁם		adv	*there*
שָׂמָה		Qal Perf 3fs	שִׂים
שָׁמָּה		adv + ה of direction	שָׁם
שְׁמוֹ		noun ms + suff 3ms	שֵׁם
שָׂמוֹחַ		Qal Inf abs	שָׂמַח
שָׂמוֹחַ		Qal Inf abs	שָׂמַח
שְׁמוֹנֶה		numeral f	*eight*
שְׂמֹחַ		Qal Inf cstr	שָׂמַח

שָׂמֵחַ		Qal Ptc	שָׂמַח
שָׂמַח		verb	to rejoice, be glad
שִׂמְחָה		noun fs	joy, gladness
שָׁמַיִם		noun m dual	heaven
שְׁמָם		noun ms + suff 3mp	שֵׁם
שְׁמֹנֶה		numeral	eight
	שְׁמֹנַת	numeral cstr	eight of
שְׁמֹעַ		Qal Inf cstr	שָׁמַע
שָׁמַע		verb	to hear
שָׁמֹעַ		Qal Inf abs	שָׁמַע
שֹׁמֵעַ		Qal Ptc	שָׁמַע
שָׁמַעְתָּ		Qal Perf 2ms	שָׁמַע
שָׁמַעְתִּי		Qal Perf 1s	שָׁמַע
שְׁמֹר		Qal Impv ms	שָׁמַר
שִׁמֻּר		noun ms	שָׁמַר
שָׁמַר		verb	to keep, guard, Hit to observe
	מִשְׁמָר	noun ms	prison
	מִשְׁמֶרֶת	noun fs	injunction, charge
	שִׁמֻּר	noun ms	vigil
	שֹׁמֵר	noun ms	guard
	שְׁמֻרָה	noun fs	eyelid
	שָׁמְרָה	noun fs	watch, guard
שֹׁמֵר		noun ms	שָׁמַר
שְׁמֻרָה		noun fs	שָׁמַר
שָׁמְרָה		Qal Perf 3fs	שָׁמַר
שָׁמְרָה		noun fs	שָׁמַר
שִׁמְרוּ		Qal Impv mp	שָׁמַר
שָׁמְרוּ		Qal Perf 3p	שָׁמַר
שִׁמְרִי		Qal Impv fs	שָׁמַר
שְׁמֹרְנָה		Qal Impv fp	שָׁמַר
שָׁמַרְנוּ		Qal Perf 1p	שָׁמַר
שָׁמַרְתְּ		Qal Perf 2fs	שָׁמַר

שָׁמַרְתָּ		Qal Perf 2ms		שָׁמַר
שָׁמַרְתִּי		Qal Perf 1s		שָׁמַר
שְׁמַרְתֶּם		Qal Perf 2mp		שָׁמַר
שְׁמַרְתֶּן		Qal Perf 2fp		שָׁמַר
שֶׁמֶשׁ		noun ms and fs	sun	
שִׁמְשׁוֹן		pr noun	Samson	
שְׁנֹא		Qal Inf cstr		שָׁנֵא
שָׁנָה		verb	to repeat	
	שָׁנָה	noun fs	year	
	שְׁנֵי	numeral cstr	two of, both of	
	שְׁנַיִם	numeral	two, both	
	שֵׁנִית	ordinal adj	second	
שָׁנָה		noun fs		שָׁנָה
שְׁנֵי		numeral cstr		שָׁנָה
שְׁנֵיהֶם		numeral + suff 3mp		שָׁנָה
שְׁנַיִם		numeral		שָׁנָה
שֵׁנִית		ordinal adj		שָׁנָה
שָׁעַר		verb	to estimate value	
	שַׁעַר	noun ms	gate	
שָׂפָה		noun fs	lip	
	שְׂפָתַיִם	noun f dual		שָׂפָה
שְׁפֹט		Qal Inf cstr		שָׁפַט
שָׁפַט		verb	to judge	
	שֹׁפֵט	noun ms	judge	
	מִשְׁפָּט	noun ms	judgement	
שְׂפַת		noun fs cstr		שָׂפָה
שְׂפָתַיִם		noun f dual		שָׂפָה
שָׁקָה		verb	Hif to give someone a drink	
שֶׁקֶר		noun m	lie, falsehood	
שַׂר		noun ms		שָׂרַר
שָׁרָה		verb	Pi to loose, set free	
	יִשְׂרָאֵל	pr noun	Israel	
שָׂרָה		noun fs, pr noun fs		שָׂרַר

שָׂרָה		pr noun	Sarah
שָׂרוֹת		noun fp	שָׂרַר
שָׂרִים		noun mp	שָׂרַר
שָׂרַר		verb	to rule, be a prince
	שַׂר	noun ms	prince
	שָׂרָה	pr noun	Sarah
	מִשְׁתֶּה	noun ms	feast, banquet
שֵׁשׁ		numeral f	six
שָׁתָה		verb	to drink
שְׁתֵּיהֶם		numeral f + suff 3mp	both of them
שְׁתַּיִם		numeral f	two
שְׁתִיתֶם		Qal Perf 2mp	שָׁתָה
תֹּאכַל		Qal Impf 3fs	אָכַל
תֹּאכַל		Qal Impf 2ms	אָכַל
תֹּאכְלוּ		Qal Impf 2mp	אָכַל
תֹּאכְלִי		Qal Impf 2fs	אָכַל
תֹּאכַלְנָה		Qal Impf 3fp	אָכַל
תֹּאכַלְנָה		Qal Impf 2fp	אָכַל
תֹּאכְלֶנּוּ		Qal Impf 3fs + suff 1p	אָכַל
תֹּאמֶר		Qal Impf 2fs	אָמַר
תֹּאמַר		Qal Impf 3fs	אָמַר
תֹּאמַרְנָה		Qal Impf 3fp	אָמַר
תֵּבְךְּ		Qal Impf 3fs apoc	בָּכָה
תִּגְלֶה		Qal Impf 3fs	גָּלָה
תִּגְלֶה		Qal Impf 2ms	גָּלָה
תִּגְלוּ		Qal Impf 2mp	גָּלָה
תִּגְלִי		Qal Impf 2fs	גָּלָה
תִּגְלֶינָה		Qal Impf 3fp	גָּלָה
תִּגְנֹב		Qal Impf 2ms	גָּנַב
תִּגְּעוּ		Qal Impf 2mp	נָגַע
תִּגַּשׁ		Qal Impf 3fs	נָגַשׁ
תִּגַּשׁ		Qal Impf 2ms	נָגַשׁ
תִּגְּשׁוּ		Qal Impf 2mp	נָגַשׁ

תִּגְּשִׁי		Qal Impf 2fs	נָגַשׁ
תִּגַּשְׁנָה		Qal Impf 3fp	נָגַשׁ
תִּגַּשְׁנָה		Qal Impf 2fp	נָגַשׁ
תֵּדַע		Qal Impf 2ms or 3fs	יָדַע
תֵּדְעוּ		Qal Impf 2mp	יָדַע
תֵּדְעִי		Qal Impf 2fs	יָדַע
תֵּדַעְנָה		Qal Impf 2fp or 3fp	יָדַע
תֵּהֹם		Nif Impf 3fs	הוּם
תַּהַר		Qal Impf 3fs apoc	הָרָה
תָּוֶךְ		noun m	*middle*
תּוּכַל		Qal Impf 2ms	יָכֹל
תּוֹרָה		noun fs	יָרָה
תּוֹרוֹת		noun fp cstr	יָרָה
תּוֹרַת		noun fs cstr	יָרָה
תִּזְכֹּרְנָה		Qal Impf 2fp or 3fp	זָכַר
תַּחְמֹד		Qal Impf 2ms	חָמַד
תָּחַת		prep	*beneath, under, instead of*
	תַּחְתָּיו	prep + suff 3ms	*under him (or it)*
תַּחְתַּי		prep + suff 1s	תָּחַת
תַּחְתֶּיהָ		prep + suff 3fs	תָּחַת
תַּחְתֵּיהֶם		prep + suff 3mp	תָּחַת
תַּחְתֵּיהֶן		prep + suff 3fp	תָּחַת
תַּחְתָּיו		prep + suff 3ms	תָּחַת
תַּחְתֶּיךָ		prep + suff 2ms	תָּחַת
תַּחְתַּיִךְ		prep + suff 2fs	תָּחַת
תַּחְתֵּיכֶם		prep + suff 2mp	תָּחַת
תַּחְתֵּיכֶן		prep + suff 2fp	תָּחַת
תַּחְתֵּינוּ		prep + suff 1p	תָּחַת
תִּירְאִי		Qal Impf 2fs	יָרֵא
תִּכְתְּבִי		Qal Impf 2fs	כָּתַב
תֵּלֵךְ		Qal Impf 2ms	הָלַךְ
תֵּלֵךְ		Qal Impf 3fs	הָלַךְ
תֵּלְכוּ		Qal Impf 2mp	הָלַךְ

תֵּלְכִי		Qal Impf 2fs	הָלַךְ
תֵּלַכְנָה		Qal Impf 2fp	הָלַךְ
תֵּלַכְנָה		Qal Impf 3fp	הָלַךְ
תַּמּוּ		Qal Perf 3p	תָּמַם
תְּמַלֵּא		Pi Impf 3fs	מָלֵא
תָּמַם		verb	*to be completed, be finished, be gone*
תִּמְצָא		Qal Impf 3fs	מָצָא
תִּמְצָא		Qal Impf 2ms	מָצָא
תִּמְצְאוּ		Qal Impf 2mp	מָצָא
תִּמְצְאִי		Qal Impf 2fs	מָצָא
תִּמְצֶאנָה		Qal Impf 3fp	מָצָא
תִּמְצֶאנָה		Qal Impf 2fp	מָצָא
תִּמְשֹׁל		Qal Impf 2ms or 3fs	מָשַׁל
תִּמְשְׁלוּ		Qal Impf 2mp	מָשַׁל
תִּמְשְׁלִי		Qal Impf 2fs	מָשַׁל
תִּמְשֹׁלְנָה		Qal Impf 2fp or 3fp	מָשַׁל
תְּמֻתוּן		Qal Impf 2mp + parag ן	מוּת
תִּנְאָף		Qal Impf 2ms	נָאַף
תְּנַחֲמֵנִי		Pi Impf 2ms + suff 1s	נָחַם
תָּסֹב		Qal Impf 2ms or 3fs	סָבַב
תָּסֹבּוּ		Qal Impf 2mp	סָבַב
תָּסֹבִּי		Qal Impf 2fs	סָבַב
תְּסֻבֶּינָה		Qal Impf 2fp or 3fp	סָבַב
תָּעָה		verb	*to wander*
תַּעַזְבֵנִי		Qal Impf 2ms + suff 1s	עָזַב
תַּעֲמֹד		Qal Impf 2ms or 3fs	עָמַד
תַּעַמְדוּ		Qal Impf 2mp	עָמַד
תַּעַמְדִי		Qal Impf 2fs	עָמַד
תַּעֲמֹדְנָה		Qal Impf 2fp or 3fp	עָמַד
תָּעַע		verb	*to mock*
תַּעֲרֹג		Qal Impf 3fs	עָרַג
תַּעַשׂ		Qal Impf 2ms apoc	עָשָׂה

תִּפֹּל		Qal Impf 2ms or 3fs	נָפַל
תִּפְּלוּ		Qal Impf 2mp	נָפַל
תִּפְּלִי		Qal Impf 2fs	נָפַל
תִּפֹּלְנָה		Qal Impf 2fp or 3fp	נָפַל
תְּפַקֵּד		Pi Impf 2ms or 3fs	פָּקַד
תִּפְקֹד		Qal Impf 2ms or 3fs	פָּקַד
תְּפַקְּדוּ		Pi Impf 2mp	פָּקַד
תְּפַקְּדִי		Pi Impf 2fs	פָּקַד
תְּפַקֵּדְנָה		Pi Impf 2fp or 3fp	פָּקַד
תַּפְקֵדְנָה		Hif Impf 2fp or 3fp	פָּקַד
תַּפְקִיד		Hif Impf 2ms or 3fs	פָּקַד
תַּפְקִידִי		Hif Impf 2fs	פָּקַד
תָּקוּם		Qal Impf 3fs	קוּם
תָּקוּם		Qal Impf 2ms	קוּם
תָּקוּמוּ		Qal Impf 2mp	קוּם
תָּקוּמִי		Qal Impf 2fs	קוּם
תְּקוּמֶינָה		Qal Impf 3fp	קוּם
תְּקוּמֶינָה		Qal Impf 2fp	קוּם
תִּקַּח		Qal Impf 3fs	לָקַח
תִּקַּח		Qal Impf 2ms	לָקַח
תִּקְטֹל		Qal Impf 2ms or 3fs	קָטַל
תִּקָּטֵל		Nif Impf 2ms or 3fs	קָטַל
תִּקְטְלוּ		Qal Impf 2mp	קָטַל
תִּקָּטְלוּ		Nif Impf 2mp	קָטַל
תִּקְטְלִי		Qal Impf 2fs	קָטַל
תִּקָּטְלִי		Nif Impf 2fs	קָטַל
תִּקְטֹלְנָה		Qal Impf 2fp or 3fp	קָטַל
תִּקָּטַלְנָה		Nif Impf 2fp or 3fp	קָטַל
תִּרָא		Qal Impf 2ms	יָרֵא
תֵּרֶא		Qal Impf 3fs	רָאָה
תִּרְצַח		Qal Impf 2ms	רָצַח
תִּשָּׂא		Qal Impf 3fs	נָשָׂא
תֵּשֵׁב		Qal Impf 2ms	יָשַׁב

תֵּשֵׁב		Qal Impf 3fs	יָשַׁב
תֵּשְׁבוּ		Qal Impf 2mp	יָשַׁב
תֵּשְׁבִי		Qal Impf 2fs	יָשַׁב
תֵּשַׁבְנָה		Qal Impf 2fp or 3fp	יָשַׁב
תִּשְׁבֹּתְנָה		Qal Impf 2fp or 3fp	שָׁבַת
תִּשְׁחַט		Qal Impf 3fs	שָׁחַט
תִּשְׁחַט		Qal Impf 2ms	שָׁחַט
תִּשְׁחֲטוּ		Qal Impf 2mp	שָׁחַט
תִּשְׁחֲטִי		Qal Impf 2fs	שָׁחַט
תִּשְׁחַטְנָה		Qal Impf 3fp	שָׁחַט
תִּשְׁחַטְנָה		Qal Impf 2fp	שָׁחַט
תִּשְׁכַּח		Qal Impf 2ms	שָׁכַח
תִּשְׁלַח		Qal Impf 2ms	שָׁלַח
תִּשְׁלַח		Qal Impf 3fs	שָׁלַח
תִּשְׁלְחוּ		Qal Impf 2mp	שָׁלַח
תִּשְׁלְחִי		Qal Impf 2fs	שָׁלַח
תִּשְׁלַחְנָה		Qal Impf 3fp	שָׁלַח
תִּשְׁלַחְנָה		Qal Impf 2fp	שָׁלַח
תַּשְׁלִיכֵנִי		Hif Impf 2ms + suff 1s	שָׁלַךְ
תַּשְׁלֵךְ		Hif Impf 2ms	שָׁלַךְ
תַּשְׁלֵךְ		Hif Impf 3fs	שָׁלַךְ
תִּשְׁמֹר		Qal Impf 2ms or 3fs	שָׁמַר
תִּשְׁמְרוּ		Qal Impf 2mp	שָׁמַר
תִּשְׁמְרִי		Qal Impf 2fs	שָׁמַר
תִּשְׁמֹרְנָה		Qal Impf 2fp or 3fp	שָׁמַר
תֵּשַׁע		numeral f	nine
תַּשְׁקְ		Hif Impf 2ms apoc	שָׁקָה
תַּשְׁקְ		Hif Impf 3fs apoc	שָׁקָה
תִּתֵּן		Qal Impf 3fs	נָתַן
תִּתֵּן		Qal Impf 2ms	נָתַן
תִּתֵּנָּה		Qal Impf 3fp	נָתַן
תִּתֵּנָּה		Qal Impf 2fp	נָתַן
תִּתְּנוּ		Qal Impf 2mp	נָתַן

תִּתְּנִי		Qal Impf 2fs	נָתַן
תֵּתַע		Qal Impf 3fs apoc	תָּעָה
תִּתְקַדֵּשׁ		Hitp Impf 2ms or 3fs	קָדַשׁ
תִּתְקַדְּשׁוּ		Hitp Impf 2mp	קָדַשׁ
תִּתְקַדְּשִׁי		Hitp Impf 2fs	קָדַשׁ
תִּתְקַדַּשְׁנָה		Hitp Impf 2fp or 3fp	קָדַשׁ
תִּתֹּשׁ		Qal Impf 2ms	נָתַשׁ

Verb tables

Table 1 Qal: strong verbs

Qal					
Strong verbs	קָטַל	שָׁמַר	פָּקַד	כָּתַב	זָכַר
Perfect					
3ms	קָטַל	שָׁמַר	פָּקַד	כָּתַב	זָכַר
3fs	קָטְלָה	שָׁמְרָה	פָּקְדָה	כָּתְבָה	זָכְרָה
2ms	קָטַלְתָּ	שָׁמַרְתָּ	פָּקַדְתָּ	כָּתַבְתָּ	זָכַרְתָּ
2fs	קָטַלְתְּ	שָׁמַרְתְּ	פָּקַדְתְּ	כָּתַבְתְּ	זָכַרְתְּ
1s	קָטַלְתִּי	שָׁמַרְתִּי	פָּקַדְתִּי	כָּתַבְתִּי	זָכַרְתִּי
3p	קָטְלוּ	שָׁמְרוּ	פָּקְדוּ	כָּתְבוּ	זָכְרוּ
2mp	קְטַלְתֶּם	שְׁמַרְתֶּם	פְּקַדְתֶּם	כְּתַבְתֶּם	זְכַרְתֶּם
2fp	קְטַלְתֶּן	שְׁמַרְתֶּן	פְּקַדְתֶּן	כְּתַבְתֶּן	זְכַרְתֶּן
1p	קָטַלְנוּ	שָׁמַרְנוּ	פָּקַדְנוּ	כָּתַבְנוּ	זָכַרְנוּ

Imperfect					
3ms	יִקְטֹל	יִשְׁמֹר	יִפְקֹד	יִכְתֹּב	יִזְכֹּר
3fs	תִּקְטֹל	תִּשְׁמֹר	תִּפְקֹד	תִּכְתֹּב	תִּזְכֹּר
2ms	תִּקְטֹל	תִּשְׁמֹר	תִּפְקֹד	תִּכְתֹּב	תִּזְכֹּר
2fs	תִּקְטְלִי	תִּשְׁמְרִי	תִּפְקְדִי	תִּכְתְּבִי	תִּזְכְּרִי
1s	אֶקְטֹל	אֶשְׁמֹר	אֶפְקֹד	אֶכְתֹּב	אֶזְכֹּר
3mp	יִקְטְלוּ	יִשְׁמְרוּ	יִפְקְדוּ	יִכְתְּבוּ	יִזְכְּרוּ
3fp	תִּקְטֹלְנָה	תִּשְׁמֹרְנָה	תִּפְקֹדְנָה	תִּכְתֹּבְנָה	תִּזְכֹּרְנָה
2mp	תִּקְטְלוּ	תִּשְׁמְרוּ	תִּפְקְדוּ	תִּכְתְּבוּ	תִּזְכְּרוּ
2fp	תִּקְטֹלְנָה	תִּשְׁמֹרְנָה	תִּפְקֹדְנָה	תִּכְתֹּבְנָה	תִּזְכֹּרְנָה
1p	נִקְטֹל	נִשְׁמֹר	נִפְקֹד	נִכְתֹּב	נִזְכֹּר

Imperative ms	קְטֹל	שְׁמֹר	פְּקֹד	כְּתֹב	זְכֹר
Infinitive Cstr	קְטֹל	שְׁמֹר	פְּקֹד	כְּתֹב	זְכֹר
Infinitive Abs	קָטוֹל	שָׁמוֹר	פָּקוֹד	כָּתוֹב	זָכוֹר
Participle	קֹטֵל	שֹׁמֵר	פֹּקֵד	כֹּתֵב	זֹכֵר
Jussive 3ms	יִקְטֹל	יִשְׁמֹר	יִפְקֹד	יִכְתֹּב	יִזְכֹּר

Table 2 Qal: weak verbs

Qal Weak verbs	Pe guttural	Ayin guttural	Lamed guttural	Pe yod/ Pe vav	Ayin yod/ Ayin vav
Perfect					
3ms	עָמַד	שָׁחַט	שָׁלַח	יָשַׁב	קָם
3fs	עָמְדָה	שָׁהֲטָה	שָׁלְחָה	יָשְׁבָה	קָמָה
2ms	עָמַדְתָּ	שָׁחַטְתָּ	שָׁלַחְתָּ	יָשַׁבְתָּ	קַמְתָּ
2fs	עָמַדְתְּ	שָׁחַטְתְּ	שָׁלַחְתְּ	יָשַׁבְתְּ	קַמְתְּ
1s	עָמַדְתִּי	שָׁחַטְתִּי	שָׁלַחְתִּי	יָשַׁבְתִּי	קַמְתִּי
3p	עָמְדוּ	שָׁהֲטוּ	שָׁלְחוּ	יָשְׁבוּ	קָמוּ
2mp	עֲמַדְתֶּם	שְׁחַטְתֶּם	שְׁלַחְתֶּם	יְשַׁבְתֶּם	קַמְתֶּם
2fp	עֲמַדְתֶּן	שְׁחַטְתֶּן	שְׁלַחְתֶּן	יְשַׁבְתֶּן	קַמְתֶּן
1p	עָמַדְנוּ	שָׁחַטְנוּ	שָׁלַחְנוּ	יָשַׁבְנוּ	קַמְנוּ

Imperfect					
3ms	יַעֲמֹד	יִשְׁחַט	יִשְׁלַח	יֵשֵׁב	יָקוּם
3fs	תַּעֲמֹד	תִּשְׁחַט	תִּשְׁלַח	תֵּשֵׁב	תָּקוּם
2ms	תַּעֲמֹד	תִּשְׁחַט	תִּשְׁלַח	תֵּשֵׁב	תָּקוּם
2fs	תַּעַמְדִי	תִּשְׁחֲטִי	תִּשְׁלְחִי	תֵּשְׁבִי	תָּקוּמִי
1s	אֶעֱמֹד	אֶשְׁחַט	אֶשְׁלַח	אֵשֵׁב	אָקוּם
3mp	יַעַמְדוּ	יִשְׁחֲטוּ	יִשְׁלְחוּ	יֵשְׁבוּ	יָקוּמוּ
3fp	תַּעֲמֹדְנָה	תִּשְׁחַטְנָה	תִּשְׁלַחְנָה	תֵּשַׁבְנָה	תְּקוּמֶינָה
2mp	תַּעַמְדוּ	תִּשְׁחֲטוּ	תִּשְׁלְחוּ	תֵּשְׁבוּ	תָּקוּמוּ
2fp	תַּעֲמֹדְנָה	תִּשְׁחַטְנָה	תִּשְׁלַחְנָה	תֵּשַׁבְנָה	תְּקוּמֶינָה
1p	נַעֲמֹד	נִשְׁחַט	נִשְׁלַח	נֵשֵׁב	נָקוּם

Imperative ms	עֲמֹד	שְׁחַט	שְׁלַח	שֵׁב	קוּם
Infinitive Cstr	עֲמֹד	שְׁחַט	שְׁלֹחַ	שֶׁבֶת	קוּם
Infinitive Abs	עָמוֹד	שָׁחוֹט	שָׁלוֹחַ	יָשׁוֹב	קוֹם
Participle	עֹמֵד	שֹׁחֵט	שֹׁלֵחַ	יֹשֵׁב	קָם
Jussive 3ms	יַעֲמֹד	יִשְׁחַט	יִשְׁלַח	יֵשֵׁב	יָקֹם

Perfect					
Weak verbs	Pe nun	Double ayin	Pe alef	Lamed alef	Lamed he
3ms	נָגַשׁ	סָבַב	אָכַל	מָצָא	גָּלָה
3fs	נָגְשָׁה	סָבְבָה	אָכְלָה	מָצְאָה	גָּלְתָה
2ms	נָגַשְׁתָּ	סַבּוֹתָ	אָכַלְתָּ	מָצָאתָ	גָּלִיתָ
2fs	נָגַשְׁתְּ	סַבּוֹת	אָכַלְתְּ	מָצָאת	גָּלִית
1s	נָגַשְׁתִּי	סַבּוֹתִי	אָכַלְתִּי	מָצָאתִי	גָּלִיתִי
3p	נָגְשׁוּ	סָבְבוּ	אָכְלוּ	מָצְאוּ	גָּלוּ
2mp	נְגַשְׁתֶּם	סַבּוֹתֶם	אֲכַלְתֶּם	מְצָאתֶם	גְּלִיתֶם
2fp	נְגַשְׁתֶּן	סַבּוֹתֶן	אֲכַלְתֶּן	מְצָאתֶן	גְּלִיתֶן
1p	נָגַשְׁנוּ	סַבּוֹנוּ	אָכַלְנוּ	מָצָאנוּ	גָּלִינוּ

Imperfect					
3ms	יִגַּשׁ	יָסֹב	יֹאכַל	יִמְצָא	יִגְלֶה
3fs	תִּגַּשׁ	תָּסֹב	תֹּאכַל	תִּמְצָא	תִּגְלֶה
2ms	תִּגַּשׁ	תָּסֹב	תֹּאכַל	תִּמְצָא	תִּגְלֶה
2fs	תִּגְּשִׁי	תָּסֹבִּי	תֹּאכְלִי	תִּמְצְאִי	תִּגְלִי
1s	אֶגַּשׁ	אָסֹב	אֹכַל	אֶמְצָא	אֶגְלֶה
3mp	יִגְּשׁוּ	יָסֹבּוּ	יֹאכְלוּ	יִמְצְאוּ	יִגְלוּ
3fp	תִּגַּשְׁנָה	תְּסֻבֶּינָה	תֹּאכַלְנָה	תִּמְצֶאנָה	תִּגְלֶינָה
2mp	תִּגְּשׁוּ	תָּסֹבּוּ	תֹּאכְלוּ	תִּמְצְאוּ	תִּגְלוּ
2fp	תִּגַּשְׁנָה	תְּסֻבֶּינָה	תֹּאכַלְנָה	תִּמְצֶאנָה	תִּגְלֶינָה
1p	נִגַּשׁ	נָסֹב	נֹאכַל	נִמְצָא	נִגְלֶה

Imperative ms	גַּשׁ/גְּשָׁה	סֹב	אֱכֹל	מְצָא	גְּלֵה
Infinitive Cstr	גֶּשֶׁת	סֹב	אֱכֹל	מְצֹא	גְּלוֹת
Infinitive Abs	נָגוֹשׁ	סָבוֹב	אָכוֹל	מָצוֹא	גָּלֹה
Participle	נֹגֵשׁ	סוֹבֵב	אֹכֵל	מֹצֵא	גֹּלֶה
Jussive 3ms	יִגַּשׁ	יָסֹב	יֹאכַל	יִמְצָא	יִגֶל

Table 3 All stems: strong verbs (קָטַל)

N.B. Tables for the other stems of the weak verbs are outside the scope of this course.
However, they can be found in Hebrew grammars.

Perfect	Qal	Nifal	Piel	Pual	Hitp.	Hifil	Hofal
3ms	קָטַל	נִקְטַל	קִטֵּל	קֻטַּל	הִתְקַטֵּל	הִקְטִיל	הָקְטַל
3fs	קָטְלָה	נִקְטְלָה	קִטְּלָה	קֻטְּלָה	הִתְקַטְּלָה	הִקְטִילָה	הָקְטְלָה
2ms	קָטַלְתָּ	נִקְטַלְתָּ	קִטַּלְתָּ	קֻטַּלְתָּ	הִתְקַטַּלְתָּ	הִקְטַלְתָּ	הָקְטַלְתָּ
2fs	קָטַלְתְּ	נִקְטַלְתְּ	קִטַּלְתְּ	קֻטַּלְתְּ	הִתְקַטַּלְתְּ	הִקְטַלְתְּ	הָקְטַלְתְּ
1s	קָטַלְתִּי	נִקְטַלְתִּי	קִטַּלְתִּי	קֻטַּלְתִּי	הִתְקַטַּלְתִּי	הִקְטַלְתִּי	הָקְטַלְתִּי
3p	קָטְלוּ	נִקְטְלוּ	קִטְּלוּ	קֻטְּלוּ	הִתְקַטְּלוּ	הִקְטִילוּ	הָקְטְלוּ
2mp	קְטַלְתֶּם	נִקְטַלְתֶּם	קִטַּלְתֶּם	קֻטַּלְתֶּם	הִתְקַטַּלְתֶּם	הִקְטַלְתֶּם	הָקְטַלְתֶּם
2fp	קְטַלְתֶּן	נִקְטַלְתֶּן	קִטַּלְתֶּן	קֻטַּלְתֶּן	הִתְקַטַּלְתֶּן	הִקְטַלְתֶּן	הָקְטַלְתֶּן
1p	קָטַלְנוּ	נִקְטַלְנוּ	קִטַּלְנוּ	קֻטַּלְנוּ	הִתְקַטַּלְנוּ	הִקְטַלְנוּ	הָקְטַלְנוּ

Imperfect	Qal	Nifal	Piel	Pual	Hitp.	Hifil	Hofal
3ms	יִקְטֹל	יִקָּטֵל	יְקַטֵּל	יְקֻטַּל	יִתְקַטֵּל	יַקְטִיל	יָקְטַל
3fs	תִּקְטֹל	תִּקָּטֵל	תְּקַטֵּל	תְּקֻטַּל	תִּתְקַטֵּל	תַּקְטִיל	תָּקְטַל
2ms	תִּקְטֹל	תִּקָּטֵל	תְּקַטֵּל	תְּקֻטַּל	תִּתְקַטֵּל	תַּקְטִיל	תָּקְטַל
2fs	תִּקְטְלִי	תִּקָּטְלִי	תְּקַטְּלִי	תְּקֻטְּלִי	תִּתְקַטְּלִי	תַּקְטִילִי	תָּקְטְלִי
1s	אֶקְטֹל	אֶקָּטֵל	אֲקַטֵּל	אֲקֻטַּל	אֶתְקַטֵּל	אַקְטִיל	אָקְטַל
3mp	יִקְטְלוּ	יִקָּטְלוּ	יְקַטְּלוּ	יְקֻטְּלוּ	יִתְקַטְּלוּ	יַקְטִילוּ	יָקְטְלוּ
3fp	תִּקְטֹלְנָה	תִּקָּטַלְנָה	תְּקַטֵּלְנָה	תְּקֻטַּלְנָה	תִּתְקַטֵּלְנָה	תַּקְטֵלְנָה	תָּקְטַלְנָה
2mp	תִּקְטְלוּ	תִּקָּטְלוּ	תְּקַטְּלוּ	תְּקֻטְּלוּ	תִּתְקַטְּלוּ	תַּקְטִילוּ	תָּקְטְלוּ
2fp	תִּקְטֹלְנָה	תִּקָּטַלְנָה	תְּקַטֵּלְנָה	תְּקֻטַּלְנָה	תִּתְקַטֵּלְנָה	תַּקְטֵלְנָה	תָּקְטַלְנָה
1p	נִקְטֹל	נִקָּטֵל	נְקַטֵּל	נְקֻטַּל	נִתְקַטֵּל	נַקְטִיל	נָקְטַל

	Qal	Nifal	Piel	Pual	Hitp.	Hifil	Hofal
Impv ms	קְטֹל	הִקָּטֵל	קַטֵּל	—	הִתְקַטֵּל	הַקְטֵל	—
Inf Cstr	קְטֹל	הִקָּטֵל	קַטֵּל	קֻטַּל	הִתְקַטֵּל	הַקְטִיל	הָקְטַל
Inf Abs	קָטוֹל	הִקָּטֹל	קַטֵּל	קֻטֹּל	הִתְקַטֵּל	הַקְטֵל	הָקְטֵל
Ptc	קֹטֵל	נִקְטָל	מְקַטֵּל	מְקֻטָּל	מִתְקַטֵּל	מַקְטִיל	מָקְטָל
Juss 3ms	יִקְטֹל	יִקָּטֵל	יְקַטֵּל	יְקֻטַּל	יִתְקַטֵּל	יַקְטֵל	יָקְטַל